CONTENTS

PREFACE

Without the written word, man cannot long retain his history. His intelligence permits him to recall events, but without writing, the tales of the past rapidly degenerate into fumbling myth and fable. The experiences encountered in this book are true. Some readers might even see themselves as part of the story. Any Midwestern farm boy would feel some kind of kinship with the author. People who grew up in the Depression years will remember the hard times and sacrifices. Those who were drafted and ended up in the Army, Navy and Marine Corps will recall the difficult times in the service in wartime. Those who went through the Aviation Cadet Pilot Training Program will remember the trials and tribulations inherent in the process of becoming a pilot and a commissioned officer. I provide a lot of detail during my pilot training as it was so very important to me. In other areas of my story, I often leave details up to the reader's imagination. Those who flew in combat will be back in the cockpit. Those who flew combat reconnaissance missions will remember that they were "eyes in the sky" or "spy pilots."

The late Gary Francis Powers did the same thing as I did only in more modern equipment. He flew twice as high and still got hit by a missile. In World War II, these "soldiers in the sky", armed only with a camera, were constantly harassed by enemy aircraft and were often hit with flak from enemy guns. Those who spent a career in the military will relive the fairly well paid gypsy lifestyle with a family move every three years. The overseas assignments to experience a new culture at every location around this big world were wonderful. Those who flew business aircraft will share in the many thrills and worldwide experiences of the exciting life of a corporate pilot that most always included dawn departures and late night arrivals.

Aviation has come a long way during this century from the Wright Brothers at Kitty Hawk to the astronauts in deep space. This book is not intended as a documentary, rather an account of things the way they were as aviation grew during my lifetime. Three long-time aviation associates have graciously written introductions. John Kane had a career as a Naval aviator and several years with McDonnell Douglas Aircraft and General Dynamics Corporation. Paul Rodgers was an airline executive with the former Ozark Airlines and later with TWA. He founded Air One Airlines and later was in a group of four people who formed the Wings of Hope Foundation. This humanitarian organization provides airplanes to fly mercy missions into third world countries. William (Bill) Nichols had a long career as a Naval aviator and, after retirement, worked as a Sabreliner simulator instructor for Flight Safety International in New York and later as Director of Training in St. Louis.

My aviation history is full of good times, humor, sadness and tears. It's not just another account of someone who flew airplanes. When I finally retired after 55 years in aviation, I became a fire-wagon horse put out to pasture. Whenever the bell rings, I stop at whatever I am doing and glance up at the passing airplane—wondering if those pilots up there are having as much fun as I had.

Flying gave me a most lasting human experience that is indelibly etched in my memory. If my story provides entertainment for you, then it was successfully told. I have made every effort to ensure the accuracy of events and information in this book. I assume no responsibility for errors, omissions, inaccuracies or any other inconsistencies herein. Any slight of people, places or organizations is purely unintentional. All pictures are property of the author.

This book is then my contribution to the history of American aviation in the 20th Century.

Thomas Gordon
Airline Transport Pilot
#296522

DEDICATION

This book is dedicated to my loving wife, Joan, and my three sons, Michael, Steven and John.

Without their encouragement and strong support, I could not have even begun to write my story. Although fate dealt them a husband and father who created for them an unusual life, they have understood and loved me. I will forever be grateful to them and to others who shared my life and helped me break into aviation at a tender young age. I learned to fly and used my wisdom to pursue my goals.

I dedicate these pages also to those of today's young people who have an ideal in life and a strong desire to be active, peaceful, helpful and happy. The words and pictures that follow are those of a human being like yourself, who was able to make his choices about life in the keen knowledge of the intellect and freedom of liberty.

Thank you Joan, and thank you Michael, Steven and John for helping me get the story of my life in aviation off the ground.

No one can predict what heights you can soar,
even you will not know until you spread your wings.

— United States Air Force Academy

INTRODUCTION

In the years since 1903, this country, and the world, saw a completely new industry develop which would have a profound effect on all our lives. From the sands of Kitty Hawk to dust on the moon in less than a century!

The biggest business in our state, and one of the largest in the country, is the many-faceted aviation industry. This industry is unique in that there is such a close relationship between military and civilian aviation. For example, the same know-how in developing power plants, airframes, navigational aids and communication facilities in the military soon found its way into the commercial aviation field.

THIRTY SECONDS OVER BERLIN, by Tom Gordon, is an interesting story illustrating the many facets of the aviation industry and how one person's career and life's work was influenced by this industry. Tom received his early flight training in the military. He flew combat missions in the European Theater of Operations in the famous Lockheed P-38 Lightning. After a long flying career in the Air Force, he became a corporate pilot and flight manager for one of the top aviation manufacturing firms in the world—General Dynamics Corporation.

I have known the author for about half of his 53-year flying career. He is a professional and dedicated aviation enthusiast. While Tom was a Nebraska farm boy, I was an Iowa farm boy. I still recall hearing the deep drone of those early picturesque bi-planes as they flew across the Iowa farmlands during my growing years. Once my parents took me to Forest Park, in St. Louis, to see Charles Lindbergh fly over in his famous Spirit of St. Louis airplane when he returned from Paris.

I was also in the Air Force in the ETO and helped start four air-carrier operations: Trans World Airline-International Division, Parks Airlines, Ozark Airlines and Air One Airlines. It was my privilege to be one of the four founders of Wings of Hope. This organization of volunteers restore light airplanes for humanitarian missions in third-level countries. Aviation is truly a wonderful industry and Tom Gordon's book will provide you interesting and first-hand accounts plus insights into the many facets of aviation. Enjoy!

Paul J. Rodgers
Former Chairman of the Board
Air One Airlines

INTRODUCTION

THIRTY SECONDS OVER BERLIN, by Tom Gordon, is a very interesting historical account of aviation events leading up to World War II and military aviation during World War II, Korea and Vietnam. The book explains the training program for pilots in precise detail and covers the lifestyle and duty assignments of military pilots. Tom gives a full account of corporate aviation achievements over a long period of time and how they relate to military aviation.

Corporate flight departments have excellent safety records due to pilot selection, pilot training programs and very high maintenance standards. General Dynamics' St. Louis flight department was one of the best, second to none, due to Tom Gordon's professional management, chief pilot skills and conscientious efforts. He also ensured that all aircraft were in excellent mechanical condition. He along with his pilots took recurrent training on a regular basis in addition to initial training in all types of aircraft they flew. I have known Tom Gordon since 1975 and have flown with him and every pilot in the General Dynamics flight department assigned to the Sabreliner aircraft. Also, I helped train his pilots in the Sabreliner visual simulators. Tom and I worked well together because we both understood how teamwork between an instructor and the flight crew was so very important in achieving the final goals. Tom was also helpful to me in locating an excellent instructor, that he had served with in the Air Force, to instruct in the military T-39 simulator. Ed Shepherd was the instructor I hired and he worked at Flight Safety International in St. Louis until he retired in 1990.

I can appreciate Tom Gordon's dedication to aviation. Like Tom, I started flying in a government sponsored college program titled Civilian Pilot Training in 1940 where I earned a Private Pilot certificate. In January 1942, I started in the U.S. Navy aviation cadet training program and graduated as an ensign and Naval aviator in September 1942. Then I completed instructor pilot training and was assigned to Naval Air Transport duty, first in seaplanes—PBY3s, later in DC-4s and DC-6s. I spent 25 years as a Naval aviator, 21 years on active duty and 4 years in the Reserves between World War II and the Korean War. I was a copilot-navigator during part of this period for Pan American Airways. I also earned a FAA Navigators certificate, which was a requirement at that time. I was recalled to active duty during the Korean

vi

War and stayed on until retirement. After Navy retirement in 1967, I was hired by Flight Safety International (FSI) as a simulator and flight instructor in Sabreliner and Hawker-Siddley jet programs at LaGuardia Airport in New York City. After 27 years with FSI, 20 years as Director of Sabreliner Training in St. Louis and 17 years as a FAA Designated Examiner for Sabreliner type ratings, I retired in September 1994. Then I worked part time giving flight checks until March 1995.

This book will provide readers with valuable information about the many facets of aviation.

Tom's chapter on transition to retirement is a good outlook for retirement time. I recommend it.

William B. Nichols
Commander, USNR (Retired)
Director of Flight Safety International Sabreliner Training (Retired)

INTRODUCTION

He came prepared. He brought with him the aircraft, the flight crew and the experience to build a Corporate Flight Department. His name was Tom Gordon. The aircraft was a Rockwell twin-jet Sabreliner. The crew was his flight team from our Fort Worth Division of its parent company, General Dynamics Corporation.

The date was June 6, 1971-the 27th anniversary of the World War II Normandy Invasion or D-Day. I had been given the assignment of organizing a flight department in St. Louis, following the move of General Dynamics Corporate Headquarters from New York City.

Chairman David S. Lewis had set the requirement for executive transport and it was up to me to start the process. Tom Gordon was the ideal man to take charge of the newly formed flight department as Chief Pilot and Aviation Manager. His background was the United States Air Force as a pilot of fighter aircraft and later as a multi-engined bomber pilot, coupled with post-war commercial flight experience at our Fort Worth Division. He was an excellent choice for the assignment.

Experience was not the only factor in Tom's favor. He had an innate sense of what action was most appropriate to safety of flight, of paramount importance in corporate aviation. He was assured by the Chairman, and by me, that he and his pilots would make the go-no-go decisions without pressure from any passenger regardless of executive position. That backing from the top assured us that our operations would be well planned and meticulously carried out.

Tom and I were of the same age, both with military flight backgrounds, but in different branches of the service. He had served in the Air Force and I was a Naval aviator. Our careers, however, were not similar. Tom was a professional pilot with thousands of hours in his flight log, while I had much less time in the air, but considerable engineering support time.

It didn't take Tom long to organize his department into a very effective support group and to bring his pilots and maintenance people to a level of outstanding performance. For the next 14 years he brought new pilots and new aircraft into the St. Louis operation. First came a modified Sabreliner version, followed by the acquisition of a Gulfstream II and then a Gulfstream III. All of these upgrades brought with them the careful planning for cockpit and cabin designs together with equipment and instrumentation needed for domestic and international operations.

Tom wrote and published an in-depth Flight Operations Manual which was then adopted by other General Dynamics divisions that operated business aircraft. The manual was cited by the National Business Aircraft Association (NBAA) as one of the best they had ever reviewed. Tom instituted a flight evaluation program for his pilots, making use of established experts among various flight safety organizations to ensure that his pilots were tops. He took the same courses and followed the same rules he required others to follow. A leader is always out in front, and Tom was always out in front.

Those 14 years with him in the General Dynamics family were full of challenges and rewards. I could say we were lucky in never having an accident or incident but that would be overlooking the firm and sensible control that Tom brought to flight operations.

Tom Gordon was, and still is, my good friend. He was more than that when we worked together. He was a man of great responsibility, common sense and a devotion to duty equal to none. I am proud to have known him in the workplace and to have him as a friend today.

John C. Kane
Former Director, Flight Operations
General Dynamics Corporation
Captain, United States Navy (Retired)

CHAPTER ONE

A DAY TO REMEMBER

*Ever since man first walked the earth, he has dreamed of ascending above it.
Man only has to observe the birds in flight to fuel the desire to achieve his dream.*

—*Wilbur Wright.*

The clock on the wall in the pilot's ready room read five minutes to seven as I walked in and sat down for the morning briefing. It was April 7, 1945, a warm sunny day in western Germany during the fourth spring of World War II. This former Luftwaffe airfield was now occupied by the 405th Fighter Bomber Group. They flew the popular Republic P-47 fighter bomber known as the Thunderbolt which initially was called the Thunderjug. Typical of a pilots' ready room, it was filled to capacity and everyone was talking at once. I didn't know a soul as they were trained in fighter-bomber concepts while I was trained in aerial reconnaissance and flew a P-38 Lightning equipped with big aerial cameras and no guns. Their aircraft were equipped with guns and no cameras. My job was to fly with this group today and record their napalm bomb strikes. It was called Bomb Damage Assessment (BDA), a very dangerous mission for an unarmed reconnaissance pilot. It was my first mission of this kind and I was very apprehensive. My airstrip was about 30 miles away, and I flew over earlier that morning so I could attend their pre-mission briefing. No, I wasn't ordered to fly this special mission; in fact, I volunteered. The photo intelligence my cameras would record was very important to the 9th Air Force and especially to the U.S. Army. Moreover, I was anxious to see how these pilots dive-bombed. I was soon to find out. I had flown over enemy territory 15 times already, and this was going to be number 16. While waiting for the briefing to start, I began thinking about my airplane and hoped the 405th FBG topped off my fuel tanks, as the target for today was no doubt deep into Germany. No one seemed to notice my arrival as they just kept up their loud banter. Precisely at seven o'clock, a side door opened and in walked the Group Commander followed by some of his staff. As if someone had flipped a switch, the room became very quiet and everyone snapped to rigid attention. Neither West Point nor Annapolis graduates could have done any better. The Aviation Cadet Program had taught us a lot more than just how to fly airplanes.

The Group Commander, Colonel John Kelleher, hopped up on the briefing platform with athletic ease. He was a 1937 graduate of Notre Dame and a star quarterback He looked about 6' 2", a good 200 pounds, and could probably still play football. He once took Notre Dame to a 42-41 victory over Michigan by running for two touchdowns and throwing for three in the second half. In a strong voice he said, "At ease gentlemen, and take your seats." The Colonel was wearing a flight suit and I felt sure he was going to lead the mission. With him were his briefing officer, weather officer and the group chaplain.

Colonel Kelleher continued: "Today we have a very special mission and the target is located in southern Germany. Before we get started, I want to introduce a guest who is going to fly with us today. He is Lt. Tom Gordon from the 33rd Photo Reconnaissance Squadron, and he will record our napalm bomb strikes with his special cameras. He will be flying a P-38 Lightning. Tom, will you please stand up?" As I stood up, all eyes in the room worked me over. I quickly sat down. Colonel Kelleher thanked me and said I would be diving down with each of the three squadrons on their individual bomb runs. He continued, "Our target for today is the ME-262 jet fighter launch strip near the city of Munich. Located on the field is a fuel dump and ammunition storage facility. We will try to knock out the runway and destroy their fuel and ammunition supply to help end the war. Without fuel or ammo, they are no threat to us. Now I will ask Major Miller to brief you on the details of the mission."

The major started out by saying, "The ME-262 jet fighter is three times faster than anything we have today. It can fly as high as 40,000 feet and its forte is to dive out of the sun and pick off fighters, bombers or whatever is out there. It does not dogfight like a conventional fighter. It's like a big hawk diving on smaller prey, and it never misses. The jet has twin engines and when it's at high altitude, you can probably see its contrails. When the contrails suddenly stop, beware! He is now coming down at nearly mach 1 speed and evasive actions had better be taken quickly." The briefing officer went on to tell us that jet fuel for the ME-262 was in short supply and our strikes on that airfield were vital to keep these jets out of the skies. The major then turned to the wall map that was covered with a curtain. After exposing the map, he said, "You will see the route of flight to the target. It's not a direct route for tactical reasons. The Initial Point (IP) is the town of Harr. From the IP you will turn in on the airfield as it is shown here." He then brought out a larger scale map that showed the airfield's location along with its latitude/longitude coordinates. "Now I want you to notice the area around the airfield; there are several major highways, railroad lines, and all kinds of strafing opportunities after you drop your napalm." He went on to tell the pilots to continue their strafing until their fuel state was down to the amount necessary to get back home. "Fire on anything that's moving," he said. I sat there and thought, "Wow," this is going to be an exciting day. Little did I know at the time just how exciting it would be.

The briefing officer then said, "Your route is as shown on this map. You all will be given a small-scale copy of this routing. Be very careful as there are pockets of German resistance that General Patton encircled during his march across Germany. These pockets have the potential of good concentrations of 88 mm anti-aircraft guns. Stay away from them at all costs. These pockets, as you see, are circled in red on the map. Make sure your maps are so marked." Then he said, "We don't expect much in the way of German propeller-driven fighters today as their fuel state is worse than the jet supply. Expect heavy anti-aircraft activity (flak) when you are near the target. Also, when strafing, expect heavy ground fire from light anti-aircraft guns including small arms fire. Engine start time for Red Flight is 0830 with takeoff at 0845."

The briefing officer then explained that the first squadron to take off would be Red Flight, the second squadron would be White Flight, and the last squadron would be Blue Flight. Red Flight Leader will be our Group Commander. The White and Blue elements would be led by their respective Squadron Commanders. Then he said, "The photo airplane will be the last airplane to take off. The group will orbit above the field until everyone is in formation. Then the group will proceed to the target area and fly at 15,000 feet. I suggest the photo ship fly just above the formation. His tactical call sign is Lancer 29. All airplanes will have their four-channel radios set up so each button is common. Able channel is our tower frequency. Baker channel is enroute radar control. You will probably lose him about an hour after takeoff. Charlie channel is our group common, and Dog channel is the emergency frequency of 121.5 MHz. Red Leader will tell you when to go to baker channel after the group has formed up. As I speak, our radio people are changing the crystals in the photo airplane so all airplanes will have matched channels. White Flight will start engines at 0845 and Blue Flight at 0900 hours. Flight element takeoffs will be 15 minutes apart. Good luck gentlemen and now here is Captain 'Stormy' Allen to tell you about today's weather." "Good morning, gentlemen. It looks like we will have a good day here and most of the way to the target. In the Munich area expect scattered clouds around 14,000 feet. This could probably change to broken or maybe overcast by the time you get there.

The winds at 15,000 feet today are from 240 degrees at 40 knots. Surface winds here are calm. On your return, expect some thin scattered clouds at around 5,000 feet. For your landing, there will be unlimited visibility. Winds from the south at 10 knots." Captain Allen turned around for a moment and then said, "I have been asked to give you a time hack. I will mark you at exactly 0745. Thirty seconds, twenty seconds, ten seconds, 5 - 4 - 3 - 2 - 1 - mark! The temperature for your takeoff will be 68F and the altimeter setting is 29.98. Now here is Colonel Kelleher."

"Okay, when we get within 10 miles of the IP, I will start a slow descent to 12,000 feet. At the same time, shift from a V formation to an element right. At the IP, I will head right for the target and Red Flight will dive down and release the napalm on my command. I want the photo ship to tack onto my tail-end-charlie (last man) and go down with him. As soon as he gets his BDA shots, the photo ship will climb back up and go down with the White Flight, and then back up and go down again with the Blue Flight. He then can stay with the Blue boys and maybe record some strafing hits. Listen up on Charlie channel and, on my command, we head for home climbing to 14,000 feet. During the climb, get back into a V formation. On your strafing runs, look for trucks, trains, ammo dumps and things like that. Now, are there any questions?" One pilot stood up and asked if he should keep his fuel drop tank when it was empty or jettison it. The Colonel said, " Keep it if you can, but if you see any bandits, get rid of it quickly." There were no more questions Colonel Kelleher continued: "Now gentlemen, if you will all rise, Chaplain Graf will give us some words to think about today." James Graf was from Sterling, Illinois, not far from Chicago. After high school, he attended a Jesuit Seminary for eight years before being ordained a Catholic priest. His first assignment was that of Associate Pastor at St. Bernard Parish on the north side of Chicago. A year after Pearl Harbor, he decided to become a military chaplain and chose the Army Air Corps over the Navy. His brother Bob was in the Navy and didn't like being at sea all the time.

Chaplain Graf got up and walked over to the edge of the briefing platform. For a minute, he just stood there looking over the assembly of young pilots. He guessed their ages to average around 22. They were in the prime of their lives. Then he said softly, "Gentlemen, as you are about to depart on a combat mission, I want you to know that you will be defending human liberty and freedom. All the eyes of the free world are upon you, wanting you to succeed. All the prayers of your family and loved ones are with you, wanting you to return safely.

When you take off in a short while, I want you to know that there is no greater love than to give your life for your God and Country. Yours is a noble calling. Yours is a courageous calling. The prayers of our soldiers in enemy prison camps will be your companions in battle. Now we pray:

Lord God, please watch over us and be our guide and protector on today's mission. Keep us mindful of the precious gift of life which we have received from you that we may not come to any harm to body and soul. Help us Lord to remain alert and careful. Help us to be mindful of the rules of safety and common sense. Help us to return safely and let this prayer be our inspiration, both when flying combat missions and throughout our lives. Lord support us with your grace when we are faced with danger. Help us to be patient in any trouble which may come our way. Help us to always be mindful of Your presence and love.

Now for your comfort and grace, I will read the 23rd Psalm,
The Lord is my shepherd. I lack nothing.
In grassy meadows He lets me lie.
By quiet streams He leads me to restore my spirit.
He guides me in paths of saving justice as befits His name. Even were I to walk in a ravine as dark as death, I should fear no danger . . . ."

As the Chaplain continued with the Psalm, I tried to concentrate on his every word. I just couldn't do it. My mind was racing with the thought of soon being over enemy territory with flak and ground fire all around me. Airplanes getting hit and screaming voices on the radio were real and very frightening. The chill of all that quickly brought me back to reality.

The Chaplain was saying, "May God be with you today, gentlemen. Trust in Him. Good luck and may God bless you."

As the Chaplain finished, Colonel Kelleher dismissed everyone. It was 0800 hours and just 30 minutes before the first P-47's would be starting engines. As the pilots filed out of the room, they again started talking all at once. A couple of them asked me how fast the P-38 could fly. I told them "about twice as fast as you guys." I was only kidding, but they acted like they might have believed me. The P-47 was known as the "Jug". Some even called it the "lead sled" because it was always loaded down with external stores (weapons) and was slow. Its cruising speed was 240 mph, while the P-38 cruised at 300. The Jug was built by Republic Aviation Corporation in Long Island, New York. More than 15,600 were built and were used everywhere. It had a big double-row radial engine that generated 2,300 HP. The Pratt and Whitney R2800 engine was very reliable and was used on several other airplanes as well. The Jug could take a pounding as it was very rugged. I would witness that to be true that very day.

Outside the briefing room, I flagged a ride in a jeep out to my airplane. I wanted to make sure she was fueled and ready to go. After taking care of a latrine stop, I was ready to go. I quickly crawled up on top of my right wing and sat down to watch the show going on in front of me. Whole groups of noisy fighter-bombers were either taxiing out or cranking their engines. There were 36 of them with three ground spares just in case. It was very exciting just to be able to watch this spectacle. Even more exciting to me was that I was going with them, if they ever got off the ground.

Each ship needed a battery cart to crank the big engine. The ship's battery just wouldn't do it. I didn't need a start-cart as the P-38 would start easily on its own battery. The right engine was started first because that's where the generator was mounted. The battery wasn't needed for starting the left engine. The generator provided power for that.

One by one, Red Flight finally got airborne. They were so heavy that each airplane used every bit of the runway. After becoming airborne, the Jug seemed to struggle until the gear came up, followed by the wing flaps. Then it seemed to accelerate pretty well. When the last airplane of Blue Flight taxied past me, I set my parking brakes and pulled the chocks myself as no one was in sight to help me. But that was okay, I didn't need any help. I settled into the cockpit, closed the canopy, and got ready to crank the engines. When only three aircraft were left to take off, I started my engines and quickly caught up to the last P-47. It was the Blue Flight's tail-end charlie. All of my engine instruments were in the "green." The only thing left to do before takeoff was to give each engine a quick magneto, propeller and power check. All items on each engine took less than 20 seconds.

The control tower was located near the middle of the airfield. Nearby, the crash and rescue equipment was positioned. I was just given clearance to take the runway and hold my position when I noticed the fire truck and ambulance suddenly take off for the far end of the field. Just then the tower said, "Lancer 29, hold your position. We have a downed aircraft off the end of the runway. Please stand by." Soon, I could see a tower of black smoke rising from that direction. I knew some poor guy must have had engine trouble and had to belly in on the overrun area. After holding in position for a few minutes, the tower said I was now cleared for takeoff.

As I became airborne, I saw the downed airplane all covered with white foam from the fire trucks. No more smoke could be seen and the tower was clearing the spare airplane to taxi out. I heard later, from Red Leader, that the downed pilot was alive but badly burned. Quickly, I got the P-38's gear and flaps up and was now aerodynamically clean. The P-47 group was at 5,000 feet and climbing and soon I was in the middle of their formation and just slightly above them. They weren't going to lose me, I kept thinking. As they were climbing at only 180 mph, I had to throttle back to equal their speed.

Finally, after what seemed like a long time, we reached 15,000 feet. Red Flight was easy to spot as each airplane had a wide red horizontal stripe on its tail. Once in cruise, I had to again throttle back as they were only doing 200 mph. In addition to reduced power, I did slow lazy "S" turns above them. I was having a good time but knew it wouldn't last much longer. Soon, we reached the IP and the weather was just as predicted. Broken clouds below us and I don't know how Red Leader found the IP, but he did. En route, I was watching constantly for bogeys or even bandits. A "bogey" is an unidentified airplane while a "bandit" is a confirmed enemy airplane.

Down below, the German countryside looked very peaceful and beautiful. One would never know there was a war going on. We saw neither bogeys, bandits nor flak all the way to the IP. That really surprised me, as I fully expected some action. On my previous 15 missions, there were many occasions of dodging flak and evading bandits. Remember, I carried no guns, zip, nothing. So when I saw a bandit, I would duck into a cloud or simply evade him with my light and fast P-38. I could outclimb him, outdive him, and outturn him. That's the only thing that got me home sometimes.

Just as he said he would do, Red Leader headed toward the target. We were now at 12,000 feet and in an element-right formation. In just a short time, Red Leader rolled over on his back and did a "split-S" straight down. Wow! When tail-end charlie of Red Flight did that, so did I. The first thing I noticed coming straight down were bursts of flak. The Germans knew we were there. Around 5,000 feet, Red Flight shallowed out their dive angle some. The flak bursts now were gray in color; higher up they were inky black. The gray color indicated smaller caliber antiaircraft guns. Also, as advertised, there were indications of small arms fire as I saw yellow tracer bullets down low when the napalm bombs were being released. I had my cameras set for two-second-interval shots. This was done coming over as I had set my camera control box, called the interverlometer. Once set, it's automatic. This would be no problem as I had 200-foot rolls of film in each camera magazine. That day, I carried two 24-inch focal length Fairchild aerial cameras in the nose section. As soon as the last napalm bomb had hit,

I stopped the cameras with my "gun" switch. Now, I had to rapidly climb back up and join the White Flight for act two.

My dive with the White Flight went okay, but I did see one P-47 get hit with gray flak. It was in the left aileron area. He just moved a little and then went right back to business. What a great airplane! My last dive was with the Blue Flight. The tail-end charlie that I was following down was the spare airplane that took over from the one that faltered earlier on takeoff. By now I was getting pretty good at dive-bombing. What a thrilling day for me, but it was far from being over.

The P-38 did a nice job of diving and I have always loved the split-S maneuver, even back in the training program. It was always a thrill to do that, but in combat, it was something else! During one of my three dives, I saw a P-47 get hit in the engine cowling. Pieces of cowling flew away, but believe it or not, the airplane just kept on going. Again, that is one rugged airplane!

After three dives, I escaped without a scrape of any kind. The Germans must have known that one single P-38, with all those dive bombers, must be up to no good, yet, they didn't seem to be shooting directly at me, though I was still in the line of fire on all three dives. After the Blue Flight dropped their bombs and I got my BDA pictures, I followed them on a wild foray of targets-of-opportunity strafing runs. One spectacular hit was on a train chugging along. The tactical objective was to stop the train, not necessarily destroy it, so the bullets were aimed at the engine. When the third P-47 poured lead into the engine, it blew sky high - what a sight! Great clouds of steam shot skyward and the train came to a stop. Mission accomplished.

Next, Blue Flight spotted a German ambulance traveling down a dirt road at high speed with a big plume of dust flying behind it. Blue Leader said on charlie channel, "Hey, that ambulance is sure moving fast." Too fast to be carrying wounded, he thought. "Let's go down and look that baby over." I followed the flight and sure enough, when we got close, the ambulance took off across a field. Now I knew it wasn't carrying wounded. Blue Leader said, "Okay, let's stop that guy." After a few bursts from his 50-caliber guns, the ambulance blew sky high with a huge column of black smoke. He must have had a load of ammunition or something on board, certainly not patients.

After the ambulance hit, I was turning around a small hill with a clump of trees on it. Something caught my eye, a flash of light or something. I came back around and looked closely at the hill and was shocked at what I saw. There, under the cover of the trees, hundreds of German soldiers were huddled close together. I guessed they were just hiding from the onslaught going on with all the bombing and strafing.

On my third pass, I was so close I could see the fear in their faces looking up at me. They just sat there; not one rifle was raised to fire. Not just because of that, I just couldn't make myself reveal their presence. I have to admit, even though it was war, I didn't want them killed. If I had said anything at all about what I found, sure enough some eager beaver from one of the flights might have made mincemeat of those guys. Those soldiers knew I saw them and did nothing about it. I hope they remember the guy in the P-38 that day that probably saved their lives. I will never forget that scene for the rest of my life. And I think those soldiers might not forget it either. I'm sure they couldn't tell if I had guns or not. All they knew was that I didn't kill them or have them killed by the Thunderbolts.

Being unarmed sometimes has its merits. Reconnaissance pilots don't win battles. With their gathering of photo intelligence, they directly help to win wars. After a few more minutes of strafing, Red Leader said, "Okay men, let's get into a V formation and head for home." A few of the airplanes were hit by flak bursts and had some damage. The only P-47 lost was the one that crashed on takeoff. Climbing out of there, I wondered how the poor guy was doing.

After reaching 14,000 feet, the group settled into a loose V formation following their leader back to home base. About 1,000 ft above them, I was again doing lazy "S" turns to match their speed. Even though they were lighter now, they still flew no faster than 240 mph. My plan was to stay with them until about 50 miles from home, then make a pass under them at high speed and then, climbing away, do a couple of slow rolls in farewell. None of that was to happen.

I was thinking about the day and how exciting it was to be a part of a dive bombing and strafing mission. My camera magazines had over a hundred 9-inch frames of exposed film. As soon as I got home, a film crew would meet the airplane in a jeep, and as soon as the propellers stopped, they would be opening the nose cowling to remove the film magazines. In a matter of minutes, the film would be processed and printed in two copies. One set would be driven over to 9th Air Force Headquarters. In less than an hour, photo interpreters at our base and at 9th AFHQ would be busy obtaining three-dimension intelligence from those pictures.

In today's photo stores they have a sign that advertises "pictures in one hour." We were doing better than that over 50 years earlier. Without any warning, my day nearly came to an end right there. Without meaning to, Red Leader must have flown over one of those red circles on our maps. Suddenly there were black flak bursts all around me. I was about to advise Red Leader when I heard a loud bang. A burst must have gone off just under me as my airplane pitched up and over. It was like Paul Bunyan had hit me with a bridge plank. When I regained control of the ship and realized both engines were still running and I didn't see any blood, I pushed everything to the firewall. Finally, at about 20,000 feet, I told Red Leader a flak burst hit me but my engines seemed to be running okay. He said the group saw the flak bursts. Why the Germans were shooting just at me, I can't explain. After asking me if I was okay, he said to come over and he would look at my airplane, especially the belly. When I told him where I was, he said he couldn't come up there. I would have to drift down to him at 14,000 feet.

When I got down there, he got under me and said, "I see a lot of holes but no leaks. Let's see, there must be over 20 of them." He then bid me farewell and thanked me for going with them and getting a record of their bomb damage. By then, they had broken left for their air strip and I turned right and headed for mine. In just a few minutes I noticed the oil temperatures on both engines were starting to climb toward the red line. Naturally, I throttled back and knew that now I couldn't get home. I had to put the airplane on the ground quickly. With both engines in idle, I was just a heavy glider coming down rapidly and still over enemy territory.

Hours later, back at my squadron's air-strip, the Operations Officer told the duty clerk, Sergeant Davis, to post an MIA (missing in action) notice beside my name on the combat mission flight board.

Aviation is proof that given the will, we have the capacity to achieve the impossible.

—Captain Eddie Rickenbacker

CHAPTER T W O

AN AVIATOR IS BORN

Man's flight through life is sustained by the power of his knowledge.

—Ralph Waldo Emerson

Early one spring morning, Dr. Frank Burgess drove his horse and buggy up the winding lane to my parents' farm. He was one of the last country doctors who regularly made house calls. His buggy was a beautiful black polished rig pulled by his black mare he called Maggie. She was plump and groomed to a fine luster. Soon Dr. Burgess was attending to the birth of my mother's sixth child. Afterward, he told her, "Ella, you have a fine healthy boy here." After having given birth to five consecutive girls, she was very happy with her first boy. It was May 26, 1922.

That's how it all started. I was named Thomas Francis Gordon after my grandfather. He was still living, so they should have tacked on a "II" to my name, but they never did. I guess a lot of attention was showered on me from all those females in the family. My father had two girls from a previous marriage. I actually had seven sisters to grow up with, ranging in age from twenty two to three. Two years later, my brother Joey was born. But after only one year, the Good Lord decided to bring him back home.

After all those sisters, I used to say I knew a lot about girls before I knew much about boys. Later, when I was about 12, during confirmation, I was given another name - Paul. Now my full name was Thomas Francis Paul Gordon. I liked the name Paul, but nobody ever called me that. Francis either, for that matter. We lived about a mile west of a small town in east-central Nebraska. The village was located on the Cedar River and was called Cedar Rapids.   That's because the early town fathers thought the spot by the rapids just might be put to good use some day. For years, the rapids drove an electric generating plant that provided power to the whole community. The village was originally named Dayton—after an early settler. I rather liked it.

My parent's farm, spread over 102 acres and, except for a small pasture, was all under the plow, as they say. We had the usual horses, cows, pigs and chickens. Dogs and cats were always around as each had a job to do. The dogs pulled guard duty and the cats kept the rodent population to a minimum. Neither were ever allowed in the house as they had their own facilities.

One day, I let one of the dogs in the house and was punished, so I never did that again. Growing up on a farm is one of the finest things a young boy can experience. All the animals, except the pigs, were my friends and most had names. We had four good work horses named Doc, Major, Dan and Prince. Doc was the youngest and always let the rest of the horses know it. We had four milk cows that I remember: Maud, Bess, Nellie and Gert. And there was Rose the young heifer. Naturally we had a bull and his name was Red. He was something else, always jumping the corral fence to find romance in greener pastures I guess. Many was the time when neighbors had to help us bring Red back home. The trick was to get one of our milk cows to lead him back home. It worked every single time.

I was always curious why the neighbors brought their milk cows over to "visit" Red out behind the barn. My father would shoo me up to the house when that happened. Curiosity finally got the best of me one day. When my mother was busy in the kitchen, I worked my way back to the barn and, through a crack in the wall, finally realized what was going on.

Life on the farm is not all milk and honey. Being the only boy, I had plenty of chores to do: feed the animals, feed the chickens and gather the eggs. All that was okay, but feeding the pigs was not any fun. Pigs are a dirty and ungrateful lot. Milking the cows, when I got a little older, was kind of fun, but hard work, too. When Rose had her first calf, that was something else. She wouldn't let any one near her except her calf. The pretty heifer calf was promptly named Rusty. That was her color and she had a perfect white heart on her forehead. Rose was so ornery, that in order to get the milk her calf didn't want, she had to be hog-tied with ropes. That ritual happened every day, morning and evening. My dad had a lot of patience to put up with that. The next year, after her second calf, she was absolutely no problem.

I took a great fancy to Rusty. I fed her from a bucket but before she would drink from it, I had to let her suck my fingers. So with my fingers in her mouth, I just put her head in the bucket. When she tasted the milk, she quickly forgot about my fingers. She quickly caught on to bucket feeding. One day when she was about 6 months old, I tried to ride her like a pony. She would quickly buck me off but I never gave up and finally, after weeks of trying, I got to sit on her back for a short period of time. Eventually I trained her to walk when I patted her on her rump and to stop, I patted her on the neck. I couldn't believe how she responded to all that. I fed her grain twice a day and she quickly became my friend. My folks could not believe it as they watched me ride her out to the pasture and then come back at a nice slow pace as I sure didn't want her to run. That went on until one day she realized that Red, the bull, was watching her. After her first encounter with Red, she suddenly dropped me. She wouldn't come to the fence when I called her as before and when I would go to her for a ride, she would just run away. Obviously, she had other things on her mind. It was fun while it lasted though.

My dad's horses were work animals and I never got to ride them. We didn't even have a saddle on the farm but I enjoyed them as they each had their own personality. Doc, the youngest, had a thing about always being first. When hitched up with another horse, and after they were brought to a stop, he invariably would take one more step forward so he always would be just ahead of the other horse. It never failed to happen while I was growing up.

Our farm had an L-shaped lane that led up the hill some 200 yards from the cemetery road. My dad and I built a wooden drag from heavy planks and we would hitch up one horse, using stays from an old buggy, and pull it up and down several times until the dirt lane was smooth. That was always fun for me to ride that drag-sled. My dad would only drag the lane and the farm yard about twice. When he finally let me do it by myself, I would drag the lane at least five times. I would have the lane and the farm yard as smooth as a race track. We always used Doc for the dragging job as he seemed to like it and would go on and on. For his good work, Doc always got an extra ration of oats at night. One day Doc got sick and before the vet arrived, he just went to the far end of the pasture, laid down and died. It took me a long time to get over that. Doc was a special animal and a real champion.

One summer, when I was about six, we all piled into my folks' 1919 Model T Ford sedan and headed for town and the annual two-day fair. There were parades and a softball game in the mornings. In the afternoons, there was always a baseball game between neighboring towns. In addition there were several kinds of rides and a midway with stalls of various games of chance. My dad always worked in the food and beverage tent. When I would pay him for a dime hamburger, he usually gave me a nickel back. That year after the baseball game, I saw my first hot air balloon ascension. What a spectacle to watch how they built a wood fire and, with local help, inflated the bag with hot air and smoke from the fire. The balloon pilot would ask for volunteers to go for a ride. The only ones he got were local chaps who had consumed a few beers. My parents had to drag me away when it was time to go home and do the evening chores. Day two of the fair had more parades, another softball game with different teams, and in the afternoon, another baseball game. This game matched the winner of the game the day before against another town team. Baseball fascinated me then as it does today, some 70 years later. Again, for the second day in a row, I witnessed something I had never seen before. An airplane flew overhead, circled a couple of times and then disappeared. Soon someone said he landed in the Gordon's hay meadow not far from town. When my dad heard that, he promptly left the food tent and, together, we drove home in the Model T to see what was going on. Sure enough, there in our hay meadow sat the small airplane. My dad and I walked out there and, while he and the pilot had a heated conversation, I just stood there in awe of that flying machine. The smell of hot oil, aviation gasoline and fabric dope (sealer) made a permanent impression on me. Instead of a tail wheel, the airplane had a skid bar. Today they are called tail draggers. Everywhere the airplane taxied on the ground, the skid bar made a small furrow. That's what my dad was upset about. He told the pilot to get his "machine" out of there and to stay out. As I watched the airplane depart, I was thrilled to see a real live airplane take to the air. If the hot-air balloon the day before didn't plant the seeds of aviation in my mind, the sight, sound and smell of that airplane most certainly did.

Twenty years later, I would give my dad a ride in a small airplane from a farmer's field. It was his first and last ride in an airplane. He enjoyed it but never asked for another flight. The weather in east central Nebraska was famous for its extremes;. very hot and dry in the summers and deep snows and well below zero in the winters. One winter day when I was 12, my parents rushed me to the hospital for an emergency appendix operation. They operated that night, and the next morning, my dad came into the room and told me it was 26 degrees below zero. His ears were nearly frozen from just walking the short distance to the hospital. The weather I feared most was the spring tornados. We had a storm cellar near the house and used it many times while I was growing up. The cellar was where the canned goods were kept along with the root beer, wine, and real beer, all homemade. One had to be careful when opening the beer bottles, as the slightest movement would cause the beer to blow to the ceiling. It was all good and every time we had company, a lot of it disappeared. When I was about 15, I graduated from root beer to the real thing. Never more that one bottle, though. When the violent spring storms turned the sky black with shades of green, we headed for the storm cellar. My dad always took along an axe and a lantern. My mother always took her rosary and a holy candle. During one especially bad storm, something fell across the cellar door, making a huge crashing noise. My dad said maybe that was the windmill, or part of the house. My mother led us in prayer that it was neither.

While waiting for the storm to ebb, we had apples and peaches to eat, but there was never any drinking during a storm. After chopping through the cellar door with his axe, my dad discovered that the loud noise we heard was only a large tree limb that had fallen across the cellar door. The windmill and house were not damaged but there were tree limbs scattered all over the place. The rest of the day was spent cleaning up. I witnessed several strange happenings during those spring storms. In 1928, using hog sale money, my dad bought a new car. It was a Chevrolet sedan, green with a black racing stripe. The car was garaged in the same building as the granary. After one bad storm, I saw oat grains driven into the car's radiator. Another time, I saw stalks of straw driven into tree trunks. I learned early on to have a healthy respect for those storms. All through my aviation career, I watched the weather like a hawk. Thunderstorms were given a wide berth whenever I encountered them while flying.

My Uncle Louie, who had a horse ranch in the Sandhills region of Nebraska, also operated a large steam engine to run grain threshing machines. During the winter months he stored it at our place. Boy, did I have fun playing in that steamer, making imaginary trips all over the country. During my early school days, my mother would drive my youngest sister and me down the hill to school. When I got older, we had to walk when the weather was decent. Finally one Christmas, Santa Claus brought me a new bicycle. It suffered a few dings while I learned to ride it. One of the first things I did was take the rear brake completely apart. Of course I had no luck at all getting it back together. After loading all the pieces in the back of the car, my dad and I headed for the hardware store. On the way back home, he said I would have to pay the $1.50 repair bill. That was a lot of money then, and it took me a long time to save it up. In the meantime, the bike stayed at the store. After I finally got the bike back, I rode it all over the area including to and from school but I never tinkered with it again. My sister had a girl's bike but I never went near it.

During my freshman year in high school, my sister, Eileen left for Lincoln to begin nurses training All the other girls were long gone so, now, I was all alone with my parents and the animals. By now Rusty was an old milk cow and as docile as they come. Through the years she had many calves but none were like her. One day she didn't come in with the other cows from the pasture at milking time. She had become ill and just couldn't walk anymore. Later my dad found her dead in the pasture. It was so sad for all of us. Rusty and I had so much fun together in her early years.

I loved and played all sports. Like in the movie "The Natural," my dad would play catch with me in the front yard. He too loved baseball and would listen to the Chicago White Sox games on the radio whenever he could. His eyes were bad, and when I threw the ball to him I had to throw it high so he could see it. He would pepper it back to me and I liked that. I was constantly throwing things, especially a rubber ball, against a building, any building, including the house. On the barn, I even outlined the baseball strike zone with a piece of chalk so I would have a target to throw at. I preferred to throw the baseball, but the barn wouldn't toss it back to me. One day I got a brainstorm and decided to fix the baseball problem. I proceeded to design and build a "battery box." I named it that because on a baseball team, the pitcher and the catcher are known as the "battery." I searched around and found some wooden planks. Using my father's tools, I sawed them to the correct size. Next, I nailed them together to form the shape of the baseball strike zone. In those days the strike zone was the width of home plate stretching from the knees to the shoulders.

Today the strike zone seems half that height and also wider than home plate; also, no two umpires seem to have the same size strike zone. There are no more high strikes. Then, I had to shape the plank so the surface was convex. When a baseball was thrown at it, the ball would react as if the plank were a large bat. Finding a solid place on the side of the barn, I nailed it up at just the right height from the ground. With chalk, I drew an outline of a batter standing next to my strike zone plank. The batter didn't last long as the rains took care of that and I decided I didn't need it anyway. I could vividly imagine a right-or left-handed batter standing there whenever I wished. But my project was only half finished. Next I had to build a pitcher's mound. Being quite young, I located it only 40 feet from the barn instead of the normal 60 feet, 6 inches. At first I didn't always hit the strike zone and would bang the barn. My dad didn't like that as it might scare the animals and chip the red paint. So I put up thick boards to outline the plank. That took care of pitches that were "balls."

Many enjoyable hours were spent playing imaginary games. My favorite team then was the New York Yankees. Many years later, I would drop the Yankees for the St. Louis Cardinals. As a result of the curved plank, I became a pretty good fielding pitcher. The top and bottom of the plank were also curved so I got plenty of grounders and pop-ups. Sometimes a line drive would come right back at me. It was great fun. When I would burn one in and it came back over my head, that was a hit. Most of my spending allowance went toward purchasing baseballs. They didn't last long against that thick plank. To grade the hits, I devised a piece of heavy cardboard and put a spinner on it. The card was marked so when the spinner stopped, it would point to either a single, double, triple, or even a home run. I would walk some batters but not many. In a couple years, I moved the mound back to regulation distance from home plate. I talked to my dad about putting up a light so I could have night games. He said no, because baseball was a day game. Playing it at night would just ruin it, he said. I painted my strike zone white and the boards around it black. Against the red barn, I thought it looked pretty good. Each fall, I would have the play-offs and then the heated "World Series." Before each game I would warm up using an old beat-up ball. But when it was time for the game to start, I would get a nice new one, just like in a real game.

In 1937, because of the depression, drought and poor crops, the folks decided sell the farm. I will never forget the auction sale. It was a nice day, so everything we didn't want was put out in the yard to sell. The place was packed with people and everything was sold. Seeing all the animals and farm equipment go to the highest bidder was very sad for me. The last thing to sell was the farm itself-so much per acre and that included all the buildings. We gave away the cats and dogs. We just couldn't sell them. It was a very emotional day. We remembered all those years and hard work my dad invested in those fields trying to raise a decent crop. Now we had very little to show for it. Life on the farm left many permanent memories. Across the road to the north was the town's cemetery. It was divided into two parts. The eastern half, covered with fir trees, was the Protestant half, and the western half, treeless, was the Catholic side. During the day it was very quiet and peaceful there, but at night the ghosts and the gremlins came out. I heard them countless times. I wouldn't even look over there when it was dark outside. In our own tree grove, we had many birds that were always singing. We had nightingales too, but they only sang at night. Our birds seemed to stay away from the cemetery also.

Life on the farm was pretty much regulated by the chores that had to be done morning and evening every day 365 days a year regardless of the weather conditions. On Saturday afternoons everyone would go to town to shop and visit. I looked forward to these times as I could romp and play with my school friends, horsing around as most of our parents called it. One Saturday several of us went up to the train depot. The agent wasn't around as the afternoon train didn't come in until later. Inside, we became curious about the gum ball machine hanging on the wall. Soon we had it off the wall and were shaking it upside down. Instead of gum balls coming out, coins came out and rolled around the floor. We were so surprised, we didn't know what to do. Some wanted to get out of there fast, but we just hung the machine back on the wall and put the coins back into the machine where they belonged. For that, we were rewarded with pockets full of gum balls. If our parents knew of that devilry, we all would have gotten a good tanning.

Every evening we ate supper promptly at six o'clock, and would listen to the news on the radio. After supper, my dad would have a cup of hot tea and a Camel cigarette. I'll never forget the aroma of that smoke, especially the first whiff. It was delightful. I also liked hot tea and still do, to this day. During the day my mom would listen to her favorite radio programs such as Ma Perkins, Vic and Sadie, and Just Plain Bill. She considered all those characters her good friends.

One Saturday night there was a dance in town and, after the shopping and the chores were done, my parents and I decided to go. Soon I had enough of the dance and wanted to go home. My parents were not ready, and said I could go on by myself. A good friend of mine was ready also, and we left together to go up the hill toward home. About half way we came to his house, and I was left to make the rest of the trek alone. It was okay until I got near the cemetery. We had an L-shaped lane up to the house, and I ran full speed all the way. Our two dogs (Toby and Rex) were on sentry duty and put out a warning bark. Quickly they realized it was me. Now I felt better as I was among friends. Together we went to the front porch where I climbed on the swing. The house was pitch black and I wasn't about to go in there. The dogs settled on the porch and resumed their sentry duty. Just before I fell asleep, I heard a nightingale sing. The next thing I knew, my mother was shaking me awake and sent me on to bed. The next morning when I looked over at the cemetery, it was so peaceful and quiet, it was hard to believe. I figured the ghosts and gremlins must sleep during the daytime.

I hated some jobs on the farm, such as cleaning the chicken coop and the barn and weeding the garden. Fixing fence was another job I detested. My mother would get upset with me for various reasons, but never slapped me, not once. She vented her emotions by pounding me on the shoulder. She was a very kind and lovable person. One time she saw a mouse in her kitchen. She yelled and ran outside and wouldn't go back in the house until I rounded up the critter. On the farm, we had a large orchard. Apple, peach, pear, cherry and mulberry trees were in abundance. My mother also had grape vines from which she made delicious jams and wine. On most Sunday afternoons, our pastor would come up and, along with neighbors, played cards. My dad didn't smoke cigars, but the pastor did. When they were through playing and were outside, I would take a couple of fair-sized butts and hide them for future use. My grandfather died when I was about two years old and he left some old pipes at our house. A neighbor friend and I would put a cigar butt in one of the pipes and smoke away out behind the barn. It wasn't long before both of us were pea green and couldn't eat much supper after those sessions with the cigar-pipe.

The same group of boys that pulled off the gum ball job got to-gether one Saturday night and proceeded to the train depot. This time we stayed out of the station, but saw an empty box car standing on a siding. One of us noticed a brake wheel and wondered what would happen if we decided to turn it loose. With lookouts posted, one boy climbed up on the car and turned the wheel. The siding must have had a slight downgrade, because the car slowly started to move away. Need-less to say, we all got out of there quickly. The next morning, my dad said he heard that the morning train lost an empty box car and it was found upside down in a ditch south of town. Soon, several boys formed a private club. We called ourselves the Pirates and our meeting place was in one boy's hay loft. That was the Pirates' Den. We had strict rules for new recruits plus an initiation to go through. After they took the oath of honor to abide by The Rules of the Pirates, they went through the initiation. First, they were blindfolded and asked to remove all their clothes-everything. At the drugstore, we had bought a bottle of what was then called mercurochrome. On their foreheads we painted the letter "P". On their chests we painted a large "P" with a skull and crossbones in the circle of the letter. Then we painted their private parts. Now, after everything dried, they were told to dress, and we took off the blindfold. The look on their faces was hard to describe. They knew we did something, but weren't sure just what. Their oath pre-vented them from saying anything. That orange colored stuff won't wash off, it just had to wear off. Their mothers must have asked a lot of questions about the orange "P" on their son's foreheads.

Jim Van der Heiden was our club president and would come up with some dandy ideas for things to do. One winter, we built a bobsled that held eight people. The next thing was to borrow a horse from some farmer to pull it on the snowy roads around town. One night we had the horse and sled all ready and recruited eight passengers, four boys and four girls. The captain of the sled rode in the number one slot and managed the one horsepower "tractor." Behind the captain sat girl, boy, girl, boy, etc. All legs had to be around the person in front of you. The sled had a little shelf for the captain's legs to ride on. With the horse at a gallop, we had a great time clipping along those graveled roads. When the snow was thin, sparks would fly from the steel runners. It was great fun even though some nights it was really cold. We never did this during the day for reasons I can't remember, just at night. One night as the horse flew around a sharp corner, we all went tumbling into the snow-filled ditch. No one was injured and all just lay there in the snow and laughed and laughed. It took a while to recover our sled and horse and we did this many times. It was always a great event, and we never had any trouble getting passengers.

One summer evening, the Pirates dispatched two of the junior members to requisition some watermelons. A farmer had a big patch down by the river, and we never had a problem getting them to the Pirates' Den. The boys said the patch had more melons than the farmer could ever sell. I guess they helped him out as we did this several times each summer. To get to the melon patch, the boys had to ford the river both ways. They said coming back with two big melons was rather difficult, to say the least. Nothing tasted better than a cold watermelon that we didn't have to buy in the store or from a passing vendor's truck. One night when the boys were just leaving the farmer's patch, they heard dogs barking and then a loud blast from a shotgun. No pellets fell near them however. The club decided to take watermelons off the menu for the rest of the summer.

The people who bought our farm let us stay in the house a couple weeks so we could pack up for our move to Lincoln. My mom wanted to be near my two sisters who lived there. With our nine-year-old Chevy packed to the roof, we headed out of town. The three of us were silent in leaving as we all felt very sad. Soon we found a house to rent in Lincoln, and bought some used furniture to make it livable.

My sisters were very happy to have us there. My dad found odd jobs around town and I enrolled in the Cathedral High School. The classes were large and I was now a sophomore in a big city school. Six months later, my dad became tired of city life and wanted to move back to Cedar Rapids. My mother liked the situation there in Lincoln, but went along with my dad's wishes to leave. I made the "B" basketball team and really liked the school. The kids were all friendly and my best friend was Jack Sweeney. One day Jack got me into some trouble in class and the nun made me stay over and write "I will not talk in class" 500 times. Jack showed me how to do that by using two pencils.

In late spring of 1938, my parents left Lincoln without me. They soon found a house to rent near Cedar Rapids, and I stayed with my two sisters and finished out the school year. My sisters had a one-bedroom apartment, and I slept on the couch. It worked out fine. For some spending money, I found a job at the Cornhusker Hotel working in the coffee shop. At first, I worked the "China Clipper" in the kitchen. The Clipper was a huge dish-washing machine that used hot scalding water and steam. Coming out, the dishes really sparkled. I had to be there at 6 a.m. and at 8:15, I had to hike on to school. Soon I graduated to the counter and served food. The hotel paid me $1.50 per day, plus free breakfast.

In June when school was out, I went back to be with my folks in Cedar Rapids. I worked on one of my brother-in-law's farm and he kept me busy from dawn to dusk. My brother-in-law (James Langan) taught me to drive a tractor, cultivate corn and do all kinds of fun things. I had all the good food I could eat and each Saturday my sister, Margaret, would give me five dollars, sometimes more. That fall I enrolled in the local high school - my junior year. I went out for football and made the team as a running back. After football, it was basketball and in the spring, track and baseball. I was very busy that year. Each summer during high school I would work on the farm again. James Langan decided to buy a threshing machine. It was great fun going around the area threshing grain for different farmers. By then, I was pretty good with the tractor and that became my job - tractor manager. It had a power take-off and, with a big long belt, would drive the thresher. At each farm, the women would bring the work crew a big basket of goodies along with iced lemonade. That happened twice a day, once at mid-morning and again at mid-afternoon. I was having a ball doing that, except for getting up each morning at 4:30 a.m. All the farmers would take an hour nap right after lunch. That sure did help my tired body, and I was surprised we could do that. During my senior year I played all the sports. Our basketball team came within one game of going to the state finals for our division. When we lost the last game, we really got down. We worked so hard all year and developed into a pretty good team. To get that close to the state finals and then lose was very disheartening.

The team felt so low about losing that last game in the district finals, we found someone to buy some beer and got pretty soused. Even the cheerleaders went along with us. The next Monday at school, all hell broke loose. The team was to immediately report to the principal's office. There behind closed doors he dressed us down good and said we embarrassed him, the whole school and the whole town. Nine of us were suspended for one week. The girls got off, because of some plea bargaining. It was all the boys' fault, they said. At home, all of us were grounded. I asked my mother to pick up a couple of history books from school. In that week, I not only read them, but wrote two long book reports that I later turned in as extra work. I was quite surprised when I got an "A" in history that year.

During my senior year, I worked each Saturday sweeping out the school gym. Then I would go upstairs and scrub blackboards. For all that, I received the grand sum of one dollar per week. The war in Europe was raging, and one day, during the lunch period, I heard a short-wave radio broadcast direct from Germany. The person who was speaking, or rather shouting, was Adolph Hitler. The Fuhrer was announcing his plans to invade Holland, Belgium and France. It was May 10, 1940. Just thirty five days later, on June 14, Paris fell to the German invaders. Everyone wondered how the United States could possibly keep out of this war. To fight the Germans from England would make more sense than to try to fight them from America. The newspapers were full of war clouds. The winds of war were blowing now and everyone was very nervous. Paris and all of France suffered severe hardships under German rule. However, after 1,533 days of German occupation, Paris was finally liberated by American forces on August 26, 1944.

Each time when I go back to Cedar Rapids and go up the hill to the old cemetery to visit the graves of my parents and brother, I can't help but look across the field to the south and see the old homestead. In my mind, I can still see the big two-story house, all the trees, the big red barn and all the other buildings that we had, the old wooden windmill turning in the breeze and the animals in the barnyard going to the big water tank for a cool drink. My old "battery box" and all the other things are crystal clear in my mind. But soon, I realize I was just looking at a mirage. When I blink my eyes there is absolutely nothing there but a large cornfield. Every last thing is gone, everything. I spent 15 wonderful years on that hill and now, only fond memories remain. Looking around the old cemetery, I wonder where all the ghosts and gremlins were. They seem to be gone, too. Leaving my parents' and my little brother's graves I have to fight back the tears.

To love what you do and feel that it matters — how could anything be more fun?

—Katherine Graham

CHAPTER THREE

BUILDING AIRCRAFT

Only the eyes and ears are able to absorb knowledge. Never the mouth.

—Benjamin Franklin

The first aviation-related event to make an impression on my mind occured when I was about six years old. That was when I first saw a hot air balloon ascension and the Curtiss Jenny war surplus airplane that landed in my parents' hay meadow during the summer fair in 1928. Except for building a lot of balsa wood models, I wouldn't have aviation enter my life again for another 12 years. During my last year in high school, the teachers were always talking about college and what to do with our lives. Much as I liked history, I was torn between teaching history and veterinary medicine as career choices. As much as I liked animals in my growing years, it was a difficult decision to make. However, after graduation, things changed quickly. First, my parents couldn't afford to send me to college and I had no rich uncle. The war news in Europe was constantly on the radio. It wasn't getting any better and I wondered how much longer it would be before the United States would be drawn into it. Along with all the other young boys, I would no doubt have to enter the service of my country.

My youngest sister, Eileen, was in Lincoln in nurses' training. Her boy friend's brother was the manager of a government contract aviation school in Lincoln. They trained pilots and mechanics for the U. S. Army Air Corps. I became very interested and another sister, Margaret, lent me the money to ride the train to Lincoln and talk to the people there. The manager, Wendel Harding, told me I had to have a college degree to enter Army Air Corps Pilot Training. Being a high school graduate, however, I qualified for the mechanics school but first, I would have to take the oath and join the Army Air Corps. That didn't exactly appeal to me and, after further investigation, I discovered that the school also offered a course in aircraft fabrication and assembly. I learned those graduates would qualify for employment in various aircraft factories around the country. The cost of this three-month accelerated course was $600 and the next class was to start in two weeks. That got my attention quickly and I was extremely interested.

Back home, I told my parents what I wanted to do. The problem was money. They didn't have $600 lying around and I became very worried. In a few days, a letter arrived from my sister in Lincoln saying another brother of Mr. Harding might loan me the tuition money. Again, Margaret came to my rescue and I returned to Lincoln to negotiate the loan. After graduation, I was to repay the loan at a minimum of $25 a month. Eileen and I both signed the promissory note and I was enrolled in the Lincoln Flying School. My parents were very happy with my good fortune but at the same time, were saddened by the fact that their youngest child, and only son, was leaving the nest. I didn't think much about that at the time but years later when my first son left home, I realized what my parents went through when I left that day in the spring of 1940, at the tender age of 18.

My two sisters in Lincoln insisted that I move in with them again. I slept on the couch and was glad to have that available. My school started on June 6 and was located at 24th and O streets just east of downtown Lincoln. I would have about a 20-minute walk to school from the apartment where I would be staying. My aviation class had about 40 students and they came from near and far. Classes were from 8 a.m. to 4 p.m. five days a week. We had morning classes and an afternoon workshop period. In class, I learned about the history of aviation and it's manufacturing techniques. I learned how an airplane is conceived on the drawing board by design engineers, and then how wooden models are made from the drawings. The models are then put into a wind tunnel to show the effects of high-speed wind on their individual airfoils. In the work shop, we learned how to build a full size airfoil by using wooden ribs and, after fastening them to the two wing spars, we proceeded to stretch and sew linen fabric over the whole thing. The workshop was on the lower level and it was quite large. Our class was split into four groups with an instructor for each group. In the morning classroom, we were always all together.

Applying dope to the fabric was interesting. Dope is the trade name for a clear mixture of acrid cellulose-acetate butyrate and can be pigmented (colored). First, a coat of clear dope would be put on and left to dry overnight, then a second coat of pigmented dope was applied, followed by a third coat of the clear stuff. Now, the fabric was nice and tight and smooth as glass. No single group would do a whole wing, just about a six-foot section. All four groups were graded on how well they did. Next, we did a similar project by building part of a fuselage. We fastened some stringers and formers and by now, we were getting rather good at it. It was like a life-size model airplane kit.

We worked on parts of the tail section and then each of the three controls—the ailerons, rudder and elevators. Those projects were full scale and complete. The instructors seemed pleased with our work. Now we were through with wood and fabrics, and graduated to metal work. Large sheets of aluminum alloy were put on a drilling machine to drill the pattern of rivet holes. When the holes were all drilled, about two inches apart, we took the "skin" to a machine that formed the dimples. This was a procedure where the holes were formed so the rivet heads would be flush when driven. Jigs were used to hold the formers and stringers so we could fasten the skin to them. Everyone took turns at driving the rivet gun which used compressed air. Then we were formed into pairs, one driving and one "bucking" the rivet from the other side with an aluminum bucking bar. It was exacting work, and it took some time to get the hang of it. A perfectly driven and bucked rivet is a thing of beauty. I enjoyed that phase very much.

Each morning in class, the instructors would demonstrate how we were going to perform the next project. Time flew by and the next and final project was to learn all about a popular airplane engine—the Curtiss OX-5. It was a V8 engine that developed 90 HP at 1400 RPM, consumed 9 gallons of fuel and a quart of oil per hour and was water cooled. The school had five of those engines and that equated to eight students and one instructor per engine. Each engine was located in an engine mount about four feet off the floor for easy access. This phase required us to completely disassemble, clean and reassemble each engine. The engines were then trucked out to the Lincoln airport test cell, where they were run and tested for proper operation.

In tearing down an engine, the minor assemblies must be removed first. When taking out the spark plugs, we had to be careful to plug each hole with a piece of soft wood. This was to prevent any foreign objects from dropping inside the cylinders. The rocker arm assemblies and water pump were then removed. After that the magneto was removed and sent to the electrical repair shop for inspection and, if necessary, repair.. Next, the cylinders came off and we had to be careful that someone was holding the pistons when they were freed of the cylinder. If left to flop down, they could be easily damaged. The oil was drained by turning the engine upside down in its stand. First to come off was the crankcase, then the oil pump, followed by the connecting rods and pistons. Finally, out came the crankshaft. The engine was now completely disassembled. All the parts were laid out on a big table covered with clean brown paper. Some of us inspected and cleaned various parts while others cleaned the crankcase. Everything had to be whistle clean. Finally a light coat of oil was carefully applied to each part.

As the crankshaft was the last part to be removed from the engine, so it was the first part to be replaced, followed by the pistons and connecting rod bearings. Now, the cylinders have to be mounted, valve-operating parts put back and the intake manifolds installed. Next, the rocker-arm assembly must be put back and the valves timed. The magneto now must be mounted and timed. All the other parts are now put back on, including the carburetor. The instructor demonstrated how to clean and gap the spark plugs. When there are no more parts left on the table, the engine is ready for a thorough and rigid inspection. We finished up on a Friday and the instructor told us the engines would be taken out to the airport over the weekend. Monday morning a detailed briefing would be given on how the engine test would be conducted. For a student to pass the engine phase of the school, his engine had to run and run well on Monday. This was very exciting work and all of us thoroughly enjoyed this phase of school. Even our instructors were excited about the tests.

While the class was sitting in school Monday morning waiting for our instructors to come in, we heard a rumor that some aircraft manufacturer representatives were coming in to interview us. That bit of news increased the level of excitement in all of us. The thought of helping to build a real live, honest-to-goodness airplane was almost beyond my imagination. The chief instructor, Mr. Faggio, came in and told the class that only one of the five engines that had been torn down and rebuilt would be tested. There wasn't time to run them all and he left us to wonder which group's engine would be tested. Now I wondered how good a job the other groups did. My group hoped our engine would be tested because we felt we took extra pains to do the build-up right. On the bus to the airport, I tried to get Mr. Faggio to confirm the rumor we heard, earlier that day about the job interviews. He would neither confirm nor deny it, and just said he didn't know anything about that. None of us really believed him. I felt that the General Manager, Wendel Harding, wanted to give us that news himself.

Arriving at the airport, the bus took us to the engine test cell located in a far corner of the field. There in the middle of a large building sat one lonely looking OX-5 aircraft engine. On each side were bleachers for the 40 students to sit and observe the test run. Quickly I noticed that on the front of the engine was mounted a small sawed-off propeller. While it was still quiet, Mr. Faggio told us the small propeller was weighted and acted like a flywheel on an ordinary engine. An aircraft engine doesn't have a flywheel and that's where the propeller came in. He then explained how they jury-rigged a water supply to the coolant connections. A small fuel tank was added and, last but not least, he showed us that the crankcase was indeed full of fresh oil.

Mr. Faggio then handed out earphones to each of us to muffle the expected noise. The muffler was left off as the short exhaust stacks expelled the exhaust gases, and I knew it would be very noisy. We were told to observe the run carefully. First, the instructor opened the fuel supply cock, made sure the magneto switch was in the off position and cracked the throttle open about an inch. He then hit the starter switch. The early engines had to be hand-propped to start them. Now they had an electric starter. With a growl, the engine turned over as we watched the little propeller turn slowly. After counting eight blades, he released the starter. With the magneto switch now on, he mashed the starter switch again. Again, with a growl the engine slowly turned over. Then without any kind of warning, the engine coughed, belched smoke out the exhaust stacks, and came to life.

The little weighted propeller was spinning in a blur. Mr. Faggio set the speed at 1,000 RPM so the engine could warm up slowly. At that setting, it was running like a sewing machine and it sounded good. The instructor was smiling as he looked around. We all let out a yell and were grinning from ear to ear. Some of the students even took off their ear phones. They wanted to hear the full sound of that beautiful little engine. The rest of the test went perfectly. We were all very proud of it. From that day on, I have always treated an engine, airplane or car, with the utmost tender loving care. My motto became "keep it clean on the outside and keep fresh oil on the inside." I was very happy I had taken that course. When the test run was over we all piled into the bus and were taken back to the school where Mr. Faggio gave us the rest of the day off. He said to be back at 9 a.m. the next day for a special meeting. We all yelled "whoopee" over that. Most of us went to an afternoon movie to relax. The movie, including a large popcorn, cost 30 cents.

Greeting us the next morning was the Lincoln Flying School's General Manager, Wendel Harding. He congratulated us on the exemplary manner in which we had completed the course, then handed out certificates of completion. I was extremely happy. Mr. Harding told us that representatives from four aircraft companies were waiting in an adjoining room to interview us. To be fair, he went on, we would enter the interview room in alphabetical order. Each student would have the opportunity to talk to Boeing, Lockheed, Curtiss-Wright and Glen L.

Martin representatives. When it was all over later that day, I accepted an offer from the Curtiss-Wright Aircraft Company in Buffalo, New York. All the offers were good but the Curtiss representative was the most impressive of the group. Mr. Mullins, from Curtiss-Wright, gave me an application and other forms to fill out. When that was completed, he gave me a travel voucher to give to the Greyhound Bus people for travel from Lincoln to Buffalo. I had two weeks to get ready and report for work. Another piece of paper directed that I take a taxi from the bus depot in Buffalo to the St. Regis Hotel. From the hotel, I was to call an indicated phone number and. they would take it from there. Les Hilger, a good friend and classmate, took the same job offer and we would ride the bus back east together. The Hilger family had roots in Cedar Rapids but Les's father moved to a farm north of Columbus, Nebraska, soon after he married.

Now, I had to go home and tell my parents the good news. I had a real job! My time at home passed quickly. My parents were very pleased but saddened that I, at such a young age, would be so far from home. I not only had a nice job, but some debts to pay. I felt very grown up. As I left my parent's house, my mother was crying, so was I. She was a very emotional person and I guess I inherited that from her.

With a new suitcase, I met Les at our agreed upon time in Lincoln and we started out for Buffalo. I had $35 in my pocket-$25 from relatives, and $10 from my dad, the last he would ever give me. The long trip to Buffalo lasted three days. The city looked nice and clean and was the biggest, by far, that I had ever seen. This was all new to me, but Les and I found the St. Regis hotel and called the Curtiss telephone number. The man who answered instructed us to stay there that night and he would pick us up at 8 a.m. the following day. He also said the bus would have the Curtiss Aircraft name on it when it came by the hotel.

At the aircraft plant, I filled out more forms in the Personnel Department. After that, I was given a physical and was processed into the company.. With a nice badge with my picture on it, I was to report to work the next day at 4 p.m. I chose the second shift because it paid more and I didn't have to get up so early. I got off at midnight and the buses ran all night because the plant ran three shifts around the clock. All the newspapers continued to remind us that we were on the brink of war. It was September 21, 1940.

During my in-processing the personnel manager, Mr. Flynn, told me about a nearby rooming house. The big white two-story house was located at 83 Hodges Avenue, just two blocks from the bus stop on busy Elmwood Avenue. Les and I wanted a car but that would have to wait for a while. My first day at work, I was assigned to the final assembly line for the P-40 fighter airplane. The line was long, I counted about 20 airplanes, nose to tail, in various stages of completion. My foreman's name was Mike Valley. He was a super person. He took me under his wing probably because I was so young. Les also picked the second shift but was assigned to another assembly line for the Navy's SB2C Dive Bomber. On the P-40 line, I was assigned to man the rivet gun. To me, that was easier than bucking rivets on the inside of the airplane. That was a hot and confining job, so I stayed on the rivet gun as long as I could. One day, Mr. Valley said I should also learn to buck rivets.

I didn't tell Mr. Valley I already knew how to buck rivets. I just kept quiet about my training back in Lincoln and he never asked. In those days, there were few labor unions but every night when I left the plant, union representatives at the main gate were handing out pamphlets and tobacco in the form of chewing plugs, cigars and cigarettes. This went on every night for the two years I was there. Mr. Valley said unions were no good so I never accepted any of their hand-outs. I did notice the representatives I saw were all rough looking people. They reminded me of movie thugs.

After a couple months, the temptation to buy a car got the better of us. One day before going to work, Les and I visited a used car lot. An hour later, we drove out of there in a blue 1937 Ford V6. It had the small engine-only 60 HP. It could barely pull itself up a good hill but, at least, we had our own transportation. Our only day off was Sunday and now we could scout around the city looking for excitement. Soon we found some action across the Niagara river in Ontario, Canada. It was the first time I was ever outside the United States. There was an amusement park there called "Two Flags Over Niagara." It was always crowded and good-looking French Canadian girls were everywhere. Les and I would go over there nearly every Sunday. There was a dance hall where you could buy tickets for 10 cents a dance and I met a lot of nice girls there.

One day Mr. Valley asked me if I would like to take on a different assignment. He took me to the end of the P-40 assembly line where the airplanes were nearly the finished product, ready to be test-flown and delivered to the customer - the U.S. Army Air Corps. He took me up on a work stand beside the last airplane on the line, then he told me to sit in the pilot's seat. Wow! What a thrill that was! Next he showed me how the sliding canopy worked by turning a hand crank that opened and closed the canopy. It seemed to work very well. Then he said,

"Tom, I want you to work with Mac and learn how to install these canopies." I couldn't have been more pleased. Mac began by taking me back up the line a few airplanes where the canopies were first set up. First, he showed me how to inspect the tracks the canopy would slide on. Using an alignment tool, the installers made sure the track was perfectly spaced and level. Next I learned how to install the hand crank assembly and the cables that connect to the canopy to make it slide open and closed. I really liked this job; it was great.

Before long, Mr. Valley went back to the day shift as he was promoted to Supervisor of Final Assembly. I was happy for him and told him so. My new foreman was Mr. Burns and, like Mr. Valley, I liked him for the way he treated his people. The canopy installation job was great. Waiting for various parts to be delivered to the airplane, I just sat in the cockpit. I didn't know what it was like to be a pilot, but I sure wanted to find out. In less than a month, Mac turned me loose and I was, effectively, my own boss. Only the government inspector had to inspect and stamp my canopy installations. I was extremely careful in my work, as those canopies had to work perfectly. Occasionaly the tracking tool detected a flaw in one of the two tracks. When that occured, I had to have Mr. Burns bring in a specialist to re-rig the track rails. While waiting for that to happen, I got in more cockpit time.

It was critical that the cables, which pulled the canopy in either direction, be adjusted precisely to the specified tension. Using a system of turnbuckles and a tension meter, I would satisfy this requirement, but, before the tension meter could be removed from the cable, a turnbuckle specialist was required to safety wire the turnbuckle to ensure that the tension remain as set. More time in the P-40 cockpit was spent waiting for the specialist to show up. Soon I knew just where everything in that cockpit was located. I could touch everything with my eyes closed and made lots of imaginary flights.

Through the company, Les and I got a package trip to Cleveland, Ohio. The package consisted of a Sunday afternoon baseball game between the Cleveland Indians and the New York Yankees, train fare both ways and food and beer on the train both ways. I thoroughly enjoyed the game that day as I watched my first major league baseball game. Bob Feller pitched for the Indians and Lefty Gomez threw for the Yankees. They were wonderful pitchers to watch, but I cannot now remember who won the game. When we got back to Buffalo, Les and I headed for the Glass Bar for a night cap and, over a couple of beers, relived that wonderful trip. Seeing major league baseball at its finest was very exciting. There were no errors and the fielders threw accurately to the correct base every chance they had. It was a low scoring game as the pitching was superb. Lying in bed that night, I thought about what a wonderful day we had.

Les soon grew tired of the little Ford 60 and wanted out of the shared ownership. So I bought his half and he got something he liked better. Fever is contagious they say because in just about a month, I traded the little Ford for a 1938 Ford V8. The real thing. It had an 85 HP engine! The color was racing green and the body had a teardrop design. It was very good-looking and ran like a top. Naturally, I took excellent care of the engine and bought a set of re-capped tires as soon as I saved the money. New tires were not available to the public at that time due to the war effort.

After I had spent a year on the P-40 assembly line, Mr. Burns asked if I would like to volunteer for a new project. He said it was classified and if I took it, I would have to have an FBI background check in order to get the clearance. If the background check was good, I would wear a second badge. Naturally I was interested and went for it. I passed the background check and then had to go through another processing to obtain my second badge. I was reluctant to leave the P-40 line but this was a challenge I wanted to take. When everything was in order and I was wearing two badges, Mr. Burns took me over to another building and introduced me to a Mr. Cooper. His title was Special Projects Manager. I thanked Mr. Burns for giving me the opportunity and then he left. Mr. Cooper took me into another building that had a large black curtain inside the door. After going through that, we came into a large hangar and I noticed there were no windows. The lights were turned up and there sat a big full-scale wooden model of the Curtiss C-46 twin engine transport. She was a beauty and, except for the wheels and landing hear, she was all wood! In Mr. Cooper's office, I learned that this airplane was right off the drawing board. The first metal ship was not even started yet. A group of hand-picked men were to fit and size the necessary jigs that would be needed to build airplane number one. My job was, again, in the cockpit measuring and helping to build the window jigs. This cockpit had windows all over it, even down to the floor on both pilots' sides. Without cockpit seats in this mock-up, I sat on a box to work. I ate lunch at 9 p.m. in a separate dining room just for this special project.

During the coming months I worked hard on the plywood mock-up. Everywhere I went my tools were a clipboard, flashlight and measuring tape. Only about 20 people worked on this project during second shift. I have no idea how many worked on it during the other shifts.

The cabin was so large, it looked like it could hold twice as much as the C-47, its forerunner. The engines would be the R-2800 Pratt & Whitney twin-row radial that developed 2,300 HP. It had Curtiss electric propellers that had four blades instead of the usual three. The big transport was given the name Commando. Finally we had the jig specifications finished for the first metal C-46. Now the engineers and technicians were ready to set up the jigs for production. After the mock-up work is finished, the jigs are set and the first assembly is started. Usually the fuselage is started first, then the nose and cockpit section, followed by the tail section. The wing is built in its own jig and, when finished, is mated to the fuselage further down the assembly line. It was quite a thrill to work on the first model of a new airplane. I had never had that privilege before and never had it again. My work was in the cockpit forming and fitting the alloy window frames in place. This was hard work and progressed slowly. The first airplane of any series is always slow work. The production numbers that followed always went smoother and faster. On number one, we learned as we went along—trial and error as they say.

I finally accrued some vacation time and Les and I arranged to take our vacation together. First, we drove up to Niagara Falls to see that spectacle. What a sight to see all that falling water. We took a tour and saw it from below also. What a grand sight. Sometime later, I saw a Marilyn Monroe movie that was filmed there. After Niagara Falls, Les and I traveled southeast across the state of New York to see the big city for the weekend. Finding a hotel room near Times Square, we saw sights that are hard to describe. 42nd Street and Broadway are the crossroads of America. They say if you wait there long enough, you will eventually see someone you know. What a busy city with taxi-cabs running all over the place at breakneck speed day and night. New York City is just as busy and interesting today as it was then. One night we went to Harlem to visit the famous Cotton Club. That night Duke Ellington's band played dance music to a full house, and it was really jumping with all the good music. Les and I really enjoyed ourselves and, after a couple of drinks, left and went down the street and had some of the best barbecue I have ever eaten.

While in New York we took in the Radio City Music Hall show with the Rockets. Those 40 girls did a magnificent job with their precision dancing. Their high kick was their specialty and they did a lot of it. Across the street, we visited the CBS Radio Studios and went on a tour. We watched a daytime soap opera. Four people were standing around a microphone in a studio and, through a glass window, we watched "One Man's Family" unfold. Their sound effects man was incredible. In another studio, they told us to turn away from the sound man and guess what each sound represented. There were horses walking, horses running, doors closing, phones ringing and many more. All the sounds were produced clearly and realistically. We also took in the big Broadway review called "Hellzapoppin," starring Joe E. Lewis. He was quite a character. JEL had lots of very funny vaudeville skits that kept the audience in stitches the whole two hours. My sides hurt from the constant laughing. Early the next day, Les and I headed back to Buffalo and our jobs.

Back at the plant, things had changed in our absence. The C-46 production was declassified and its assembly line moved to the main plant alongside the P-40 line. Now I was back working for my old boss, Mr. Burns. He put me on the Navy SB2C Dive Bomber line helping with its canopy installation. On this airplane, a crew of three worked together doing that task. It was fine, but I liked working alone on the P-40 and the C-46 lines better. Les received some bad news from home. His father became quite ill and his mother wanted him to come home and help with the farm. Les didn't want to leave but knew he had to. I hated to see him go as he was a very good friend and we had lots of good times together.

Coming home one Sunday afternoon, I heard on the radio that the Japanese had attacked our Navy port at Pearl Harbor, Hawaii. It was December 7, 1941. The next day at work, everyone was talking about it. Now we were getting into the war with Japan instead of Germany. In just a matter of days, war was declared on Germany as well. Like a lot of others, I visited the Army Air Corps Recruiting Office the next week and saw the waiting line stretched around the block. I decided not to pursue the issue right then and would wait for a while. However, I still, very strongly, wanted to become a pilot. After being around airplanes for over a year, there was absolutely no doubt in my mind. Flying airplanes was my goal, and nothing could change that now that World War II had started in two very distant parts of the world.

A lot of people enlisted in the service and the Curtiss-Wright work force was noticeably thin in places. If someone didn't show up for work, it was assumed he had joined the service. One day a letter came from my sister, Agnes, in Omaha. She included an article from the Omaha World Herald newspaper that told of the Glen L. Martin Aircraft Company's plans to open a new assembly plant at the Fort Crook Army Base south of Omaha. The airfield there was known as Offutt Field. The article went on to say they expected to start operating the plant in early summer of 1942. Before going to work the next day, I stopped at the library on Elmwood and had the lady look up the Glen

L. Martin Aircraft Company's address in Baltimore, Maryland. I wrote immediately and said I was interested in working for them in Omaha. By now I had well over a year experience in aircraft manufacturing. In about ten days, I received a reply. They thanked me for the letter and included an application form to complete. Mr. Valley and Mr. Burns wrote letters of recommendation and, with the application, it was all sent to Baltimore via air mail. At work, my canopy assembly team shrunk to two people because of workers joining the service. One day, Mr. Burns took me over to the O-52 Army Air Corps assembly line. He said I might as well work on every airplane built there. I was happy for the opportunity. I learned how to install the movable flight controls and hook up the control cables that moved them. It was a small airplane and fun to work on. It had a high wing and one 650 HP engine. The small observation plane would carry a pilot and two observers.

Another letter arrived from the Glen L. Martin Company's personnel office. They received my application and said, that if I wanted the job, to be at their Omaha plant personnel department not later than May 1, 1942. I had nine weeks to make up my mind about this offer. One night, at the Glass Bar, I met a very nice young girl. Her name was Helen Murphy and she worked for Bell Aircraft Company there in Buffalo. They were building the P-39 fighter aircraft for the U.S. Army Air Corps.

Helen worked in the office of the Production Manager as a secretary. We hit it off really well and she liked to dance to the slow music as I did. I soon learned that she lived only four blocks from me at 35 Days Park. I didn't tell her I was going to be leaving in two months. No use spoiling a good relationship. How wrong I was. Being a local girl, Helen knew all about the Two Flags Amusement Park. One Sunday we went there and had a good time on the rides. I wanted to take her up to Niagara Falls but she had seen it and didn't care to go back. She claimed there were too many people for her comfort. The Glass Bar was open seven days a week till 2 a.m. So every night, after work, I would go there and look for Helen. She worked second shift at Bell for the same reasons as I did at Curtiss.

Behind the Curtiss-Wright plant was a small airstrip just long enough for the P-40, the O-52 and the SB2C to depart for the short flight over to Buffalo's main airport. That is where all Army Air Corps aircraft deliveries were made. Before the C-46 could depart from the plant, they would have to add a couple thousand feet to the runway. It would be awhile before that aircraft would be ready to fly anyway. Occasionally the chief inspector would call me out to the ramp behind the plant to adjust a canopy or its crank mechanism on a P-40. I mentioned to one of the test pilots that I wanted to be a pilot in the Army Air Corps. He told me to go down to the recruiting office and sign up right away. I told him about going back to Omaha soon and would do it there. He said, "Don't forget now, it's a real nice job." Time was going by quickly now that it was getting on into April. In just two weeks I would be leaving for Omaha and still didn't have the courage to tell Helen. By now, I was seeing her almost every night after work at the Glass Bar. It looked like it might get serious at any time. My landlady Mrs. Snyder was an understanding soul, and one day I told her about Helen. She scolded me severely and said I should have told the poor girl a long time ago. Now I didn't know what to do.

It was April 20 and I planned to leave Buffalo on the 23rd. This would give me plenty of time to drive out to Omaha and get settled in. Friday was my last day at work, and about all I did was attend to the out-processing that needed to be done. My security clearance was revoked, my badges were turned in and I was issued a temporary badge just to leave the plant. The final thing, before saying goodbyes, was to receive my final pay. This time it was in cold cash and a $50 bonus was included. From whom, I never learned. I was allowed to leave two hours early and, when going out the gate, the union people were just arriving. This time I took a package of three cigars, and then asked for a second package. Those goons didn't know what to say. But I got the cigars.

That night at the Glass Bar I kind of hoped Helen might not be there, but she came in right after work. I bought her a beer and said I needed to talk to her. She said it was too noisy and she wanted to dance. I always drank the local beer called "Downs" but that night it just wasn't appealing. When Helen came in with her girl friends I asked her if I could take her home later as I had a special reason. Sitting in the swing on her front porch later that night, I told her of my plans; the tears came and I said I was terribly sorry and felt awful. With her sobbing, I don't think she even heard me. She quickly got up and ran inside the house.

I hated to leave Buffalo as I thoroughly enjoyed my job at Curtiss Wright and met scores of very nice people. Some, I didn't treat very well, I am sorry to say. The trip to Omaha went without a hitch as the Ford ran perfectly. Being in a grumpy mood over Helen, I thought about writing her but decided it would serve no real purpose. I blew it and keenly knew that. The first night in Omaha, I stayed with my sister Marie. She had four daughters so I slept on the couch. The next day, I went up to visit with my folks. They were fine and were happy that I was back in Nebraska.

The Glenn L.Martin Aircraft Company was starting operations in brand new facilities. Soon, it was called the "Bomber Plant." During in-processing, I again selected the second shift as it paid 50 cents more per hour and I didn't have to get up so early. I was the 211th employee hired and; today my old wooden tool box still has the Martin decal on it that reads #211. My old aircraft fabrication tools, including several of my favorite rivet bucking bars, are still in it.

The Martin Company was building the B-26 Medium Bomber and my job was on the final assembly line. I worked inside the bomb bay of the aircraft, adjusting the cable tension. I would go to the tool crib and check out a tension meter; then go inside the bomb bay where I first adjusted the cable tension to my satisfaction. Next, I would attach the tension meter and continue the adjustment until the tension met specifications. When that was done, I would notify Mr. Minter, my supervisor, who in turn would notify the govenment inspector. The government inspector, accompanied by a specialist, who would safety-wire the turnbuckles, would sign off on the job with his stamp of approval on his worksheet. At this point, the job was done. There were control cables for each control surface, each set of cables where checked and signed off in this manner. Needless to say, there was a lot of waiting time and I didn't wait in the bomb bay for the government inspection. I seized the opportunity and waited in the cockpit where I familiarized myself with the B-26 cockpit. I soon could locate every guage and control from memory. That cockpit time would help me a lot, later on, in getting familiar with the airplanes I would fly.

My other sister in Omaha, Agnes, had a spare room and I gratefully stayed with her. She and her husband, Elmer, had no children and both worked; so the arrangement worked out very well. I paid modest rent, but rarely ate my meals there. All this time I was paying off my debt to Niles Harding, the person who loaned me the money to attend the Lincoln Flying School two years earlier. I now owed him only $75. When he found out I was in Omaha working for the Martin Aircraft Company, he wrote me a curt letter saying it was high time I paid off the debt. Our original agreement was to pay it off at $25 a month until it was satisfied. Now, suddenly, he wanted the balance right away. The first chance I got, I went over to Lincoln and met with him. He wanted all his money. I argued that we had an agreement and the discussion heated up. Finally, I told him if he was that worried, I would manage to get the $75 and pay him off. That really upset me. I appreciated what he had done for me but didn't like his attitude. Soon, I scraped up the money and mailed it to him with a curt note attached.

There is nothing like the aroma of a brand new airplane. Working on the Martin B-26 was easy and exciting and I was getting in a lot of cockpit time waiting for the inspector. Each night at the end of my shift, I would have to turn in my tension meter to the tool crib. I wasn't allowed to keep it in my tool box and that was just fine with me.

Rapidly, the plant's work force expanded. Each night at 8 p.m., I ate lunch in the plant's new cafeteria, where the line seemed to grow longer each night. Very few women worked for Curtiss Wright in Buffalo. Here at Martin in Omaha, there were lots of women of all ages, and they did everything.

At the first opportunity, I went to the Army Air Corps Recruiting Office in Omaha. There was a large crowd but, after a long wait, a sergeant had me fill out some forms. After the forms were completed, I was given a preliminary physical examination and some psychological tests. Then I had to take another physical examination and more psychological tests. When I told the sergeant I worked from 4 p.m. until midnight, he scheduled the tests for one morning of the next week. I felt good about all this and now I must pass the full physical and the other tests. They were tough, but I passed. The sergeant checked my position on the waiting list for the Army Air Corps Aviation Cadet Training Program and informed me that I was number 406. Not expecting to be placed on a waiting list, I asked the sergeant if being on the list would protect me from the draft. He replied, "No, but if you get drafted, they'll find you." I didn't like that at all as rumor had it that, once you got into the Army, you could easily get lost in the numbers. After fretting about this for a couple days, I went back and looked up the same sergeant. By now, my number was 348. The rate of progress was too slow for me as I had just received a card from the draft board showing my status as 1A. I was ripe for the draft - no question about it. Then the sergeant mentioned a possible way to avoid the draft. My defense work only protected me from the draft for six months at a time.

The new "deal" was to sign up with the Enlisted Reserve Corps. (ERC) in the Field Artillery. They had a program where light airplanes were used to spot artillery hits on a target. I would be flying a cub, or something like that; and would emerge from flight training as a Staff Sergeant Pilot. To me, it was better than being drafted into the Infantry. They wanted my decision by the next Monday as slots were filling up rapidly. After talking to my boss and friends, I made up my mind that I wouldn't be drafted. Back to the sergeant I went and signed up with the ERC. The program called for completion of two phases of flight training and lots of ground schooling. From start to finish, the two phases took six months to complete. It was the middle of May and in just 11 days, I was going to be 20 years old.

A lot of water had passed under the bridge in the last two years. I was earning good money and had paid off all my debts, including my '38 Ford and my tuition loan. My savings account wasn't large but it was respectable. I was told at the Omaha recruiting office that I was to report for duty at Fort Hays, Kansas on September 8, 1942. That gave me about 15 weeks to wind up my civilian affairs and get ready for induction into the United States Army.

One day while in South Omaha on some business, I happened to drive by a used car lot and there sat my next car. My Ford was fine but the maroon 1939 Buick Coupe had a straight eight-cylinder engine and the trunk was big enough to sleep in. Little did I know that would actually happen later on. The tires were in good shape and probably were recapped but it didn't matter.

The Ford and I had treated each other well and it was a sad parting; but that Buick drove like a dream-quiet with a soft ride. My savings account took a hit, but I still had some left as I put something into it every payday.

Unlike Buffalo, Omaha's bar closing time was 1 a.m. After work, some of the people I worked with would all go to a pub called "Peanut Island." It was no Glass Bar but it was fine. Storz Grainbelt beer was one of the local brews and tasted wonderful after eight hours work in the bomber plant. By the time we got there, there were only 45 minutes before it closed. If you bought a last round of drinks at 12:55, you could stay there as long as you wanted. They just closed the bar and locked the doors. Everywhere you went in that place were large baskets of peanuts in the shell. House rules were you could pitch the spent shells on the floor and, by closing time, the floor was a sea of shells. There were no stringent fire rules in those days.

Peanut Island had four pool tables, one of which was a 9-foot snooker table. That was my favorite and we kept it busy. Sometimes the police would come in to see if the bar had really closed. When they realized we were "aircraft factory workers" with our badges, they never said a word to us. The summer passed quickly and before I knew it was early August and I only had a month left in civilian life. After talking with my supervisor and discussing my military plans, we set the date for my termination at the bomber plant for August 24. That gave me just two weeks before leaving for Fort Hays. Bob Ritzdorf, a school mate and best friend of mine, and I talked about taking a little vacation first. He was also working at the bomber plant, and would try to get a few days off.

One night at Peanut Island, after a couple of beers, Bob and I decided to ask one of our chums from school, Loretta Wetovick, to go with us. She had just come back from a couple years working in California. She had a sister and a brother to look after her out there. Her nickname was "Chub," and she was back in Omaha visiting with another sister. The next day, I called her and asked if she would like to have dinner with Bob and me. She went for that and we picked her up that evening in my Buick. After some discussion, we picked out a Chinese restaurant in downtown Omaha. As we finished, the conversation got right down to our proposal. At first, Chub laughed and thought it was silly for two guys and a gal to drive around the country by themselves. We were all just past 20 years old. Leaving the restaurant, we went to the "Cave Under the Hill" night spot and talked some more about the trip. After a couple drinks and without any warning, Chub blurted out, "Okay, I'll go with you guys; but this trip cannot be mentioned to anyone." We all shook on it and agreed to leave Omaha on August 26 for parts unknown. We had no particular plans, we just planned to see more of the United States.

After dropping Chub off that night, Bob and I wondered if we knew what we were getting into. If word leaked out, our parents would just "fry us." On the morning of the 26th, Bob and I picked Chub up at her sister's house, and on driving away, she said, "I just had to tell my sister." Bob and I just looked at each other in utter profound disbelief. We couldn't believe what we just heard her say. Leaving Omaha, our first stop was St. Louis, Missouri. The 1942 World Series was going on and the third game between the St. Louis Cardinals and the New York Yankees was in St. Louis. I stopped and inquired about tickets but was told it was a sellout, so we drove by Sportsmans Park and could hear the fans yelling. Leaving the city, I found the ball game on the car radio over a St. Louis station, KMOX, and listened to the rest of the game.

Bob, Chub and I had a ball driving around the country. It was exciting doing something that we knew wasn't exactly correct for three very young people to do. Each night we would find either a rooming house, or a low-cost hotel room. We always let Chub sleep in the bed while Bob and I slept on the floor. We were all brought up correctly and no "hanky-panky" was anticipated. Soon we found ourselves in Alabama. There, we located another high school chum, Fritz Korth. He was in the Army Air Corps, and we found him at the airbase near Selma. Fritz was happy to see us and thought our vacation plans were just great. The four of us went out for a good meal and, the next morning, we three vagabonds headed for parts west. Some states had gasoline rationing and some did not, so we had to be wary. Our funds were still in quite good shape, but Chub didn't bring along much money. Now we were on a strict budget and, a lot of times, we would go to a grocery store and buy picnic type food. It worked out just fine. Arriving in Arizona, we visited Bob's sister in Mesa. She let us know right away she didn't think much of our vacation plans. Bob and I had to sleep on the porch at her house. As we were leaving the next morning for home, Bob said, "Don't tell the folks you saw us." Driving away, we all knew she would write her mother and dad that same day. We saw a lot of sights on our trip but our funds were now getting critically low. We had to set aside gasoline money and the rest would go for food.

The last three nights on the road our sleeping arrangements changed. With no money for a hotel room, we had to sleep in the car. Bob slept in the trunk and Chub and I in the front seat. We had to crack the windows for air and Bob used a stick to prop up the trunk lid. The first night we did this we all broke up. A couple hours after we settled down, I heard Bob laughing back in the trunk. Soon we were all laughing so hard that our sides hurt and tears were streaming down our cheeks. We laughed for a long time. After a lull, one of us would start up and then all of us were laughing again. We were in a city park somewhere in Colorado. We hoped no one heard us carrying on into the night.

While driving east the next day, we couldn't imagine what was so funny that started the outburst. Bob said he could shed some light on the reason. He said he dreamed he died and then came back to earth as a donkey. That night, the laughing started again. But we were pretty tired, and it didn't last long. The third and final night on the road, we were too exhausted to laugh any more. Finally we arrived back in Omaha and in dropping off Chub, her sister came running out shouting, "I'm sure glad you're back. Everyone was worried about you." It seemed the cat was out of the bag. Before splitting up, I made Bob and Chub promise to drive me out to Fort Hays when the time came in just a few days.

The three of us left Omaha in the Buick early in the morning of September 8, 1942. When we arrived at Fort Hays, I told them to wait while I checked into the Civilian Pilot Training Program. As soon as I got a mailing address, I returned to the car and gave it to them. I wanted each to write me while I was in Kansas. Bob wished me good luck and we shook hands. Chub gave me a big hug and both promised to write. Without any further fanfare, they drove away in my Buick.

The plan was to take the car back to my parents in Cedar Rapids where my dad would store it in their garage. They didn't have a car then and that would be just fine. My dad had someone help him jack it up, drain the radiator, disconnect the battery and "put it to bed". In the first letter from Bob, he told me the trip back was uneventful except for one thing. As they neared home, they drove by his brother's farm. As luck would have it his brother, Gil, was working in the field near the road and noticed them. Before Gil could see who was in the car, Bob pushed Chub to the floor where she couldn't be seen. Bob couldn't afford that explanation.

I was now duly enlisted in the service of our country. The Civilian Pilot Training Program (CPTP) was located on the campus of Fort Hays State Teachers College. Our quarters were built under the football stadium-nothing fancy, but okay. My class was not very large-about 50 students. We were wearing the summer tan uniform and would change to the olive drab (OD) winter uniforms on the first of October. Our quarters under the stadium were all in one big room filled with Army style cots. Each of us had a locker and that was all. Latrines were at each end of the building and our meals were taken in the college cafeteria three times a day. Each morning we had drill practice and physical training - PT. In the afternoons we had classes in various subjects relating to aviation. Theory of flight, navigation, meteorology, military tactics, mathematics and aircraft systems made up the class curriculum. Some afternoons we had two long classes and other days we had three shorter ones. In six weeks the classes came to an end. After we all passed the final examinations, the afternoons were spent learning to fly airplanes. The CPT program at Fort Hays had several types of small airplanes such as the Aeronca, Piper Cub, Taylorcraft and the Interstate Cadet. All had 65 HP engines and were called tail draggers. On the first day, I met my instructor, Mr. Haughlan. With four airplanes we got right into dual instruction. Normally, it takes a student from eight to ten hours of dual rides to be ready to solo. To solo means a student takes an airplane up alone, flies it alone, for a short period, then lands it alone and walks away from it alone. That's exactly what I did on December 18, 1942 in the Interstate Cadet airplane. Upon landing, I noticed several people standing alongside the runway. It is always windy in Kansas and they were there to catch the "solo pilot's" wing tips so he wouldn't groundloop. The feeling of soloing an airplane for the first time almost defies description—a feeling of complete freedom from Mother Earth. That night the eight of us, who had soloed that day were permitted to go into Fort Hays for a few hours to celebrate. The only place we could buy a beer was in the

American Legion Hall. We congratulated each other for what we accomplished that day. Feelings were mixed with pride, emotion and a deep love for aviation. A pilot gets only one first solo in his lifetime.

Phase I of the CPT program progressed smoothly. On solo rides, after that first one, I practiced S-turns across a road, lazy eights, partial stalls and many, many takeoffs and landings.

We were called Aviation Students and of the original 50 to start the program, every one finished with flying colors. Mr. Haughlan said that was very unusual as there were always some "washouts." A washout is someone who couldn't cut the mustard, either in class or in the flying phase. Not having seen a washout, I could not know the emotional effect it might have on young men who aspired to become aviators.

We did have one student ground loop an airplane but only minor damage was done and he seemed to have control after that. That was the only incident during phase I- a great credit to our very fine instructors. Each Saturday afternoon and evening, we were given a pass into town. Fort Hays didn't have a lot to offer but they did have a nice USO (United Services Organization) Club where we could relax, play cards, pool and ping pong, and write letters to family and friends. It was fun writing them I was now a real pilot—having flown it, landed it and walked away from it, all by myself. When a pilot walks away from his landing, it is a safe one.

My friend Chub wrote a few times and said she went back to Washington, DC, and applied for a "government girl" job. In her next letter, she told me she had gotten a job with the Coast Guard and was very excited about it. The third letter said she met a person named Olson and they were planning to get married. That was my last letter from Chub.

One weekend in Fort Hays, I met a nice girl by the name of Louise Green who was attending the local college. We went to several movies and spent some time at the American Legion Hall. There she could have a beer, too. At her dormitory, I couldn't go past the lobby. That was one of the house rules. Louise was from Dodge City and was kind of lonesome. We became good friends, but both of us knew we would have to part when my training ended.

My instructor, Mr. Haughlan, left for another job, and was replaced by a Mr. Harris.   Everyone liked him but we were going to leave soon. During phase I, my flying time totaled 61 hours. All students were within five hours of each other. I flew all the four types of airplanes the school had, but liked the Interstate Cadet best. It just seemed to fly better and it was the airplane in which I had soloed. On

February 28, 1943, CPT Phase I came to an end and we all went to the Legion Hall for a party. All the instructors were there and we had a good time. After a two week leave, I was to report back to Fort Hays to start Phase II. That would be in a bi-plane called the Waco. After telling everyone that I would see them in two weeks, I rode the train to Omaha for a couple days. I then went to see my folks to tell them all about my experiences in Kansas, especially my first solo flight.

While I was home, a letter came from the Omaha Recruiting Office. On the envelope a notice said to forward it to the addressee without delay. My Aviation Cadet number had come up. Whoopee!!!!! I was to report as soon as possible. After saying my goodbyes, I was on the morning train for Omaha. After a complete physical and a battery of tests, I was sworn into the United States Army Air Corps. My parents knew that pilot training was what I really wanted; and they also knew that it would take me into the war either in the Pacific or in Europe. With all that, they were happy that I was going to be an Aviation Cadet and be trained to fly big military aircraft. Before I could start the Aviation Cadet Program, I had to become a soldier first. This meant that in a day or two, I would be on another train going to six weeks of "hell" - Basic Training.

On March 6, 1943, I was to report to the Army Transportation Office at the Omaha train depot. Only bring a minimum of civilian clothes and little to no personal effects, they said. That morning at the depot, there must have been nearly a hundred "potential" Aviation Cadets standing around in civilian clothes ranging from rags to riches. I put myself somewhere in the middle of that scale.

My orders indicated that my basic training would take place at Sheppard Field near Wichita Falls, Texas. The train ride there was kind of fun as all the guys suddenly realized that no matter where or what class of life we came from, we were now all in the same boat. We played cards, talked, and had fun. The last fun we would have for the next six weeks.

Basic training turned out to be just as advertized; it was pure hell. Fraternities have their hell week but this was going to last for six long weeks. At the train depot, we were met by a big burly sergeant from the base. He told us to get our gear and board the waiting bus on the double. I noticed it was very warm and this was only March. At the base, we were marched to base supply where we were issued regulation clothing which I stuffed into two big duffle bags. We were also issued our bedding of sheets, blankets and pillow cases. It was quite late that night when we got all of this together. The sergeant said lights out at 10 p.m. We were housed in two-story wooden barracks in open bays on each floor. The bunk beds were placed about six feet apart. It was rather cosy and we were placed in order alphabetically. As a "G," I was on the lower floor. We flipped coins for upper or lower bunks and I won a lower, which is what I wanted. When leaving us that day, after evening chow, the sergeant said we would be awakened early in the morning for our first day in the real Army. We were to dress in our olive drab class B uniforms and be in front of the barracks in formation 30 minutes after reveille sounded. I don't remember his mentioning what time that would be.

When we received our clothing issue, naturally we said to the clerk behind the counter that we wanted small, medium or large in everything we got. At the time, I didn't notice, but I didn't always get what I ordered. The ritual of trying on our uniforms that night was a riot. Everything was either too large or too small. It didn't matter, we wore it anyway. This was the Army. We were jarred out of sleep the next morning when a loud blast of reveille came over the big speakers in front of our barracks. It was 5 a.m. and right after reveille sounded, a loud voice over the speaker told us to be shaved, showered, dressed and out front for roll call in 30 minutes. There were two latrines in our barracks, one upper and one lower. Each contained about 30 sinks and as many open stools and urinals. The big shower room had shower heads all around the wall with one large center drain. Each morning the action in those latrines was something else. At each station, whether it be a sink, urinal, stool, or a place in the shower, there would be a line of new recruits, all buck naked, waiting their turn.

If you didn't answer your name at roll call, you were either on sick call, or AWOL (Absent Without Official Leave). At every meal there were always lines. Inside the chow hall, a sign read: "Take what you want, but want what you take." After eating, each metal tray had to be doused in hot soapy water three times and then three more times in plain hot water. We went through this ritual three times every day. In basic training, most of the time was devoted to making soldiers of us. Every morning it was drill, drill, drill; how to salute, when to salute and when not to salute. At mid-morning we changed into gym shorts and tennis shoes for two solid hours of physical education, called PE. The first half was stretching and exercising. That was okay and it always started out with the old favorite, the side-straddle hop. The second half was not so much fun, we ran, and ran and ran some more.

The finale was the obstacle course where we had to jump ditches which were full of muddy water. There were ropes to climb, walls to climb, tunnels to crawl through and much more. After PE, the shower room was again full of naked bodies waiting their turn to wash off the sweat and grime. Everyone lost a good deal of weight from this rigor.

44

In the afternoons, there were classes in military doctrine, firearms of all kinds and chemical warfare. Next came classes in military bearing-how to look and act like a soldier. At the end of each barracks floor was a large mirror with a sign over it that read, "Do **YOU** look like a soldier?" We couldn't get out of the building without encountering that big mirror.

After three weeks of morning drill, we started doing cross-country marches, short ones at first, then several miles - both day and night. What made it tough was the fact we had to carry a 20-pound pack on our backs. Canteen belt and leggings were also part of the uniform of the day. The sandy soil in that part of Texas is not easy to walk on and a lot of feet were blistered as a result. After every march, those with foot blisters had to take off their shoes and socks. Lying on the ground with their blistered feet up in the air, the bottoms of their feet were painted with a purple substance by a person dressed in white. Those with purple feet were excused from marching for two days. They did odd jobs around the barracks - no loafing permitted.

Never once, during my stay in basic training, did the instructors let up on us. They knew that someday we would be officers. They also kept saying only half of us would make it through.

Our spirits were high in spite of this constant hazing. There was little time for recreation. We were kept so busy all day that at night, when lights went out at 10 p.m., we were ready to crash into our bunks. The post exchange was open for us two hours each evening. There we could buy a cold soda, malted milk or, if you wanted, some 3.2% beer.

One day near the end of training, we all had to report to the base theater for a briefing. A major got up on the stage and, before he started to speak, I noticed he was wearing pilot's wings. He began his talk by saying, "I know you are anxious to get into the Aviation Cadet Program and I can't blame you one bit. There is, however, one more obstacle for some of you. Until about two years ago, a person had to have a college degree before he could be accepted into the program. For the past two years, we have accepted young men with only two years of college credits. In going through your records, I see where some of you have less than two years of college. Now, those with two years or more of college credits will be going on to the Aviation Cadet Program in just a few days. The rest of you will be going to a new program called College Training Detachment - CTD. Several colleges around the country have set up programs that consist of six months intensified college level courses. The classes will be all day five days a week. Drill and PE will be done on Saturdays. There is one part of this new program that I know you will like. You will be given 10 hours dual (with an instructor) flight time in a Piper Cub! At the completion of your courses, you will be given a written test on each subject taken. These tests must be passed. After that, you will proceed, by fastest means, to the Western Air Training Command in Santa Ana, California, to start your Aviation Cadet training." For a few seconds the theater was quiet, then, as if someone had turned on a switch, a loud cheer went up. The thought of getting out of basic training and going to some college was wonderful. One of the last things we did was go out to the firing range. There we had field classes on several weapons including pistols, rifles and machine guns. We tore them down and put them all back together with no parts left over. On the range, we fired the M-1 rifle at some stationary targets. I hit very few, as I recall, but it was fun anyway. Each time a firing range is open, a special red flag is flown to let everyone know to stay away unless they are required to be there. This special red flag is called "Maggie's Drawers."

The six weeks of torture finally came to an end and I was getting out of that hell hole. With all our newly issued gear, we boarded a train in Wichita Falls and headed for Cedar Falls, Iowa. There, at Iowa State Teachers College, our College Training Detachment was located. It was just breaking dawn on April 28, 1943, when the train rolled into Cedar Falls. From the station, we marched through town to the college campus. During that whole trek, we sang our hearts out. I guess we just felt good about our future. Later we heard the College President was awakened by the noise and didn't like it. The campus looked green and beautiful with lots of trees and nice red brick buildings. I was going to like this assignment

Due to the war, the college enrollment was down and to make room for the CTD program, some of the girls' dormitories were given up for us. That got a lot of chuckles out of everyone. There were 250 student cadets there, a lot of civilian girls and, to our surprise, about 400 female Navy clerical students right out of Navy Boot Camp. We were all fresh out of "Basic Training" and that gave us a common bond. With over 600 girls on campus and only a few 4-F male students, the 250 cadets were going to have an exciting summer indeed. Today, that college in Cedar Falls is known as Northern Iowa University.

Classes met from 8 a.m. to 4 p.m. and we had two free hours before evening chow. All students, male and female, ate in the student cafeteria. Each morning, we marched from our dorms to breakfast, so did the Navy Waves and, while waiting to go through the chow line, the Navy girls gave us a bad time - said we were cute and stuff like that. The same thing happened at each meal. Even in town on the weekends, we couldn't escape them. Sailors are sailors and even the females take advantage of the situation when they outnumber the "foe."

Soon, we got to know some of them and the hazing stopped. They were only there for four weeks, then another group would come in. The same routine would start all over again. The latrines in our dorms were different as there were no urinals. We lived four to a room using double-deck bunks and everything worked out just fine. On some of the walls, we noticed a lot of telephone numbers. None of them were useful to us as those girls were long gone.

Because we were to get ten hours of dual instruction in a Piper Cub, we had to take some related subjects - theory of flight, meteorology, navigation and more military doctrine. I had all those courses back in Fort Hays, so it was a snap for me. I was the only one in the group of 250 that had prior flight experience. I was bombarded with questions in the bull sessions in the dorm. They wanted to know if I was scared when flying alone, how I avoided getting lost, what I would do if the engine quit and all kinds of things like that. I had to explain those events in great detail.

Our courses at the college were mathematics through calculus, English, history, science and an elective. The instructors were from the college and were very good. They knew what they had to cram into our heads and were good at it. First, they taught us how to properly take notes in class as that was the key to the test we would take later. One instructor said, "Study your notes and do not waste time reading the books, unless I tell you to." Every night after the evening meal, we had a two-hour mandatory study period and lights had to be out at 10 p.m. The latrines did not have windows so some went there to study or write letters after 10 p.m. Soon we were able to finish drilling and PE by noon on Saturdays. We were off until 11 p.m. and all day Sunday until 10 p.m. Most of us went into town where they had a big USO club. Waterloo, Iowa, was a much bigger city than Cedar Falls and only a short bus ride away. I liked Waterloo because of its large amusement park and of course there were Navy Waves everywhere. They were very nice girls about our age or younger. May 26 was my 21st birthday. That weekend a group of us went to Waterloo and had a blast. Now I could legally drink beer in public. Some Navy girls came with us and that was great. We had fun at the park and later found a pub where we drank beer, sang songs and danced a little. The last bus back to Cedar Falls was jammed full of happy Cadets and Waves. It was a great weekend and I could not buy one beer because the gang said, on your birthday, your friends treated you.

Building Aircraft

One morning during our theory of flight class, the instructor said we only had one more session in aviation subjects, after that, we would be going to the airport to start the flying phase of CTD. We were all happy about that and couldn't wait. I felt I didn't need an instructor but knew I'd have to fly with one anyway. The following Monday, we boarded a bus after class and drove to the small airport on the edge of Cedar Falls. It wasn't much of an airport, a couple of hangars and a square mile of grass field. The chief instructor and several of his assistants were there to greet us. They were very cordial and showed us the Piper Cub airplane. Six of the planes were sitting in front of the hangars. The class broke up into groups of six. It had been decided earlier that the student body had to be split into two groups-the A Wing and B Wing. The wings were then divided into five squadrons. I was assigned to the 2nd Squadron of A Wing.

My group was to be given instruction by Mr. Gifford. That afternoon he took each of us up for a 20-minute orientation ride. When my turn came, Mr. Gifford took the plane off and, after climbing to about 3000 feet, said, "Here, take the controls and see if you can make a coordinated turn. Try one in each direction for 90 degrees." I made two smooth coordinated turns without losing or gaining any altitude at all. Quickly he said, " What are you doing? You have flown before, haven't you?" I told him about the CPT program at Fort Hays and that I had flown 61 hours. He took the controls and back to the airport we went. On the ground he said, "Why didn't you tell me before we went up? You have just wasted government time and money." The next time I flew with Mr. Gifford, he put me in the front seat and he got in the back. After making the takeoff, he said, "Now, show me what you learned out there in Kansas."

After climbing to 3,000 feet, I did all kinds of turns, level, climbing and descending. Then I did lazy eights, chandells and some partial stalls. He motioned me to go back and enter the traffic pattern for landing. You had to enter the left hand rectangular pattern on a 45 degree angle and when opposite the control tower, watch for a green or red light from the tower. As we had no radio, traffic was controlled with an electric light. It was called the "biscuit gun" and was operated by the tower controller. Takeoffs were handled the same way. Green meant you were cleared for takeoff and red meant you were to hold fast and wait for a green. In the air, green meant you were cleared to land, and red meant you could not land and had to make a go-around and fly the pattern again. On the downwind leg, a green light flashed at me and I turned base leg, rolled out, then turned onto the final approach and came in and landed the cub with a fair landing. Mr. Gifford said,

48

"Mr. Gordon, you should not even be in this program." I guessed that was meant to be a compliment. He went on to say that the next time he and I flew, we would go on a cross-country. That was just fine with me. Before leaving the airport, I bought an Iowa sectional chart for 25 cents. Back in the dorm, I put the aerial map of Iowa on the floor and, with a straight edge, drew a course line from Cedar Falls to Morrison, up to Waverly and back to Cedar Falls. I couldn't wait to show it to my instructor on the next flight.

We were now half-way through the CTD program and everything was going pretty well. I had one midterm exam in each subject and somehow I managed to pass. I really felt good when the instructor said our final exam would not cover any first half material. We still had mandatory study periods and it was paying off. Occasionally a tutor would come over and help us and everyone liked that.

One day the leaders of the Student Cadets and Navy Waves got together and decided on some diversion for Saturday morning PE. Soon we were playing softball, volleyball and other games. That was great fun! The girls in their white tops and blue shorts and the boys in their white tops and tan shorts were a good-looking group. There were so many of us we took up the entire play area including the football field. On one of these occasions, I met Mary Lou Reitz.

She was from Bayonne, New Jersey, and said her mother did not want her to join the Navy but her father overrode the decision and here she was. We became good friends and one weekend I took her to the amusement park in nearby Waterloo. I was very good at throwing a ball and I knocked over a lot of wooden milk bottles on the midway. Soon she was carrying three Kewpi dolls and a wearing a funny looking straw hat. Late in the evening we were so tired we just got on the big Ferris Wheel to relax. Before long, both of us were sound asleep. The man operating the ride finally shook us awake. He said he knew we were tired and he just let the wheel keep going even though we were the only ones on it. The last bus had left and we had just enough money to take a taxi back to the Cedar Falls campus.

The time at CTD was passing rapidly and my progress in class was fair to good. Thanks to an exceptional math instructor, I understood calculus well enough to get by. Those instructors taught us how to study and we followed the study instructions to the letter. I have never forgotten that technique. The Saturday PE games went on and everybody looked forward to that morning of fun. The girls were good in all the sports and that made it even more fun.

Every four weeks we watched the old group of Waves leave and the new ones come in. It was exciting to see this every month. By now, we knew how to handle the mild hazing and we just gave it right back to them. I lost Mary Lou as she had departed for her next school. She promised to write but never did. Every Saturday afternoon and Sunday the Waterloo amusement park was jammed with girls in blue and boys in tan. At last came the final examinations and that weekend we stayed on campus and studied like crazy. It took all the next week as they only gave us one final test each day. Thank goodness for that. As miracles sometimes happen, I passed all the exams and was never happier. I worked hard and perseverance paid off; prayers did, too.

At graduation each of us received a certificate indicating that we had earned 60 college credit-hours. I still have that piece of paper buried in a footlocker somewhere. Now we were fully qualified to go on to Aviation Cadet training. About a fourth of the group went to the Western Air Training Command in Santa Ana, California. The rest went to the Southern Air Training Command in San Antonio, Texas, to train. I enjoyed my six months at Cedar Falls, and kind of hated to leave. In a few days, we boarded the train for sunny California and never looked back.

Integrity is doing the right thing, even if nobody is watching.

—James Stovall

CHAPTER FOUR

AVIATION CADET PROGRAM

Once you have tasted flight you will always walk the earth with your eyes turned skyward: for there you have been and there you will always be.

—Leonardo Da Vinci

The Aviation Cadet Program was an elite aircrew training program that, year after year, produced highly trained pilots, navigators and bombardiers for the United States Army Air Corps and for the air forces of Canada, England and other allied nations. The civilian flying schools simply could not produce the numbers that were needed in the war effort. Four Air Training Commands were established in 1940 and were located in the west, south, southeast and on the east coast. Before the war started, only Randolph and Kelly Fields in San Antonio, Texas, produced Army pilots. Randolph was known as the "West Point of the Air." The Aviation Cadet Aircrew Training Program extended that Randolph/Kelly concept all over the country.

The Air Training Commands were located in four regions. The Western was located in Santa Ana, California, the Southern in San Antonio, Texas, the Southeastern in Montgomery, Alabama and the Eastern in Miami, Florida. Each command had scores of airfields where the training was conducted. Pilot training was given in three phases - primary, basic and advanced. Navigators received their training in the Western Command at Mather Field, Sacramento, California. Bombardiers were trained in the Southern Command at Ellington Field, Houston, Texas.

All cadets were required to be classified as either pilot, navigator or bombardier before their training could begin. A stringent physical was given; a battery of complex written tests was administered and each cadet filled out a form indicating his classification preference and reason for that preference. After all the results were sifted and sorted, each cadet was classified for training as a pilot, navigator or bombardier. No appeals were accepted and the decision was final.

It was October 10, 1943 when the troop train pulled out of Cedar Falls to begin the long trip to the Western Training Command Headquarters in Santa Ana. From the original CTD group, about 60 of us were assigned to the Western Training Command. On the train ride out, we talked constantly about how we might be classified. Nobody wanted to be a navigator or even a bombardier. We all had one goal - to become a military pilot. I noticed that the train was taking us through the beautiful Colorado Rocky Mountains. The scenery was out of this world but I felt a strange sensation. I wasn't ill but something was wrong and I just associated it with the high altitudes. Later I would find out why I didn't feel well. The train arrived in Santa Ana on the 14th and I had my first look at palm trees as we rode a bus from the train station to the air base. It was a bee-hive of activity. Santa Ana didn't have a runway, but there was one nearby at El Toro and planes were flying around every day. At the base, we were put up in two-story wooden barracks. I got the lower floor but lost the coin-toss for a lower bunk.

At the Classification Center we could sleep until 6 a.m. each morning. That was quite a treat from the past year of getting up with the chickens. The food was really good and I found out that everyone had to pull KP (Kitchen Police) duty. I didn't mind that as we were permitted to eat all we wanted and could take fruit back to the barracks after getting off duty. In addition to KP, I had to pull guard duty and that was tough because I had to memorize the Military General Orders. The classification process took about three weeks. The first thing on the agenda was the tough aviation physical exam. This physical was designed to check every function of the body and the tolerances were narrow. It was the toughest physical exam I had ever taken and I was worried like everyone else. If you didn't pass the physical, the fat lady began to sing and the ball game was over.

Next, I took a battery of written tests. These tests were psychogical in nature, widely varied and all were timed. I knew that if I were to be classified as a pilot, I would need very high scores. There were some psycho-motor coordination tests using a machine that, like a simulator, required that you make coordinated movements with different levers and controls. After coming out of that, I wondered how anyone could pass. I hoped my previous flying training would help me there. When all the testing was finished, there was nothing to do but wait. A notice on the cadet bulletin board indicated that we would be notified as soon as the results were known. Talk about sweating something out, we were all as nervous as cats.

In our barracks area, was a center courtyard where a large bulletin board was mounted like a leader board in a golf tournament, only this board was smaller and you didn't need a ladder to read it. After two days of sweating, I was relaxing on my bunk after lunch and trying to get my mind off the current situation when, suddenly, I heard a loud noise outside. Getting up to see what was going on, I noticed a sea of cadets running toward the big bulletin board. They were yelling that the classifications were out and being posted. I ran out in a crowd of other cadets to learn my fate.

The board contained several long lists of names and classifications assigned to each. I could get nowhere near the board as cadets were 30-deep at each list, so I just waited it out. Soon I spotted one of my good friends, Fred Goodwin, running toward me yelling, "Whoopee!!! I made the pilot's list and Tom, you did too." He did a flying leap and grabbed me. We were so full of emotion we couldn't even talk. Other cadets were screaming and shouting that they too, made the list. I then heard some groans from those who did not make the coveted pilots' list. They would become navigators or bombardiers. I felt sorry for them as I could have very easily been among them. I was extremely thankful for my good fortune that day.

After lights out that night, everyone talked in the dark about going into pilot training. Some said to shut up, as obviously they didn't make the "list." Nobody slept very much that night as we were just too wound up with emotion. The next day I would move to the next phase known as Preflight. Now everything would be pilot-oriented, or so I thought.

For preflight training, I was assigned to class 44F, the class I should graduate with and the sixth class to graduate in 1944. We were further assigned to the 47th Aviation Cadet Pilot Squadron which contained four flights. I was now a full-fledged Aviation Cadet. I don't recall ever being happier. The routine in preflight was reveille at 5:30 A.M. followed by a full day of activity. The mornings were dedicated to drill and physical education. The PE instructors were more demanding than any we had encountered up to now. They put us through long stretching exercises, then, we ran for 50 minutes, rested for 10, and ran some more. We ended each morning by running the obstacle course; but this one was harder and longer than any I had seen before. By noon we were ready for the sack, but no. After lunch, back to the classroom we went. Military doctrine, military tactics, chemical warfare, weapons and the usual firing range kept us busy in the afternoons.

Each Sunday a dress parade was held on the large parade grounds. All squadrons were graded on their marching ability. On the reviewing stand was the Commandant of Cadets, the Base Commander and the Western Air Training Commander and their staffs. On some occasions, additional guests were present for this spectacle. Over 1,000 cadets would be involved in the dress parade every Sunday afternoon. We would assemble around 1 p.m. but wouldn't "pass in review" until around 3 p.m. For nearly two hours we stood in formation at "parade-rest" in the hot California sun.

On October 1 of each year the military changed uniforms from summer khakis to winter woolens called OD, for olive drabs. Each April 1, back we went into khakis without regard to the temperature. Those Sunday afternoons were not something we looked forward to. On one such occasion, it got so hot I thought I would pass out; a lot of cadets did, every Sunday. Even after the parade was over and I got out of the heat, I didn't feel well for a considerable time. On Monday morning I decided to go on sick-call at the base hospital. After a long wait, I got to see a doctor and I was sure it was the heat from the day before. After a lot of tests, including x-rays, I was told to wait there in the examining room. Finally the doctor came back and asked me questions of where I had been and what I had been doing for the past several weeks. I traced my activities all the way back to Cedar Falls, Iowa. He asked if I had spent any time in the mountains lately. The troop train did go through some mountains in Colorado, I told him. He left again, came back shortly and told me, "Son, some how, some way, you contracted Rocky Mountain Spotted Fever." I just looked at him; I didn't know what to say.

He explained that I had an acute infectious disease called "rickettsia", which is transmitted by ticks endemic to the Rocky Mountains and characterized by high fever, muscular pains and skin eruptions. The doctor went on to tell me I would have to enter the hospital so they could control the effects of the disease. I still have some spots on my chest that remain today, over 50 years later. After two weeks of treatment, the doctor said I was ready to go back to my unit, but before I could leave, I had to take another physical. I thanked my lucky stars I was 100% fit again. Back at the squadron I discovered that my class, 44-F, had already shipped out, and I was put back with the class of 44-G to complete my preflight training and, hopefully, would stay with them until graduation at advanced flight school.

Quickly I made new friends, especially with the family of G's, as we slept, ate and worked alphabetically. After my physical at the hospital, the doctor gave me a "light-duty" slip. This meant I wasn't required to drill, run or participate in the weekly dress parade. I was free but not quite. The squadron's grass detail was formed from the light-duty cadets. On Sunday afternoons when everyone else was at parade, we cut and watered the grass around the cadet barracks area. Sometimes we would still be working when the marchers returned to the barracks. I was able to attend the afternoon classes and participate on the firing range. That was fun and I did well enough to qualify as marksman. They forgot to give me the marksman badge, but did mail it to me weeks later during primary flight training.

Many nights before going to sleep, I wondered what my fate would have been had I remained in class 44-F. Much later, I heard from one of my 44-F friends that it looked like most of the class was headed for the heavy stuff - bombers, transports and the like. One day we were marched to the gymnasium where the Commandant of Cadets told us, class by class, where we would be going for primary flight school. He finally told us we were going to Thunderbird Field Number One at Glendale, Arizona. Glendale is a northern suburb of Phoenix. The whole class was delighted as they considered that good news.

Thunderbird One had a reputation of being a top-notch primary school. That was the scuttlebutt anyway. We found out about Thunderbird One on a Wednesday and the following Monday, my class of 44-G boarded the troop train for Glendale. As the train pulled out of the Santa Ana station, we all sang the Air Force Song as loud as we could. "Off we go into the wild blue yonder - climbing high into the sun. Here they come ... "

For evil to triumph, all that is necessary is for good men to do nothing.
—John F. Kennedy

My first birthday - 1923
Author's collection

First day of school - 1928
Author's collection

Aviation Cadet Gordon - 1943
Author's Collection

Boeing PT-17
Primary Trainer
Thunderbird Field
Glendale, Arizona 1943
Author's Collection

Aviation Cadet Barracks - 1943
Always had to be left in
inspection order each morning
Author's collection

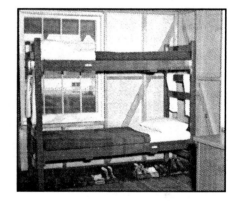

Consolidated-Vultee BT-13
Basic Trainer -Lemoore Field,
California
Wide landing gear made landings
very manageable - 1944
Author's collection

North American B-25 Mitchell Advanced Trainer
La Junta, Colorado - 1944
Also flew it after the war as an instructor
at Lowry Field, Denver, Colorado - 1951-54
Author's collection

Brand new Flying Officer home on short leave
before heading off to war - 1944
Author's collection

CHAPTER FIVE

PRIMARY FLIGHT TRAINING

Plans are only good intentions unless they immediately degenerate into hard work.

—*Peter Drucker*

It was my first Christmas in warm weather and kind of hard to get into the spirit of things. All the cards from home helped a lot, as each contained a long letter with all the family and local news. It was December 29.1943, as the buses rolled into Thunderbird Field. Thunderbird was operated under contract with civilian management. Colonel Butler, Commandant of Cadets, and his staff were the only military present. All the rest of the instructors and check pilots were civilian. The line mechanics were civilian as were the ground school instructors. This was quite a change for us, after Santa Ana. Our housing consisted of small two-bedroom units that allowed four cadets to live comfortably. Two single beds were in each bedroom and we had to manage with one bathroom. Now we could sleep until 6 a.m. and, after breakfast, we had until 7:45 to make our beds and clean up the unit. We had a kitchen but we seldom used it. No beer was allowed in the icebox, only sodas that we could buy at the post exchange.

Our routine consisted of classroom instruction and flying. One week we attended class in the morning and flew in the afternoon; the next week that would be reversed - we flew in the mornings and attended class in the afternoon. There would be no night flying in primary training. On the second day, an upperclassman took a group of us on a tour of the field. He pointed out and explained all the buildings, including the flight line hangars. There on the ramp, sat row upon row of blue and yellow Boeing primary trainers. Boy! They looked good and I couldn't wait to get into one. It's designation was the PT-17 Stearman. Our guide said that until we soloed, we would be called "Dodoes,." then "Misters." Saturday mornings were, again, devoted to drill and PE. We were trained in gunnery using the 45-caliber pistol and nobody could hit a thing with it. The gun was just too heavy to hold in one hand and fire accurately. Later, the rules were changed and we were permitted to use both hands. Our accuracy improved considerably with that change. I was grateful for the pistol training, as I would carry this same type of handgun on every combat mission I flew.

It was satisfying to have it with me, as it was the only gun on the airplane.

The first day on the flight line, I met my instructor, Mr. Anderson. He was a slight soft-spoken man in his early thirties. After the introductions were made, he looked at his four young students and said, "Misters, I am only a civilian pilot. I don't have any bars on my shoulders, but from now on, I'll demand the same respect and adherence to discipline I would expect if I held a commission in the Army Air Corps. It's my job to teach you how to fly this airplane. To do that, I will have to have your complete cooperation." Each of us nodded in agreement.

The nearby flight line was very active and so noisy we didn't need a morning reveille-call. Mechanics were out very early running engines; and two dozen airplanes all running up at once makes a lot of noise. The early flying period started at 8 a.m. and the afternoon group took off at 1 p.m. There was no night or weekend flying and I needed the time to clear my head after five days of strenuous activity. As our records had yet to arrive from Santa Ana, the only processing we could do was to draw our books, bedding and flying equipment. The January weather in Phoenix was mild on the ground but it got really cold in the air in the open cockpit. For that reason we drew heavy fleece-lined flying clothing and helmets. Before I could fly, I had to go the parachute loft and watch the rigger "open" a parachute. Then he would hang it up in the tower to dry out. Moisture in a chute is as bad as rust in an airplane. I then watched him pack a chute into a small bag that was part of the pilot's back-pack. The rigger's work was very impressive. I would wear a parachute every time I flew for the next 20 years.

One of the subjects in ground school class was "theory of flight." This would be the third time I had taken the course, and I believed I could have taught the subject. We had navigation, meteorology and now, aircraft systems. The flight instructors were very good, especially Mr. Anderson. During the second session with him on the ramp, he said, "Listen to me carefully. After you solo and I tell you to take an airplane up and practice maneuvers at 2,000 feet, don't get the idea you can fly around at 1,800 feet or 2,200 feet just because I'm not there to watch you. I will soon learn whether you are carrying out my orders. Those who do not will find themselves out of here fast. I will do everything in my power to see that you become pilots but its mostly up to you. Now, do you understand?" We all nodded to that very soberly. Mr. Anderson then showed us how to handle a parachute, placing emphasis on never laying it on wet or sandy ground. "It's your life preserver. Treat it right and, if the time ever comes, it will treat you right," he said. Then he put on a chute and showed us how to adjust it to a nice tight fit. "One more thing," he added, "if something should go wrong up there and I order you to bail out—**do it!** Don't wait for me to tell you a second time, because I won't be there."

Next came instructions on starting the engine. Before doing that, Mr. Anderson gave us a little history of the airplane. He said the Boeing Aircraft Company had built over 10,000 primary trainer aircraft like this one for the military. It had a Continental radial engine that developed 225 HP. Its top speed was 125 mph, it cruised at 105 mph and landed at 70 mph. It had a range of 450 miles and a service ceiling of 14,000 feet. Finally he said, "It will tend to ground-loop on every landing if you let it." He got our attention really quick with that statement.

Mr. Anderson then emphasized that airplanes have engines not motors. It took two cadets to start the engine, one in the cockpit, and one on the starting crank above the left main wheel. The starting procedure had to be memorized, and memorized that afternoon. He told us he would keep us on the flight line until we knew the procedure by heart, even if it meant missing our evening meal .

This is the engine starting procedure we were required to memorize that afternoon:

Crank Man	Cockpit Man
Safety-belt fastened?	Safety-belt fastened!
Controls free?	Controls free!
Brakes set?	Brakes set!
Gas on fullest tank?	Gas on fullest tank!
Fuel pressure up?	Pressure up!
	(using wobble pump)
Throttle cracked?	Throttle cracked!
Magneto switches on?	Magneto switches on!

As the crank was turned, the inertia starter began to wind up. After 15 turns, the crank was removed and the crank man pulled the "T" handle out. The propeller started to turn and as the engine caught, the cockpit man moved the mixture control forward to full rich. Now the propeller was a blur and the engine ran nicely. The cockpit man would now set the throttle at 1000 RPM for warm-up. The stopping procedure was simpler: throttle closed, mixture off, magnetos off, gas off, wheel chocks in place, brakes off. When all four of us got our turns at both the crank and in the cockpit, we had the procedure pretty well fixed in our minds. It was still a lot for a new cadet to remember.

That evening at dinner, every cadet had to recite the correct starting procedure before he could begin eating. After eating, and before we could leave, we had to recite the stopping procedure. We had to do this at every meal until we soloed. The next afternoon we began flying. After having learned my lesson in Cedar Falls, I told my instructor I had 71 hours flying light airplanes. He said fine, but I was still going to have to show him that I could fly the Stearman. We sat on the ramp beside the airplane and he explained that he would take each of us up for an orientation ride. I was second to go up. The PT-17 had a one-way intercom system called the "gosport." It consisted of a long piece of rubber tubing with a funnel at the end in the rear seat and connected to the headset in the front seat. The instructor could talk to the student, but the student could only reply with a head bob.

The instructor did all the talking and there was plenty of it. After engine start, he taxied the airplane to the takeoff area. On the way there he told me never to get any closer to another airplane than two lengths of the ship. He showed me the run-up procedure of setting the brakes, running up the engine to 1800 RPM and checking the magnetos. We waited for a green light from the tower and then he made the takeoff. We were airborne after a very short run. Mr. Anderson said never to fly near Phoenix, and to stay north in our practice area. East of Phoenix was another training field called Thunderbird Two. That's where foreign students were trained and we should not fly near there either. He made a few turns, some level, some climbing and some descending. Then he told me to do the same thing. The controls were a little heavier than the Piper Cub; but I did a decent job, or so I thought. He took the airplane over, came back in and landed; then he said, "We have a lot of work to do."

The upperclassmen in primary were called "Dodo Beaters" and they made sure we knew the starting and stopping procedure perfectly. We could not start eating our evening meal until they said so. One evening as I went through the ritual of stopping the engine, I got up to leave. A Dodo Beater said, "Mister, where do you think you're going with that chair?" I'd forgotten to unfasten my imaginary safety belt. I sat back down, clicked the belt free and went on my way. Every cadet had similar experiences with the upperclassmen. In six weeks, if all went well, I would be an upperclassman - a Dodo Beater.

The West Point hazing system was earlier passed on to Randolph and Kelly Fields and it got to be rather severe. Students were put inside a metal barrel, covered up, and someone would beat on it with a club for a long time. Other times, they would be put into a six-foot hole in the ground that was filled with water up to their chins and covered with a lid. They were then left there for long periods. When the Aviation Cadet Air Training Program first started, hazing was allowed. But after a congressional investigation, it quickly began to decline. There was still some hazing, but not much. The upperclassmen ruled the roost and that was okay because in just a few weeks, every lowerclassman would then become an upperclassman. This "conditioning" system seemed to work for things to come.

I loved flying the Stearman, and the open cockpit added a little excitement to the whole thing. The hardest part was the landing. Mr. Anderson was absolutely correct when he said the airplane would ground loop if you let it. With just the slightest cross wind at touch-down, it wanted to turn into the wind every time. Once I learned to control that, everything else was fairly easy. Before I could solo, I was required to demonstrate that I could land the airplane three-point. That is, make all three wheels touch at the same time. Later we practiced wheel landings; they were much easier. On wheel landings, the main wheels touched first and you let the airplane roll down the runway a ways and then let the tail wheel down slowly. But as soon as the tail wheel touched — **watch out!** — that's when she wanted to ground loop.

When a tail wheel airplane ground loops, it turns into the existing crosswind and tends to make at least one complete revolution. As it is turning, the outside wing scrapes the ground and usually causes some damage to the bottom of the wingtip. Once, when I was on final approach, ahead of me I saw two airplanes ground loop. It was scary and what every cadet feared—washing out because of too many ground loops. After a few hours of dual, I was mastering the airplane. I loved the stall, where you kicked it over into a spin. Three turns were the most we could do before pulling out.

After eight hours of dual, Mr. Anderson taxied the airplane over to the staging shack in the middle of the field. Thunderbird Field was a mile square area with the big wind sock and staging shack in the middle. Both halves of the field were always in use, one using left-hand traffic and the other right-hand traffic. At the staging shack, Mr. Anderson got out and crawled up the wing next to me in the front seat. He shouted the words that makes a cadet's heart jump, "Take her up alone, Mister." Then he said, "Leave the pattern as you were taught, do some turns while climbing up to 2,000 feet, fly around, and be back in 30 minutes." - and suddenly he was gone.

I managed to taxi the airplane to the takeoff point without hitting anyone. When I got there, I noticed three airplanes in front of me, so I waited my turn and finally the green light came and I knew it was my turn to take off. As I was rolling down the dirt runway, I had the horrible thought that I'd forgotten to run the engine up for a magneto and power check. I prayed that my instructor didn't notice that. I raised the tail wheel as soon as I could and then nursed the airplane off the ground very carefully. Suddenly I was airborne! I brought the throttle back to climb power setting and then left the traffic pattern in the way I was taught. 90-degree turn and then a 45 degree turn to depart. I even remembered to climb to 2,000 feet but didn't do many turns, just flew straight-away. I was impressed with the way the airplane responded to my every movement. After flying around the training area for a while, I decided to do a few lazy eights, one of my favorite maneuvers. Suddenly I realized that I had to get back to the field. I dove down to pattern altitude, entered it and came in for a landing. On final approach, the question crossed my mind whether to make a wheel landing or a three-pointer. Realizing my instructor would be watching, I decided to land on all three wheels. This was not the time to ground loop as I would be on the brakes and throttle in anticipation. Luckily, the wind was down and the Stearman rolled straight down the runway.

When I taxied back to the staging shack, my instructor was there waiting and signaled to me to cut the engine. He climbed up on the wing and said, "Congratulations, Mr. Gordon, you did a fine job." Of his four students, I was the first to solo. Mr. Anderson taxied the airplane back to the ramp and I rode the shuttle bus to the operations building. Soon my instructor called me to the side of the briefing room and said he would like to ask a favor. He said the other students didn't have any prior flight time like I did and asked if I would help them. He said, "After the study period tonight, take the other three students and have them sit on the edge of their bunks and demonstrate for them using your imagination, how to fly the Stearman. With stick and rudder, do the coordinated turns, climbs and descents." Being that I was the first to solo, they listened to me and we had a lot of fun "flying" the Stearman there on the edge of those bunks. Coordination is hard to learn and that exercise helped them a lot.

A week later, Mr. Anderson told me my nightly instruction helped and they were doing much better. Those cadets did not have any flying experience at all before coming to primary training.

Many is the night I thanked the Lord that I had that prior experience in Fort Hays and Cedar Falls. It got me off to a good start. It wasn't long before the other three cadets soloed and how happy the four of us were. Now we could fly solo for a couple of flights, followed by a ride with our instructor about every third flight. During our dual rides, we would often get the engine cut back for simulated forced landings. Mr. Anderson taught us how to glide the airplane to the nearest suitable landing area. A hay field was the best as they were usually soft and smooth. The worst thing was to undershoot the emergency field. We soon learned how to play the wind in making those gliding turns. The propeller was just windmilling in idle to simulate a failed engine. Someone said it was like flying a glider.

My fellow students were Oscar Graves from Roswell, New Mexico; Rodney Worrell from Huntington, West Virginia and Bert Brown from Electra, Texas. Our instructor, Mr. Anderson, grew up in Kansas City, Kansas. Before coming to Thunderbird One, he instructed CPT students at the University of Kansas at Lawrence. Mr. Anderson's wife, Mary, was a registered nurse and worked at St. Joseph's Hospital in Glendale. We would meet her later.

Midway through primary, we were introduced to the famous link trainer. It was the forerunner of today's aircraft simulators. This little blue box with stubby yellow wings drove everybody nuts. Its sole purpose was to teach us "blind" or instrument flying. An instructor sat at a nearby desk that was electrically connected to the trainer. The desk contained the same instruments that the trainer had so the instructor could tell exactly what we were doing. He gave instructions over headphones that we both wore. Inside the closed trainer, it was hot and dark as night. Every cadet had vertigo sooner or later from that blasted box. Vertigo is a state of disorder in which your surroundings seem to whirl dizzily. Instrument flying in the airplane was much easier; but we had to log 25 hours in the blue box to get past our final phase in primary.

All the link instructors were NCOs (Non-Commissioned Officers) and they loved to give us cadets a hard time whenever they had the chance. Many cadets, during the course of an hour's lesson, would eventually spin in. When the trainer "hit the ground," there was always a loud crashing noise. The instructor would then yell, "Another cadet just bit the dust."

Just like West Point, we had a flag system for the uniform of the day. In front of the cadet administration building were three flagpoles. Old Glory flew from the higher center pole. On another pole next to it flew the "uniform of the day" flag. In the summertime, a white flag indicated the khaki uniform was to be worn. A red flag meant raincoats and service cap. In the winter time, a white flag meant no overcoat. A green flag meant overcoats; and a red flag indicated a need for raincoats. A third flagpole gave indications of what the flying clothes would be for the day. A white flag meant we were to wear just our flight suits. A green flag meant for us to wear our heavy sheep-lined leather suits. A red flag meant no flying that day. There was a universal code to indicate whether a cadet had soloed. If he wore his flight suit pant legs rolled up the prescribed eight inches, he had not yet soloed. If the flight suit pant legs were worn all the way down, he had soloed.

As underclassmen, we could only go into Glendale on weekends and had to be back at the field by 11 p.m. After becoming upperclassmen, we were now allowed to go into Phoenix. That was a big deal and we always went to the Westward Ho Hotel. The manager had a big sign out in front that read, "Welcome Aviation Cadets." We could drink beer in the lobby, but not in the bar. One weekend the manager said from now on, there would be a Sunday afternoon tea dance sponsored by the local mothers. They would bring their daughters and the hotel would supply the cadets. The first dance was a little slow in getting started. Finally the mothers announced that we all must dance, so we all lined up and picked a partner. That broke the ice and after that it was lots of fun.

Every Sunday after that, we all made it a point to be at the Westward Ho for the tea dance. Beer was never allowed before, during or after the dancing. The mothers needed to see to their satisfaction that we were training to become officers and gentlemen. The girls would give us their names but never a phone number. Mothers' orders, I suppose.

One day, while we were on the parade field, the wife of the Commandant of Cadets walked by on the sidewalk. I didn't hear it but apparently someone let out a loud whistle or two. She promptly reported it to her husband. Soon a jeep pulled up and the Commandant got out in a rage. We all had to stand at attention while he dressed us down with a tongue lashing on proper behavior. He continued with, "My wife has just been verbally insulted right out in public. I will not tolerate this kind of behavior. Will the person responsible for this act please step forward?" No one moved. Then he said, "All right, you are all confined to quarters until the guilty party comes forward."

Back in our area we wondered what was going on. Later a couple of tactical officers (training officers) came by and told us they found the culprit. It wasn't a cadet after all. It seemed some street workers nearby did the whistling. They were promptly fired and shown the front gate.

For not keeping our quarters in perfect shape, or for other misdemeanors, discipline was meted out in the form of "gigs." Each gig was an hour of personal time marching, with rifle, around the Cadet Headquarters square. The correct procedure was to march singly around the square five times, then repeat the routine in the other direction. Goofing off was not possible, as it was right in front of the Orderly Room where eyes were on you constantly. Too many gigs were cause for the Maytag Machine, which means reporting to the Elimination Board with a high probability of washing out. Nobody wanted any part of that.

During Primary Flight Training, cadets usually flew a minimum of 65 hours. If anyone had to retake a check ride, more hours would be added. When we were about ten hours from finishing the course, Mr. Anderson mentioned that he had some plans for us the next Saturday night and not to plan on going into town. He said his wife would bring some student nurses out from the hospital. We would all meet at the Anderson's house for a barbecue. That sounded great and we all looked forward to the event. . When Saturday came, Mrs. Anderson came by in the afternoon and picked us up and drove us to their modest home in Glendale. The student nurses were already there and wore smiles as only nurses can. The hosts served soda and beer and we all helped with the outside grilling. We had steaks, baked potatoes and all the trimmings. When everyone was stuffed, we went inside and listened to some good music by Benny Goodman, Harry James, Tommy Dorsey, Clyde McCoy and other popular bands of the time. Before long, the rug was rolled up and everyone was dancing. We just sang along with some of the music but there was a lot of dancing too. Someone said they wondered if the boys overseas could listen to such good music. We all hoped they could and I wondered if that music would be available when I got over there. Later that night, Mr. Anderson took the girls home, then he came back and took us home. We profusely thanked the Andersons for a memorable time.

We wished the Andersons would do that again; but it never happened. I guess instructors and their students had to keep their social distance. I'm surely glad they made that one exception to the time-honored rule. During primary training, I was introduced to elementary acrobatics. I practiced and learned how to do a slow roll, barrel roll, split S, immelmann turns, and lazy eights. The lazy eights were, by far, the easiest of all the maneuvers. Spins happen when you deep stall an airplane and it falls off on one wing, and just spins. An airplane will spin right into the ground if you let it. When the PT-17 was deep-stalled, it would just fall straight ahead; so, to get it into a spin, I had to push a rudder pedal really hard to make it spin.

Acrobatics were fun and I would get more in basic flight school. A week before we finished Primary, we were informed that everything had to be completed. Every square had to be filled - academics, drill, PE, flight hours and number of landings. No one could proceed to basic flight school until everything was completed satisfactorily. All my squares were filled except one - airplane landings. I discovered that my records indicated that I was three landings short of the minimum required. Quickly, I located Mr. Anderson. He said there must be some mistake as his records showed all his students had completed the necessary flight hours and landings. Together we went to the Administration Office to report this mistake. They insisted I was three landings short. Outside, Mr. Anderson told me to sit tight and on Saturday his wife would come by and pick me up. That's all he said. Now I was confused and scared of being held back to the next class. That happened to me once in Preflight Training and I sure didn't want it to happen again.

Sure enough on Saturday, right after lunch, Mrs. Anderson came by and I got in the car with her. She said hello, but no more. As we went out the main gate, I wondered what the guard thought when he saw this lady with a cadet. I hoped he figured she was just giving me a ride into town. Anyway, he didn't stop us. Outside the gate, I asked her what was going on. She replied, "Didn't Ron tell you?" After convincing her I was in the dark, she told me her husband volunteered to fly a rare weekend test flight on one of the Stearmans. He was taking it out to one of the auxiliary fields and we were to meet him there. Upon arriving, there sat the PT-17 with its engine idling. Mr. Anderson waved me over and motioned me to get in the front cockpit. Through the gosport speaking tube he said, "Now, let's get three of the fastest landings you can get." I could not believe what was happening. After landing the third time, I jumped out and he took the airplane back to Thunderbird One. On the way back to town, Mrs. Anderson said she would drop me off at the USO Club. I could catch the shuttle bus back to the field later. I thanked her and never saw her again. It seems my instructor took his log into the Cadet Administration building and convinced them I had my required number of landings in the Stearman. No more was said about it. Now, all my squares for primary training were filled.

The day of graduation from Primary Flight Training was drawing near and was going to be a big day. As all squares were filled, we had to dress in clean Class A uniforms and march to the parade field. There, we would pass in review for the final time at good old Thunderbird One. As we marched to the parade field that final day, we broke out into song. All soldiers like to sing when they march; it just makes the event all the more enjoyable. At Fort Hays, Cedar Falls and Santa Ana, we always sang as we marched. It was encouraged by our leaders and somehow, singing made it easier to keep in step.

Our two favorites went like this:

Now be kind to your web-footed friends,
For a duck may be somebody's mother.
She lives in a creek by a swamp,
Where the weather is always damp.
Now you may think this is the end;
Well - it is!

A well-drilled group of aviation cadets could really put a song over. One that will always be remembered by every man who was a cadet:

I've got six pence,
Jolly, jolly six pence,
I've got six pence
To last me all my life.
I've got two pence to spend,
And two pence to lend,
And two pence to send home to my wife . . .
poor wife.

Chorus:

Oh, no cares have I to grieve me,
No pretty little girls to deceive me.
I'm happy as a king, believe me,
As we go rolling home.
Rolling home, rolling home,
By the light of the silvery moo-oon,
Happy is the day when an airman gets his pay
As we go rolling, rolling home.

I've got four pence
Jolly, jolly four pence,
I've got four pence
To last me all my life.
I've got two pence to spend,
And two pence to lend,
And no pence to send home to my wife...
poor wife.

(Chorus)

I've got two pence,

Jolly, jolly two pence,
I've got two pence
To last me all my life.
 I've got two pence to spend,
And no pence to lend
And no pence to send home to my wife . . .
poor wife.

(Chorus)

I've got no pence,
Jolly, jolly no pence,
I've got no pence
To last me all my life.
I've got no pence to spend,
And no pence to lend,
And no pence to send home to my wife . .
poor wife.

(Chorus)

Marching to the parade field that day, we belted the songs out
with all the lung-power we had. After we passed in review for all the
brass on the reviewing stand, we came back around and assembled in
mass in front of the reviewing stand. After all the cadets were assembled, we received the command to stand at parade-rest. The Commandant of Cadets told us we were an above average class, no accidents, no incidents and no disciplinary problems. He ended by saying,
"God Speed and good luck on your next phase of flight training."
Everyone in my class of 44-G graduated, except one. The poor
guy could not land the PT-17 and keep it under control. He ground-
looped too many times. There was no particular damage to the airplanes, just his pride and future. We all felt very badly about that. After
65 hours in the Stearman, I felt like a million dollars. Now, basic flight
school was ahead of me and I couldn't wait. My instructor and his wife
had a lot to do with my pleasant stay at Thunderbird One Primary
Flying School. It took two more days before my class was scheduled
to depart for basic flying. Everyone wanted to go back into Phoenix
one more time but our request was denied. Early on March 10, 1944,
Aviation Cadet Class 44G quietly boarded the train that would take us
to Lemoore Field in California and Basic Flight School.

Never be afraid to sit a'while and think.
—*Lorraine Hansberry*

CHAPTER SIX

BASIC FLIGHT TRAINING

Knowledge is the frontier of tomorrow
—Denis Waitley

The train arrived in Lemoore, California, late at night on March 11, 1944. The class was bused out to the airfield and the gate guards would not let the busses pass until everything was checked and in order. Even late at night, it looked like a military compound because, as the buses came to a stop, there were military people all over the place. They were a combination of tactical officers and upperclassmen and all they did was shout orders and make life miserable for us. As we got off the bus, orders were shouted to fall into columns of two and we marched to the mess hall and had to sing the whole way. After the long train and bus ride, we were tired. It didn't matter, we had to march briskly and sing anyway.

At the mess hall, before the food was brought out, we had to sing again. All the tactical officers would say was, "Louder, louder." Finally, we got to sit down and eat our first decent meal of the day. While we were eating, the tactical officers came around and made some small talk. That seemed to ease the tension a little. After the meal, we went to supply and checked out our bedding and then carried it over to our assigned barracks. Our duffle bags were dumped off a truck outside in a big pile. It took a long time to find my two bags. It was after midnight when I got my bunk made up and fell into it. As the tactical officer left, he shouted, "Reveille at 5:30, breakfast at 6:00 and an orientation meeting at 7:30." I was suddenly back in the Army. Here in basic, we were required to wet-mop the area around our bunks each morning in addition to the regular clean up chores. There were a limited number of mops and we had to hurry to finish in time. At 7:15, we marched over to the base auditorium for orientation to Basic Flight Training. As the Base Commander, Colonel A.J. Malone, entered with his staff, everyone jumped to attention. Along with Colonel Malone was the Commandant of Cadets, Major Eubanks; the Director of Training, Major Ketchler; and the Director of Flying, Captain Slate. Colonel Malone then put us at ease and said to take our seats.

He started out with, "Misters, your flying for fun ended at Primary. From here on your training will become grimmer. There will be but one purpose behind the instruction you get here. Everything you do and learn will be aimed at making you the most scientific pilots and the best equipped killers in the world." The rest of the staff spoke a few words about sincerity, dedication to duty and staying out of trouble, both on and off the field.

Lemoore was located about 40 miles south of Fresno and 20 miles west of Hanford It would be a while before we could get a pass anywhere. At Lemoore, we had a choice of continuing the second half of the flying program in either single-engine or twin-engine airplanes. As a result of this, we would be better prepared for various airplane assignments later. There was much spirited rivalry between the fighters and the bombers. My hope was to fly fighters.

Regardless of whether I received single-engine or twin-engine training, I would develop a spirit of teamwork and confidence in my ability to meet the enemy anywhere, anytime, and smash him. Here at Lemoore, I would be flying the Vultee BT-15 single engine basic trainer for at least, the first half of basic flight training. Vultee Aircraft Company produced over 10,000 of the trainers during WW II. It had the Wright R-975 radial engine that developed 450 hp. Top speed was 155 mph and it cruised at 130 mph. Landing approach speed was 75 mph. The airplane's nickname was the "Vibrator," as the instrument panel shook whenever the airplane was stalled and spun.

Halfway through the basic flight training program, my class would be split in half—one staying with the BT-15 and the rest going on to twin-engine training. We all wondered how we would be split. We quickly settled into our routine. Half the group attended classes in the morning while the rest reported to the flight line. Each week it would be reversed. I liked the morning flying as the air was smoother. Even though it was March, the San Joaquin Valley in California got pretty hot in the afternoons. Hot weather means choppy air and training became more difficult. The first day on the flight line, I was introduced to my instructor. His name was Lieutenant Lancaster. I was in "C" flight and my fellow students were H.B. Groom, F.J. Goodwin, W. Green and J.P. Greeves. The BT-15 looked pretty big but I noticed it had a wide landing gear. The PT-17's landing gear was much narrower. The wide landing gear, to me, meant "anti-ground-loop." I hoped I was correct. Lieutenant Lancaster took us on a detailed exterior inspection of the airplane, then, each student had to sit in the cockpit for half an hour familiarizing himself with the instruments. The BT-15 was equipped for instrument flying and it would be my first experience flying just by the gauges. I had a feeling I was going to like instrument flying. I had quite a lot of experience sitting in cockpits, so this would be fun for me. We drew numbers for this task and my turn would be third.

Rumor had it that we had to pass a blindfold cockpit check before we could learn to start the engine. The rumor proved to be true and on the next flying session, we all took the blindfold check. I passed mine easily. Under the blindfold, I had to point to or touch various gauges and controls in five seconds or less. Next we had drills on starting the big engine. Before long we got the procedure down pretty well. The first several flight hours would be dual lessons with the instructor. When he felt we were ready, we could take it up alone. I had done that in the Cub and the Stearman, but this was a much bigger and more powerful airplane. On my first dual ride, I didn't touch the controls until Lieutenant Lancaster demonstrated several maneuvers. Then he gave me the stick. The controls were heavier, but the airplane responded very nicely, that is, until I tried a loop. Not having the proper airspeed, I stalled out near the top of the loop. As the airplane stalled, my instructor kicked the rudder and suddenly we were spinning. Through the interphone, he said not to worry as he needed to show me a spin anyway. As the airplane was spinning, the instrument panel was shaking like crazy. Now I knew why they called it the Vultee Vibrator. After a lot of practice, I could do the loop quite well. My next maneuver was the Immelmann turn. This maneuver was invented by a German Ace in World War I—Oberleutenant Max Immelmann.

The Immelmann turn started out exactly like a loop, but at the top, while on your back, you simply did a half roll and suddenly you were going the other way—a neat maneuver indeed. My instructor tried two of them and then let me try one. I did quite well for my first time and he said, "We'll do more of those later." We then entered the landing pattern and shot some landings. I was correct about the airplane's wide landing gear. After touchdown and during the roll out, the airplane rolled straight as an arrow, and it certainly made me feel good. I was really going to like this bird. After each student in Lieutenant Lancaster's flight had an orientation flight, he sat us down by the airplane one day and gave us a little pep talk, "It's my job to start you on your way to becoming combat pilots. Some of you will be fighter pilots while others will be bomber or transport pilots. In either case, your job will be to stop the enemy. I'll expect your full cooperation here at Lemoore. That's all."

That same day I had my first session with the link trainer. It was the same trainer we had in primary training, except these had a few more instruments. At first, all I did was some simple turns, climbs and descents to certain altitudes. Some of the turns were "timed." Three degrees per second at 30 degrees of bank angle was the norm. The cooling fans in those trainers were just too small as it was always hot in there; but our complaints fell on deaf ears. A new subject in ground school was Morse Code. The instructor said this was just an introduction to the course. We would just become familiar with the alphabet and numbers. There would be no final test. He did warn us that in advanced flight training, the ability to copy twelve words per minute would be required. Now everyone was concerned.

For the first time, I was flying an airplane that had wing flaps. We didn't need them for the takeoff; but did use them to slow the airplane for landing. To my dismay, the flaps were manually moved with a hand crank located to the left of the pilot's seat. Fifteen cranks gave you full down flaps. There was no indicator. You just counted the turns of the crank If the flaps were stuck in the up position, you just landed the airplane that way but at a faster speed. Besides the link trainer, we were doing some instrument flying in the back seat of the airplane where a white curtain was pulled over our heads. No outside references, such as the horizon, could be used.

During basic flight training, from the time we were blasted out of bed in the morning until lights out was announced, we were in high gear. Our training in neatness and order might qualify us to one day make some woman a good wife. On the other hand, she might be driven crazy by our acquired habit of insisting that everything be kept in its proper place. Every cadet was given an absence card. These cards stated why a cadet was absent from his area. He could be on leave, in charge of quarters, in the hospital, the junior officer of the day, off post on pass or the cadet officer of the day. If he was absent for that day, he simply checked his card and signed it. The card was part of the honor system and a cadet was never questioned about it; however, if he ever violated the system, he was a goner.

Primary flight school was a plush flying club compared to basic. There was no question we were back in the Army. Carrying out the Commandant's administrative duties was a corps of cadet officers. At the top was the wing commander, followed by the flight commanders and then the lowly cadets. That was the chain of command. Aviation Cadets were neither enlisted men nor civilians; we were considered potential officers. Discipline was the order of the day every day. Slowly, we were being trained as leaders. A few cadets failed to recognize this and took the attitude that they were being trained to become little tin gods with silver wings. They failed to visualize the responsibilities that lay ahead, or to understand that their training was not for personal gain, but for the sole purpose of fighting the enemy. Those cadets did not survive.

There was some idle time at basic, but that depended on marks in ground school and how well we did in flight training. "Gigs" were now walked off on the flight line and you had to wear a parachute and walk around a prescribed area one hour for each gig. If, however, we did find a free moment or two, facilities for relaxation were close at hand. The base had a large facility where you could relax, play cards, play pool or ping pong, listen to the juke box, just talk or write letters. It was known as the Cadet Day Room.

Part of our PE class was practicing sit-ups, pull-ups and push-ups. Before I could leave basic I would have to do 114 sit-ups and a minimum of 5 pull-ups. Push-ups were the easiest of the three. We had to do at least 25. Some cadets could do that with one hand. I needed both hands for everything. The post theater ran an 8:00 movie every night. If our studies were up to date, we went to the show. If a movie was long, we had to leave early in order to be back in the barracks by the 10 p.m. curfew. I had to leave a lot of movies early, so I never knew how they ended.

Food at the cadet mess was very good but discipline reigned there too. At breakfast, as we entered the hall, every cadet stood at attention behind his chair. The Cadet Wing Commander, from the front of the hall, sang out, "Take seats." This was the command to take our seats but we had to remain at attention. Next, the CWC moved to the center of the big aisle and held a piece of paper in front of him at arms length. From this paper he read the Orders of the Day. He then gave the command, "Rest." This command signaled that we were free to start eating. If the CWC added the phrase "Take off at will," you could leave when finished.

The cadet mess hall was new and beautiful. It was nicely painted and decorated and the windows even had fresh-looking curtains. The place was staffed by a mess sergeant, 6 cooks, 8 cook's helpers, a head waiter and 20 waiters. Except for the man in charge, all the rest were civilians. No KP duty for cadets, and that was fine with everyone. Tables were arranged to seat 10 cadets, five per side. A cadet officer sat at the head position bringing the total per table to 11. The two cadets near the aisle were called "gunners." It was their duty to call attention to a waiter to refill any empty bowls. There was only one topic of conversation at meals and, of course it was flying.

At the front of the cadet mess hall sat an additional table which seated 12 and where the Cadet Wing Commander and his staff ate their meals Sometimes there were guests and, occasionally, these "visiting firemen" were high ranking officers. Occasionally there were stars on their shoulders and wings on their chests. It was difficult to believe that they too, had once been a cadet just like me.

Lieutenant Lancaster and I had been flying instruments one day when he chewed me out for not being precise with my rate of climb and descent. He wanted 500 feet per minute rate of climb, not 400 or 600. Never, except for takeoff, did we climb straight ahead. It was always climbing turns and descending turns. He always said, "You can't see well enough ahead when you're climbing with level wings. He was, of course, correct.

One day near the end of the flying period when both of us were exhausted, he did not shut down the engine when he parked. Jumping out of the back seat and shouting over the idling engine noise, he spoke those famous words that makes a cadet's heart jump, "Take her up alone Mister. Look the flying area over and be back in 30 minutes. Make only one landing." Then he was gone. There I sat alone in the BT-15 with its engine idling. I just sat there for a few seconds and did not move a muscle. Finally, I saw the lineman signal that the chocks were pulled and I was clear to taxi. I remembered to do the "S" turns while taxiing so I could see ahead and not run into anyone. At the hold line, I even remembered to set the brakes and run up the engine. It purred like a new sewing machine. The airplane had a basic radio and I asked the control tower for permission to take off. The takeoff went smoothly and before I knew it, I was climbing away reaching for the sky.

I felt so good that I just flew around and looked over the country-side. We could not fly west of highway 145 or east of highway 41. After doing a few lazy eights, it was time to head for the field. Down I came at exactly 500 feet per minute. I could hear my instructor's words about precision flying and he was not even in the airplane. I entered the landing pattern and the tower cleared me to land. My first solo landing in the BT-15 was actually a good one, to my surprise. I was going to like this airplane.. As I taxied into the parking ramp, an earth-shattering thought struck me right between the eyes. I had totally forgotten to lower the wing flaps for landing. Nobody noticed and I certainly never told anyone.

Flying cross-country was always fun as I liked the detailed planning. I'd put a sectional aerial map on the floor of operations and, with a straight edge, drew a red course line representing my intended route. The planned route was always from home base to another airport about 100 miles away, then I would turn around and come back. Later on, I would fly a triangle route which was even more fun. If I was ever in doubt about my position along the route, I would go down over a town and "shoot the station." This meant I would fly by the train depot and read the name. Water towers sometimes had names also. Discovering that I was still on course gave me great confidence. The weather in the San Joaquin Valley was always good at that time of year. In the valley, airfields were everywhere. I had to keep my head on a swivel to watch for other solo cadets like me. I suspected combat pilots swiveled their heads a lot looking for enemy aircraft. The very thought of combat flying was very exciting and stimulating.

The Western Air Training Command used every bit of the state of California they could to build airfields. So, on cross-countries, we had to keep our heads on a swivel as there were so many airplanes in the sky every day. Every pilot likes to do some low-level flying as its fun and exciting. At higher altitudes one has no reference for his speed; but down low when you see the trees and other objects whipping by, you have a much better perspective. Flying low can also be dangerous. A particular hazard is birds. Our speed was about six times as fast as the birds and there was no way to miss them if they got directly in front of you.

Basic flying was going along very well in spite of the constant pressure from the tactical officers. "You can always do better," was their motto. The cadet officers usually mirrored the tactical people. One day I noticed a crowd around the area bulletin board as mid-term check ride schedules were out. Sure enough, I saw my name for a check ride, two days hence, with Captain Milford. The notice went on to say that my takeoff time was 1 p.m. and to be there, with parachute and goggles, 30 minutes early. Notices like that will start your knees shaking. Nobody likes a check ride as nerves get in the way and you just don't do as well as you would like to. The next day, Lieutenant Lancaster took me up and gave me a practice check ride. He had me do everything in the book. Lazy eights and landings were my forte. Later, on the ground he said, "Try to relax and every time the check pilot tells you to do a maneuver, repeat it to him for clarification. If you do well on the first couple maneuvers, he might not spend much more time with you." He went on, "Before each maneuver, be sure you yell out "clear left," "clear right," "clear above," "clear below." He will grade you on that— believe me." I did not sleep well the night before my check ride. The next morning at PE, my heart was not in it and I asked the PE instructor for a favor. I told him I needed to leave a little early as I had to shower, change clothes, eat an early lunch and be at the flight line at 12:30 for an important check ride. To my surprise, he let me go early. That was the first break of the day and maybe my only one.

Precisely at 12:30, I was standing by the BT-15 that was assigned to Captain Milford. I had already made the walk-around pre-flight inspection. Soon it was 1 p.m. and no check pilot was in sight. Soon it was 1:15 and still no check pilot. At 1:20, a jeep roared up and out jumped my check pilot, Captain Milford. He was in his class A uniform and service hat. He left his blouse and hat in the jeep and told the line boy to park it somewhere. I was standing by the airplane with my parachute and goggles stacked in a neat pile beside me. As he neared, I gave him my best salute. He said, "Are you Mr. Gordon?" "Yes sir." I replied. Then he said, "What's this stuff doing on the ground?" "For you to inspect, Sir" I replied. He told me to get into the front seat pronto. Quickly Captain Milford started the engine from the back seat and got the clearance from the control tower to taxi out for takeoff. When parked at the hold line by the runway, he told me to make the magneto and power check of the engine. That being finished, we received clearance from the control tower to take off.

Captain Milford shouted over the intercom, "Make the takeoff and fly to the alpha practice area while climbing to 5,000." "Yes sir!" I shot back at him, "Alpha area at five thousand." During the climb out, he again shouted over the interphone, "Why are you climbing at such a slow rate?" I said that was what my instructor trained me to do. With that, he yanked the stick back and added full power. Now we were going up at 1,500 feet per minute. It didn't take long to reach 5,000 feet that way. At level off, he stood the airplane on one wing tip then the other. That is a clearing maneuver prior to doing acrobatics. Then he said to me, "Give me a slow roll to the left." I started to say; "Clear left," when he cut me off and told me to knock that crap off. I took a few deep breaths and did the slow roll as well as I could. Now he said, "Give me a snap roll to the right." Snap rolls to the left are fairly easy, but to the right they are tough, as you are going against the torque of the engine.

I yanked the stick back to the five o'clock position and, at the same time, jammed in full right rudder. To my surprise, the airplane snapped to the right and rolled over and I recovered it straight and level. Then he said he wanted the airplane and promptly did a snap roll to the left. It was perfect. "Okay," he said. "Now do an Immelmann turn." Diving to get the proper airspeed, I cleared myself and pulled up into the Immelmann. It wasn't perfect, but not bad either. He asked, "What's your favorite maneuver?" I said the lazy eight. "Do a couple, then." he said without shouting—for once. I went on to do four perfect lazy eights.

He then took over the ship and dove at redline speed, entered the pattern and landed the airplane. I just sat there in awe at how he mastered that trainer. After parking, he jumped out and said to tell the next cadet to be in the front cockpit as soon as possible, then he dashed into operations. The next student, Fred Goodwin, came walking out and I told him the check pilot wanted him in the front seat right away. Fred asked if I passed the check ride. I said, "I don't know. He never said."

Back in operations, I located my instructor and told him I didn't know if I passed or failed. He said Captain Milford was like that. "But if you failed, you'd have known about it." He added. All Lieutenant Lancaster's students passed the mid-term single engine check ride. He was proud of us but never came out and said it. He just started treating us better. None of his five students performed the same maneuvers on their check rides. How I yearned to be a check pilot! I thought that would be the greatest job. Many years later, I would become an instructor and check pilot and would hold that satisfying job for a long time.

Until phase one of basic was finished, all our flying was solo. I took several three-legged cross-countries and loved every minute. I never became lost but do admit to shooting several stations. Sometimes on a cross country leg, if there were no other airplanes in sight, I would do a couple of lazy eights. They were very relaxing and lots of fun. Thank goodness I never got caught.

When phase one of basic flight training was finished, I had flown 36 hours in the BT-15 airplane. I had to fly five hours of night time and get ten night landings. That was scary but I managed to get that square filled on time. Right after my last flight in the BT-15, a notice appeared on the area bulletin board for all cadets to stop by the cadets' administration building and pick up a form. It was to be filled out and returned the following day. The form contained many questions on how we liked basic flight training, including ground school, PE and military drill. Then came the 64-dollar question. Would we like to continue the second half of basic in the single engine airplane or change to the twin-engine Cessna Bobcat known as the UC-78. Its official name was the AT-17 Advanced Trainer.

The last item on the form was for the cadets' reason for their choice to stay in single-engine or switch to twin-engine training. That was a tough one to answer. I liked single engine flying and it would eventually lead to flying fighters. On the other hand, twin-engine training would involve a whole hoard of multi-engine bombers and transports. I had quite a lot of experience in building twin-engine aircraft, such as the C-46 transport and the B-26 bomber. I was quite impressed with them. My many hours in the P-40 cockpit back in Buffalo also brought back fond memories of that airplane.

I was perplexed over making this decision. Before we filled out this form, a lot of barracks talk centered around both avenues in our careers. I was at the fork in the road and from peer pressure, I finally chose single-engine and thought I gave good reasons for that decision. At the bottom of the form was this statement: Whatever your personal choice is, the final decision rests with the Commandant of Cadets. Personal choice is but one part of the final decision. Other factors are cadet grades in ground school and overall aptitudes displayed in the first half of your basic training. Lastly, your instructors, ground and air, have input also. You will be notified of the final determination of your path of training for the last half of basic training and, later, advanced training.

Every cadet was sweating this outcome. Nothing happened for two days. We just continued our ground school classes, PE and drill. Flying was stopped pending the decision. Everyone was nervous as cats on a hot tin roof. During the night, you could hear cadets turning and tossing trying to get to sleep. The next morning, after roll call and breakfast, we were to report to the base theater to hear our fate. The place was packed with the entire cadet class of 44-G and it was strangely quiet. As the Commandant of Cadets entered, everyone rose to attention. He then asked everyone to take their seats and went to the microphone. He began by saying, "Good morning Students of class of 44-G. You have reached the fork in the road here at basic flight school. The selections for single-engine and twin-engine training have been made and will be read to you shortly. There is no appeal to our final decision. Even if you know someone in the Military or even in Congress, don't bother them. It will do you no good as our selection list is final. Now, my aide, Captain Roberts, will read the lists." Captain Roberts started by saying, "I will read the single-engine names first - followed by the twin-engine list. Both lists are in alphabetical order." He started reading the names and as he got close to the "Gs", I held my breath. Then I heard him say "Gordon" and my heart jumped. But in the next half second, he said, "George." Now my heart sank. I knew George Gordon; he was in another flight. I also knew that I was now headed for twin-engine training.

That afternoon the same lists were put up on the area bulletin board just for confirmation and for checking on some of our friends. There was a lot of talk about the decision. I was rather disappointed, but not overly so. The old saying goes: two engines are better than one; and I accepted that. That same afternoon, the single engine guys moved to their own barracks and I stayed put. My friends, Fred Goodwin, Harold Groom, Willie Green and John Greeves all stayed with me. We all would go through twin-engine training together. At the same time, the upperclassmen moved on to advanced training. Now we were upperclassmen and watched the new lowerclassmen move in from primary training.

The airplane I would be flying was the Cessna UC-78 Bobcat, sometimes called the AT-17, the Ucey-Ducey or the Bamboo Bomber. Its two radial-engines were the Jacobs R-755-9 rated at 245 HP each. Top speed was 175 mph, cruising speed was 150 mph and it landed at 75. Over 5,000 ships were built. Before starting twin-engine train-ing, I had to bring my link trainer hours up to date. I had fallen behind with all the BT-15 flying and check rides going on. I "flew" the link trainer twice a day for three days in a row. I hoped never to see one of those things again. I had to master the radio range instrument approach and it was tough in that little blue sweat-box with stubby yellow wings.

The next Monday morning I reported to the twin-engine flight line and met my new instructor, Lieutenant Bass. Being that Fred, Hal, Willie, John and I were in the same flight, we shared the same instruc-tor. Lieutenant Bass took us out to one of the Bobcats and said to get under the wing where it was shady. We all sat down and he leaned against the main wheel landing strut. He told us some interesting things about this airplane, like; "Once you get it into the air, it gets along very well. But on the ground, it's a bear to taxi and control. Ground opera-tion is by a combination of inputs from the brakes and throttles. It takes a while to get used to, as you will find out. This will be the first airplane you will fly that has a retractable landing gear. The gear is moved up and down by electric motors and has a hand-crank backup system. Let's hope we never have to use it."

Lieutenant Bass went on to explain how the flight instruction would proceed. He would take three of us up on an orientation ride. He would occupy the right hand seat and do instructor/co-pilot duties. That mainly dealt with the radios and reading the checklist. Each of us would get about 30 minutes in the left seat and then change around, so all three got a taste of twin-engine flying. He would then demonstrate a typical landing, change students and do it all over again with the last two. He said he would pick us in alphabetical order of our first names. I was in the second group that day.

In ground school, we each received a handbook on the airplane and its systems, including the engines. Now we were issued a chest-pack type parachute. They were fine as all we had to wear was the light-weight harness. The chest pack itself would be stored on the floor of the airplane. All you had to do was snap the pack on the large rings on your harness and be ready to jump. When I taxied the Bobcat, my instructor wanted me to use the engines to make the "S" turns that were necessary. This was a difficult maneuver until I learned the correct throttle inputs.

A cadet really had to stay ahead of this airplane. One day, at the hold line, waiting for takeoff clearance, I saw the crash and rescue trucks go racing down the runway. The tower announced that a Bobcat was coming in to land with its gear stuck in the up position The crew could not get the gear down by either the normal or back-up systems, so had no choice in the matter. A belly landing was the only option left. Training fields did not have foam in those days so the fire truck sprayed water on the runway so the airplane would slide better. Soon the Bobcat came in very slowly and, when over the fence, the crew shut down the engines. Then, to my amazement, the props were "motored" to level position thus preventing damage at touchdown. It looked like a perfect job. I found out later the instructor did all the work and was a good friend of Lieutenant Bass. All flying was suspended for the day as the airplane had to be removed from the runway. I taxied back to the ramp and got the rest of the afternoon off. A rare privilege in flight training, to be sure.

The instruments in the Bobcat were similar to the BT-15 except for dual airspeed and altimeter indicators and, of course, dual engine instruments. A nice feature was an electric fuel pump for starting engines. On my first flight in the airplane, the instructor made the take-off and then handed it over to me. I was surprised at how nice and easy it handled. The weight of the engines seemed to help the ailerons when banking in a turn. I climbed to 5,000 feet and Lieutenant Bass demonstrated power-on and power-off stalls, both with and without flaps. He said, "You don't want to spin this baby." Sitting side by side, no intercom was needed; we just talked normally. Next, he showed me how the airplane handled with one engine cut back to idle. I had to crank in a lot of rudder trim and opposite aileron trim, but it flew well enough, rather slowly-about 100 mph. Before Lieutenant Bass let me crank in rudder trim, I had to show him that I could hold the airplane straight with opposite rudder pressure. I developed strong leg muscles very quickly. I enjoyed landing the Bobcat, because if you had the correct landing attitude, when coming in over the fence, all you had to do was bleed off the power and the airplane would settle in to the runway nicely with a soft touchdown. It sounds easier than it really was.

After about ten hours of dual, I was allowed to fly "buddy" style. Two cadets would fly for a while, come back and land, park and change seats, then we went back for another hour. This was fun, especially when we went on cross-country flights. With this airplane, we could fly somewhere, land and change seats, then fly back to Lemoore. Now I could pick up radio ranges and homing beacons as aids to navigation. I didn't have to go down and "shoot stations" anymore.

All the instructors were harping on the cadets for taxiing too fast. It came to a head one day when two cadets were coming in from their final landing of the day. As usual, they were taxiing much too fast and when it came time to stop on the ramp, they had to jam on the brakes. Then it happened; the brakes locked and the airplane tipped over on its nose. One of the instructors came over and proceeded to pull the tail back down. Then he went around and viewed the dented nose and bent props. Those two cadets each received 15 gigs for that trick and after that, they had a velvet touch on those brakes. They also taxied more slowly from then on.

Another thing that bugged the instructors were those cadets that ignored time limits. When Lieutenant Bass sent us up for an hour, he meant an hour, not an hour and ten or fifteen minutes. I, myself, became a victim of that rule. One day, Fred Goodwin and I went up in the Bobcat for an hour to practice stalls, power on and power off as Lieutenant Bass said we would get stalls on our final check ride. There were puffy white clouds that day at 4,000 feet so we climbed above them to 6,000 feet where the air was silky smooth. We were having so much fun doing the stalls that time got away from us. When we landed, Lieutenant Bass met us at the parking ramp. We were gone an hour and a half. As I was in the left seat, he said, "Mr. Gordon, here is a piece of white chalk. Walk yourself down to the far end of the runway and autograph it." It was a long walk as the runway was almost a mile long. After I signed my name on that runway, and while walking back, I resolved always to be on time after that embarrassment.

Soon, I had completed all my link trainer time. My ground school classes were finished, but I still had good old PE and drill. I flew every day now and could handle the Bobcat quite well but keeping the engines synchronized was difficult. The instructor said to keep the engine tachometer needles together. That was okay but I could do a better job by ear. When the beat was just right, my ears told me that the engines were perfectly synchronized.

My Bobcat final check ride went well. I had an engine cut back right after takeoff and the check pilot said to take the airplane back and land it, just as if the real thing had happened. I managed to get it back on the ground, and the check pilot said, "Okay, take off again, stay in the pattern and make a no-flap landing." After I did that, he said to take it in and park it. I couldn't believe it. It was, by far, the easiest check ride I ever had.   Basic flying training suddenly came to a close. I had to turn in my equipment, books and flying clothing issue. There were a few meetings but that was about it.   During basic flying training, I flew 36 hours in the BT-15 and 52 hours in the AT-17.   I enjoyed my stay at Lemoore Army Air Base but was anxious to get on to the next phase. That would be Advanced Flying School and my coveted silver wings.

There is never a better measure of what a person is
than what he does when he's absolutely free to choose.

—-William Bulger

CHAPTER SEVEN

ADVANCED FLIGHT TRAINING

Love is perhaps the only glimpse we are permitted of eternity.

—Helen Hayes

In one of the meetings before leaving Lemoore, the Commandant of Cadets told us our advanced flight school was scheduled for La Junta Army Air Base in Colorado. I never heard of it but guessed it was somewhere in the eastern part of the state. We were shocked when the Commander informed us that we would no longer be flying the AT-17 Bobcat. We would be going right into the big stuff and flying the AT-24, a modified version of the B-25 lightweight bomber. Wow!!

Aviation Cadet Class 44-G arrived in the small hamlet of La Junta, about 40 miles east of Pueblo, and about the same distance west of Lamar on highway 50. The nearest town of any size at all was Rocky Ford, 15 miles to the northwest. The elevation at the La Junta air field was 4,066 feet above sea level. As we rode the train out from Pueblo, the land looked pretty barren with hardly any trees. There was very little vegetation along the Arkansas River. As at Lemoore, the new base was all military and the only civilians were clerks and line mechanics. Arriving late, we were taken directly to the mess hall and fed, no singing this time. The tactical officers and a few upperclassmen who met us were cordial and did not chew us out, to our surprise. Here, two story wooden barracks, to which we had become accustomed, were replaced by austere tarpaper huts.

Eight cadets were assigned to each hut and there were no latrines. Tarpaper outhouses had been placed about 40 feet behind the huts and were connected with the huts by boardwalks. We had electricity and, for heat, a big stove which was oil-fed from a tank located behind the hut. It was May 25, 1944, one day before my 22nd birthday. The eight cadets assigned to my hut were Goodwin, Groom, Green, Greeves, Gordon, Garvey, Grace and Gomez. Bill Garvey was voted the Hut Commander. The latrines out back were lighted and heated and each had a big shower room where eight of us could shower at once. That happened many times with absolutely no embarrassment. Each cadet had a single bed, a footlocker in front of the bed and a combination wall-locker-desk behind the bed—not fancy but adequate. Four beds on either side of the room gave us a reasonable amount of living space. Both the footlockers and wall cabinets could be locked except during inspection periods. It took 32 of those huts to house my class of 250 cadets. As lowerclassman, we were the greatest distance from everything on base. A large bulletin board with a little roof had been placed in front of the housing area. We had to check it daily for any special assignments or any messages. It took a while for my mail to catch up with me and when it did, I had over 20 letters from family and friends. I read some of those letters over and over, especially those from my mom. The food in the cadet mess hall was outstanding; even though our living quarters were not.

At our first orientation meeting, the Commandant of Cadets, Colonel Moore, said, "Good morning Misters! I hope you have found your quarters comfortable. It's not the Conrad Hilton, but it will seem like it when you get overseas and live in cold and wet tents." He continued, "You have just nine weeks to complete eleven weeks of classes, flying, PE and drill. We have but one objective here, and that is to get you prepared to fly a bomber, loaded with bombs, toward an Axis target to hasten the end of the war." He paused for a moment to let that sink in, and then said, "You probably noticed two types of airplanes on the ramp here at La Junta. The fighters are Bell P-39s that belong to the 21st Fighter Group. They rotate training squadrons here every two weeks. The present squadron is the 7th. There is also a ramp full of AT-24s. It's actually a stripped down B-25 Michell Light Bomber." Pausing to take a drink of water, he continued, "The AT-24 is a very good and stable ship and you should adapt to it quickly. Army intelligence reports dealing with combat work in the war zones, are being furnished all advanced flight schools weekly. From these reports of pilot experiences in actual combat, much useful information can be passed on to us. Good luck with your training and Godspeed."

Like the other schools, we had a half day of classes and a half day of flying. In ground school, there were new subjects—aircraft and naval ship profile recognition for the Allied, German and Japanese planes and ships. We were first shown a black profile of the plane or ship projected on a large screen during which time, pertinent details were pointed out. After several exposures to the profiles, we were then shown quick flashes of the objects and expected to identify it.. Flash cards were also used for the buddy-study periods in the tarpaper huts. Morse code was now being taught in earnest and we had to master 12 words per minute to pass the course. There were more classes on chemical weapons and the use of the gas mask; we even got a whiff of some of the different gases. Instead of going to the firing range, we went to the skeet range and fired at clay pigeons. That was actually fun even though every cadet had a bruised shoulder from the shotgun's kick. Other classes were military doctrine and protocol. One day we did go to the firing range after all. It was a special indoctrination to the 30- and 50-caliber machine guns. From a moving truck, we fired at a moving target going the opposite way. Man, did those machine guns ever shake you up, especially the 50s. The skeet range was more fun. Our instructor said it was a good hand-eye coordination exercise. Another good hand-eye exercise was playing ping-pong as much as possible. Several tables were in the dayroom and they were always in use. I became rather good at ping-pong. Even today, I can usually beat people half my age.

At PE, push-ups, pull-ups and sit-ups were stressed. We also ran the two-mile obstacle course twice a week, rain or shine. By now, most of us were in pretty good shape from all that PE stuff. The first day on the flight line, some upperclassmen took us, in groups, on a tour. We visited all the hangars first, then the flight line. There, these "dodo-beaters" tried to tell us all about the Mitchell Bomber and how tricky it was to fly. I personally interpreted that as a scare tactic.

I didn't listen very closely to the upperclassman. I wanted to hear all that from my instructor. One of the things the upperclassman said that I did remember was, "You better hope you don't lose an engine on take off because she's a bear to handle." After this so-called tour, we all assembled in a hangar where we would be briefed by the Chief of Air Training, Major Sands. He started out by telling us how our group would be separated into four flights, Able, Baker, Charlie and Dog. All the "G"s wound up in Baker flight. Now the flights were separated and Baker flight met their instructors. My instructor introduced himself as Lieutenant Lewis, and he quickly told us we were only his second class. He had graduated with the class of 44-E. He seemed like a decent sort, about our age and just a little cocky, I thought. He said to follow him out to the ramp where a new-looking B-25 sat gleaming in the sun. Starting from the nose section, we slowly walked around the airplane while Lieutenant Lewis pointed out its features. When we got back to the nose section, he said, "The only check ride you will get here at advanced flying school will be a comprehensive instrument check, that's all, just an instrument check." I couldn't believe what I had just heard.

Leaning against the airplane's nose, our instructor gave us some history of the bomber. It was built by North American Aviation Company in California. In addition to the Army Air Force, other countries such as Britain, Holland, China, Russia and Australia also flew the airplane. It became famous during the Doolittle bombing of Tokyo in April 1942. It had two Wright R-2600 radial engines that developed 1,700 HP each. Maximum speed was 275 mph, cruising speed was 230 and it landed at 90. Lieutenant Lewis then added: "I didn't lose any students in my first class and I don't intend to lose any with this class. When we start flying, I am not going to teach you how to fly this airplane, I'm going to show you how to fly it, then, you fly it just like I do. Remember, instrument flying is the big thing here so get all the Link trainer time you can. You will be notified when to show up for your orientation flight."

One at a time we got to sit in the left seat and stare at all the instruments, levers and controls. Our ground school would have classes in aircraft systems and the B-25 Mitchel had a lot of them. Fuel, oil, hydraulic, electrical, pneumatic and mechanical were the major systems we had to learn. The first day in ground school, I was issued a thick book describing every inch of the airplane. It had two long checklists, normal and emergency. The bold face items on the emergency checklist had to be memorized. My thoughts went back to all the cockpit time I had in the aircraft factories.

The day we reported for our first flight, Lieutenant Lewis took the six of us on a detailed walk-around inspection. He especially emphasized the down lock pins in each main wheel well. The airplane had two lower entrance hatches, one up front for the crew, and one in the back for extra students or passengers. Opening and closing of those hatches were demonstrated at least twice. Lieutenant Lewis pointed out that this would be our first experience with a tricycle landing gear.

No tail wheel was on this aircraft. Now we had a nose wheel instead; which eliminated the need for "S" turns while taxing. I could taxi straight down the taxiway as visibility ahead would be excellent. Lieutenant Lewis told us, "I've said it before and I will say it again, here at advance, we stress instrument flying, day and night cross-country flights and day and night formation flying." The airplane looked mighty big to me for cadets to be flying. He then said, "You will have to memorize the outside preflight inspection. Everything inside will be done according to the printed checklist. The person in the right seat, instructor or student, will read the checklist items. The person in the left seat will verbally respond from memory. Any questions on that?" "No sir!" we all responded together.

"Today, you will get your first ride in the airplane. Remember I said ride as each of you will sit in the right seat and watch me carefully. You won't even touch the controls today. I will do this in two short flights. The first flight will be Gordon, Goodwin and Groom. When we land, they will depart and Green, Greeves and Garvey will get on board. After that, the last two will get their flight. You're getting a free ride, make the most of it."

After lunch, I checked out my chest-pack parachute and harness. Lieutenant Lewis told me to get in the right seat first and I was thrilled over that. Fred and Hal climbed in behind me and sat on the shelf just behind the entrance hatch. After strapping into the seat, the instructor handed me the checklist and said, "Read it to me slowly." After each item I read, he responded. Soon we got to the engine start section. Deftly, the instructor primed the right engine and then pushed the start button. The big propeller started to turn, the engine coughed, shook and finally fired up and ran quite roughly. He set the RPM at 1,000 and went through the same starting procedure with the left engine. It, too, ran roughly, and he said that all radial engines run rough at low speed To prove his point, he advanced the throttles so both tachometers advanced to 1200 RPM. At that speed, the engines ran smoothly.

I finished the checklist and we were ready to taxi. The tower gave us clearance to taxi to runway 30. The designation 30 indicating that the runway's magnetic bearing was 300 degrees. The opposite direction was 120 degrees and was called runway 12. On that day we had a northerly surface wind as a cold front had come through the day before. Even in idle rpm, the airplane taxied right along with no extra power needed. Near the runway, I was shown how to "power check" each engine. First, the prop had to be exercised, so hot oil would be distributed evenly throughout the propeller's governor system. This was necessary in case of the need to "feather" (stop) the engine after takeoff. Next, both magnetos were checked for any rpm drop while running on only one set of spark plugs. Each cylinder in the engine had two spark plugs—each fired by separate magnetos. The engine was run up to 1800 RPM and the manifold pressure was set, by the throttles, to 25 inches of mercury. If the engine was happy (less than 200 RPM drop on one magneto), then the airplane was ready to fly. Each engine was checked in this same way. I read the final checklist items and Lieutenant Lewis asked the control tower for clearance to take off. Wow! This was big time aviation for a young cadet.

On the takeoff roll, I was impressed with three things—the noise and vibration of the airplane, plus its acceleration. Going down the runway, I was pushed back in my seat like never before. As Lieutenant Lewis pulled back on the control yoke, the airplane left the runway very smoothly. He braked the wheels to a stop and raised the landing gear. He told me that braking the wheels was necessary so that when they retracted up into the wheel well, the wheels would not be turning. If still turning, they could rub against something and be damaged. After climbing a few thousand feet in just minutes, the instructor did some turns en route to the practice area. After awhile he said, "Okay, let Goodwin come up here for a while." As I passed Fred coming up to the flight deck, he was grinning like the cat that ate the canary. In about 30 minutes, we headed back to the airfield. We landed on the main wheels, while the nose wheel was held off as long as possible. Later we were told that this was called "aerodynamic braking." No wheel brakes could be used until the nose wheel was on the runway. I was totally impressed; and on getting out, I thanked Lieutenant Lewis for the ride. He shot back, "You won't be saying that after the next flight."

It was two days before I got my next flight. As before, we were separated into two groups of three. This time Fred, Hal and I flew the second trip. When the first three left the airplane, they all looked beat. I learned why very quickly. Fred got into the left seat first and all I heard from the shelf was yelling and cussing. The shelf on the B-25, where extra crew members sit, is located behind the flight deck. I was next and in passing , Fred said to me, "He said I didn't know how to fly very well." After I strapped into the left seat, Lieutenant Lewis made some 90, 180 and 360-degree turns. I noticed the altimeter hardly moved from 4,000 feet. In those days, we would take off with the altimeter set at zero. So the 4,000 represented that altitude above the ground. Years later, all altimeters were set at the field pressure setting. On a normal day of 59 degrees temperature at sea level, the pressure would be 29.92 inches of mercury. Then, the altimeter would read the elevation above sea level.

When Lieutenant Lewis had completed the demonstration of turns, he told me to do the same thing. My first turn was okay, but when I tried the 180-degree turn, I lost some altitude and promptly got chewed out; " Damn it, use your elevator trim when turning." So I did the 180 again and it was some better. Next I started the 360 degree turn. He did his to the right so I did too. In a second he stopped me and I got chewed on again!, "Damn it, I did mine to the right because I was on the inside of the turn and its much easier. Whenever you're told to do a turn, do it toward your side of the airplane." So, I set up again, and turned to the left. Halfway around, I did pretty well but then the altimeter started dropping -3900 feet, 3800 feet and then 3700 feet. When I rolled out I was almost 400 lower than where I had started. Here he came at me again, " Damn it, when you saw you were losing altitude, why didn't you do something about it. You weren't flying the airplane; it was flying you." That evening at the mess hall, I was so tired and down that I could hardly eat. Now I knew what my instructor wanted—flying with much more precision. There was no question about that. I was embarrassed about not being able to hold my altitude in the B-25. I could do it in the other airplanes I flew. Now I was going to have to bear down and fly right.

In those days, the B-25 nose wheel tire had a round bead like the main wheel tires—only smaller. When parking the airplane on the ramp it was very difficult to keep the nose wheel straight as the airplane came to a stop. It would simply flop over to one side and it was embarrassing to have that happen. It drove the instructor up the wall. When that happened, I would have to power up the engines and go around the flight line on the ramp and come in again. After many reprimands, I finally learned that for the last few feet before stopping, I would have to "ride the brakes" in order to keep the blasted nose wheel straight on stopping. There was no hydraulic nose wheel steering like in today's airplanes. Years later the B-25 was equipped with a nose wheel tire with a flat tread. It never flopped when you parked it.

During my first few flights, I quickly learned two things—make turns without losing altitude and to park the beast with a straight nose wheel. When I mastered that, Lieutenant Lewis was half way decent to me. Single-engine work was something else. This was a big airplane and when an engine was reduced to idle in flight, there was a tremendous amount of directional control lost, or yaw to handle. My instructor insisted that I learn to control the airplane's direction using the rudder pedals. That was a big order but when I showed him I could do it, even for a little while, he then let me use rudder trim to keep the airplane going straight. The airplane stalled at altitude with no falling off to either side. It just fell straight ahead and by quickly adding power, you could recover without losing very much altitude. I was finally learning to handle this monster. Some of the cadets had a little trouble with landings. But for some reason, I found it rather easy. Years later, when I became an instructor in this airplane I knew it like the back of my hand.

Lieutenant Lewis finally let us go up alone. Two cadets in a B-25 - that was something we had never dreamed of a few weeks earlier. Now it was fun and I found the airplane easy to fly and land. I could even park it correctly every time. The first thing we did was take some daylight cross-country flights. In eastern Colorado, there weren't many towns to "shoot stations" on but the airplane did have an ADF (Automatic Direction Finder) radio and when you received a good signal, you could "home" on the ground station by keeping the ADF needle pointing at the twelve o'clock position. The B-25 also had a low frequency radio range receiver. That was used for finding an airport and making an approach by instruments. The system used two signals, an "A" which was Morse Code "dit dah" and an "N" which was "dah dit." When you were on the proper path to the station, you received a steady tone. This was the way we found these stations and from there you followed the indicated magnetic bearing to the nearby airport. I would do this procedure in the Link trainer many times before attempting it in flight.   Radio range orientation was a tough procedure to master. The ADF was much simpler but it had a shorter signal range.

After several daytime cross-countries, Lieutenant Lewis told us to prepare for our first nighttime cross-country. Navigation required careful planning. Before this announcement, we did do some local night flying and just stayed in the landing pattern for night landings. The B-25 had rather dim landing lights, so night landings were sporty to say the least.

The ritual at the cadet mess hall was not as harsh as it was earlier in basic flight training. All cadets had to stand behind their chairs at the table, waiting for the Cadet Commander to give us the "be seated" command. Every evening meal was "Sunday cooking," if it wasn't steaks, it was chicken, pork chops or roast beef and all the trimmings. If it wasn't for PE and the rigors of flying, we all would be as fat as pigs. Life in the tarpaper huts went along very well. It was June now and the weather was mild to warm in the daytime and cool at night. The base boasted a huge recreation center, a place for cadets to relax whenever there was time. We were kept busy as bees. A continuous ping-pong "ladder" tournament was established at the recreation center. The ladder board held about 30 names and the bottom name could only challenge the one above him and so on up the ladder. The lucky man at the top could only be challenged by the cadet below then only after he had been challenged by the man below him. That was great fun.   I once managed to reach the top of the ladder. Once removed from the top, down you went to the very bottom to start all over again.

In ground school, the only problem I had was with Morse Code and the flash cards of airplane and ship recognition. Halfway through advanced training, I had been able to take Morse Code at ten words a minute. I had two more words to go and I honestly didn't know if I could do it. When a cadet could do 114 sit-ups, 25 push-ups, 10 pull-ups and run the obstacle course in the prescribed time, he passed the physical education class.

Fred Goodwin and I were paired to go on our first night cross-county flight and were given ample time to plan and prepare for it. I got the sectional maps out on the floor in operations, and drew the course lines. We planned to fly from La Junta south to Lubbock, Texas, land and take on some fuel. From there we would fly over to Goodland, Kansas and, without stopping, turn west and return to La Junta. That sounded to us like a dream trip. The weather briefing officer said the night's weather generally should be good except for some isolated thunderstorms forming over the southern Rocky Mountains. He signed the flight plan and, after the operations officer approved our flight, we were set to go.

During preparation for the flight, Fred said, "Tom, you fly down to Lubbock and then we can switch seats." That sounded good to me and that's the way we set it up. Departure time arrived and, after an early dinner, Fred and I headed for the flight line. With all our maps and other things, such as flashlights, we headed to the B-25 sitting on the ramp. The preflight was routine. Soon the engines were started and Fred got our clearance to taxi to the takeoff hold point. After running through the usual engine power checks, I waited for our trip clearance to come through. Finally, the tower said we were cleared to the Lubbock airport indicated by our flight plan. We were given departure instructions and cleared for takeoff. Five minutes after takeoff, we were to contact en-route traffic control. I took the runway and let the B-25 race down the concrete strip and suddenly we were airborne. It was as black as the ace of spades that night and I turned south on course. There were five other cross-country flights that night. All were recalled due to bad weather building up in the region. Fred and I never heard the recall and flew merrily on into the black night.

Fred and I were the first to take off out of six scheduled that night. We tried unsuccessfully to contact en route air traffic control. All we could hear was noise that sounded like eggs frying in a pan. We had been cleared to climb to 9,000 feet and in the climb we soon entered some clouds. The wing tip lights were just round glows, red on the left and green on the right. We couldn't see the white tail light from the flight deck. As we climbed toward 9,000 feet, the air started to get bumpy. Soon I felt rain hit the airplane and we both thought of ice but the outside temperature gauge indicated our temperature was above freezing. Fred tried again to contact en route traffic control but the noise was just too great. Now the air was really getting rough. I had already reached 9,000 feet and asked Fred what he thought. At first he didn't answer but finally said, "Let's descend to 7,000 feet; it might be smoother there." I said to check the map to see if 7,000 feet would be safe where we were, or thought we were.

After checking the minimum enroute altitudes, Fred said, "No, we can't go any lower; in fact we need to climb to 10 or 11 right away. While he was checking the map, I noticed lightning flashing all around us now. Heavy rain and some hail noisily pelted the airplane hard. The air became rougher and I moved the mixture controls to full rich and advanced the prop and throttle levers for the climb up to 11,000 feet. The carburetor heat was also turned on for each engine. Constant calls to the en route air traffic controller were in vain. The thunderstorms the weather briefer had told us about were obviously right in our path. Not long after reaching 11,000 feet, two things happened simultaneously. First, air traffic control came booming in on the radio and second, we abruptly broke out into the clear! It was the most beautiful sight you could imagine. Lights on the ground were visible and the stars above big and bright. Off the front of the nose sat the large cluster of lights that was the city of Lubbock. Our ADF receiver was picking up the Lubbock signal loud and clear. ATC had been trying to contact us for the last hour. They had wanted to warn us of the bad weather that had suddenly moved into the area. ATC also said the other five B-25s had been contacted and recalled to the base.

After telling ATC we had Lubbock visually in sight, we were told to descend to 5,000 feet and to contact the Lubbock control tower. The tower cleared us to descend and to report on the downwind leg. Soon I landed and taxied to the ramp. While the airplane was being refueled, I tried to call La Junta on the military network. Unable to make any contact, I filed another flight plan at base operations to fly to Goodland, Kansas, turn west and head for La Junta. Fred and I were very lucky to get through those thunderstorms. The rest of the cross—country went uneventfully. When we landed back at home base, it was nearly midnight and the ramp was quiet. As the engines were being shut down, I noticed a car approaching at a fast clip. Out jumped the AO (Aerodrome Officer) and, as I slid the cockpit window open, he shouted, "Where have you guys been anyway? Everybody's been looking all over for you."

By the time Fred and I arrived in base operations, the AO had made some calls to let everybody know we were back safely. Then the AO told us that the Operations Officer wanted us, along with our instructor, in his office at 8 o'clock the next morning. Going to bed without eating was not my immediate concern. What the Base Operations Officer might say to us in the morning was definitely a concern.

The next morning we met our instructor at 7:45 in base operations and told him exactly what happened and why. He said to relax; he would do what he could for us. Soon the three of us were ushered into Major Blair's office to face his wrath. After hearing in detail what happened, he said, "When you hit the storm and couldn't contact ATC, why didn't you just turn around and come back?" To that, I said, "Sir, we were briefed that our course was clear of any bad weather. When we got into some rough air, I thought we were probably on the eastern edge of it and would soon fly out of it." The Major pulled on his mustache and said, "I guess you two know how lucky you were. A bad storm like that can tear an airplane apart. Stay out of any kind of storms from now on. I'm going to have a little talk with that weather officer. Dismissed."

My knees were shaking the whole time we were in the Major's office. When outside, our instructor said, "Go on to class and I'll see you this afternoon." "Yes, sir!" we said as we saluted him. As luck would have it, Morse Code was my first class that morning. Many times through the years Fred Goodwin and I talked about that night cross-country. Toward the end of the war, Fred suffered a severe head injury in a P-47 landing accident. It resulted, later on, in the total loss of his vision. At this writing, Fred lives with his wife, Helen, in Winterset, Iowa.

The next night cross-country Fred and I flew went without a hitch. The next phase in advanced training was day formation flying. It was all dual with an instructor in each airplane. We went out to the far edge of the practice area and joined up in a three-airplane "V" formation. One airplane led and the other two formed up one on each wing of the leader. It was fun, as Lieutenant Lewis let us do most of the flying. I have always liked formation flying, except at night. Night formation was tough as nails. The only lights on the airplanes were small blue lights on top of the wings. Again, Lieutenant Lewis was with us to keep us out of any trouble. We only needed two hours and were grateful when it was over.

Daylight bombardment was the next type of instruction.. Our simulated bombardment missions might be compared to the shadow boxing of a prize fighter preparing to meet his next opponent. Nine B-25s would take off on a staggered time schedule. Each plane represented a formation of bombers. We formed up in a wide formation using some high and low elements, just like the big boys do it. Our simulated target was supposedly heavily defended with antiaircraft batteries. As we approached the initial point (IP), all went into the target at different levels. Closing in, I flew straight and level so the bombardier could make a quick adjustment to his bomb sight, then he released his "bombs." The target was a blazing shamble as we assembled and flew home in blissful victory.

I was now an upperclassman in advanced flying school, the highest status an aviation cadet can reach. We had moved from our original tar paper hut to a similar one, but near all of the "action," including the flight line. I was rapidly accruing flying time and I loved flying the B-25. It was noisy, yes but very stable and reliable. Anyone who has flown a short-stacked B-25 will eventually suffer a hearing loss. I flew the Link Trainer as much as I could because the only thing standing between me and a pair of silver wings was that final instrument check. Lieutenant Lewis gave me a lot of instrument practice. Behind the pilot's seat was a white curtain that could be drawn forward, on overhead rails, toward the instrument panel and snapped in to stay there. Now all I could see was the panel of instruments and, of course, that was the object of the curtain. This was known as flying under the hood. My instructor told me I just might get an instrument takeoff (ITO) on my final check ride. For an ITO, the instructor would taxi the airplane onto the runway and line it up straightaway and set the brakes. When the student was ready for takeoff, he added power and released the brakes. By using the gyro directional compass, he tried to keep the airplane going straight down the runway. When the air speed was adequate, he slowly pulled the yoke back and became airborne. This maneuver represented a takeoff in zero visibility conditions. I practiced this many, many times before I could keep her rolling straight.

Ground school was now finished; I still had PE but no more drills. I had been drilling for a year now and felt drilled out. Our graduation was originally set for July 28; but due to some administrative reasons, it was re-scheduled for August 4, 1944. That was only two weeks away and there was a lot to do. Two squares remained to be filled, the instrument check and a final flight physical. Both had to be passed to graduate and every last cadet had that on his mind.

One day the May Company sent two representatives down from their Department Store in Denver to fit us for our new officers' uniforms. What an exciting day! My graduation outfit— blouse, trousers, shirt, tie, service hat and brown shoes cost $235.00. I had the money saved up for some time. In a few days a man from the Balfour Ring Company came to take our class ring orders. They offered us a choice of settings but the basic ring was the same for everyone. I chose black onyx. Against the solid sterling silver ring, it was beautiful. I still wear the ring today, over 50 years later. The rings cost $25 and the man promised to deliver them himself before graduation day.

As an aviation cadet, I was paid $75 a month and had minimal expenses so I had saved a tidy sum of money. We usually were too busy to spend much, even playing cards in the outside latrine. Besides my uniform cost, there were the brass insignia, gold bars and silver wings. That all added up to $40.

All in all, each of us had to pay out $300 to be properly dressed for the graduation ceremony. A notice was posted one day on the area bulletin board informing us that we were responsible for scheduling our own physical. It had to be completed by July 25. I went to the base hospital and scheduled mine for the morning of the 20th. On the way back from the hospital, I passed the building where I had taken Morse Code. I could not believe I actually passed 12 words per minute. Through the window, I could see some cadets still in there struggling with the "dit-dahs" and the "dah-dits."

The day before my final instrument check, my instructor gave me a good workout in the airplane while under the hood. I practiced about everything he thought the check pilot would give me during my final check ride. I even made three ITOs, two of which were pretty darn good. Lieutenant Lewis said I was about as ready as I could get. He said to try to relax, have a good meal, forget about instrument flying, and get a good night's rest. All night, I tossed and turned and had crazy dreams. I was worried about that final check ride. By morning, I felt more exhausted than when I went to bed the night before. After a light breakfast, Fred Goodwin, Bill Garvey and I reported to base operations at 8 a.m. to meet our check pilot. We had been told earlier that the three of us would go up on one flight together. The check pilot would have each of us do whatever maneuvers he chose.

We waited about ten minutes and here came an officer in a flying suit. He introduced himself as Captain Black. Walking out to the airplane, he said to me, "Mister Gordon, you get in the left seat first." "Yes sir!" came my reply. I was glad that I was first because now I wouldn't have to sit back on that shelf sweating out my turn. As we sat in the cockpit before starting the engines, Captain Black said to me, "I know you can fly this airplane or you wouldn't be here. I just want to know if you can fly by instruments." With that, he proceeded to start the engines. I began to read the checklist to him, and he stopped me with "I'll do everything, you just relax." Taxiing out for takeoff, I just knew he was going to ask me to make an instrument takeoff under the hood (the good old ITO). To my surprise, I was actually ready for it.

At the hold line by the runway, he did the usual engine check and run up. He then asked the tower for take off clearance. I could not

believe what I was witnessing. Captain Black made the takeoff and
climbed to 5,000 feet, leveled off and set the power for cruising at
precisely 200 mph. Then he looked over at me and said, "Are you
ready? " When I nodded, he continued, "You take the airplane and do
a few turns and get comfortable." After doing that, he took over the
airplane controls and told me to bring up the curtain to the closed position. Now I was sitting there in a white cotton cage. Before returning
control to me, he turned the aircraft due north. He then covered the
directional gyro with a piece of round black cardboard. Now he said,
"When I give you the airplane, here is what I want you to do. You're
on a heading of due north and when you're ready, I want you to give me
a 360 degree timed turn. Keep your altitude at 5,000 feet and your
airspeed at 200 mph during the turn. Are there any questions?" "No
sir," I replied.

Captain Black then said, "It's your airplane." Talk about pressure; this was big-time pressure. With the directional gyro covered, all
I had for directional reference was the "whiskey" compass. It was the
standby compass that every airplane has, even today in the big jets.
Somewhere in the cockpit of every airplane, there is a small "whiskey"
compass. The reason it's called "whiskey" is that the compass card is
encased in a small chamber filled with alcohol. That type of fluid
dampens the rotation of the compass card that floats freely in the little
chamber of the compass housing.

The "whiskey" compass is reliable only when you're flying
straight and level at a constant speed. But if you are turning, climbing,
descending, accelerating, or decelerating, the compass goes wild. It
starts swinging back and forth and is not reliable until the airplane is
back on an even keel. Once I started the timed turn, all I had for
reference was the airspeed indicator, the altimeter, the bank angle indicator and the clock. The bank angle determines the rate of turn. If I
wanted to turn at two degrees per second, I had to use a certain bank
angle. But if I wanted to turn at three degrees per second, the bank
angle had to be increased slightly. One type of turn took 180 seconds
and the other 120 seconds. I decided to do the 360-degree turn in 120
seconds, or two minutes.

With a deep breath, I entered the turn to the left adding a little
power to keep the airspeed constant and rolled in some trim to help
maintain constant altitude. Now it was a game of chance. I must keep
everything constant as the second hand on the clock told me where I
was, or where I was supposed to be. As I came around, I felt good
about keeping my airspeed and altitude on the money. About five seconds before the two minutes expired, I did a slow roll-out. At the same

time I reduced power slightly and rolled out some elevator trim to keep my airspeed and altitude steady after roll out. When I rolled out after two minutes, and had the wings level, I looked up at the "whiskey" compass that had now finally settled down. The "N" for north was absolutely split by the center lubber line.

To my shock, I had just made a perfect 360-degree timed turn. I sat there staring at that little compass. As I looked over at Captain Black, he was staring at it too. Then he said, "Okay, I have the airplane. Go back and have one of the others come up here." I don't know when I said "Yes sir!" so loud. I felt like a million dollars. The other two cadets did some other maneuvers under the hood and soon we were heading back to the field. We all three made the grade on our final cadet flight check. I was walking on air the rest of the day.

Soon, I received some more good news. I passed my final physical examination. Now, all my squares were filled in advanced flying school. As the day for final graduation from the Aviation Cadet Program drew near, I found it increasingly difficult to imagine myself an officer. During aviation cadet training, I had been accustomed to looking at any man with rank as a god, and an officer with pilot wings on his chest, as a couple degrees above Superman. Despite my training, I did not feel qualified to join their ranks. Even up to the day before graduation, I was more in awe of an officer than I had been when I stepped off the train at Santa Ana nearly a year ago. One morning, after breakfast, the entire class was to report to the assembly hall where we would be graduating in just a few days. There in the hall were the men from the May Company with our new uniforms! The whole class of 44-G were acting like ducks around spilled corn. Needless to say, I checked everything very carefully before trying it all on. When everything was okay, I paid the man and proudly took my brand new officers uniform back to my tarpaper hut.

With time running out, most of my cadet gear and other items were already turned in. I was allowed to keep my flight suits and my GI watch. The last few days, we just wore our flight suits, as we couldn't leave the post anyway. In those last days, two unfortunate events occurred. First, one of the cadets from a hut down the street, was sitting on a stool in the latrine reading when he suddenly passed out and fell to the floor. One of his buddies found him and of course, off to the hospital he went. Everyone knew the poor guy would not graduate, at least, not with class 44-G.

I was the victim in the second event. A hut inspection was scheduled for sometime on the morning of our last Saturday. As usual, we had everything in perfect order since we were scheduled to graduate the following Wednesday. With "scouts" posted at the windows of the hut, everyone would get an early warning of the approaching inspection team of tactical officers. Everyone was at the ready; our shoes had a high shine and we were all set for this last one. Finally a scout shouted, "Here they come." Everyone scrambled and stood at attention in front of his bed and foot locker.

The inspection team consisted of two tactical officers and a cadet officer who carried a clipboard for any notations from the inspectors. They started across the aisle and inspected those four cadets with no comments that I could hear. On my side of the hut were the other four areas. Mine was third from the door. They approached me and proceeded with my personal inspection during which I heard no comments. They continued with the inspection of my combination desk and wall locker and I heard some talking which I couldn't make out. One of the tactical officers came to me and asked why my book shelf was out of inspection order. I replied, "Sir, I had it in regulation order." The inspector then said, "Well, it's not and that will be two gigs." With that, they quickly checked the last cadet and walked out. I was so shocked my heart almost stopped. All through cadet training I had had only three gigs and that was in primary training. There were none in basic, and none in advanced flight school until now. I immediately went to my bookshelf which was mounted just above my desk and checked. Sure enough, a magazine was lying there out of place. Apparently while we were waiting for the inspection team to arrive and when I wasn't looking, one of my "friends" had been looking at one of my aviation magazines. When the scout warned that they were near, he must have tossed the magazine on the shelf instead of stacking it where he found it. I got mad and yelled, "Who's the son-of-a-bitch that did this to me?" No one said a word; they just stood there looking at the floor "Fine friends I have." I said as I left the hut. Before closing the door, I heard Bill Garvey, our hut commander, say, "Ok, who's the bastard that did this awful thing to Tom?"

I went directly to the Cadet Administration Office to see about my penalty. Usually penalty gigs are walked off on the flight line. As this was an administrative penalty, they let me walk for two hours in front of the building. Up and back, up and back I marched. After 50 minutes, I could stand at parade-rest for ten minutes and then do it all over again. I was the only cadet in my entire class of 249 to receive a gig that day. I was mortified. The next day my hut-mates apologized, as a group, on behalf of the perpetrator, but they never identified him. The day before graduation, everyone tried on their new uniforms for the last time as a cadet. What fun it was to parade around the hut acting like an officer. That afternoon, at the cadet recreation center, I won the ping-pong ladder finals. My name was on the top rung.

Wednesday, August 4, 1944, finally arrived. My hut was buzzing well before reveille and, after a special breakfast, the class had to report to the assembly hall for an important briefing. Extra folding chairs were brought in as the class was 249 strong and about 50 guests were expected to attend. The guests would include families of the cadets and others. At the hall, the Commandant of Cadets explained exactly how the ceremony would proceed plus all the other details of the graduation. I didn't know my next assignment yet, that was part of the mystery. The brown envelope that everyone would be given would contain new assignment orders. Everyone had speculated for weeks about that. Also in the envelope would be our coveted silver wings— our badge of honor.

Everyone would be given a two-week leave enroute to his next duty station. So, I already had my train reservations and tickets in hand. My ticket was long as I had to make three connections, one in Denver, one in Kansas City and the last in Omaha. After a special farewell lunch, we all hurried back to our huts so we could "suit up" for the big event starting at 1 p.m. My baggage, which consisted of two duffle bags and a B-4 bag, had to be tagged and placed in front of my foot locker. They would be picked up later and taken to the train station. Putting on that new officers' uniform was a thrill like no other but there were no bars. They would be in the brown envelope along with our wings. The age-old military ritual called for family or friends to pin on the bars and wings right after the ceremony.

At high noon, the class formed for the last time in front of the cadets' quadrangle. As a group we marched over to the auditorium. By prior arrangement, we formed alphabetically, as our names would be called in that order. As we entered the building, the base brass band was playing light marches. After everyone was seated, the band continued playing. Everyone felt great and the euphoria spread like fever. Sitting on the speakers' platform were the Commandant of Cadets, Colonel Moore, his wife, his staff and their wives. The main speaker was Colonel James H. Bagley of the Western Air Training Command. He would address the graduating class. Sharply at 1 p.m., the band stopped playing and everyone rose for the National Anthem. It never sounded better to me in my life.

After the anthem, Colonel Moore went to the podium and said, "Aviation Cadet Class of 1944-G and guests, please be seated." He introduced first, his staff and then the guest speaker, Colonel Bagley, Chief of Training for the Western Air Training Command located in

Santa Ana, California. Colonel Bagley moved to the podium and began to speak, "Since your days at Santa Ana you were called Misters, today I will call you Gentlemen. I hope that for the rest of your lives everyone will call you Gentlemen." Colonel Bagley had completed 50 missions flying B-24 heavy bombers over Europe. He had been shot down and imprisoned, escaped and, with help from the French underground, rejoined his unit and completed his tour of duty. He was tall and resplendent in his uniform with ribbons and silver wings. As he looked over the large group of cadets, he was probably thinking when he, too, sat out there as an aviation cadet in great anticipation of big things to come.

Colonel Bagley related some of his life experiences. His father had worked in the southern Illinois coal mines for many years, as did his father before him. He joined the Army Air Corps in 1937 and earned his wings at Kelly Field in 1938. He then said, "I know how hard you have worked in this program. I know because I helped set it up when it was realized that Randolph and Kelly Fields could not possibly produce the number of pilots, navigators, and bombardiers needed in the war effort. When your wings are pinned on you in a short while, wear them proudly wherever you go. You have certainly earned them. They are your badge of honor. Do not ever, not ever, forget that. Throughout your training you received the best attention possible. You were disciplined to a high degree, probably higher than you thought necessary. That training will pay huge dividends in your lives. You will wear two hats, first that of an Officer of the United States Army Air Force. Second, you are pilots of the first order, the best trained pilots in the world. By its nature, a military force must be a disciplined force. There must be rules. Someone must be in charge. The freedom of choice available to most individuals in our democratic society needs to be constrained. You can hardly expect an officer or a senior NCO to lead an enlisted man by saying, If it's all right with you, many of us believe it might be a good idea if you would do the following . . .

It just doesn't work that way. In the Army, your superiors say do it and you do it. I think that men in uniform still retain some rights and are still entitled to a degree of freedom. Your Commanding Officer may well have to send you on a dangerous mission from which you may not return. But should that very same CO tell you what music to listen to or how to behave toward your wife or girlfriend? I don't think so. Since you were all trained in twin-engine aircraft, you will no doubt go on to fly a bomber or a large transport. Our bombers of today, the B-17 and the B-24, are the last of the small bombers. Just around the corner are bigger and better aircraft that will soon be in our inventory. Now, go serve your country with honor and distinction and be proud and successful aviators, no matter what you fly. Good luck in the skies, and may the Lord protect you."

As he stepped away, we all rose and gave him a rousing round of applause. Colonel Moore then stepped to the podium and said, "Here on the table behind me are 249 brown envelopes.   I think you all know what's in them. But for the sake of our guests, the envelopes contain a set of orders for OTU (Overseas Training Unit) training, and when and where to report. Also, in the envelopes are a pair of silver pilot wings and two gold Second Lieutenant bars. Before I hand these envelopes out, I want the class of 1944-G to stand and take the oath of a commissioned officer."   Everyone rose and automatically stood at attention. In taking the oath, we all agreed to honor and obey our superiors and fight for our country even if it meant giving up our lives. We all continued to stand. It would be the last time class 1944-G would stand together as a group. Row by row, we slowly moved toward the reviewing platform to receive our brown envelopes. This was the hour. This was the moment I had been waiting for. Two years earlier when I first signed up for Aviation Cadets, I never thought I would be standing here waiting for my brown envelope. It was one of the highlights of my life. I was so excited I could hardly stand it. The same excitement was in each newly commissioned officer's eyes. No one said a word while waiting to file up to the stage where the big table, piled high with brown envelopes, stood. They didn't need to.

Finally my turn came to walk across the stage and, as Colonel Moore handed me my brown envelope; I took one step backward and executed a smart salute which both Colonels returned. Walking out the side door of the building, I couldn't wait to open my envelope. All around were brand new Second Lieutenants being hugged by their parents or friends. A few had wives; some had girl friends, or just good friends. I had nobody to pin on my bars and wings, or so I thought.

As I was tearing my envelope open, I heard someone say, "Hello there." I looked around and there stood my best friend, Bob Ritzdorf. A couple of years earlier he and Chub had driven me down to Fort Hays.   Since then, Bob had enlisted in the Army Air Corps and had applied for pilot training. We had written back and forth a few times. In my last letter to him, I casually mentioned that my graduation from aviation cadets was scheduled for August 4 at La Junta Army Air Base. Never did I dream he would get leave and ride a train all the way from California to be there for me. My folks couldn't come, nor could anyone else. So earlier, several other cadets and I agreed we would "pin" each other. They had nobody there either. After a handshake and a hug, I thanked him for taking the time and effort to come to my graduation. Then I said, "Bob, I just have to look at my next assignment and see what I will be flying." The orders read: "Special Orders Number 44-07926. The following named officers are to proceed to Will Rogers Field, Oklahoma City, Oklahoma, to undergo overseas training in the Lockheed P-38 Lightning aircraft. You will report no later than August 18, 1944 to the OTU Training Command Headquarters. Travel by government transportation is authorized." The orders were dated August 4, 1944. I was so stunned I couldn't say anything for a minute. Never in my wildest dreams did I think I had a prayer to fly the famous P-38 Lightning. Bob said, "Is there something wrong?" "No," I replied, "Something is finally right!" Besides the special orders, the envelope contained my silver wings and officers bars. Bob started to pin the bars on first but I said, "No Bob, pin the wings on first; I worked so hard and so long for them." When all were pinned on, Bob stepped back and gave me my first salute. Military tradition has it that when a newly commissioned officer receives his first salute, he gives that person a dollar bill. As luck would have it, the smallest bill I had was a fiver. So I gave it to him and said to keep the change. I had to catch a bus to the train station and asked Bob if he would like to ride along. He did. After spending some minutes shaking hands with my fellow officers, Bob and I headed for the bus. During the ride to the station, Bob was thinking that he had a good chance to get into the Aviation Cadet Program. The war in the Pacific was expanding and more of everything was needed there. I thanked him again, wished him luck and got on my train for Nebraska. Bob headed back to California.

A lot of new officers were on the train that afternoon and everyone proudly wore a new pair of silver wings. Most graduates went on to fly bombers. Only eight of us out of that whole class got the coveted P-38 Lightning. My mind went back to the Curtiss factory in Buffalo when I talked to the P-40 test pilot about getting into cadets. I could still remember his words: "Get into Aviation Cadets and become a pilot, it's a very good job."

At the train station in Denver, part of the gang departed with goodbyes. Again in Kansas City, more departed and in Omaha the same routine was repeated. Now I was the only pilot officer on the train to Columbus, Nebraska. There were only two other military in my car - an NCO and a private. The poor private got as far away from me as he could. The NCO finally asked me if I was a new graduate. We talked for a long while and he said that he would give anything to fly airplanes. I said, "You can. When you get back to your base, apply for Aviation Cadet Training. They can't turn you down for wanting to improve yourself. The physical and some testing is all you have to worry about." He acted as though he might just do that.

At the station to meet me in Columbus were my parents, two sisters and their families. After hugs and kisses, we all went to a cafe and had a nice long lunch. Everyone was talking at once and I never felt better in my life. They were so pleased that I was going to fly the airplane I really wanted. Also, it pleased them that I now had 90 college credit hours, 60 from the CTD program and thirty more for becoming a Commissioned Officer. That was three quarters of the credits required for a college degree. Later that day we drove to my folks' place in Cedar Rapids and had a grand time. There, I met a girl named Lucille and we went out several times. I'm sure it was the uniform that attracted her.. She promised to write me if I would send her my address. I said I would and, later, did receive some V-Mail from her. She was not the only girl I would be writing.

My time at home passed quickly. I think something was going on every night and I surely was ready to get back to an environment that included airplanes. My folks were deeply concerned about my flying in the war. I told them it was safer in the skies than it was on the ground fighting the enemy. I promised to write often and I did. So did my Mom. I caught the afternoon train out of Cedar Rapids and was gone again. This time I was off to war.

On the long train ride to Oklahoma City, I did a lot of thinking. I looked back on the Aviation Cadet Program to a lot of fond memories. The training was rigid and I sometimes thought the instructors unduly harsh. I can forgive them now, if they can forgive me for being such a slow knucklehead. The discipline was strict, but necessary. There were moments of despair and moments of joy and encouragement. There were humorous incidents to leaven the moments when I felt certain I'd never make the grade. Classification, Preflight, Primary, Basic and Advanced all were hard work and at times pure drudgery, but I would gladly endure it again that I may fly.

Into the air, you sons of Liberty,
From every blessed state,
Blast the evil sons of perfidy,
Who were suckled on greed and hate.
Yours is the fight for freedom,

For all peoples, regardless of creed,
To live on God's earthly kingdom,
Forever from tyranny freed.
God has given you silver wings,
To soar the Heavens blue,
And through your missions, He will be near
To steer your course for you
- Harold Mavre

CHAPTER EIGHT

OFF TO WAR

*I have observed that in war nothing ever goes according to plan,
except occasionally, and then by accident.*

—Winston Churchill

After a long day, my train pulled into the Oklahoma City station the afternoon of August 17, 1944. Catching the military shuttle bus, I soon arrived at Will Rogers Field. By then it was too late to check in at Training Headquarters so I found the BOQ (Bachelor Officers Quarters) and was given a single room. It was the first time I had the luxury of having a single room since joining the Army Air Corps two years earlier. Directly across the street was the Officers Club and I went over for a cold beer before having my evening meal. It was after duty hours and the place was jumping with young pilots fresh out of flight school. As I was paying for my beer, I heard someone call out my name. At the other end of the bar were my good friends Jim Foster and Fred Goodwin. They had arrived earlier that day and had already checked in at OTU Headquarters. Jim said they were assigned to the 25th Tactical Reconnaissance Training Detachment. After a couple beers we ate dinner and then retired to our rooms. Fred had been to see his folks in Iowa and Jim had visited his family in Los Angeles. Jim had been with me in cadets since the beginning but he had always been with the "F" people and lived in different barracks. Jim and I would be together for the rest of the war. He was very young and everybody called him Junior. Jim got into the program at 18 and was two years younger than most of his class. The next morning, after a good breakfast, I checked in at OTU Headquarters and sure enough, was assigned to the same training detachment as Jim and Fred. There was an atmosphere of efficiency about Will Rogers Field as everything was in apple pie order; acres of green grass and lots of flowers planted everywhere. I was impressed and knew I was going to like this place. That morning, as I walked over for the orientation briefing, I saw some P-38's taxiing out for takeoff. Boy, did they ever look and sound good. During the briefing we were told what to expect in the next few weeks. The new class was going to learn all about aerial reconnaissance work with the P-38. The briefer said the aircraft we would be flying had been modified in that the guns were removed from the nose section and replaced with large Fairchild aerial cameras. The photo intelligence we would be gathering would be used by the Allied Armies in Europe. The photos would help them in their march through Germany. That made their work much easier and safer. The briefer said that P-38's were used in the Pacific also. The idea of flying into combat without armament didn't set very well with me. Someone had put up a large poster that read, "Photo Joe - Alone, Unarmed and Unafraid." That made me wonder what I was getting into. The schedule called for classes all day for the first two weeks. The briefer then surprised us by saying everyone had to get five hours in the AT-17 and ten hours in the B-25 before they could check out in the P-38. No problem, we all had lots of time in both airplanes and I was sure the requirements would be waived, but no dice. We had to fly it off anyway. In checking out in the P-38, I would get one "piggy-back" ride with my instructor, and that was it.

Because I had prior time in the AT-17 and B-25, the school did allow me to fly using the buddy-system without an instructor. We paired off and in a short time, met the requirements. Now I could concentrate on P-38 aircraft systems in ground school. The airplane had quite a number of systems but none were very complicated. I could hardly wait to start flying this machine. Another subject in ground school was the Fairchild aerial camera. Several different models were studied in detail. Some had 6" focal lengths, some had 12" focal lengths and one had a 24" focal length. The ones we would be using in our training missions were the 12" models. Soon, everyone learned the detailed use and care of the camera. The operation of the camera was controlled in the cockpit by an intervalometer box. It sat on the floor in front of the pilot's seat. Using the intervalometer we could tell the camera to take a single shot or several shots in rapid succession. It was nice of the installation engineers to put the camera switch on the control wheel. I guess we could pretend it was a machine gun switch if we wanted to. The film rolls in the removable magazines were large and could hold 100 feet of 9-inch film or even more for combat missions. I also learned how the exposed film was processed. One day we all went to the big film laboratory to watch this procedure first-hand. It was extremely interesting, and even today, I have a small film lab of my own.

Now that I was an officer, I didn't need a pass to go into town. After a week or so Fred, Jim and I made our first trip into Oklahoma City. Someone mentioned we should check out the Black Hotel. I hadn't been paid yet, and didn't have much cadet money left. The monthly pay for a Second Lieutenant was $150 base pay, $75 flight pay and $40 quarters allowance. Living on base, I didn't get the $40.

There was a $21 ration allowance that I did get but I had to buy all of my own meals.

The three of us managed to find the Black Hotel in downtown Oklahoma City. From the outside, it appeared to be an ordinary hotel but downstairs was a bodega (night club). Oklahoma was a dry state. You couldn't buy a drink anywhere. The hotel did, however, allow people to bring in their own bottle. The hotel provided ice and setups for a small price. The American Legion Club sold beer, but only beer. Someone said you could bring a bottle in there too. Soon I discovered that the hard stuff could be purchased from a bootlegger, an illegal source.

The bellhop supplied the name of a bootlegger who said he would only deliver to a hotel room. That meant we had to spend $8 to rent a room and the bootlegger delivered as promised. The price for a fifth of Four Roses 86-proof blended whiskey was $12 but with Coca-Cola or 7-Up, it made a rather decent drink. The hotel had a small band that played dance music almost every night. Somehow the local girls knew this was a new pilot hangout and they came in droves. They would have one drink but no more. I'm not sure they trusted us yet. We were brand new commissioned pilots and the girls were always asking us for a pair of pilot wings. I told one girl I was only issued one pair and I needed them for my uniform. I could have bought her a pair at the post exchange but I didn't tell her that.

Every time the new pilots went into town it was always directly to the Black Hotel. Great fun was had there and Albert, the bootlegger, always came through with the spirits. After two solid weeks of ground school, the schedule called for us to report to the flight line to meet our instructor. He introduced himself as Captain Henry Neilson—a soft-spoken man with a nice personality. He said he hailed from Mankato, Minnesota. I walked around the airplane in awe and could not imagine myself in that beautiful thing. Just sitting there, it looked like it could leap into the air at any moment. Captain Neilson was assigned six student officers and he told us some things about the airplane.

The P-38 Lightning was built by Lockheed Aircraft Company in Burbank, California. Starting in 1939, more than 10,000 would be built before the war ended. It had a wing span of 52 feet, a length of 38 feet and a height of 13 feet. Its loaded weight was 17,500 lbs. The fighter was powered by two Allison V-1710 liquid-cooled engines that generated 1,475 HP each. Its top speed was 450 mph; it cruised at 300 and landed at 90. Its service ceiling was 40,000 feet, and its range was 1,100 miles. The Germans called it "Der Gabelschwanz Teufel." The forked-tailed devil.

Captain Neilson explained that several of the airplanes were converted to the piggy-back model. This was to allow a student pilot to sit behind the instructor and watch him fly the airplane for just one flight. Then it was ours to master by ourselves. To modify the piggy-back, the radios had to be removed from the shelf behind the pilot's seat and put in the nose section. Those trainers didn't carry any cameras, just ballast weights. My instructor dismissed me with these words, "Go back to your room and read the airplane operating manual. You will need to know it in order to solo and you will have to answer my questions about the airplane and its systems." He added; "Be back here tomorrow at 1 p.m. in your flight gear and parachute and don't forget the leather helmet and goggles. Forget the oxygen mask. You won't be needing that for some time."

The propellers on the P-38 were Curtiss Electric with three blades. That was a rather complex system for us rookies. Captain Neilson said not to worry as he would demonstrate everything during our orientation flight in the piggy-back. He further said, "When you get back there on that shelf and when I close the canopy, it gets really cozy. Don't get sick on me!" He went on to say that the flight would take less than an hour and would be at a relatively low altitude, no higher than 15,000 feet. Everyone hoped there would be no aerobatics because if we got sick on him, it really would be "on him." He gave us all a good explanation of the exterior walk-around preflight inspection and the operation of the ladder and canopy. As he started the engines he stressed attention to detail as we would only get to watch him once. He said, "Watch everything I do and listen to what I say because I will be explaining everything as I do it. Remember, when you solo you're all alone up there." The following day I was scheduled for my piggy-back ride. As I met Captain Neilson on the flight line, he said to me, "Tom, are you ready to fly?" "Yes sir!" I replied, just like a well trained aviation cadet.

Climbing into the airplane was easy but getting back on that shelf wearing a backpack parachute was another story. Finally we were ready to go. Captain Neilson said, "If you have any questions, tap me on the shoulder. If not, just listen and watch." The canopy was left open until engine start; then he carefully went through the ritual of starting the engines. I watched him like a hawk. When the engines were running nicely, he called the tower for taxi instructions. Will Rogers Field was quite large with three major runways and a lot of taxiways. As we taxied out to the takeoff runway, he mentioned the brakes. You did not just apply them. They needed to be pumped up first, then applied, then pumped again and applied again and so on. It sounded to me like a lot of work. Why did Lockheed install brakes like that anyway, I wondered.

Talk about an excited young pilot, I was beside myself experiencing this important event in my young career. At the runway hold-line, my instructor .proceeded to instruct me in exercising the props and conducting the power check which was similar to that of other engines in which I had gained experience. When all was done, the tower cleared us for takeoff. The acceleration was unbelievable. I was holding on to the back of the pilot's seat for dear life. We became airborne in seconds and then Captain Neilson raised the landing gear and the wing flaps. Now that the airplane was aerodynamically clean, it accelerated like a greased monkey. Everything was happening so fast, I had a hard time taking it all in. Climbing above 10,000 feet, my instructor did a climbing slow roll. I was really impressed with the way he handled the airplane. The Lightning flew so beautifully and it was so quiet in the cockpit, we just talked in normal tones. The engine exhaust was routed through a supercharger and the noise was muffled to a hum. Next, my instructor demonstrated some simple maneuvers and then did a loop. In the loop, we must have pulled several "G's," as I could hardly hold my head up against the negative force. He then showed me how to shut down an engine and feather the prop. After that, he restarted it by turning the prop governor and when the prop was spinning in the slip stream, he turned on the ignition and fuel and the engine caught and ran perfectly. I hoped I could remember all that in case I ever needed to do it.

Then Captain Neilson said, "Okay, that's about it." Now he started to descend to traffic pattern altitude. The tower cleared us for an overhead approach for landing. This was new to me and I was going to like it. In the overhead approach, you come in over the landing runway at about 1,500 feet. Then when exactly over the end of the runway, you suddenly do a break (bank) left with a very tight pattern while bringing the engines back to idle. Halfway through the break, the gear and flaps were lowered and we just came around and landed. Rarely was any power needed after the initial break. Captain Neilson made a great landing and then left the runway at the end and taxied back to the ramp. Now my knees were shaking as I knew when he parked the airplane and got out, I was going to be there all by myself. He told me, after parking, that he would sit on the wing on the way to the runway. When I reached the hold line by the runway, Captain Neilson suddenly slid off the wing, and was gone.

I just sat there at the runway hold line for a moment: then I remembered to close the side windows before power-checking the engines. In ground school I was told the power boost on the aileron controls would be safety-wired off. I guess the school didn't want us overcontrolling the wings after takeoff. Finally, the tower cleared me for takeoff. As I released the brakes, the airplane moved on its own without additional power. It was so "clean" that idle power was all it needed to taxi. Captain Neilson had taught me to pump up the brakes and hold them while applying takeoff power. Before I had full power set, the airplane started to move. I released the brakes and let her roll and roll she did. Before I knew it, I was airborne! I don't even remember pulling back on the yoke at 100 mph. I was just hanging on. After becoming airborne, the first order of business is to assure a positive rate of climb then raise the gear and flaps. Power then had to be reduced to climb setting to avoid reaching the airspeed redline. This was a great airplane! It was hard to believe I was actually flying a P-38. Then again, maybe it was flying me.

I was to stay up no longer than 30 minutes so I climbed up to 10,000 feet and just flew around the area west of Will Rogers Field. I tried some lazy eights and boy were they ever a joy. That airplane amazed me, it could really zip along. I scanned the checklist so I wouldn't forget any chores to be done before landing. The main things were to check the fuel selectors on the fullest tank, set the power (in case of a go-around) and lower the gear and flaps. The only thing left to do was land the airplane. I even remembered to not make a three point landing. I wanted to hold the nose off for some aerodynamic braking. The landing was better than I expected. As I taxied in to the ramp, Captain Neilson was there waiting for me. He kidded me by walking around the airplane looking for dents. I don't know when I felt so good! I fell in love with the P-38 that day. Another thing I liked was the 360 degree overhead traffic pattern we used. That was great fun. My instructor's only comment was, "Good job Tom and welcome to the world of fighter aircraft."

That night at the Officers Club, those that soloed that day were given free drinks before dinner. I don't know who paid for them but it was a nice gesture. Later that night I was so wound up it was difficult getting to sleep. All my flying now would, of course, be solo. After I had about ten hours in the P-38, I was among the half of the class that would go TDY (temporary duty) to Coffeyville, Kansas. There we would fly off the balance of our training; which was supposed to be some 50 hours.

Coffeyville was an auxiliary field for Will Rogers Field and was located north just across the Oklahoma-Kansas state line. Upon arrival, one of the first things I heard was that the town was quite famous as part of the old west. Outlaws such as the Dalton Gang operated around there for a while. The story goes that one day the Dalton boys got greedy and tried to rob both the town's banks at once. The three Dalton brothers and five accomplices were all shot and killed. This happened in broad daylight and when the dust settled, all eight outlaws were laid out in a row in front of one of the banks for the town folks to pass in review.

At Coffeyville, we had about ten modified P-38's that were technically called F5's. We all said the "F" must stand for "fool" as the airplane was armed with cameras but not guns. Rumor was that at the factory in Burbank, California, one of every eight P-38's built was modified as an F-5, a photo reconnaissance model.

Now some serious aerial reconnaissance training began. First, the camera people took us out to the airplanes and made sure we understood how the camera was operated. The sergeant cautioned us about taxiing over mud or water that might spray up on the glass ports where the cameras looked out. As weather was a big factor in getting suitable pictures, the target had to be in clear conditions or with not more than scattered cloud cover. That's from one-tenth to four- tenths sky coverage. When the weather was good, I flew every day and sometimes twice a day. My flight time was building up and the days were passing quickly. Most of my training targets were military airfields around the Midwest. Sometimes I would be asked to shoot marshaling yards— sometimes called train or rail yards. All my first ten missions were at altitudes between 8,000 and 10,000 feet. On each flight, I liked that airplane more and more. I had no idea that it was so much fun to fly and it was very quiet.

Since the class had not been through the altitude chamber, we couldn't fly above 12,000 feet. The only chamber near us was at Will Rogers Field and it was presently down for maintenance; so we just flew our missions at 12,000 feet or below. I shot lots of airfields in Kansas and Nebraska that fall. In the photo lab I watched most of my film being processed and some of the pictures looked very good. The lab chief told me that photo interpreters, using 3-D magnification equipment, could tell what people at these military bases were doing when the pictures were taken. The shadows would tell them the time of day, heights of buildings and a lot more. There was a lot to photo-intelligence and I could see how the allied ground forces could use this information in combat areas.

The P-38 did not have very good heaters. The sun would keep the upper half of our bodies hot, and whatever was out of the sun rays would freeze. The use of fleece-lined boots was a must as the ship was not wired for heated suits like the bomber airplanes. On each of our targets, an initial point (IP) needed to be established about three to five miles away. I would fly to the IP, turn and make a beeline for the target at top speed. I had to be straight and level if I hoped to get any usable pictures. The flying time from the IP to the target was called "pucker time" in combat. Targets, such as enemy airfields and rail yards, would be heavily defended with anti-aircraft batteries. During pucker time, I flew the airplane at full throttle just to get out of there for obvious reasons.

One day a C-47 transport came up from Will Rogers Field to take the group down for the altitude chamber course. Horror stories are told about that training. The transport was drafty and chilly but better than the train ride we had anticipated.. The altitude chamber was a two-day course. First, there was a classroom session emphasizing the dangers of oxygen deficiency and how it struck without warning. I learned all about the oxygen equipment and was given a detailed briefing on how the "ride" would go the next day. That night and the next morning we were cautioned about what not to eat. Gas-producing foods were a no-no.

The thought of sitting in a large steel cylinder while the life-giving oxygen was pumped out was hardly reassuring. The chamber was a steel tube about 40 feet long and 10 feet in diameter. It was painted silver, and on one side were the dials and controls to regulate the pressure inside. Located on the opposite side of the chamber were giant vacuum pumps to evacuate the air inside.

Several thick glass portholes were located along the side where technicians and medical people could observe the activity inside. An intercom system provided communication between the technicians on the outside and instructors inside the chamber. The whole scene was awesome and not unlike some kind of strange execution device. Medics in white jackets were standing around as though they were waiting for a victim. This was a weird scene indeed. Before entering the chamber, the 12 of us had to strip to the waist and a flight surgeon gave us a good checkup. Special attention was given to the ears, nose and throat. Once inside the chamber, our oxygen masks were fitted to assure an air-tight fit. At the far end of the chamber was a small room where one person was sitting. It had a big window facing us. I asked an instructor what that was and he replied, "That's a medical officer and he has been breathing 100% pure oxygen for the last half hour. It eliminates the nitrogen in his body, and he will be in the main chamber with us."

A voice over the loudspeaker announced that the chamber doors were closing. The loud clank sounded like a large jail cell door. Now the loudspeaker said, "Don't put on your masks yet. We will tell you when." Now I could hear the big vacuum pumps start up and I knew it was pumping air out of the chamber. On the wall of the chamber was a large altimeter, that indicated an altitude of 5,000 feet. The medical officer said, "We will pause here for a moment." When everybody was acclimated, the vacuum pumps started up again. At 10,000 feet, we paused again, then at 15,000 feet, and again at 20,000 feet. Now the medical officer told us to put on our masks, except one student. "Now Lieutenant," the medical officer said as he handed him a copy of the Reader's Digest; "Read something from that aloud." He told the rest of us to watch him closely. He continued, "Watch the effect of oxygen deficiency on him. I'm doing this so you can better see the effect, otherwise it would hit some of you so fast you could not observe the effect. I want you to remember what you see today. Let it be a serious warning. Don't wait until you feel the need of oxygen before putting on your mask. You may never feel it."

The vacuum pumps started up again and the big altimeter on the wall started climbing. The student with no mask kept on reading from the magazine. He did fine for a while, then began to stumble over simple words. He started gesturing with his free hand. Then he grinned as though he were drunk. At 23,000 feet, the student began to nod and drop his head. An instructor quickly put a mask on him. Now the medical officer said, "Don't wait to put on your mask. Act before you feel any effect." The vacuum pumps started again. We leveled at 25,000 feet and I had no sensation and no discomfort. Everyone passed wind in the chamber. We were told in class to expect that. Suddenly one student was waving his hand and pointed to his jaw. The medical officer took him to the small room and we were told it was the decompression chamber. They would take him to ground level in there. Next a student with a stomach pain had to be taken down to ground level the same way. The vacuum pumps started up again and soon we were at 30,000 feet. When no one had any problem, we went on to 33,000 feet. The medical officer wanted another volunteer. When no one volunteered he picked one, and it wasn't me. The student was asked to read the Reader's Digest again. In a matter of seconds his lips turned blue. Quickly his mask was put on with 100% oxygen flowing at full pressure. In just seconds, he was fine. Those exercises were mighty impressive and would be vivid in my memory for the rest of my flying days.

That was as high as we went in the altitude chamber. Now the descent began and it was much slower than the ascent. The first thing affected by a too-rapid descent is the ears. Great discomfort can be felt and often it can be very painful. This happens when the eustachian tube is swollen shut from inflammation or infection, usually as a result of a head cold or a sore throat. Coming down too rapidly can cause the tube to open under pressure. The result is that the infected matter is carried into the middle ear and causes inflammation. Bottom line: If you have a cold or a sore throat, don't fly! After a lengthy descent, the chamber finally got to ground level. The big doors swung open and everybody heaved a big sigh of relief. My first thought was of the two who had to be brought down because of severe discomfort. An improperly filled tooth was the first man's problem, and the second man simply had too much stomach gas, probably the result of something the guy shouldn't have eaten the night before.

l learned a lot the last couple of days about the body's need for oxygen. Before catching the C-47 back to Coffeyville, we all went to the auxiliary mess and made up for what we couldn't eat the night before. All twelve of us were fine with no side effects from the steel monster. As long as I flew in the military, the altitude chamber ride had to be repeated every three years. Back at the field in Coffeyville, I had five missions to go before completing the overseas training course.

Naturally these last five missions were going to be at high altitude as most combat aerial reconnaissance missions, we were told, were flown above 25,000 feet. "The eye in the sky had to be high" was the saying. Four of these missions were to be four hours in duration and the last was five hours. For these missions, tear-shaped fuel drop-tanks were attached to shackles under the airplane. They came in two sizes, 150 gallons and 300 gallons. I would take off using the main fuel tanks, and later, switch to the drop tanks and run them dry. They could be jettisoned if need be. I supposed that in combat, that happened a lot and it did, as I learned later..

The first three missions were flown at 25,000 feet. I had two 150-gallon drop tanks slung under the wings. I hit targets in Colorado and Nebraska and most of my shots were rather good. It's hard to get the airplane exactly over a target at high altitude. After I stopped the camera on a run, I quickly rolled on my back to see how close I was. If it didn't look right, I would go back to the IP and do it again. In combat you wouldn't take that second risk, you were expected to get it right the first time. On my last training mission, two 300-gallon drop tanks were hung on my airplane. The extra weight required a little more distance for takeoff, but not much. Those engines were just great.

My targets were in Iowa and Nebraska. With excellent weather, I shot all the targets with no problems. The last target was the Air Base at Grand Island, Nebraska. With a little time to spare, I took advantage of the opportunity to fly over to Cedar Rapids and give them a taste of what the P-38 Lightning was all about. After raking the town over at 400 mph a couple of times, I flew over two of my sisters' farms and did some slow rolls. I learned, in letters, that my presence made the chickens fly the coop and the cows didn't give any milk that night. My family never let me forget that day. Even so, they enjoyed seeing their son and brother flying that sleek and fast P-38 Lightning. They told me later that the airplane really whistled as it zipped by.

Flight training at Coffeyville was now finished, but we had to return to Will Rogers Field for our graduation and overseas orders. The ceremony was short and simple as each of us received a certificate that said we were qualified P-38 Reconnaissance Pilots. The colonel briefing us then said, "I have your overseas orders. Some of you will proceed by train to Hunter Field, Savannah, Georgia, and the rest will go to Travis Field in California."

Special Order # SO 287 sent about 30 of us to Hunter Field. Out of the 50 or so new P-38 pilots, only about 20 went to Travis. Being in the Hunter group was just fine with me. There was too much water in the Pacific Theater for me. As this was our final night at Will Rogers, a big group went to the Black hotel for the last time. Different girls were there but they liked to dance and we had our usual supply of Four Roses. At closing time, there was a little left in my bottle so I gave it to the girl with the largest purse to take home. She said she would give it to her dad. Yeah, I bet she did.

After a long and grimy ride, the train pulled into the train station in Savannah. A short bus ride took us to Hunter Field just west of town. My orders were to proceed to Hunter for overseas processing. Soon I would find out what that meant. First, it was back to the two-story wooden barracks and for the first time, we didn't have to bunk alphabetically. Jim Foster and I got adjoining bunks on the second floor. This also was a change, as I was always on the lower floor with the G's in aviation cadets. The next morning we assembled in the base theater for briefings. This was the 3rd Air Force Overseas Staging Wing and there were air crews from everywhere representing all types of airplanes; fighters, bombers and transports. The briefer stated that he was waiting for authority to cut further orders for us. It was yet to be decided whether my group was going to the European or the Mediterranean Theater.

The next day the schedule called for overseas shots and a clothing issue. We were issued a steel helmet, leggings, an Army great coat and a Colt .45 automatic pistol. On the Hunter gunnery range, I had to qualify with the M-1 rifle of all things. Rumor had it that we would be taking this rifle on the ship with us. We all hoped not as it was big and heavy. The Officers Club at Hunter was a plain building with a bar, lots of tables and chairs and, of course, a large mess. One of the things that caught my eye were rows and rows of nickel slot machines along the walls. It was my first experience with these one-armed bandits and I liked them.

I was signed up for the free $10,000 GI life insurance and I listed my parents as primary beneficiaries. The pay section handed out some forms to be filled out. If I wished, I could have half my monthly pay sent to my wife, parents or a bank of my choosing. I decided to have mine deposited in the First National Bank in Omaha. Most of the guys went along with the plan, however, some wanted all their pay no matter where they were. Next of kin forms had to be filled out, too. After two weeks at Hunter, we all assembled again in the base theater. Now I would find out if I was going to the European Theater of Operations or the Mediterranean Theater. I was hoping for the ETO but either would be better than the Pacific Theater and all that water. Many years later, I would get to fly over that huge lake west of California.

The briefer had two sets of special orders that included all of us. First, he read SO-FJ505.

"The following named officers will proceed by train to Camp Kilmer, New Jersey, to await ship transportation to the European Theater of Operations." In two days I was on the train for Camp Kilmer. Those last two days gave me lots of time with the slot machines and I won my share. At Camp Kilmer, it was all Army and they were everywhere. We had to get some more shots and to my surprise, everyone was paid to date. Money in my pocket and no place to spend it. I bought a money order and sent it to my folks. All Camp Kilmer offered was a canteen and a post exchange. My overseas baggage was limited to one B-4 bag and two duffle bags. I carried the rest on my back in a big pack. I not only felt like a foot soldier, I even looked like one - steel helmet, back pack and all. The news of the war in Europe was grim, and the outlook was even grimmer.

In a couple of days, buses took us to the New York docks near Fort Hamilton. There we all boarded a Liberty ship named the USS Hershey. Expecting a big troop ship, I didn't know what to think when I saw this small Liberty ship we were about to board. The ship had a crew of 30 and lots of freight lashed down on the deck. The passenger list contained 37 names-all replacement pilots going to the war in Europe. The next day the ship milled around the harbor, setting up in a huge convoy that would cross the Atlantic Ocean. That evening, November 14, 1944, the huge convoy departed at a snails pace. Departing

New York harbor, I watched the Statue of Liberty until she was lost in the darkness. A strange feeling crept over me as I wondered if I would ever see her again.

Following a zigzag course along a circuitous route, it took 14 days to get to England. The small Liberty ship was doing nine knots and, I'm sure, set the pace for the entire convoy. One day I noticed a small aircraft carrier loaded with airplanes. Most of the time the sea was so rough, you couldn't even see the rest of the convoy. Everyone got sick from all the tossing around and no one ate much. Hot tea was the only thing I could handle. The big concern in a large convoy, was enemy submarines. Almost every night, we were called to "battle stations." Everybody had a certain place to go and don a life vest. It was all for drill. One night when battle stations sounded, a voice from the ship's speakers said, "This is not a drill." That scared the hell out of us. We just knew a German submarine had spotted us and was ready to fire his torpedoes. It turned out that a life vest, with a flashlight burning, had fallen overboard from one of the ships. Wow!

One day while browsing through a book in the ship's small library, I noted the name of the girl who had donated the book to the U. S. Navy. She was Mary Katherine Rellahan from Upper Montclair, New Jersey.. Later in England, I sent her a V-Mail letter. Sure enough, she answered promptly. She was in college and her brother was an ensign in the Navy. We traded letters about once a month and one day I received a large photo of her in her nurse's uniform.. She had just graduated and received her "cap." What a beautiful girl. I told her in a letter that, if I came back from the war, I would try to look her up. Finally, land was sighted and we docked at Port Talbot in Swansea Bay. Terra firma never felt better to me in my life. I don't ever want to live the life of a sailor. It was November 28, 1944, when I got on the narrow-gage train headed for the town of Stone, England. Stone was about a hundred miles west of London and was the location of the 70th Replacement Depot (tent city). A better description would be "mud city" with tents.

It rained nearly every day while we were at Stone and the mud was ankle deep. Each tent contained four army cots and a small "coke" stove. Beside the stove was a box of fuel that contained coke pieces about the size of baseballs and instead of burning nicely, they just sat there and smoldered like charcoal. Those sorry stoves didn't generate much heat. I slept in my clothes under several blankets and still froze. Here I was in a foreign country in the middle of a war—what a culture shock. The tents had just been put up and had no floors yet. Soon some lumber arrived and the four of us built a makeshift floor. That helped a lot and we smuggled some of the lumber scraps and had ourselves a real fire for a few nights. Our first briefing in the tent theater was how to behave in England. The British had a saying, "The Yanks are over-paid, oversexed and over here." The Yanks had a saying, "The Brits are underpaid, undersexed, and under Eisenhower."

In England, it was the Queen's this and the Queen's that. Having endured over four years of war, the British felt that if the allies could run the Germans out of France, the war would then be down hill. The British RAF bombed Germany by night and the US Army Air Forces bombed them by day. The Germans were now getting hit pretty hard around the clock. The morale of the local people around Stone was now upbeat. Everyone wore his .45 pistol cowboy style and the British just shook their heads when they saw us. Rumor had it that German paratroopers might be landing at any time, day or night. I felt that if they did land in England, it would be near a large city, not out in the boondocks where we were. In the evenings, my three tentmates and I would walk into Stone as it was only about two kilometers away. Someone at the base said to look for the Blue Boar Pub. Soon we found the small establishment with a big bar and a bigger barmaid. Molly was friendly though and asked us to try some "mild and bitters" ale. It wasn't bad at all. Because it was early December, the ale was cold. Promptly at 10 p.m., Molly would bellow out "toy'm" (time). That ended the evenings drinking with never an argument. On the walk back to the base, when nature called, we just used the road. Someone said, "I wish the Queen could see what we are doing on her road." The next time we went to the pub, Molly said to try half and half. She called it "arf 'n arf." It was a better drink. Old British veterans in the pub would be throwing darts or playing cribbage. They rarely spoke when engaged in those games. When just drinking, they talked of their Yank friends from World War I. There in that little pub, I learned two things—how to throw darts properly and how to play the game of cribbage. (I still do both today). One night some local lassies came to the pub. They didn't want to dance but sure liked the free drinks we bought for them. I tried to take one of them home after closing but she wouldn't have any part of it. She said her grandmother would not allow it. The lassies always came and went in a group. I suppose they felt there was "safety in numbers", as the saying goes.

Soon, more orders came. Six of us were to go, by surface transportation, to an airfield south of London. There we would be flown to Paris and report to the 134th Pilot Replacement Battalion. That sounded good to me; anything to get out of muddy Stone. I would miss Molly.

On December 15, 1944, a British bus took us to the airfield in dense fog. By noon the fog still hadn't lifted so we were taken to a British Officers Club for lunch. That was a joke—cold mutton and some awful tasting cheese. The hot tea was about the only thing I could handle. On that same day, Glenn Miller, the famous big band leader, was also scheduled to fly over the English Channel to Paris.

Glenn Miller was born in Clarinda, Iowa on March 1, 1904. Shortly, the family moved to Fort Morgan, Colorado. Glenn learned to like music very early in life and at the age of ten, was given his first trombone. Glenn took lessons and practiced constantly. By the time he was 17, he was playing in a band. Three years later, at the age of 20, he moved to Los Angeles and did some arranging. He discovered that he not only liked arranging, but that he was good at it. Soon he joined the Ben Pollack band. Ben had one of the first well-known dance bands. The band slowly moved across the country playing at many famous dance halls. In New York, Glenn made contact with all the well-known musicians of the time. His arranging expertise soon became known and Red Nickels and his Five Pennies hired him as their arranger. It was not long before Glenn was also playing in the band. After a long stint with the Red Nickels band, Glenn continued his arranging. In 1934, when the Dorsey brothers formed their band, they asked Glenn to join them. Besides being a very good and highly paid arranger, he was a good business man. When the British band leader, Ray Noble came to America, Glenn helped him recruit and form an American band.

In 1937, Glenn Miller formed his first band in New York City. Two years later, he had the most successful and popular band in America. When the country entered the war in 1941, Glenn and other band leaders began losing musicians to the war effort. After a year of that, Glenn decided to join up himself. That September, he joined the Army Air Force. Just 12 days earlier, he had been turned down by the Navy. Basic training at Fort Mead, Maryland took two months after which he received a field commission as a captain. Quickly he became director of military bands for the Southeast Training Command. Glenn knew what kind of music the young men and women in the service wanted. Soon he formed several service bands.

In the spring of 1943, he formed his own AAF band and enlisted many musicians from other big bands. Glenn's hardest thing to learn in the Army was getting up when most musicians were just going to bed. The band played every Saturday night on the NBC Radio Network. On June 21, 1944, Captain Miller left for England, as the Supreme Headquarters Allied Expeditionary Forces (SHAEF) wanted the

Miller band to play for the allied troops there in England. They also played over the BBC network. In London, the band stayed at the Royal Hotel which was first class according to European standards.

General Dwight D. Eisenhower, the SHAEF Commander, liked the Miller music and listened to it whenever he could. German V-1 flying bombs drove the Miller band underground and they slept in bomb shelters many nights. Glenn Miller concluded, "London is rotten to the core and they ought to tear it down and start all over again." He wanted to get his band out of London quickly. In Bedford, about 40 miles north of London, accommodations were arranged. The band would stay there until December when Glenn planned to move the band to Paris. He insisted to the Transportation Commander that they all fly to Paris. He wanted nothing more to do with water transportation after his tossing and heaving Atlantic crossing.

At Bedford, Glenn and the band finally got their first good night sleep since arriving in Britain. As there were many RAF and 8th Air Force bases around Bedford, the band kept busy playing good American music for the boys. The day after the band's arrival in Bedford, Glenn learned that their previous quarters in London had been wiped out by a German bomb. The BBC and the Armed Forces Radio kept the band busy too. They could have played every day in the UK but Glenn limited their engagements. He had new arrangements to work on and they always practiced a lot. The Glenn Miller band now had grown to 40 members and soon formed three bands within the big band. These small bands could play dance music for some of the military clubs on Saturday nights. The Miller music was in demand everywhere. One Saturday night at the 8th AF base at Thurleigh, the band played to a hangar filled with some 3,500 airmen and officers. After each number, the crowd gave the band a standing ovation. When the concert was over, Glenn talked to General Jimmy Doolittle and told him, "General, if I had all the money in the music world, I wouldn't feel as rich as I do tonight."

Her Majesty, Queen Elizabeth, came to Bedford one day and visited the American Red Cross Club, where she drew huge crowds. The streets were filled with people and flags were flying everywhere. In the ARC Officers Club, the Queen met Captain Miller. She mentioned that Princesses Elizabeth and Margaret Rose were great fans of his music. They listened to him on the BBC whenever they could. Occasionally, the big 40-piece band would be invited to London to play concerts and all were total sell-outs. On October 1, Captain Miller was summoned to SHAEF Headquarters in London. There he met with General Bedell Smith, Chief of Staff to General Eisenhower. General

Smith said, "Major Miller, we want you to go to Paris. General Eisenhower is already over there and wants you to do your magic in Paris. You can use the military shuttle. It flies to Paris every other day." Glenn was promoted to Major on the spot.

During the next ten weeks, the Miller band was busy as bees. It could not possibly fill all the requests for appearances. Glenn brought out new arrangements, and a lot of time was needed to work them out with the band. From the October meeting with General Eisenhower, the plan was for the band to move to Paris in December before the holidays.

December 15 began with dense morning fog. Glenn decided to fly over with one of his staff in a small plane. The band would follow in two C-47 transports. After lunch at the Officers Club at Milton Earnest Hall, the fog started to lift. At Twinwood Farm Airfield, a single engine C-64 Norsman airplane took off carrying Major Glenn Miller and Colonel Baessell. The plane was piloted by Flight Officer John Morgan. They departed at 1:45 p.m. and should have arrived in Paris in about three hours. The single-engine Norsman aircraft never arrived at Orly Field.

As the fog started to lift, the replacement pilots left for Bennington Field. There on the wet ramp sat three C-47s - Gooney Birds, as we Yanks would call them. A sergeant entered our bus and told us to board the third airplane but to stay put until he gave us the "ready" signal. In a few minutes, two other buses arrived, and the passengers promptly boarded the first two airplanes. The signal was then given for us to board our transport. In boarding, someone said that the Glenn Miller band were in the first two airplanes. No one saw Glenn as he was already airborne in the Norsman. The three airplanes were to fly over to Orly Field in Paris that afternoon. As we started to taxi out, I looked at my watch and it read 2 p.m. December 15, 1944.

The flight across the English Channel was uneventful and fairly smooth. We were above a deck of scattered-to-broken clouds, but I could see the white caps in the channel quite well. In a couple hours, our airplane was approaching the famous city of Paris. Looking out the window, I was awestruck by the size of the place. The Eiffel Tower was majestic. Years later, at the very top of that tower, which is called the crow's nest, I took lots of pictures of the city. The crow's nest has been closed to the public for years because of people jumping off. At Orly Field, we heard a rumor that the C-64 Norsman had not yet arrived. I wondered how much fuel they had on board. A military bus took us out to the famous French banker's estate called Rothchild Acres. The 134th Replacement Battalion located there processed aircrews, coming and going. The Rothchild family estate looked like a big college campus. Unfortunately, most of the grand buildings were bombed out. Only two were livable, one for the 134th and the other for aircrew billets. The mess hall was in the 134th building. There was no bar, you had to go into Paris for that.

The next day, December 16, 1944, the Germans launched the Ardennes Counter Offensive known as the Battle of the Bulge. Hitler's objective was to capture Antwerp, Belgium, because of its large seaport. It was the third largest seaport in the world after Rotterdam and New York City. After the capture of Antwerp, Hitler planned to move further west. Air raid sirens kept us awake almost every night as the rumors ran rampant of German paratroopers in the area. We also heard that English-speaking German paratroopers were jumping all over France and Belgium and they were not taking any prisoners. Reports also said the Germans captured some 350 Americans who were taken into the woods and shot. "Nervous in the service" was the theme at the Rothchild Estates. About 100 pilots were there being processed in or getting ready to go home. About half were replacement pilots, like myself, who were waiting for assignment to a unit.

We now were under the command of the 9th Tactical Air Force. It was mobile and moved with the front lines, as the 9th directly supported the ground forces. The 8th Air Force Bomber Command flew all their missions from England, and never moved around. After my shot records were checked to assure they were up to date, I checked the notice board daily for assignment listings. The six of us took turns checking the large bulletin board to look for orders assigning us to a combat unit.

After checking the bulletin board each morning, we were free, so the six of us went into town-the big city of Paris, France. Jim Foster and I had gone through the entire Aviation Cadet Program together and at Stone, England, we met Bill McGrath, Everett Phillips, Burl Stokes and Roland Sanderson. By the time we arrived in Paris, we called ourselves the "Salty Six." We did everything as a group and stuck together like glue. The first night in Paris turned out to be a memorable one. First, we found a cafe that offered black market steaks. I don't know where they came from but they were delicious. The wine that was served with the meal was some of the finest I have ever had. In Paris, the merchants accepted francs, green or script; it didn't matter to them. Script was the military currency used in lieu of U.S. green currency. One had to be very careful how the exchange rate was handled. After our wonderful meal, we discovered a night spot called The Black Cat. In front of the place, the name was shown both in French and

English. French beer was not the greatest, but not too bad. Wine on tap was always available in those places too. The Black Cat had a small French band that tried to play American music; but they butchered it so badly that it was hard to recognize any number. They did their best with "One O'Clock Jump" and must have played it 20 times that night. The place was full of French girls learning to jitterbug and some were very good at it.

Under German occupation, the trams, buses and the popular subway system were kept in good working order. The Germans, like us, needed transportation around town. The girls in the Black Cat didn't want to admit it at first, but finally said they danced with the Germans too.

At the time, nobody knew how the war was going to turn out, so the French just took life in stride and kept producing good wine and raising beautiful women.

The Armed Forces published a daily newspaper called "The Stars and Stripes." About a week after arriving in Paris, I picked up a copy of the paper and saw this article:

Major Glenn Miller Lost on Flight From England

Major Glenn Miller, Director of the USAF band which has been playing in England, is reported missing while on a flight from England to Paris. The plane in which he was a passenger left England on Dec. 15. Major Miller lived in Tenafly, N.J. where his wife resides. No member of his band was with him on the flight across the channel.

In Paris, the men in the Miller band, still dazed by the disappearance of their leader and commanding officer, were naturally worried that, once it became known that Major Miller was missing, their families back home would think the whole band was lost. A popular singer, Joey Hodges, who was in Paris with a USO tour, was about to leave for New York and she agreed to call everyone's family, when she got home, to put their minds at rest. Rumors were flying that if Major Miller was not found, the band might be disbanded and the men redeployed as stretcher-bearers or ambulance drivers, or even sent to the front with the infantry. None of them had ever fired a rifle before. The military situation in the Battle of the Bulge was worsening daily. Bad weather prevented Allied air forces from using their fire power to halt the German breakthrough.

The need for more support personnel was growing daily and that made the boys in the band very nervous. They spent most of their time in their billets trying to keep warm and listening, as if nothing happened, to the radio play recorded Miller music. The music they listened to had been recorded in England just weeks before by this same group. Before long, Jerry Gray and Ray McKinley asked the Army Air Force if they could play some concerts around Paris for the Allied troops. At first, Jerry Gray led the band but soon, Ray McKinley became the new conductor and CO of the group. Although Major Glenn Miller was lost, his objective was not. Even without him, the band carried on just as he would have wanted, bringing to the Allied troops a "hunk of home." The Glenn Miller Band was to continue its work for another seven months. In July 1945, the Army Air Force called it back to America. The Glenn Miller story was gathered from the archives of the Stars and Stripes military newspaper.

One morning after breakfast, the bulletin board finally listed the six of us for an assignment. The orders read that we were being assigned to the 43rd Fighter Squadron. We all jumped with joy and then someone said, "Hey, we never had any gunnery training at Oklahoma City." We didn't care as the unit could teach us when we got there. But it was not meant to be, as the following morning, the orders were canceled. Now we had to wait for more news and, after checking the board each morning, everyone headed into town to relax at the Black Cat. The Battle of the Bulge was raging not far away, and here we were drinking and dancing in a Paris night spot. C'est Le Guerre.

One night at the Black Cat I asked the head waiter about a barber shop. The Rothchild Hilton didn't have one and I needed a haircut badly. The next afternoon I located the place and it was not a barber shop, but a beauty shop. I hesitated about going in, but finally decided to go ahead and try it anyway. It was advertised as a first class salon. As I entered, there was no one in sight. As I was about to leave, a young girl came out from behind a curtain. She was wearing a black dress with a white collar and cuffs. She smiled and said in fair English, "Monsieur, welcome to my shop, we do nice work here." Her name was Annette, and she was supporting her parents and two younger sisters. She then said she never cut hair that wasn't washed first, so I had a shampoo. What I didn't know was there wasn't any hot water. A cold shampoo is an experience I wouldn't recommend to anyone. With just a pair of scissors and a comb, she cut my hair as I sat there nervously. It wasn't a military hair cut but at least it was shorter and clean too.

Christmas was drawing near and I wanted to attend midnight mass on Christmas Eve at Notre Dame Cathedral. No one wanted to go with me so I went alone. By now, I knew my way around Paris pretty well.

Their subway system was clean and well designed with routes all over the big city. Arriving at the Cathedral, I found standing room only but decided to stay anyway. In a few minutes, a voice behind me said, "Come with me and I will find you a seat." Looking in that direction, a young friar was motioning me to follow him. Weaving through the large crowd, he led me right up to the sanctuary. On a long bench sat many priests and bishops. They moved over a little and I sat on the very end. Here I was, right in the middle of all the action. Mass was beautiful and the choir was outstanding, and, of course, everything was in French. Here I was, headed into war and I felt that "peace on earth, good will toward men," offered a keen irony.

The bishop next to me offered me a prayer card but it was in French. As I handed it back to him, he smiled understandingly. The long ceremony took the better part of two hours and by then the only transportation left for me was a taxicab. After a long wait, I hailed one down and arrived back at the Rothchild Hilton in the wee hours, dead tired, but happy that I had gone to mass at Notre Dame that night.

On December 27, orders were finally posted sending the "salty six" to the 363rd Tactical Reconnaissance Group, then further assignment to the 33rd Photo Reconnaissance Squadron. We would be flying the modified P-38 Lightning called the F-5. We were all excited about being assigned to a unit-we had been waiting a long time. Late on Sunday night, December 31, 1944, a military bus took us to the Paris train station. All we could learn from the Army Transportation Office was that our new unit was located somewhere in Belgium. When the train started to move, I settled down and quickly fell asleep. Everett Phillips and Bill McGrath played gin rummy. I don't remember how long I slept but when the train suddenly came to an abrupt and jerky stop, I was wide awake. Soon the conductor came through our car and said the tracks ahead had just been bombed out by German planes. He continued, "We are very near Laon, about one hour north of Paris." After a discussion among the six of us, we decided to find our gear and hike on into Laon.

Soon we came upon a road sign that read, "Chalon-Sur-Marne .5 kilometer." It was a small village with one hotel and it was late at night by then. After banging on the front door, we managed to get the hotel manager out of bed. He was not very friendly, but after we related our problem, using pantomime, a little French and a lot of English, he let us in. They had only one room left. The hotel had no hot water and the water closet was down the hall. Being very tired, we really didn't care much right then. That night, I slept soundly on the floor in my bedroll. In the morning, we decided that we were in a war zone and didn't shave-not in that cold water anyway. The hotel did muster up some hard french bread and some awfully thick black coffee. The coffee was heated on a coke stove in the kitchen. The hotel manager told us that he occasionally saw some American soldiers nearby. Scouting around that day, we discovered an Army Anti-Aircraft Battery a short distance from town. Using the radio link with their headquarters, they sent a message to our unit requesting rescue on our behalf.

It had been snowing for three days and it was getting rather deep. So that we could eat their delicious soup, we gave the hotel a little extra rent. Soup and bread was our diet for a week. Bill McGrath soon found a blonde French girl, and didn't care if he ever left France. Bill just vanished and we hardly saw him anymore. Up in Belgium, our unit, the 33rd Photo Reconn Squadron, finally received the message that six of their new replacement pilots were stranded in France. They dispatched Lieutenant George Coffee in a six-by-six truck to come down to France and pick us up. It was not easy. With the Battle of the Bulge going on and the deep snow, the roads were choked with military traffic. On top of all of that, George's truck broke down. But he managed to trade down to a weapons carrier with an Army unit. A weapons carrier is sort of like a big jeep with side curtains. When the sounds of a honking horn got our attention one night at the hotel, I looked out and there was the vehicle. George was irritated that we weren't out front with all our baggage waiting for him. We finally got the baggage loaded, but only five of us left. Bill McGrath decided he was too sick to travel. I thought he looked more lovesick than anything else. The hotel manager said he would try to locate a doctor for Bill. With over a foot of snow on the ground, and a bitter cold wind blowing, the loaded weapons carrier started out for Allied Air Strip Y-10 near Brussels. It was cozy in that vehicle. That's the only way we kept warm. George drove all night and told us horror stories about combat flying and all the flak and German fighters flying around. Again I wondered what I was getting into. Finally, we arrived at Chateau de Meldert just before dawn. The Chateau was where the 33rd officers were billeted. After finding some army cots, we bedded down for some much needed rest.

An elderly Belgian couple ran the Chateau and cooked our breakfast and dinner. The meals were always good with lots of soup in the evenings. There was no night flying, so we always ate on time-6:00 on the dot. In about ten days, Bill McGrath showed up looking a little pale. The five of us gave him a bad time, as we knew why he looked so drained. The 33rd air strip at Y-10 was five kilometers from the Chateau. Early every morning, all the pilots and other squadron officers rode to the airstrip in the back of a six-by-six truck. We froze back there, huddling together like a bunch of puppies. A few days after arriving, I flew a test flight for the camera repair shop. It surely felt good to be back in the P-38. The mobile control tower only operated when our own aircraft were up. About 30 miles away was an Aircraft Control and Warning Station called Orchard Control. I always talked to them going and coming from missions. They gave me reports of "bogey" aircraft, plus a steering heading in order to find Y-10 air strip. The field did have an ADF (automatic direction finder) radio beacon for us to home in on but its range was quite limited.

The Battle of the Bulge made us nervous. A straight line between the Ardennes, where the German tanks were gathered, and Antwerp fell right on top of Air Strip Y-10. Each P-38 was parked in its own revetment and they were spread all over the airfield. The runway was steel matt-large sheets of perforated steel fastened together to form the surface. Some of the taxiways were steel matt and some were crushed gravel. When taxiing on the gravel paths, one had to be careful not to rev up the engines too much, as the loose stones could be sucked up and nick the tips of the propeller blades. Way out in revetment number 15 sat P-38, Serial Number 44-23245-my airplane. The previous pilot, Captain Bill (Sonny) Clevenger, had already rotated back to the States. Sonny had named the airplane Queenie. As soon as possible, my name along with my crew chief's name was painted on Queenie's nose.

My personal crew chief was Technical Sergeant Woodrow "Deacon" Grainger who had two assistants to help him care for my P-38. The weather got worse and dense fog set in; now even the birds were walking. A few of the pilots found some German rifles in a storage building and went hunting for game. All we found were some quail. The ammo we used contained some tracer bullets and they helped to zero in on the quail. A tracer bullet is visible in that it trails a yellowish visible path. That night at the Chateau, a wonderful feast of baked quail was served.

A squadron dance was scheduled for the next Saturday night in nearby Tirlemont. It turned into a fiasco and was referred to thereafter as the "200 men and one girl" party. The girl was from the American Red Cross. Either the Belgian band failed to pass the word of the dance or the local mademoiselles decided to stay away from the drinking Americans. Soon it was forgotten, as nightly liberty to Brussels became available. A six-by-six truck left the squadron area each afternoon at 5 p.m. and we could stay in town until the following night.

Every night the squadron truck would depart Brussels from a certain place at 10:30 p.m. If you missed the ride, you had to get back to base any way you could. War can be hell at times.

On January 25, 1945, Captain Paul Miller and I were briefed on a mission over enemy territory. This would be my first combat mission. Our targets were deep in Germany; and I would be flying on Paul's wing. Paul had flown more than 50 missions and was looking forward to his 75th, which would allow him go home. The weather that morning was a low overcast and over the target, the weather was forecast to be suitable for intelligence gathering. As I taxied out of the revetment, Sergeant Grainger gave me a salute, which meant he would like to have his airplane back in one piece. While taxiing down the steel matt to the runway, I managed to slide my left main wheel off into the mud during a turn-talk about embarrassment. Paul, being ahead of me, was told by the tower to hold fast. No amount of power from my engines could get me out of that muck. Soon a tug with a tow bar came and pulled me out. I was as humiliated as I could be over that goof on my very first mission. The runway wasn't wide enough for a formation takeoff, so I waited until Paul was airborne then I followed him and, after a couple of low circles, joined up on his right wing. He said over the inter-plane radio frequency, "Tom, we are going to be climbing through a lot of clouds, so stick on my wing and don't lose me." Climbing out, I got so close to Paul that I could count the rivets on his fuselage boom panels. I didn't want to lose him and I didn't. After climbing for a long time in dense clouds, we finally broke out on top at 31,000 feet. Paul said, "Good job, Tom. Now back off a little."

Flying on Paul's wing, it was my job to look around for any bogeys or bandits. It wasn't very long before Paul said, "We're over Koln now. I'll shoot the rail yards. You get the bridges." First, we had to drop down to about 25,000 feet. Running a target, I never flew at even altitudes, usually a few hundred feet above or below. I shot the bridges at 24,400 feet just to confuse the anti-aircraft gunners. While shooting my target, I saw my first flak bursts. They were big, black, ugly puffs and they were full of shrapnel flying out in every direction. The puffs you could see; the shrapnel you couldn't. Soon Paul said, "Let's get out of here," and we climbed back to 30,000 feet and turned west for home.

As we started to descend, I had to fly tight formation again because of the dense clouds. After a long flight against the wind, Orchard Control gave us a vector heading to the Y-10 Air Strip and said the ceiling was still low. After contacting the Y-10 control tower, we were cleared to shoot the ADF instrument approach. Here I am coming home on my first combat mission and I have to shoot an instrument approach to land. Paul went first and, after a couple of circles, I went down on the beacon's beam and broke out of the clouds with the runway right in front of me. What a good feeling that is to a pilot, new or old. On the taxi-in after landing I noticed my crew chief waiting to direct me into the parking revetment. As I got closer I noticed him grinning from ear to ear. The Photo Lab sent out a photographer and I had my "first combat mission" picture taken. This was an aviation tradition in war-time. Quickly a jeep came up to the nose section and in a wink, the camera magazine was removed. It was then taken to the big laboratory on the field where the film would be processed in minutes. That included several prints of each shot I got. The prints were nine-inch square glossy black and white contact prints of high quality with good resolution. On later missions, I would "walk through" my combat film in the photo lab. Being able to do that was a fascinating experience. Of every combat shot taken and processed, several sets of prints went immediately to 9th AF Headquarters. There all but one set were dispensed to various Army units. General George Patton's 3rd Army was a regular recipient of our photo intelligence. The 33rd also had their own photo interpreters to see what the Germans were up to. The Chinese say one picture is worth a thousand words. With that first mission out of the way, I flew quite regularly. Of course after each mission, I would catch the R&R (rest and recuperation) truck into Brussels. Before I arrived, the 33rd pilots had found their favorite night spot in downtown Brussels called the Corso Club. It was only four blocks from the famous Metropole Hotel. The club had three stories. On the street level was an ordinary cafe. The second floor had a first-class restaurant where everyone always dressed up to eat and the waiters wore formal attire. Below ground level was the "real" Corso Club. It was a bodega type of night spot and that was where the 33rd pilots and other officers gathered. They had a band which could play any and all of the American tunes very well. Next to the bandstand, in the corner, was the 33rd squadron's private table. It was quite large and could seat about 12 people.

On my first visit to the Corso club, I met Freddie Roulez (pronounced Rulay). She was a local girl about my age and worked for the English Army Headquarters in Brussels. We hit it off right from the start and she loved to dance. After a few dances when I was tired, she would ask one of the other pilots at the table. She danced every dance, without exception. All you could buy in the place was wine and beer. The wine was good but the beer was not. After meeting Freddie, I was never in the Corso Club when she wasn't there. Her friend Simone was the girlfriend of another 33rd pilot, Robert "Bake" Baker. The four of us would have some great times in Brussels. After some dancing, we would go to the Metropole hotel and get a black market steak with all the trimmings. Steak wasn't on the menu, you had to ask for it. After eating, we always went back to the Corso to dance until ten o'clock curfew. The pilots would always bring knapsacks full of fruit juice, whiskey and cigarettes to the Corso. The girls would quickly drink all the fruit juice if we didn't ration it. They were just starved for it. During four years of occupation, the Germans had consumed all the available fruit juice.

The Corso Club had an old maitre d' named Jacque. "Jock" always protected our table and we would give him a glass of scotch whiskey. Our table always had a big bucket of ice and several bottles of soda water, nobody knew, or even cared, where they came from. Jock was always in splendid formal attire, and his conduct with customers could have earned him a job at London's Buckingham Palace. Jock would only let certain girls sit at our table-those he figured the 33rd boys would like. One evening when some of us arrived, our table was full of girls. Jock would quickly scatter them so we had a place to sit. When the band started up at 6 p.m., if there were not enough pilots, or other officers to dance with, the girls just danced with other girls . They were very good dancers, especially to American swing music. Freddie, working for the English Army, was still learning to speak English. When excited, she would break into rapid French that I could not understand. Simone also worked for the English and had good command of the language so she would always tell me what Freddie said. I first met Freddie on January 29 and the relationship would last until the end of the war.

Most of my combat missions were flown in two-ship formations. The leader would navigate to the target area while the wing man would cover and look for bandits. After shooting our targets, we reversed the role going home. The wing man would lead and the other ship would cover. Sometimes I was sent out by myself with the old adage: "Alone, Unarmed and Unafraid."

The first two words were true, but the last can be argued. On my tenth mission, I was sent out alone to shoot a target deep inside Germany. During the mission briefing, the weather officer said the trip would be in "CAVU" conditions. That meant the ceiling and visibility should be unlimited. To me, that meant no clouds to duck into if jumped by Me-109 or FW-190 enemy fighters. Cameras could shoot pictures but not airplanes. On the way to the target, my head was on a swivel looking for somebody who would try to shoot me out of the sky. As I left the Orchard Control radar coverage, the controller said, "Good luck, and check in on your way back." That was the last person I would speak with for two hours. I managed to find my two targets and shoot them without any opposition except for some off-target flak. Looking down on Germany on that beautiful clear day, I found it hard to imagine a war was going on in such a peaceful setting.

Minutes later, on my way home, my heart almost stopped cold as, ahead of and below me, I could see an Me-109 coming at me from the opposite direction. During the mission briefing, the intelligence officer said, "If you see one lone German airplane, look out!. His friends will be coming at you from out of the sun. Do some evasive action quickly or you will be a dead duck." I watched the Me-109 like a hawk and also looked in the direction of the sun and saw nothing. The ME-109 kept coming straight ahead and went right under me. I rolled over on my back and did a 'split-S' to see what he was up to. To my amazement, he just kept on going like he hadn't even seen me. I found that hard to believe but it happened, so I did a loop and at the top, watching him still flying eastward, I did a half roll and headed for home. Whew! What a lucky break that was. If he tried to fire at me, I could only do my best to evade him. There were no clouds to duck into that day. Continuing home, I kept thinking about the ME-109 . Maybe he was low on fuel. Maybe he didn't see me. Maybe he didn't care anymore. Nevertheless, I still had big goose bumps.

On another mission with Paul Miller, we flew into some heavy flak, but got away from it with no damage. The flak gunners were a crafty lot. If you just flew straight and level, and never changed airspeeds, they soon would have you boxed in, then — "ker-boom!" To outfox them, I was always changing speed, heading and altitude. Like a bomber from the IP to the target, I was vulnerable because over the target I had to fly straight and level for about 10 seconds. During the return flight home, Paul said to me on the inter-plane frequency, "Get on my wing. We're going to have some fun." Down we dove at redline speed and leveled off just above the tree tops. Over a large hay field, we blew the tops off several big stacks. I liked to fly formation, but not that close to the ground. Later, after landing, Paul told me that every once in a while you just have to let loose. Otherwise the pressure of combat flying will get to you; that is when you get yourself in trouble. Paul flew for a long time after the war but is no longer with us. He was a good fiend and a great flyer.

On my 15th mission, I had the pleasure of flying with Bill "Lover Boy" McGrath . On the flight to the target, Bill flew on my wing and covered for me. At the IP, we split up and headed for our separate targets. Our plan was to meet back over the IP and go home, then I would fly on his wing. Back over the IP, I circled twice, and no Bill, so I flew home alone. The flight home went well with no incidents and as I was parking my airplane, I mentioned to the Deacon that Lieutenant McGrath was missing. He pointed over to another revetment and there sat Bill's airplane. Arriving early over the IP, Bill became impatient and came home alone. He thought I was missing. We had a good laugh over that one.

When on liberty in Brussels, I usually stayed at the Metropole hotel as they were very accommodating to the 33rd squadron people. I discovered that the hotel got their steaks through the black market. The steaks actually came from Argentina. They were better steaks than our squadron's military source and I wondered why the Army never bought meat from places like Argentina like the Belgian black market did.

On one occasion in Brussels, Freddie wanted me to bypass the Metropole and stay at her apartment where she lived with her mother. I told her I would do it on my next liberty and I could bring some provisions from the mess hall. The next day, I gave my crew chief a list of things to get for me. I "greased his palm" well for that. My knapsack was so full of stuff for Freddie's mom that this time I couldn't put in any liquor or juice. The Corso Club closed promptly at 10 every night. That night, Freddie and I took the last streetcar toward her apartment. At the end of the car line, we had to walk a couple of blocks. On her kitchen table, I unloaded two cans of coffee, butter, salt, sugar, chocolate, canned peaches and some bars of Dial soap. They were extremely grateful and I received big hugs from both of them. Freddie's father had been killed in a streetcar accident several years earlier. They left their house and moved into an apartment. Their only income was from Freddie's job with the English Army. The money from her father's insurance had been spent long ago. Freddie's mother came up with a bottle of wine and we had a night cap. The apartment had two bedrooms and I slept in the small one while Freddie and her mother occupied the larger one.. Sometime in the wee hours, I was awakened by a hand on my shoulder. It was Freddie in her nightgown. She whispered in my ear, "I cannot get myself to sleep this night, mon Cherie."

Soon I heard a rumor that the squadron might be moving east. The 9th Air Force and all its units moved with the ground forces. Every day at about 8 a.m., two airplanes would take off and fly over the front lines at breakneck speed shooting pictures as fast as the cameras would take them. The run was flown low level and we did that every day when there were no clouds. The front lines themselves were usually quiet, but on either side, artillery batteries would be firing at each other all the time for mutual harassment. The first part of March, our Squadron Commander, Major T.A. "Pop" Roberts, put out a notice, "No more liberty in Brussels as we are going to be moving soon." That night, some of us pilots went into Brussels and the Corso Club anyway. At the door of the club, Jock was trying to tell us something, but in his excitement, he was gesturing in rapid French. Moving over to the 33rd's table, we ran into heavy flak. There at our table sat the Squadron Commander, Major Roberts. In his unmistakable Texas drawl, he said, "Y'all might as well come on in and sit down; everybody else is here." I asked one of the girls if Freddie was there and she said, "Yes, she's out there dancing with a Canadian pilot." Suddenly a pang of jealousy came over me. When she came over to the table, I noticed tears in her eyes. She already heard the news of our moving. When I left her that night, she was crying. I gave her my mailing APO (Army Post Office) number and she promised to write.

Moving day came on March 12, 1945, and we were heading for Allied Air Strip Y-55. It was located on the German side of the Holland-German border. All the buildings were located in Venlo, Holland, however.the runways were located across the border in Germany. The airfield belonged to the Germans before they were driven out by General Patton's ground forces. The squadron was now in permanent buildings and it sure was nice. In the Stars and Stripes newspaper, the 33rd Photo Reconnaissance Squadron laid claim for being the first USAAF unit to operate from a German airfield in WW II. Just before we left Y-10, a call came in from the main gate saying two girls were there looking for a couple of pilots. Major Roberts came into the pilots' ready room and said, "Somebody tell Baker and Gordon to get those girls out of here pronto." Bake got a jeep from the motorpool and we took Simone and Freddie back to Brussels. Very late that night, Bake and I crawled into our bunks at the Chateau dead tired.

Soon after operations started at Y-55, we were jarred out of our bunks one night when a German ME-262 jet fighter buzzed the field. All hell broke loose as our anti-aircraft guns began to fire, and we all dove for cover. After a couple of passes, the airplane left. He never hit anything, nor did we. The runways and taxiways at Y-55 were concrete and I felt good about not having to deal with the steel matt stuff anymore. In their hasty departure, the Germans left hoards of wine. After some horrible hangovers, we decided that the wine was still "green." That explains why the Germans left it, I'm sure. A way to "enhance" over 400 gallons of green wine had to be found. Before long, my crew chief, Sergeant Grainger, came to our rescue.

Behind the building that was used as the squadron's chapel stood a dense grove of trees. On a clear and calm day one just might notice a thin column of smoke rising above those trees. My crew chief, Sergeant Grainger, was the NCO in charge of the Squadron Distillery. With the help of several people, needed equipment and supplies were commandeered to erect and operate the still. The alcohol was boiled off the green wine and flowed into a large container. After being bottled, it was labeled "Grainger's Gruel." Captain Mitzloff, the squadron flight surgeon, tested the stuff and warned everyone to use it very sparingly as it tested out at 190 proof. Potent wasn't the word for it; just a little in a bottle of Coke or 7-Up took care of any sinus problems anyone had. A small bottle went for five dollars or twenty marks. Another claim the 33rd PRS made was that it was the first American unit to make real moonshine on German soil in WW II. A Lightning squadron producing "White Lightning." This claim did not make the Stars and Stripes newspaper, and for good reason. To protect the Sgt. from any personal damage, the labels on the bottles were soon changed to read "P-38 Punch."

One night, some nurses were invited over from a nearby evacuation hospital for a punch party. Someone provided a record player for dance music and the party turned out great. The nurses had such a good time they had to be helped home. The next morning, a lot of 33rd'ers were sick in quarters. Thankfully, it was an overcast day all over Europe and no missions were scheduled. We told the nurses if anyone asked where we got the punch, it was from a passing Army Tank Unit. When visiting firemen came to the 33rd, we told them the same story. Several even asked the name of the tank unit as the punch was outstanding. No one ever questioned our story.

In Germany, there was a hard and fast rule against fraternizing with the enemy, especially the females. Nearby in the village of Hinsbeck, we discovered some Russian women working in a field. They were five by five and looked as though they could play for the Dallas Cowboys. Some of the enlisted men went into the village that night and later reported "a bang-up time." I'm sure they took along some squadron punch. The squadron Line Chief, M/Sgt Marshall Batchelor, loved to spin yarns about his life in the hills of Kentucky before the war. He told one about a recent visit to a German village nearby. The good Sgt. was walking down the street when he came across a German soldier sitting in a rocking chair on the front porch Well now, Sergeant Batchelor stopped and went over to the house and ordered the soldier to surrender. The soldier just leaned over and said,

"The Geneva Convention prohibits the capture of a soldier home on furlough." Sergeant Batchelor just walked away shaking his head.

More replacement pilots kept coming in as the older ones, when completing their 75 missions, rotated back to the States. One of the new pilots was Lieutenant Bill Graunke from St. Paul, Nebraska. Being from neighboring small towns in east central Nebraska, we became good friends. Bill loved to fly and did so at every opportunity. Bill was a good man and a very good pilot. Every single squadron member liked Bill a lot.

After 15 combat missions, I was eligible for a week of rest and recuperation (R&R). I could go anywhere Army transportation would take me. Several pilots went down to Nice, France, where, rumor had it that the French "dollies" lay on the beach with not much on. Jim Foster and I decided to fly over to London for our week off. The 363rd Tactical Reconnaissance Group had a C-47 Goony Bird that gave us a ride over to London's Heathrow airport. Jim and I caught the shuttle bus into London and got off at the famous Grovner's Square Allied Officers Club. The military billeting office directed us to an area nearby where we found a small flat that was for let. We rented it for the whole week. The flat had two beds, a small kitchen and a bath. That's all we needed; it was perfect. After checking in, the first place we headed was Piccadilly Circus. It was sort of like Times Square in New York City, only better. The two of us went from pub to pub that first night and had a ball. On the second night in Piccadilly, Jim found a girl he really liked. It was four days before I saw Jim again.

I had a cousin stationed north of London near Birmingham so I decided to catch the train and go visit him. At the main gate to this huge army supply depot, a guard took me to a room where a phone was available. In a few minutes my cousin, S/Sgt Jim Gordon, was located. After I told him where I was, he said to stay put and he would be over shortly. Jim and I had a good visit and he took the next day off so we could get in some sightseeing. Along with that, we did some pub-hopping too. Jim's brother, Bill, was just there for a visit the week before. Bill was a captain in the Army's Red Ball Express Transportation Battalion. The Red Ball Express supply truck company supported General Patton's Third Army during its sweep across France and then Germany. Bill was the company commander of an all-black unit. He was the only white man in the company and his first sergeant was the one who kept unruly drivers in check. The morning of the third day, after telling my cousin goodbye and good luck, I was walking across a park to take a short cut to the train station, when all of a sudden, I heard some talking behind a large grove of trees. When I reached the end of the grove, I heard a loud command, "Achtung!" Stopping to see what this was all about, I found, behind a wire fence were several hundred German POWs. Everyone was at attention, and their leader gave me a smart salute. Using sign language, I told the Oberleutnant to put his men at ease. He shouted something and turned back to me. Talking rapidly in German that I could not understand, he pointed to my wings. He said something about "Lotse." I then nodded my head and again he pointed to my wings, "Ya Lotse," he kept saying, and the men started grinning. Using sign language, I told him I flew an airplane called "Der Gabelsschwanz Teufel." That's what the Germans called the P-38-the "Forked Tailed Devil." As I started to leave, he again called them to attention, turned and saluted me. Now here I was, a Second Lieutenant getting all this attention. I just couldn't believe it, but I returned the salute. As the Geneva Convention says, officers of all nations should recognize each other. I guess the Oberleutnant put them at ease as I never heard any more commands as I left the park. Back at the squadron, Major Roberts got a big laugh out of my experience. He said the Germans never showed him any such respect. They just shot at him.

When I returned to the flat in London that afternoon, I didn't notice any evidence that Jim had spent any time there at all. After freshening up, I walked the four blocks to the Grovners Square Allied Officers Club to have a cold beer and see who was there. The only reason the beer was cold was because the Americans had installed a large cooler. Everyone but Americans accepted beer at room temperature. My thoughts about that were, "Bad in the summer but okay in the winter. Later on while I was eating dinner, in walked Jim with his girl friend. She was quite young, very pretty, and unusually shy for a British girl. They joined me for dinner and I heard all about their three fabulous days together. Jim then shocked me by saying that he and Jenny planned to stay in the flat that last night in London. I said, "Jim, there is no way I'm going to sleep in that flat if the two of you are staying there tonight." He said he was nearly broke and had to stay there. On leaving, I asked Jim which bed he was going to sleep in. He gave me a big grin as I headed for the BOQ (bachelor officers' quarters) to spend the night. On the flight back to our squadron, Jim talked some more about what a grand time he had with Jenny. She had taken him to her house to meet her mother and grandmother. Her father was in the British Army somewhere in Italy. Jim became the man of the house and they pub-hopped every night until closing time. Where he slept was not discussed.

The day after my R&R, I was briefed on a special mission to support the nearby 405th Fighter Bomber Group. That mission was initially described in Chapter One. Now it continues:

After being hit by flak on that day in April, I tried to steer my airplane past the front lines. With both engines at idle RPM, my P-38 was just a big glider descending rapidly. Knowing I couldn't stay airborne much longer, I looked frantically for a place to get the airplane on the ground in one piece. Soon I noticed a meadow that looked level and I circled it once. Now I had to come in and put her down. To get as slow as possible, I put the gear out and lowered all the flaps. In those days, the thinking was that an extended gear would slow you down, even if it broke off. Coming in gear up on your belly might break up the airplane and cause a fire. Staggering in over the fence, I set the airplane down and, to my surprise, the main gear was rolling along on the meadow. When I lowered the nose wheel, all hell broke loose, as it went too far down. My first thought was that my nose wheel didn't extend but the gear indicator, called the "barber pole," showed all three struts and wheels down and locked.

As the airplane was plowing through that meadow, I was afraid of flipping over and catching fire as I had quite a bit of fuel left in my tanks. Thankfully the airplane came to a quick and sudden stop. Turning off all fuel and electrical switches, I opened the canopy and scrambled out like a scared rabbit. Looking at my nose landing gear, I realized that there was no nose wheel, just a piece of strut. A big chunk of shrapnel from the flak burst must have hit the nose wheel well, which was just under my feet in the cockpit The large piece of shrapnel pierced the nose wheel door like it was paper and blew the wheel off along with a piece of strut. Before coming in, when I lowered the gear, the nose strut came out and told the indicator it was down and locked which indeed it was. My nose wheel, along with a piece of the strut, must be lying somewhere in a German field If the flak burst had not hit the nose wheel, it would have been all over for me in a second. Besides the nose wheel strut damage, I counted 27 shrapnel holes on the bottom of my airplane.

There was a hole in the oil cooler on one engine and flak holes on the oil lines of the other. Now I knew why my oil temperatures were high; most of my oil must have leaked out. Here I was in this meadow and I couldn't tell which side of the front lines I was on. There was no artillery noise. It was very peaceful but the poor airplane looked a sight sitting there with its nose resting on the ground. First, I removed my .45 pistol and hid it in the airplane. If I was captured by the Germans, I didn't want to be armed. There were rumors of Germans shooting downed pilots that still wore side arms. I had to decide whether to stay with the airplane or try to escape and evade. Finally I decided to stay with the airplane. Before long, I saw a vehicle coming my way. From a distance I couldn't tell if it was German or American. I said a quick prayer that it wasn't German. As it got closer, I saw the white star on the side door and knew it was American. Four soldiers greeted me with, "We saw you circling and figured you were in trouble." Boy, was I glad to see them. They marveled at the number of flak hits and said that the burst must have been pretty close to the airplane. Before I abandoned my airplane, I had to get the film magazine off the big camera in the nose section. They helped me and soon we had it off and were getting ready to leave when one of the soldiers said, "Let's get out of here; we're right in the middle of no-man's land." That's the area between the front lines. I then remembered my pistol and parachute. After I recovered them, we boarded the truck and drove back to their unit. They insisted I ride up front with the driver. I inquired as to their unit and it turned out that they operated a Field Artillery Battery. Arriving at their site, I arranged to have them send a message to my squadron to let them know I was safe and sound. I was put up in a tent that had a small coke stove. The chow that night was in cans, but when heated on the little coke stove, it was quite good. In jest, I mentioned that earlier, I was afraid I might be eating sauerkraut that night. The Battery Commander was a young lieutenant and we talked long into the night.

In the flight operations room back at my squadron, Sergeant Davis was removing the missing in action notice beside my name on the daily flight board. They had just received a message from 9th Air Force Headquarters saying that I had been rescued by the U.S. Army and was okay. The next day the Field Artillery site received a message asking them to take me over to an auxiliary field a few miles away. I would be picked up that same afternoon. I told my Army friends that I sure wished I had known that emergency landing strip was there, I could have used it. After a few hours, here came a piggy-back P-38. To my surprise, the pilot was my squadron commander, Major Roberts. He insisted that we visit the site where my airplane was located so he could assess its condition. He said he needed to brief Captain Frush, our aircraft maintenance officer, on the damage.. I had already told him but he wanted to see for himself.

Major Roberts noted that the airplane needed a nose landing gear strut and wheel, two propellers and some extensive skin repair. Last but not least, he said, "And two oil coolers and new oil lines." We found a place for my film magazine in the nose section of his plane and climbed aboard. I would like to have flown the airplane back to Y-55, but didn't have the nerve to ask Major Roberts to sit on the shelf. It was to be my second piggy-back ride in a P-38, the first was at Will Rogers Field during overseas training. Major Roberts repeated over and over how lucky I was to survive that flak burst. He then said, "That nose wheel saved your life, Tom." I couldn't have agreed more.

After a thorough de-briefing by squadron intelligence and maintenance people, I went to see the flight surgeon, Doc Mitzloff. He wanted to make sure I was okay to return to flight status. I now had 16 missions under my belt. In two days, I was flying again and it sure felt good to see those engines running smoothly with normal oil temperatures.

While I was gone, a letter from Freddie arrived. She was terribly lonesome and wanted to come and visit me. I thought to myself, "My God woman, don't you know there's a war on?" I tried to find Bake to see if he heard from Simone, but he was flying a mission and wouldn't be back for a while. Later, when I saw him, he said yes he did get a letter from Simone. Both of them wanted to come for a visit right away. Robert (Bake) Baker was beside himself trying to figure out what to do with Simone as he was getting close to eligibility to rotate home. I suggested he talk to Major Roberts about it and Bake said, "Tom, you go and try him out first. You know Freddie is hot to go home with you." I waited until Major Roberts was in a good mood; then I asked him for some private conversation. Before I could say anything to him, he said, What are you and Baker gong to do with those two camp followers?" "I wish I knew," was my reply. We went on talking about my options, and marriage was one of them. Major Roberts said he didn't think marriage was a good idea, but that I should talk to our Group Commander, Colonel Shelley. It took a while, but I finally got up nerve enough to request a private meeting with the Group Commander. In the meantime, letters arrived like the morning paper. After I told Colonel Shelly about my dilemma, he said, "It's not a good idea right now but if you want to come back after the war, marry the girl and then take her home with you, it just might work." End of meeting.

I didn't know it at the time, but I learned later that Freddie had borrowed money from her mother to buy a wedding dress and other things. I guess she thought she had me hooked and there were times when I thought she did too. I wrote Freddie a long letter explaining that due to Army Regulations and counseling, marriage could not be approved at this time. Maybe after the war, if she still wanted that, I could come back and get it done. We would have one more get-to-

gether. I was there to fly photo intelligence missions and I thought I
had better get back to reality and my work. This social whirl had to
come to an end. I received two more letters before they finally stopped.
Both really scorched me and I couldn't blame her, I no doubt led her
on during the past three and a half months. Maybe she had a good case
for "breach of promise" against me.

On April 16 my squadron relocated our operations again. This
time we occupied another former German airfield at Gutersloh-
Marienfeld. The field was called Air Strip Y-99 and had very nice
facilities. The runways were in good condition as were the buildings.
Now the scent of war's end was in the air. I flew several missions from
there and never saw any opposition-neither fighters nor flak. We called
those missions "milk runs"-a piece of cake. The front lines were moving so fast toward Berlin that in only eight days, we moved again! To
say that the 9th Air Force was mobile was an understatement. On these
frequent moves, the pilots flew the airplanes, followed by a surface
caravan of all the men and ground equipment, including our baggage.
The photo lab moves required several trucks since it was a large operation with lots and lots of heavy equipment. They were always the last
ones to arrive at a new base of operations known as Allied Air Strips.

This move brought us to still another former German airfield at
Brunswick-Waggum. Its designation was Allied Air Strip R-37. My
mission total was now up to 24 and it looked like the war was winding
down quickly. Major Roberts had rotated back to the States and our
new commander was Major Harry Trimble, a West Point graduate.
Major Trimble, through some of his West Point buddies, arranged a
trip to the front lines to see the action for himself. Three other pilots
and I decided to volunteer to accompany him. Little did I know what
I would experience at the front lines. Early one morning, we got into a
weapons carrier (large jeep) and drove all day. Everyone had to wear
steel helmets and carry rifles. Being at the front lines is an indescrib-
able experience.. I had flown over the front lines many times but this
was my first visit on the ground. Earlier, when I had to make an emergency landing between the front lines, I didn't see much activity. Now
Field artillery barrages were continuing both day and night. At every
check point, an MP would warn us to stay on the road because land
mines could be anywhere. I had seen war from the air but this was
something else. The sounds of war are not very pleasant. Now I knew
what the foot soldier had to endure.

The captain driving the weapons carrier said we would be staying
the night in an old bombed- out hotel in a nearby village. We ate C-
rations right out of the can and the captain found some Cokes some-

where. It's too bad we didn't have any P-38 punch, someone said. There wasn't much sleep that night as German shells hit pretty close, causing the old building to shake a few times. The pilot-visitors were huddled together like four puppies. Dawn came to a very quiet war zone. The captain said it usually is that way at dawn after a long night of shelling. I think both sides just went to bed. After a breakfast of more C-rations, the weapons carrier was turning around leaving the village when suddenly there was a very loud explosion. The vehicle leaped and fell on it's side. We had driven over a land mine. It felt like the left rear wheel had run over it. None of us were injured, but the poor vehicle was knocked out of commission. Now we had no vehicle and were afraid to walk anywhere for fear of more land mines. Soon, the captain flagged down a military vehicle and, after some conversation, he came back and said someone was going to send transportation. After we had sat on the road for about an hour, a six-by-six truck came and picked us up. We headed out of there quickly. Every MP that stopped us warned that rumors were flying that German soldiers, dressed in American uniforms, might be in the area. Each time the MP's stopped us, our credentials were carefully checked. They asked questions, to check our accents, I think. After a long and dreary ride in that truck, we arrived back at our air strip safe and somewhat sound. I had always been told, since my first day in the Army, never volunteer for anything. I had not listened very well to my subconscious mind that day.

For extraordinary performance of duty in action against the enemy, the 33rd PRS was awarded a Presidential Unit Citation. We saw action in every battle on the Western front. The war was winding down now. On my last two missions I didn't see a thing-no flak and no enemy airplanes. I had now flown 25 missions over enemy territory and wished for more.

Quartered near our air strip were literally hundreds of displaced persons (DPs). We hired several of them to work on the airfield. A young unwashed, but eager, Soviet DP quickly won a place for himself in the pilots' ready room. We called him Mike; and he became our coffee and sandwich boy and mascot. He thought Spam was the greatest thing ever invented. For every sandwich he made for the pilots, I think he ate two. Mike was gaining weight and growing up daily, it seemed.

Thirsty for knowledge, Mike picked up English very quickly He could take a wrist watch completely apart, clean it and put it back together. The watch would always run. The young lad's name was Michael Ferapentow, a 15-year-old orphan from the Ukraine. He looked no more than 12, and said he had no desire to go back home after the war. One day he said he only wanted three things out of life: learn English, go to America and join the American Air Force. Mike's dreams would later come true. Mike learned English and, dressed in an Army Air Force uniform, went to the United States aboard a troop ship. An after the fact act of Congress legalized his entry. He completed high school in just two years and joined the United States Air Force. His American name became Michael Ferris. After 20 years, he retired as a Master Sergeant, USAF. I have never heard a more beautiful success story. Harry Trimble deserves all the credit in the world for paving the path for that boy to realize his dreams.

On May 1, reports came that Adolph Hitler was found dead in his Berlin bunker. That same day, three new pilots checked in - Lieutenants Devoe, Cunningham and Flippo. As Jim Foster was TDY at another air strip, Lieutenant Flippo became my new roommate. The next day the three new pilots went up on a local training flight. Only two came back. Lieutenant Devoe said the three of them were in a formation turn and flew into some clouds. That was the last they saw or heard from Lieutenant Flippo. Ground observers reported a P-38 coming out of a cloud upside down, and flew straight into the ground. Lieutenant Wilson M. Flippo had only been married a month. I had the very difficult job of packing his personal effects to be sent back home to his young wife.

On a sunny spring day in early May, I taxied my P-38 out of the revetment with my wing-man right behind me. He was a young 2nd Lieutenant on his first combat mission. Our targets were at Leipzig, about 90 miles south of Berlin. My target was the bridge that spanned the wide Gisterbecken canal. My wing-man was to shoot the city's marshaling yards. After shooting our targets, I radioed my wing-man to join up as I decided to go after a "target of opportunity"- Berlin. I took the chance because I was young and adventurous and had plenty of fuel. As we reached the famous city, I signaled my wing-man to start his cameras. We made a pass over the city with our 24-inch vertical cameras rolling. Suddenly, I noticed flashes on the ground. Thinking it was flak guns shooting at us, we tore out of there at full throttle. My first flight over Berlin lasted about 30 seconds. When we landed back at R-37, my crew chief crawled up on the wing like always, except this time he was all excited and yelled, "Sir, guess what happened, the Russians took Berlin today." That explained the flashes on the ground, the Russians were firing artillery in their wild celebration. It wasn't flak after all. I had just completed my 26th and final combat mission of WW II. When the photo lab processed my film, I was called over there. The lab chief, Captain Warendorf, wanted to know what the "unscheduled pictures" were. I told him the truth and he smiled and said they were very good. They were the first combat pictures the squadron had of Berlin. He'd take them right over to Group HQ. Group liked them so much, they took copies to 9th AF HQ. Soon I was standing before my squadron commander trying to explain all this. When I finished he said, "Well, Tom, we have just received orders to stand down and no more missions are scheduled. It looks like the war is finally over. By the way, your request for a week's R&R has been approved." On the way into Brussels in a jeep for my R&R, I heard Winston Churchill's famous speech. It was Victory in Europe - **VE Day!!**

Loudspeakers were blaring as my jeep snaked along the streets of Brussels heading for the famous Metropole hotel. It was the oldest and grandest hotel in the city at the time. The lobby was full of people celebrating and drinking from wine bottles. I was assigned a room and had a bellboy take my luggage up, as I had important business ahead. I had to find Freddie. She no longer lived in the apartment with her mother. It seemed an aged sister needed her mother to care for her out in the suburbs. Freddie now lived with her best friend Micky in another part of town.

With some difficulty, I found the apartment and rang the door bell. Nothing happened. I rang again-still nothing. Now my heart was beginning to sink as I was sure everyone was downtown celebrating, lost in a sea of humanity. Now I would never find her. After the fourth ring, I heard some voices on the second floor balcony. Looking up, I saw Freddie and Micky waving and shouting.

That night and the following night, we had little sleep. The whole city of Brussels saw no sleep. Freddie, Micky and I were caught up in the huge crowd downtown, and we marched up and down the streets singing. Bottles of wine and French bread were passed around. Soon I found myself singing French songs right along with the rest of them. By afternoon of the second day, I was so tired I just had to get some sleep. Micky decided she was a third wheel and went home. Soon Freddie and I found a park and immediately stretched out on the soft grass in the shade of a large tree. Using her lap for a pillow, I was soon dead to the world. Here I was sleeping in a public park when I had a nice comfortable room at the Hotel Metropole.

Hours later I awoke to the sounds of a bird singing just above us. I mentioned to Freddie that it sounded like a nightingale but I thought they only sang at night. She said they sing whenever they are happy. With that, Freddie started singing softly to me in French. Later in a small cafe, Freddie and I stuffed ourselves on crepe suzettes. That week in Brussels was one I will never forget. After all this celebrating, Freddie was sure I was going to take her back to the United States with me. I tried to explain the only way I could do it was to go home, leave the Air Force and come back as a civilian. She didn't go for that at all. She was afraid I would soon find an American girl when I got home. Having had such a good time, I was going to find it tough leaving her there. The air courier was to leave the next day for my base at Brunswick. Freddie insisted on going to the airport with me to catch the C-47 courier. The farewell was sad as there are no words to describe the parting of two people who loved each other so much. After much hugging and kissing, I had to say goodbye. To leave her standing there crying was one of the hardest things I have ever had to do. The last thing she said to me was, "If I can't have you, I will go with the Red Cross and work in Poland." Ironically, our paths would briefly cross again 24 years later in Meridian, Mississippi, at a squadron reunion. When she saw me in the hotel lobby, her mouth flew open and her eyes got really big. She abruptly turned and ran down a hall. I never saw her again and never found out why she was even there. No one at the reunion seemed to know either, or they just weren't talking about it. I was inclined to believe the latter.

Back at Brunswick, the VE-Day celebration was still in progress.. Most looked like they had hundred dollar hangovers. Soon we moved again to a former Luftwaffe airfield east of Kassel, Germany. The air strip, known as R-11, was located near a small town called Eschwege on the river Werra.

If you smile when nobody else is around, you really mean it.
—Andy Rooney

My airplane - her name was Queenie.
Resting at Allied Air Strip Y-10 near Brussels, Belgium 1945
Author's collection

Before going on my first
combat mission over
Germany from Allied Air
Strip Y-10 near Brussels,
Belgium
January 23, 1945
Author's collection

Just returned from my first
combat mission.
Because of clouds, saw no
German fighters.
1945
Author's collection

Pilots of the 33rd Photo Reconnaissance Squadron
Allied Air Strip Y-55, Venlo, Holland - 1945
I am in the first row, fifth from the right
Author's collection

With fellow pilots Bill McGrath and Burl Stokes
at Allied Air Strip R-37, Brunswick, Germany - 1945
Author's collection

P-38 Cockpit
Author's collection

With my friend Freddie
Roulez in front of her
Brussels apartment - 1945.
We had a close wartime
relationship. She very nearly
became my war bride.
Author's collection

I was shot down by flak on my 15th mission. The airplane was badly damaged, but I was not injured.
Author's collection

The skies over Germany were filled with flak bursts on most combat missions.
Author's collection

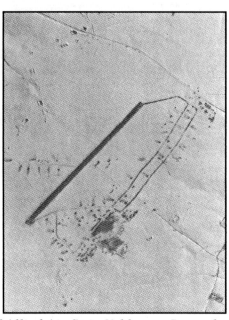

Aerial view of Allied Air Strip Y-10 near Brussels. Aircraft were
parked in individual revetments for safety. 1945
Author's collection

POW barracks at Nazi concentration camp
Buchenwald, Germany - 1945
Author's collection

*POWs taking a break from cleaning bits of bones out of
the crematoria
Buchenwald, Germany - 1945
Author's collection*

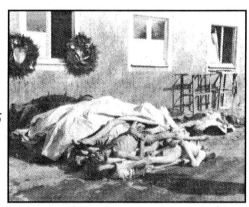

*Bodies of POWs waiting
for the furnace
Buchenwald, Germany - 1945
Author's collection*

*Buchenwald Cremation
Furnaces - 1945
Author's collection*

Body specimens used in weird experiments by Ilse Koch, known
as the Bitch of Buchenwald
1945
Author's collection

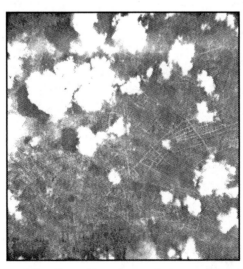

Photo of Berlin taken on my last combat mission
May 3, 1945
Author's collection

CHAPTER NINE

THE AMERICAN CENTURY

Work is not an end in itself; there must always be time enough for love.

—*Robert Heinlein*

Now that the fighting had stopped and the war was officially over, German ground and air forces were surrendering to the American forces in droves. At Brunswick, I saw three different German aircraft come in over the field with their landing gear down and landing lights on. That was the international signal of surrender. Sometimes, they had a white flag flying out the cockpit window to make sure we didn't shoot them.. It was unbelievable how many people climbed out of those airplanes after landing. An FW-190 came in and three people piled out of it. It was only a single seat airplane! Another time, a Stuka Dive Bomber, the JU-188, came in and 11 people climbed out of it. That airplane carried a crew of three! After getting out of the airplanes, the Germans put their hands over their heads and were peacefully taken away by the MP's to a quickly improvised POW camp. We had won the war and the Germans had surrendered quickly. They did so because they felt they would get better treatment from the Americans than they would from the Russians. They were right.

The end of the war triggered wild celebrations by the Americans. People who never drank quickly became drunk as skunks. Some of the nearby DP's came over to the squadron, near Brunswick and became totally drunk after only a couple of drinks. At the squadron, the enlisted men did their drinking outside while the officers celebrated in their club. It got really loud and the OD (Officer of the Day) went in and tried to quiet them down a little. The revelers just ignored him, whereupon, the OD took out his .45 pistol and fired into the ceiling to get their attention. The celebrants would have none of that and promptly took the pistol away from him. The party went on almost all night. Some P-51 pilots came in and it wasn't long before a donnybrook broke out. No one could stop the mayhem, and nobody cared much-the war was finally over. The next day, Doc Mitzloff had a long line of patients waiting for him. Nobody knew, or really cared, who started or ended the fracas.

After looking over his sorry-looking crew the next day, Sergeant Marshall Batchelor, our line chief, said, "I don't think we were indoctrinated right. We were told that if we were captured to do this and so forth but nobody told us what to do if we won!" One day some Army tanks came rumbling by the airstrip and wanted to do some bartering. They had a bag full of German cameras and pistols they wanted to trade for American whiskey. Each officer in the squadron received a monthly ration of whiskey and cigarettes. I traded two bottles of Three Feathers blended whisky for a 35mm camera and a new Mauser hand gun. Others in the squadron did well too. I felt sorry for my crew chief and gave him a bottle to barter with, instead, he just kept it for himself. After all the horse trading, the tank guys left in their noisy machines happy as larks with their catch of many bottles of American whiskey. They didn't care how good or bad it was, they drank it straight from the bottle-no chaser needed.

Our new air strip at Eschwege had one grass runway and the parking areas were also grass. Most of the buildings were made of stone and were in pretty good condition. Even our big photo lab was situated in a large building instead of the usual tent. The river Werra, about 60 yards wide, ran right by the edge of the field. The town of Eschwege was off limits to everyone as we still couldn't fraternize with any of the local females. One day one of the enlisted men, who spoke some German, shouted across the river to a fraulein. He said he would give her a candy bar if she would take off her clothes! Yelling back she said, "For a candy bar, I am yours." That scene caused unbelievable excitement among the troops. That same night, several of the men forged the river looking for some fun. The P-38 punch was long gone and so was our squadron distillery non-commissioned officer. He had rotated home some time ago.

Soon, word came down from the 363rd Group about a big mission they had for us. All of Western Europe needed to be photo-mapped since existing maps were old and inaccurate. Three reconnaissance squadrons would be assigned certain areas to cover. The aerial photos were taken in long, overlapping strips suitable for forming into a huge mosaic of the area. This job took a long time, since we could only work in good weather. We stood down a lot of days because of the clouds. To get good detail, the photo runs were made at 15,000 feet. All the new pilots were put to work on this project; most of the older ones had rotated back home. Two of the older pilots made a deal with the Air Force. Instead of rotating back to the States, they asked for a 30-day leave and then volunteered to come back to the ETO to assist in this large mapping project. To their surprise, the request was granted.

One day, less than a month after Captains Miller and Scott had come back to the ETO, Captain Scott's plane, while on a mission, caught on fire. Instead of bailing out, he tried to ride it in. In the process, the airplane exploded and Scotty was killed. Before the squadron went home, we lost a total of ten pilots, seven to the war and three in local accidents. One of the local accidents involved Captain Fred Evans flying a piggy-back P-38. His passenger was an American Red Cross woman. For some unknown reason, the airplane hit a mountain peak and both were killed.

In early June, word came down from Group that if anyone wanted to visit one of the Nazi concentration camps, a trip was being arranged. Several others and I decided to take the trip. In a couple of days, a six-by-six truck came by and off we went to Camp Buchenwald, armed with our cameras. The camp was located about 60 miles east of Weimar, Germany. Upon arriving, we encountered a horrible sight. Human bodies were piled high waiting to be cremated. Those still alive were skin and bone and they just stared at us with blank expressions. The camp had been liberated April 12, the same day President Roosevelt died. Some of the POWs had left, but most of them stayed-they had no place else to go. I noticed piles of ashes everywhere. Buchenwald was only one of many such camps located in Germany and Poland. The guide told us of a German woman named Ilse Koch who was known as the Bitch of Buchenwald. She did a lot of weird experiments on human bodies. I didn't really want to but, as I had my camera with me, I took a lot of pictures that day. I still have the album today but find it difficult to look at it even 50 years later.

During the summer of 1945, between mapping missions, we played a lot of sports. There were leagues for volleyball, baseball and softball. On the pilots' baseball team, I alternated between third base and pitching and everyone had a grand time. A short distance from the airfield was a public spa and strangely enough, we could go over there. A lot of girls were there but no amount of candy bars could bribe them into doing anything. One saucy fraulein had the nerve to wear a cardboard sign on her butt that read: "VERBOTEN."

One day, arriving back at the airfield, I found all kinds of excitement going on. It seemed that one of the new pilots was up on a local flight and he landed so hot he slid into the Werra River! All you could see of the airplane was the top of the canopy. Army engineers were summoned and, after a long struggle, managed to pull the airplane out of the water. George Kovich, the pilot, said his brakes failed-nobody believed him for a minute. The P-38 was a slick airplane and hard to slow down. It was difficult to get rid of excess speed on short final approach. On that day, the runway was just not long enough for George to get his airplane stopped in time. He soon was known as "Deep Six George."

On July 25, I was sent out on a single mapping mission. I was to reshoot some of the areas as the original pictures didn't turn out so well. That turned out to be the last official photo mission flown by the 33rd Photo Reconnaissance Squadron in WW II. The squadron now had two piggyback airplanes and they were put to good use. Every pilot treated his crew chief and other deserving ground support personnel to a "joyride." They couldn't believe the speed of the airplane. I didn't subject my passengers to much in the way of acrobatics as I didn't want someone's lunch in my lap.

Reports came in saying we were going, not home, but to the Pacific Theater of Operations to fly a new airplane, the Lockheed P-80 Jet-the Shooting Star. All the pilots were elated as jets were the coming thing. We were to go to the states temporarily for training in the P-80 and then on to the Pacific Theater. On August 8, notice came from Group that we had to ferry our P-38s to France where they would be stored in a bone yard. The depot storage yard was near Reims. Flying the P-38 for the last time was a very moving and emotional experience. I'll never forget that last flight, especially the landing; those main wheels just hummed as they kissed the runway. My airplane, along with a lot of others, died that afternoon. They were bulldozed together and then burned. The pilots were all torn up over that and it took me a long time to purge my mind of that awful event. When I returned to Eschwege, official word was received that the squadron had to pack up. We were going to France where we would board a ship for home.. It turned out to be not that simple. On August 10, a train pulling "forty & eight" boxcars came rolling in. We all laughed at this sight. It wasn't so funny when we learned that was our transportation to France.

During WW I, the forty & eight trains were used a lot. The story goes that each boxcar held forty men and eight horses, hence the name Forty and Eight. We soon learned that on this trip, twenty men and one officer would be assigned to each car. Of the 15 boxcars, I was assigned to car number 7. I wasn't looking forward to the train ride to France in a small boxcar full of thirsty, hungry and girl-starved men.

The higher ranking officers went to western France by air. Facilities for the rest of the squadron would be ready when the train arrived in a couple of days. During the months in Germany, the squadron acquired some extra equipment for the motor pool. There were four BMW motorcycles and three Mercedes-Benz sedans. When first acquired, they quickly received a military olive drab (OD) paint job with white stars on the hood and each front door. The motorcycles had a white star painted on the front and rear fenders. Our top officers rode around in style. Before we left Germany, there was a meeting of the top officers and top NCO's. Nobody questioned where these vehicles came from but now everyone wondered what to do with them. It was decided that seven of our craftiest horse traders would drive them to Paris. The paperwork was arranged so they appeared to be on official business, if any MP questioned them en route. The only logical place to get rid of this equipment was the Paris black market. Later, when the horse traders showed up at Camp Detroit, in western France, they were toting six bags full of French francs. By prior arrangement, all squadron members received an equal share, regardless of rank. Most military units acquired some foreign vehicles during the war and what they did with them at war's end, nobody really knows. I suspect most units did what the 33rd did, the only practical thing to do.

The war in Europe was over but World War II was still going on in the Pacific and that's where we were headed. The little boxcars had ample C-rations, sodas and water aboard for my train ride to France, but it was not very pleasant as it was bumpy and hot. After two days and nights, we arrived at Camp Detroit not far from Le Havre where the ships were. I had 20 men when I started out from Eschwege, but upon arrival at our destination, I counted only 18. During the last night, two had jumped ship and went AWOL. Camp Detroit was a huge tent city and, of course, it was muddy. There was one very large tent which served several purposes. There we ate our meals, held meetings, attended church services every Sunday and watched nightly movies. The chow was so-so but always hot which made it better than C-rations. From somewhere, quantities of French beer and wine showed up. The wine was much better than the beer. During the day, we played cards and just relaxed. The nightly movie had standing room only crowds, no matter what was showing. It was too muddy to play any type of sports so we just waited for word of our moving closer to Le Havre. Some of the men were concerned about the large amount of French francs they suddenly had acquired. Our leaders said that if anyone questioned them, to say that they had won it in a poker game.

On August 14, 1945, all hell broke loose in camp. Word was received that the Japanese had surrendered. The war in the Pacific was over! World War II was finally over! **It was V-J Day!** Immediately a drinking party broke out and lasted for two days. Now that the war was over, there would never be any more fighting, or so we hoped. Now the Army didn't know what to do with us because we were not going to the Pacific and didn't have enough "points" to go home. Units accumulated a certain number of points for each month of over-seas duty. Others behind us had more points and should go home ahead of us. In typical Army fashion, we moved to Camp Lucky-Strike, even closer to the harbor at Le Havre where the troopship was anchored and waiting to take us home.

Camp Lucky-Strike was another tent city but not as large as the previous ones. We fell into the same old routine-eat, sleep, read , relax and watch the nightly movie. We soon moved again, this time to Camp Twenty Grand, another much smaller tent city.. We stayed there until September 25 when we finally boarded the big troop ship, the USS General Richardson. After the gangplanks were lifted, we steamed out of Le Havre for the promised land-the good ole USA. I had come over on a Liberty ship with 37 passengers; now I was going home on a troop ship with 1,200 passengers. For the first two hours, the ride was smooth; but when we hit the ocean currents of the Atlantic, the big ship pitched and heaved day and night. My stateroom probably accommodated two in peace time; now eight of us shared the same space, thanks to double and triple-decker bunks. The only luxury we had was our own bath. Everyone just talked, played cards a lot and ate meals in shifts. When the last breakfast shift was finished, the first lunch shift started. It went that way for six days. All meals were very good and, at the evening meal, ice cream was always served for desert. I couldn't get enough of that wonderful stuff. Enduring life without ice cream for a whole year had indeed been a sacrifice.

Onboard were two famous people: Lieutenant Dan Daily, the Hollywood singer/actor, and the well known "Glacier Priest" Father Bernard Hubbard. Dan Daily gave nightly performances for the troops and they cheered him wildly. I was very fortunate to be assigned the same dining table as Father Hubbard. I had the distinct pleasure of eating three meals a day with him the whole trip. At each meal, he sat at the head of the table of about 20 people. Before eating, he always said Grace and invited everybody to join him. He talked constantly about his life with the Eskimos in Alaska. Father Hubbard was born in San Francisco in 1888. During his 30 years in Alaska, he had taught, written books, lectured and had been an outstanding photographer. He developed and printed his own pictures so that he could control the quality of his work. During WW II, he was an advisor to the U.S. Army on cold weather clothing and equipment. He also taught classes in Arctic survival. At one time, he was Chaplain for the Navy Seabees on the island of Attu. During the latter part of the war in Europe, he gave lectures to the armed forces. On May 28, 1962, while preparing to say his daily Mass, Father Hubbard suffered a heart attack. Fifteen minutes later, the famous Glacier Priest was dead.

On October 3, 1945, the USS General Richardson, pulled into Boston harbor escorted by several large tug boats shooting large sprays of water into the air. The atmosphere on the ship was electric with joy. We were safely home from the war. A brass band was playing when I stepped off the gangplank onto American soil. I wanted to bend over and kiss it. Right in front of me stood a pretty young Red Cross woman who handed me a cup of coffee and a doughnut. The 33rd Squadron members were then bused to nearby Camp Miles Standish for processing. All my gear was in two duffle bags and one B-4 bag. The sergeant that checked me only wanted my .45 pistol. He let me keep all the rest of my original issue of government clothing and supplies, some of which I still have today.

On October 4, 1945, without ceremony, the 33rd Photo Reconnaissance Squadron was quietly deactivated. The officers slowly made the rounds wishing the men well. There was talk of having a squadron reunion someday and everyone thought it was a good idea. Thirteen years later on July 4, 1958, the 33rd PRS held their first squadron reunion in Chicago. I couldn't attend as I was stationed in Spain on active duty with the Air Force.

From official records located in the archives of the United States Air Force at Maxwell AFB, Alabama, the following is noted:

The 33rd PRS had distinguished itself, it was the first:
- Air Force Tactical Unit to go overseas trained and equipped to provide both day and night photo reconnaissance.
- To develop and use photographic procedures and equipment modification that greatly increased reconnaissance unit production and efficiency under field conditions. Many of its recommendations were adopted by the Air Force.
- Photo Reconnaissance outfit to "liberate" France between Orly Field and Versailles, thanks to three C-47s that landed 33rd personnel at the wrong airfield.
- Photo Reconnaissance outfit to fly under the Eiffel Tower.
- Photo Reconnaissance outfit to photograph more than 1,000 square miles of enemy territory in a single operation using 12 unarmed P-38s, despite heavy enemy opposition.
- US photo unit to operate from German home soil in WW II.
- USAAF unit to make "white lightning" or P-38 punch.
- And only Photo Reconnaissance unit in the ETO whose pilots were credited with downing a ME-109 enemy fighter.

- Reconnaissance unit to photograph the city of Berlin.
- The only American photo unit awarded the Order of the Belgian Fourragere for the squadron's role in the liberation of Belgium and its defense in the Ardennes Campaign.

In addition, the 33rd PRS earned battle stars in five campaigns:
- Normandy
- Northern France
- Ardennes
- Rhineland
- Central Europe

The pilots earned a sixth battle star for the Air Offensive Over Europe. For its outstanding performance in action against the enemy, the 33rd PRS was awarded the Presidential Unit Citation. During our out-processing at Camp Miles Standish, I received orders to report to the Western Training Command Processing Center, Santa Ana, California, on December 5,1945. Including travel time home and out to California, I had some well-earned leave coming. My orders further stated that use of Government transportation was authorized. On the morning of October 5, three of us, Bill Graunke from St. Paul, Everett Phillips from Grand Island and I boarded a military train headed for Omaha, Nebraska. The coach car wasn't very comfortable, but we didn't care. We were only 23 years old and heading home as combat veterans of World War II.

Before parting in Omaha, Bill and I agreed to meet later and plan our trip to Santa Ana. Everett Phillips was married and said he and his wife would meet us there. Again, I met my family at the train station in Columbus, Nebraska. They were very happy to see me safely home from the war. I had only been away for a year, but everyone looked older than I expected. After a good reunion at home, and a lot of my mom's good cooking, I headed for Omaha to see my friends there. While at home I saw my friend Lucille, who had faithfully written to me while I was in Europe. It was nice to see her, but the spark was just not there anymore and that was that.

Bill Graunke met me in Omaha and we had a ball going to bars and dances. Omaha has more bars than you can shake a stick at. Our favorite dance hall was the Chermont Ballroom. We also liked Peony Park, but only in the summer, as they danced outside. Bill and I decided to go to Offutt Air Base to inquire about government transportation to the west coast. They said we could take the train, but we didn't want any more train travel. Also, we could hitch a ride on a military plane, transport or bomber, by just showing the pilot a copy of our travel orders.

Right after Thanksgiving, Bill and I met in Omaha and decided to buy a car. The uncertainty of catching a ride on a military aircraft seemed too risky. After looking over the Omaha used car lots, we finally picked out a maroon 1942 Mercury 4-door sedan. The engine looked and sounded good and the oil was not black-a good sign. The only thing needed was tires. New tires could not be found; so we had the old ones retreaded. We were warned not to let the tires become overheated. We allowed ourselves ten days to drive to California. Together, we planned a route that included many stops so we could enjoy the countryside. The trip went well and we had a great time. We wore our uniforms and were treated with free drinks everywhere we stopped. During the drive, Bill and I talked a lot about our future. He wanted to return to civilian life and use the GI Bill to become an airline pilot. I was undecided and wanted to talk to some of the other guys when I got to Santa Ana. On our trip west, the only mishap was a blown radiator hose.

At Santa Ana, there were mixed emotions about our futures. Everett Phillips wanted to get out and go to the University of Nebraska on the GI Bill. He was interested in pharmacy and his wife wanted to go to nursing school. Jim Foster was the only one who wanted to stay in and he strongly urged me to join him. By this time, I was more confused than ever. During the war I had dreams of going to college and becoming a history teacher. I also thought a lot about becoming a veterinarian. Talk was that the two best veterinary schools were Iowa State University and Cornell University. Jim Foster had been in Santa Ana for several days since he lived only a few miles away in Hollywood. He had already extended his active duty status and received an assignment to Rapid City, South Dakota, to fly the A-26, later called the B-26 attack bomber. In a few years he ended up in Korea.

I guess I didn't want Bill Graunke to drive back to Nebraska alone because I decided to separate from active duty and drive back with him. That night at the Santa Ana Officers Club, we all drank our fair share. The next day was a sad parting of good friends. Nothing tightens the bond of friendship more than serving in combat together, where the enemy wants to shoot at you every chance he gets. Bill Graunke went on to a wonderful career flying for Continental Airlines. He rose to full captain status quickly, became chief of training and then picked a plum assignment. He was Chief Pilot of the subsidiary of Continental-Micronesia Airlines. They flew Boeing 727's from Hawaii to the Micronesian Islands and back. He truly loved it and, in a letter, said it was the last of the good old type of flying. Soon Bill upgraded to the DC-10 and flew another plum assignment from Los Angeles to Hawaii. Out one day and back the next. He did that four times a month, and had homes in both Hawaii and Tucson, Arizona. It's easy for an airline pilot to commute to his place of work. In spite of his success, Bill met an early and tragic end. In 1980, he died of a reaction to a double inoculation shot. He had cut his thumb severely while opening a bottle of wine. He died in the emergency room of a Denver hospital.

I last saw Bill about two months before his tragedy. I was flying my company's Gulfstream II back from a trip to Australia and we had a rest stop in Hawaii. I took a chance and called Continental Airlines Flight Operations. Sure enough, Bill was there on a turn-around and would be at the airport soon. I told the dispatcher where Bill could find our Gulfstream II. That afternoon, my copilot, Frank Beeby, and I were supervising the changing of our APU (auxiliary power unit) starter motor. Busy with the work at hand, I heard a voice say, "Do you think I could hitch a ride back to the mainland with you guys?" Turning around, I saw Bill Graunke standing there grinning from ear to ear. We had a good visit there on the ramp at the Honolulu International Airport. He marveled at the new avionics I had in the Gulfstream. Before he left for his DC-10, I took his picture in front of my airplane. That was the last time I saw Bill. I lost a very close friend.

Upon my return to Omaha from Santa Anna, I immediately went to Offutt Air Force Base and joined the Army Air Force active reserves. I considered joining the Air National Guard as they were just getting brand new Lockheed P-80 fighters, but upon further checking, I learned that I would have to give up my Air Force Commission and take a National Guard Appointment. Not wanting to do that, I felt good about being in the active reserves. My new squadron was the 51st All Weather Fighter Squadron. It was somewhat a joke, since our resources consisted of one P-51, two AT-6 trainers, two C-45 small transports and one C-47 transport. The reserves were fun as we met once a month in Omaha for meetings. I could fly our "fighters" anytime I wanted. The check-out in the AT-6 went quickly and I had a ball. I could fly it solo anytime I wanted. It was like a private flying club. I spent a lot of time at the air base south of Omaha.

Countless times I flew up and down the Platte River chasing ducks. Often I would find some quiet farm land and do acrobatics. The AT-6 was very good for that and I did hundreds of lazy eights. Sometimes I would take one of the reserve airmen along for a ride. They always liked to do that when they could get off work. I didn't particularly look for work because I was having too much fun just flying. During the war, I had saved a tidy sum of money and wanted to buy a new car. Well, that seemed impossible since one had to get on the waiting list. Greasing some car dealer's palm would improve the list position. That was not acceptable to me. Because all the good used cars were gone, I decided to buy an airplane instead. Taking a leave of absence from the reserves, I went back to Cedar Rapids where I visited with my good friend Bob Ritzdorf who had just gotten out of the service. He was well into the Aviation Cadet Program when it was cancelled due to the war's ending. He did get his ten hours in a cub at a college in the CTD Program, however.   Bob and I had a good time taking in all the dances in surrounding towns. Every Sunday night at a town west of Cedar, called Greeley, they had a super dance and I met a very sweet girl, Mary Jane Rooney.   Mick McQuillan, the town banker, intro-duced us one night at the dance. Mary Jane and I went to many dances around the area during that time. She was only 16 and I was 23. The uniform must have made me look younger because her parents let her go with me a lot. We had excellent body chemistry and we got along very well without a lot of conversation. We both felt very comfortable with each other and had mutual respect. Our favorite song was "To Each His Own." One can occasionally still hear that song today on the "oldies" radio programs.

Every month the aviation trade paper, called "Trade-a-Plane", is published. There I saw an airplane listed for sale that caught my atten-tion.   It was a Piper Cub Cruiser known as the J-5. It seated three, pilot in front and a two-seat bench in the back. The engine was a 75 HP Continental. Terry Flying Service of Waterloo, Iowa, offered it for sale for $2,500. The ad said it was newly overhauled and had a fresh fabric covering. The next day I called Mr. Terry and he said to come over; he would hold it for me. That's all it took; I was going to be an airplane owner. Not many people get to do that. When I asked my best friend, Bob, to come with me, he was all for it. That gave me a good feeling to have Bob go with me to buy this airplane. He also could help me fly it home.   We left the next day on the train for Omaha, then took a Grey-hound bus to Waterloo. Mr. Terry picked us up at the bus station and, during the drive to the airport, he gave me the history of the airplane. It had been owned by a doctor who wrecked it in a bad landing on a windy day.

The Terry Flying Service bought it from the insurance company and restored it, including an overhaul of the engine and a new propel-ler. The standard color for a Piper Cub was factory yellow, with a thin black speed stripe down the side of the fuselage. Mr. Terry decided to stray from the standard yellow. He painted it silver with a blue speed stripe. When we arrived at the airport, there sat my airplane in the sunshine looking like a million dollars. We did a careful walk-around exterior inspection. It looked good to me. Mr. Terry said, "Let's go take it around the pattern so you will feel comfortable in it." The engine had to be hand-propped because it had no electric starter. In fact, it had no electrical system at all except for the ignition system. The engine ran great and I soon completed three circuits of the traffic pattern and executed three supervised landings. After writing out a check for $2,500, I was ready to take my new cub home. Mr. Terry topped off the oil and gas tanks, then waved goodbye as Bob and I taxied out for takeoff. It was quite a long flight home and we took turns flying. A sectional map of Iowa and Nebraska was all we needed to find our way back to east central Nebraska.

Drawing on residents of several surrounding towns I gave hundreds of people their very first ride in an airplane. Every day, if the weather was good, I would fly somebody. The fare was $2 a head for about 15 minutes of sightseeing around the town, or around their farm or ranch. They all loved it and wanted more. I named the airplane "Jane" after Mary Jane Rooney.

While flying the J-5 Cub, I took it easy on the very young and the elderly but the robust got their money's worth. About the only acrobatics I could safely do in the Cub were lazy eights, loops and spins. At the very top of a loop, when it got very quiet, I could always hear sounds behind me ranging from yelps to prayers. Most often it was a combination of the two. The few women I flew were the best at that during a loop or when spinning down.

Once a month I was required to attend a Reserve meeting in Omaha. They were held at the Fontanelle Hotel on Saturday nights. After a short meeting, some combat films were shown. The bar was near and most of the pilots would end up there trading war stories until the place closed. While in town for the mandatory meetings, I would go to Offutt the following day and fly the T-6 all over eastern Nebraska. Its engine had a horsepower rating of 650. That, compared to my Cub's 75, made for quite a difference in performance.

One day my sister Eileen needed a ride to Lincoln and, of course I offered her my private airline and at no cost. Departing Cedar Rapids, I made the mistake of giving the town a little notice that they finally had an airplane based there. While I was doing the low passes, my sister became sick and put her "cookies" all over the floor of my airplane. Needless to say, we returned to the landing strip and, using strong cleaning materials, took the time to clean it up. Finally, we took off again and made a very smooth, no-nonsense flight to Lincoln.

I had lots of fun playing on the town's baseball team. A huge storm developed one Sunday while we were away playing baseball in another town. Hail the size of baseballs fell and my airplane was riddled. I had it trucked down to Grand Island where the folks at the airport repaired it. During that time, I went back to Omaha and flew the T-6 at every opportunity. It was going to take two months to have my J-5 repaired so I took a temporary job in Omaha with a farm management company which oversaw the operations of farms in western Iowa and eastern Nebraska. My job was keeping track of the income and the outgo-bookkeeping. How I got that job, I'll never know. I noticed the ad in the paper and applied and to my amazement, they gave it to me. I told them I was a World War II veteran and was good with figures.

When my airplane was repaired, I had to leave the job and go to Grand Island and pick it up. It flew like new on the flight back to Cedar Rapids. I had taken out insurance with Mr. Jackson and the repair costs were covered. There were no deductibles or co-payments in those days. Now I was back to my barnstorming career. A friend who operated an air service in nearby Albion, asked me to consider joining him in a crop dusting business. That just didn't appeal to me and I had to say no.

Every month when I went to Omaha, I took the opportunity to fly the T-6. I really loved flying that WW II advanced trainer. We flew as one, and when I decided to do something, the airplane would seem to sense it. That meant I could do things without thinking and as a result, I became very comfortable in it. Today, when I see some "line boy" fly a T-6 in an air show, I just cringe. I'm not trying to be cynical, but only money can get those "junior birdmen" into those war birds. Another year passed while I barnstormed around Nebraska. During that time many schools would ask me to drop leaflets for special events. That was fun, as I would take a couple of high school students with me to pitch them out over neighboring towns. I was paid very well for this service. A lot of ranchers hired me to fly them over their vast spreads on inspection tours. They had never seen their ranches from the air before. I would always have a camera aboard and would take aerial pictures for those folks. I seriously considered going into the aerial photography business. People would pay good money for a picture of their farm, ranch or home in town. I already had the camera picked out. It would be a war-surplus Fairchild K-20 aerial camera with a six-inch focal length-perfect for the job. I even had my game plan worked out. After randomly shooting a farm or ranch, I would fly by low and slow and drop them a little parachute that contained a weighted self-addressed post card listing prices and sizes of pictures they could order. One of my war buddies was doing that same thing in Muncie, Indiana and was quite successful with it.

That fall, the local school system hired two Omaha girls, just out of college, to teach in the local high school. Pat Green and Mary Jane McGowan arrived and soon I had the pleasure of meeting those two very lovely ladies.

When I offered them a ride in my J-5, they eagerly accepted. I became very fond of my second Mary Jane. Her parents operated a large food manufacturing business in Omaha. We got along famously-maybe too famously.. When I took the new Mary Jane out to give her a ride in the J-5, she said, "You certainly put my name on your airplane quickly." Little did she know that the name was that of a special girl in Greeley.

That summer in 1948, while I was away, a Nebraska tornado came up. That one was big time and it did my airplane in for good. The storm totally wrecked the poor thing and then it had to be salvaged. Once again, Mr. Jackson came to my rescue. He arranged for full coverage of the loss. The only thing I saved was the propeller. Today it hangs in my office with a clock mounted in the hub. Every time I look at it I can't help but think of the many hours of pure joy that little propeller gave me pulling my J-5 through the Nebraska skies.

The next fall I entered the University of Omaha and decided to take a shot toward my earlier goals of history or veterinary medicine. Under the GI Bill, I received $75 a month for tuition. To add to my income, I took a job driving a Yellow Cab after classes. That was fine except that it offered little time for study. Cab business was very good from four in the afternoon until mid- night. A lot of my fares would take me over to Carter Lake, Iowa, where they could gamble. Some of my fares would tell me to wait until they were ready to leave. Lots of times it was very late when I finally got home but the tips were excellent.

At the University, I made the baseball team and played third base. Our coach was Virgil Yelken, a demanding fellow; but I had fun anyway. He made us run three laps around the field after each practice. It was a great feeling to be on a college baseball team. Each summer, towns in Iowa recruited college players and I ended up playing for the Remsen, Iowa, semi-pro team. We were in Yankton, South Dakota, playing a game and during pre-game warm-up, young kids came up and asked for autographs. Wearing the Remsen Hawks jacket helped, I'm sure. Another time in Storm Lake, Iowa, the same thing happened-young kids asking for autographs from college players. Nothing can make an athlete feel better than when asked for an autograph. Playing semi-pro baseball was an experience that I will never forget.

For playing baseball, I received $200 a month and we played every Wednesday night and Sunday afternoon. The town gave us the opportunity to earn extra money by working at different establishments in town. I took a job in the lumber yard delivering lumber. That was fun and I felt very fortunate for having the opportunity to do it. Virgel Yelken, my coach back at OU, did his job well teaching me the fundamentals of competitive sports. Soon, to my great delight, the Remsen manager made me a relief pitcher. Baseball is, by far, my favorite sport. It always has been and always will be.

In Washington, D.C., the Senate Military Affairs Committee was working on a bill that provided a Department of Defense with separate Departments of the Army, Navy and Air Force. Each of the Departments would be headed up by a civilian Secretary. It was called the National Security Act of 1947. The Marine Corps would remain part of the Navy and Naval Aviation would handle naval reconnaissance, antisubmarine warfare and protection of shipping. Hearings were held in the House and Senate, and in early June, the Senate Committee on Armed Services approved the bill.

A Conference Committee crafted final legislation and, on July 26, 1947, President Harry Truman signed the National Security Act of 1947, establishing the Office of the Secretary of National Defense and co-equal services including a brand new United States Air Force. The new National Security Act allowed the Air Force flexibility in organizing its headquarters and field structure. Like the Army and Navy, the Air Force would be an Executive Department of the Federal Government. The Department of the Air Force would be headed by the Secretary of the Air Force, a civilian appointed by the President and confirmed by the Senate. The US Air Force was established under the Department of the Air Force. The USAF Chief of Staff would be appointed by the President for a four-year term. All officers, warrant officers and enlisted men of the Army Air Forces would be transferred to the US Air Force. New blue uniforms with black shoes were approved. One of the pilots in my reserve squadron came from a family of clothiers. Jacobson Clothing Store in Omaha very quickly ordered a large supply of the new uniforms. My blue blouse, trousers, three shirts, ties, top coat, service hat, and shoes all came to $350. Mr. Jacobson let all the reserve pilots pay by the month with no interest added.

On March 21, 1946, the Strategic Air Command (SAC), was established at Bolling Field near Washington, D.C. It was later relocated to Maryland's Andrews Field with General George C. Kinney at its head. In November 1948, SAC moved to Fort Crook in Omaha. Fort Crook, named for Indian campaigner General George Crook, was founded in 1891 to relieve the crowded conditions at Fort Omaha. It initially housed the 22nd Infantry Regiment and later became home to the 61st Balloon Company. In the next three years 260 acres of farm land were leveled for use as a landing field. Many of the fort's original structures remain in use today and are registered as National Historic Landmarks. In 1924, the name was changed to Offutt Field, named after First Lieutenant Jarvis Offutt, Omaha's first air casualty of World War I.

War clouds gathering during the 1930s brought realization of America's lack of air superiority over Germany. Soon, the Glenn L. Martin-Nebraska Bomber Assembly Plant was constructed at Offutt Field. The plant, completed in December 1941, had built 1,585 B-26 Marauders and 531 B-29 Superfortresses. Enola Gay and Bock's Car, the two B-29s that dropped atomic bombs on Hiroshima and Nagasaki, were built at this plant. When SAC relocated to Omaha in 1948, utilizing the former bomber plant buildings, Offutt Field and Fort Crook merged as Offutt Air Force Base. Also, at this time, Lieutenant General Curtiss LeMay began working with SAC to instill discipline and build up forces. During his leadership from 1946 to 1957, he successfully converted crews, pilots and planes into disciplined, global powerhouses capable of fulfilling SAC's motto: "Peace is our Profession." SAC was a "star performer" from 1946 to 1992. However, Pentagon leaders during the early 90s consolidated all nuclear weapons-bombers, intercontinental ballistic missiles and anti-ballistic missile submarines-under a new streamlined command called STRATCOM (Strategic Attack Command). This consolidation and renaming could not, in any way, diminish SAC's role in aviation history.

By winning World War II, America reshaped her future. On September 1, 1939, World War II began with Germany's invasion of Poland. Some thought the 20th Century might evolve as the Nazi Century, the Soviet Century, or the Japanese Century.

It turned out to be the American Century. American ideals of self-governing nations, democracy, fair play, freedom and the dignity of the individual would be spread around the world. At the start of the war any complaints about wartime shortages had usually been met with the phrases "We are all in this together." and "Don't you know there's a war on?" It resulted in a teamwork that made possible the twin miracles of the American Republic in WW II-the creation of the U.S. Armed Forces and the production of war materials in unimaginable quantities.

In 1939, the US Army numbered 175,000 officers and men. It ranked 16th in the world, right behind Romania. The German Wehrmacht, meanwhile, was many millions strong and very well equipped. Hitler was certain of two things: The Americans could never outproduce Germany and young Germans brought up in the Hitler Youth Program would outfight young Americans that were brought up in the Boy Scouts. He was dead wrong on both counts. In 1940, President Roosevelt called for the production of 50,000 airplanes a year, ten times as many as were built in 1939. People thought he was crazy but in 1944, American factories produced 96,318 military aircraft. The Germans built 40,593 that year, the Japanese, 28,180. By 1945, one half of all ships afloat in the world had been built in the United States. All this was accomplished while the US Army grew from a cadre of 175,000 to more than eight million, the Navy from 125,000 to more than four million, the Marine Corps. from 19,000 to half a million. Thanks to American industry, they were the best equipped armed forces in the world, by far. Could they fight? The Americans came at Omaha Beach, at the Battle of the Bulge, at Iwo Jima and at Okinawa. The US Army lost only one battle against the Wehrmacht in WW II, it's first, at Kasserine Pass in February 1943. The American Navy lost only one battle against the Japanese Navy in WW II, its first, at Pearl Harbor.

American citizen-soldiers were characterized by their determination, courage and willingness to take the initiative against whomever they fought. The biggest single difference between America in the 30s and America at war, was that everyone had jobs. A steady job and money in the bank meant financial security, something most Americans under 35 had never before experienced. Another new experience was travel. Many Americans in 1940 had never been out of their home state, most of them never out of the country. Between 1940 and 1945, some 12 million young Americans, men and women, went overseas and into a different culture. By 1945, the American people were far better off financially than they had been in 1940. The war had greatly expanded the role of the government. In 1939, despite the New Deal reforms, the government did little for the people. Social Security was new, offered limited benefits and did not cover large parts of the work force. There was no medical help whatsoever for most Americans from any agency of the government. The GI's - the very name standing for "government issue" - bespoke the new role of government in everyday life. GI wives grew accustomed to government services - a certain degree of government paternalism. Servicemen's wives received a government allowance of $28 a month, plus $12 for the first child and $10 for each additional child. Far more important was the wisest piece of legislation Congress ever passed, the GI Bill of Rights in 1944. It provided support for college education and home and business loans for veterans. Nearly eight million veterans received educational assistance from the GI Bill. Other millions were able to get loans. The total cost to the government was about $30 billion, which was recovered many times over in taxes from the recipients.

The effect of the GI Bill on America's colleges and universities was simply staggering. Home loans got the suburbs started and business loans spawned a boom in small businesses. The role of women in the "shaping of America" during the war changed dramatically. They entered the work force in record numbers. It afforded them a previously undreamed of independence. Many of them were married with small children. "Quickie" marriages was the norm in the atmosphere of the day. If a couple wanted to have a sexual experience before the soldier left for war, they had to stand in front of a preacher first. Parents worried that hasty marriages followed by long separations would never work but most marriages did. As war transformed boys to men, the girls became women. They traveled alone, or with their infants, to distant places on hot and stuffy, or damp and cold, overcrowded trains. They quickly became good cooks and housekeepers. They managed finances, learned to fix the car and wrote upbeat letters to their soldier-husbands, telling everything the baby did. Curiously, war produces more disruptions in the lives of women, who stay at home, than men who go off to war. American women who stayed at home played as large a role as the men who went off to war in making victory possible. They held the family together. The theme of WW II was national unity. During the great depression, people had felt isolated. During the war, people felt a sense of belonging. Obviously in the armed forces but also on the home front, there was a commitment to the idea that society's needs came before personal desires. The war had created a "we" generation.

Those Americans born in the first third of the century did great things for the country and the world. They had enough of destruction. They came home and busied themselves with the task of re-construction. They built the Interstate Highway System, the St. Lawrence Seaway, great corporations and tens of thousands of small businesses. They ended public segregation in America. They paid the taxes and provided the leadership to rebuild Germany, Western Europe and Japan, and the military preparedness to hold the Soviet Union in check, and finally defeat it. They played the leading role in ending colonialism around the world. They made the Century American. Thanks to them, democracy is on the march today. Americans born in the first third of the 20th

Century stood up to Hitler, Tojo, Mussolini, Stalin and their successors and met their challenges head on. Nazism, Fascism, Japanese militarism and communism were all relegated to the ash can of history. The American Century had paved the way for the Democratic Century.

Ten miles south of Omaha at Offutt AFB, I was flying the T-6 so much, my reserve squadron commander decided to designate me as an instructor. A lot of the pilots in the reserve squadron had never flown the T-6 advanced trainer before. Now I had the nice job of checking them out. The only tricky thing about the trainer was in landing. If you didn't keep it rolling straight down the runway, it had a tendency to ground loop. I taught them to make two-point rather than three-point landings, as that made the task of keeping the bird rolling straight much easier. I gave up the cab-driving job and the balance of my college education would have to wait for a while. I had accumulated 90 credit hours during military training. One day I decided to apply to the US Post Office for the position of railroad mail agent. The exam was long and difficult but I passed it. I bid for, and was awarded the Omaha to Cheyenne run, but before I could begin work I was required to know the location of every town in the state of Wyoming. That took a while and it was very interesting. In the meantime, I learned the ropes in the Omaha Railway Mail Terminal.

In the summer of 1949, there was a rumor that the Air Force Reserve structure was going to be overhauled. Soon all the reservists were called out to the base for a meeting. The rumor turned out to be true; the 51st All-Weather Fighter Squadron was being deactivated. All the former reserve squadron members were to become part of the 322nd Troop Carrier Wing and would fly the Curtiss C-46 Commando transport. I had grown so fond of my little AT-6 trainer that I almost cried over losing her. Over the last three years I had checked out a lot of pilots in the AT-6 and she was a pure pleasure to fly. Ironically, the C-46 was the same type airplane that I had helped build back in Buffalo eight years earlier. The Commando was a big airplane by any standard. First, I had to attend ground school classes to learn the various aircraft systems. Under the new reserve alignment, I had to spend a minimum of two days a month at the base for training, and two weeks active duty in the Air Force each year. The best thing about this arrangement was that we would be paid for the monthly meetings. The active duty time was at full pay according to rank. Because everyone worked, our two days of training each month were naturally on weekends. The Air Force soon sent in some instructors to get us checked out in the big transport. The airplane was heavy and slow, but sort of fun to fly. It could haul a tremendous load of cargo, troops or both. It was a good cross-country airplane and even had an auto-pilot. Once it was set, you could just sit there with a cup of coffee and watch the world cruise by. Later in the fall of 1949, I went on active duty for two weeks. The Postal Service had no problem giving me a two week leave of absence. By then the squadron had 12 airplanes and almost everyone was checked out. Our new Troop Carrier Wing contained three squadrons, two from Nebraska and one from Iowa. Early one Saturday morning after all the airplanes were loaded with troops and a couple of jeeps, we took off and flew in a trail-formation to Atterbury Air Force Base, Indiana. We had nice quarters and flew almost every day. The flights were cross-country navigation flights and we would be back to Atterbury the same evening. Most weekends in Omaha, I would go out to the base and fly the C-46 but I had to have a crew consisting of a co-pilot and a crew chief or engineer. Recruiting a crew was difficult especially since arrangements had to be made in advance. This arrangement did result in some very good cross-country flights for me. There were no restrictions on my destinations as long as I had the airplane back by Sunday night. My favorite places to fly to were Denver and Minneapolis. The two pilots always paid the crew chief's expenses on those trips. In the summer of 1950, our summer camp was at Memphis Air Force Base, Tennessee. We were in the same hangars that Federal Express operates in today. Of course they have updated the facility so much that it's not recognizable now.

With the insurance money from my little J-5 Cub, I purchased a 1940 Plymouth coupe. It ran pretty well and was dependable transportation. It didn't have a radio so I bought a used one and installed in on the shelf behind the seat instead of in the dash. It worked out fine. The girls that I gave rides to thought it was swell-an early version of background music. One Saturday night when all my roommates were out, I decided to drive downtown to the Pine Board Bar in Omaha. It was my favorite place to go when I had the time. They had an organist, Blanche Peterson, who played outstanding music The bar employed the "red star system." If a red star appeared on the cash register receipt when you paid for a drink you were awarded a second drink free. It was a popular promotion and I won several times. That night Blanche was out sick.

With no organ music, the Pine Board was dead so I had a beer and left. Outside I noticed a sign across Dodge Street that read, "The Music Box." Below that, in smaller letters, the sign read, "Dancing Friday and Saturday Nights." It was still early so I decided to go over there and check it out. The bar and dance hall were on the second floor and on the third floor was a bowling alley. At the bar, I ordered a bottle of

Storz Grainbelt beer and just as I took a sip I felt a tap on my shoulder. I looked around and there stood my friend Doris DeFore. She was the sister-in-law of Dick Friesz, one of the pilots in my reserve squadron. Doris said, "Hi Tom, come over and meet my friend, Joan Puckett." After finding a table near the dance floor, the three of us had a good time talking and dancing to the music of the time. Later, I offered them both a ride home. I dropped Doris off first and then Joan. Why in that order, I'm not really sure.

The Korean war was heating up and I was worried about being called up to active duty. I wouldn't mind that but I sure didn't want to fly the C-46 on active duty. The P-80 Shooting Star would be my choice. At the next weekend meeting, the wing commander said that if each officer recruited two enlisted men, all the billets in the wing would be filled. Then our chances of being called up would diminish. With some effort, we accomplished that but the effect was just the opposite of what we had been told.. The whole wing was being recalled to active duty effective February 1, 1951. I had two weeks to get my affairs in order because the whole wing was going back on active duty in the new United States Air Force. I was going back as a first lieutenant. Everyone was given two weeks to acquire the new blue uniform and black shoes. No problem there; thanks to Mr. Jacobson, I already had my new blue outfit.

At the next reserve meeting, the Wing Commander explained that we were going back on active duty but not as a regular Troop Carrier Wing. Our wing was selected to fill slots in other wings by individual member's MOS-Military Occupational Speciality code. Pilots with four-engine time went to bomber units, twin-engine pilots went to troop carrier units and single engine pilots went to fighter units. My MOS was 1062 (Reconnaissance Pilot) and wing personnel tried to tell me it was a typographical error; it should be 1052, a fighter pilot speciality code. By then I was proud of my 1062 code. Sure enough, in the MOS Code Book, 1062 was listed as the code for a reconnaissance pilot. Now, they didn't know where to send me as reconnaissance units no longer existed. After a long hassle, I was assigned to the USAF Photo School of the Air Training Command at Lowry AFB, Denver, Colorado. My job there was a photo mission pilot for the school. That was dandy since living in Denver sounded good to me. I was the only one in the whole wing to be assigned to Lowry.

Time was getting short and I had to wind up my affairs but first, I drove up to see my parents. They were pleased that I was going back on active duty but hoped I wouldn't have to go to Korea. I didn't think my 1940 Plymouth would make it to Colorado so I traded it for a 1947

Buick Century Sedan, my first automatic shift car. I called it my "Black Beauty." It was tough saying goodbye to my good friends in Omaha, especially to Joan. We had become quite fond of each other since that first night in the Music Box six months earlier. I told her it would be a year before I could get any leave so if she wished, she might consider traveling to Denver sometime for a visit and we left it at that.

Early in the morning of January 28, 1951, I left Omaha with all my possessions packed in my black Buick. I didn't look forward to driving out there alone but had no choice in the matter. I traveled at a leisurely pace and stopped at North Platte the first night. The next morning was cloudy with a threat of snow in the air. The snow soon began to fall and the closer I got to Denver, the heavier it fell . The last 50 miles I was lucky enough to follow a snow plow. By the time I reached the outskirts of Denver, there was over a foot of snow on the ground and it was still coming down in big flakes. I knew Lowry AFB was on the east side of Denver but had trouble finding the correct route. After stopping for directions, I finally found the base. The secondary roads weren't plowed very well and it took considerable effort to handle the big Buick in the snow. After locating the billeting office, I was assigned a room and unloaded the car. By that time I was quite hungry and walked through the snow to the Officers Club. The club was still open and only a few people were sitting at the bar. When I asked for some food, the bartender said the kitchen was closed because of the storm. Asking for the night manager, I went on to explain that I had driven all day in the snowstorm. He then mellowed and came up with a ham sandwich and a bottle of beer. For that act of kindness, the Club at Lowry became my favorite hangout for the next four years.

Nothing ages so quickly as yesterday's vision of the future.

—Richard Corliss

CHAPTER TEN

LIFE IN THE SERVICE

It's not what the teacher says, but what the student hears, that matters.

—*Harvey Penick*

When I checked in at Technical Training Headquarters, I was given two choices. I could choose between a 22 month tour or an indefinite tour of duty. When I asked how long I had to decide, the sergeant said I had four days. My boss at the Photo School Flight Section, Major Floyd Blackburn, said I was the fourth pilot in the photo section which operated five airplanes- three C-47's and two B-25's. All aircraft were modified with mounts and special windows for aerial cameras. The B-25's were further modified for three cameras mounted so tri-metrogon (horizon to horizon) pictures could be taken. The size of the "photo fleet" was staggering-four pilots and five airplanes. Major Blackburn explained that, of the five ships, one or two were usually out of service for scheduled maintenance. He also explained that Headquarters pilots were frequently used as co-pilots in flying the photo airplanes. My first task was to get checked out in both airplanes and, after 100 hours in each type, I would be certified as an instructor pilot. Then I could use HQ pilots to fly with me as a co-pilots. The policy was that if the pilot was an instructor, the copilot did not have to be qualified in the airplane.

Captain Elmer Wasche was Major Blackburn's assistant, and was assigned to qualify me as an instructor. In less than two months, I was an IP (instructor pilot) in both airplanes. I liked the B-25 better because I had flown it over 100 hours previously in flight school. At Lowry, I flew nearly every day with aerial photo students. If the weather wasn't good for photography, I flew local transition to keep my proficiency sharp. Most months I flew 100 hours or more. The Photo School offered three courses-aerial photography, ground photography and camera repair. It was a big school and was very busy. Chief Warrant Officer Grover Gilbert, a retired National Geographic Magazine photographer, was the chief instructor.

Back in Omaha, my friend Joan wrote me a letter saying she was planning a trip to Denver to pay me a visit. During my many visits to the Lowry Officers Club, I met some Air Force nurses but no serious relationship had developed. I drank at the bar with them, ate with them and occasionally attended a movie with them. When Joan arrived, I greeted her at the train station and secured a room for her at the Shirley Savoy hotel in downtown Denver. During the three days she was in Denver, I showed her around town and we ate and danced at the Lowry Officers Club. We had a very nice time. When I put her back on the train for Omaha, I said to her, "Maybe you should come back this summer and live here." She didn't comment on that, but gave me a sweet smile as she climbed on the train that would take her back to Omaha.

Mr. Gilbert, the Air Force Photo School's Chief Instructor, was one of the nicest persons you could ever know. One day he came over to photo flight-operations and briefed us on a special mission. The Air Force Training Command had bases all over the country and they wanted aerial photos taken of them every six months. Mr. Gilbert needed an overhead shot from about 4,000 feet plus oblique shots from each of the four cardinal points of the compass-north, east, south and west. Those shots were to be taken from 2,000 feet. I was selected to go on the first trip and would be gone for a week flying the B-25. The crew was made up of two pilots and an aerial photographer, who was usually an instructor from the school. When the weather was good, we tried to shoot one training base each day, then go on to the next base, RON (remain over night) and shoot that base the next day. These trips were lots of fun for me as I did this type of "shooting" in combat, only at high altitude. This work was at much lower altitudes and it was a piece of cake. Anytime we got near the Mexican border, the crew would go into Mexico, get a good steak and bring back a couple bottles of rum. The Bacardi rum came in glass gallon jugs wrapped in cane mesh. Those bottles, when empty, made excellent lamps. With a kit from a lamp store, anyone could make them in short order. Every pilot in the section had several, and brought back some for friends. In those days, a gallon of rum cost two dollars

I participated in a lot of those summer trips photographing training bases. A new pilot who had just been recalled became our fifth pilot. Burt Emerson was a B-17 pilot in the war and had been shot down by the Germans. His crew managed to bail out safely but, unfortunately, the plane was still over Germany. Burt landed safely, buried his parachute in the forest and did his best to escape and evade the enemy as he was taught in training. He succeeded for a while, sleeping in the forest during the day and moving to the west during the night. One day he was awakened by the sounds of an advancing search party. The sound of barking dogs made him very nervous, since they could usually find their prey. It wasn't long before the Dobermans found him. The two dogs were ahead of the search party and acted as their "radar." Fortunately Burt kept his .45 caliber pistol and it saved his life. When the first dog found him, it made a giant leap for him. Calmly, Burt aimed his pistol and shot the dog dead. The second dog followed and met the same fate. Now the search party knew exactly where the downed airman was located. There were no more dogs, so Burt just threw the pistol away before the Germans reached him. Then he had no choice but to surrender. They roughly took him into custody and hauled him off hog-tied in a truck. He was taken to a POW camp and severely interrogated. The Geneva Convention Rules stated a prisoner of war was only required to give his name, rank and serial number, nothing more. Burt did that repeatedly and was roughed up by rifle butt pops to his head. Finally, they took him to one of the Stalag prison camps. There his fellow prisoners nursed his wounds and in a few days he was back in good shape. More intense interrogations were to fol- low.

Burt's crew had all bailed out safely but landed in a widely scat- tered area. All were captured but none showed up at Stalag 15 where he was. During his next interrogation, Burt was asked if he had any relatives in Germany. When he replied in the negative, they showed him a list of his relatives still living there. Burt knew his ancestors were from Germany but didn't realize any were still alive. They then asked if he would like to fly a B-17 again. When he looked surprised at the question, the interrogator explained that Germany had captured, in fly- ing condition, several American war planes of different types. Two B- 17s had become lost on a bombing mission and landed in Finland. The crews were interned, and the Germans took the airplanes. Now they were asking American POWs if they were interested in flying these bombers which still had American markings and insignia. The planes, acting as decoys, would join up with a bomb group on a bombing mis- sion. At the appropriate time the planes would signal on a special radio frequency the German fighter command, warning them of the upcom- ing bombing raid.

To this Burt said; "Hell no!" and was promptly popped hard with a rifle butt by one of the German guards. They carried him, still groggy, back to his bunker. Burt told me that when the movie "Stalag 17" came out, it was very much the same at Stalag 15. They too had Saturday night dances using homemade instruments. Half of them would fix their hair like girls and everyone had a ball. They also had Sunday "horse races" using captured mice that were trained to run for food. The betting was as fierce as at any horse track. All the POWs looked forward to the Red Cross care packages each month. The special foods in them were carefully guarded like gold. They passed the time by playing poker and other mind games. An escape committee was formed and Burt was on it as Vice Chairman. They drew up three different escape plans but never got the chance to use any. One of the plans consisted of digging a tunnel from their bunker out to the perimeter fence. That project was started but never finished. Burt spent 28 months as a POW before the Russians liberated the camp in May, 1945. After arriving home, he soon separated from the service. After three years of struggling, Burt tried to go back on active duty. He now had a wife and two children. The only way he could go back was as an NCO.

Master Sergeant Burt R. Emerson was assigned to Lowry AFB on January 15, 1948. I first met Burt when I went into the officers club one day to pay my monthly dues. There in the office was a short and very friendly master sergeant who helped me with my business. From time to time in the club, we would talk, mainly because he was wearing a pair of pilots' wings-quite unusual for a master sergeant. Later in 1952, at my urging, Burt applied for and was recalled to active duty as a first lieutenant. He was assigned to the photo flight operations and Major Blackburn turned him over to me for training. Burt first went to Randolph Field in San Antonio, Texas, to receive some flight indoctrination before being assigned to us. There he flew 10 hours, dual, in an AT-6 advanced trainer.

When I started Burt in his training program, it was shocking to me how much he had forgotten about flying. In the cockpit, he didn't recognize half the gauges and controls. I had my work cut out for me but Burt was such an enjoyable guy, we had fun and a million laughs in the process. Burt had trouble landing the C-47 in a cross-wind, but with the B-25, he caught on quickly. Soon, he was having fun flying again. In a few weeks, I took him with me on a week-long trip in the B-25 to photograph some training bases. We had shot a field in Iowa and then went to Des Moines to RON (Remain Over Night). In Iowa in those days, you had to join a private club to get a drink. That night we had a heavy rainstorm and the next morning, we couldn't get either engine started. The airplane had been parked outside all night in the rain and the engines had gotten so wet we had to get some help from a fixed base operator (FBO) to remove the spark plugs. All 32 spark plugs were put out in the sun to dry. Back at Lowry, they would just put in new ones; but on the road, we had to clean and dry them out. The second morning, both engines started like gang busters and we were on our way. During trips like that, Burt told me bits and pieces of his war experiences. I tried to get him to write a book about it but he didn't seem interested. That was unfortunate because he would have had a great story to tell.

Most of our missions with aerial photo students were up and down the east side of the Rockies south of Denver toward Colorado Springs. Before the Air Force Academy was built there, we photographed that same area hundreds of times. Later, when the Air Force decided to locate the new Academy there, the very first class was located on the east side of Lowry AFB. Many of the cadets in that first class got their first ride in a military airplane with me. Each Saturday, I would take six of them up in the B-25 for an indoctrination ride over the Rocky Mountain Range. I would do that every Saturday morning when the weather was suitable. Not a single one got sick and they all took turns riding in the glass nose section where they could see the world in all directions.

Fitzimmons General Army Hospital was located just northeast of Lowry AFB. Injured soldiers from the Korean War came there for re-habilitation. One day I received a letter from my mom telling me that the son of one of her friends was there and that I should go and see him. I finally located the young man and, in our conversation, asked him if he could get free for a ride in a B-25. After verifying that he could, we set a date for the following week. When he arrived at photo flight op-erations, I showed him everything about the Mitchell Light Bomber, the B-25, the airplane General Jimmy Doolittle made famous on his Tokyo raid in April, 1942. The young man said that he was familiar with that story. He was surprised that the B-25 was as big as it was. I found a chest-type parachute for him, grabbed a copilot and away we went. For the takeoff and landing, he had to ride on the "shelf" behind the flight deck. After that, I told him to crawl up in the nose compart-ment for a good view of the world. We flew all over the Colorado rockies and skimmed the peaks at about 50 feet or less. After an hour of this we came back and landed. Over a cup of coffee, he told me he had one lung shot away in Korea. Had I known that before hand, I would never have taken him up to those altitudes. He claimed to enjoy the ride and seemed to have no discomfort. Whew!!!

Back in Omaha, Joan took me up on the offer to move to Denver-arriving in the summer of 1951. We found a nice girls' rooming house on University Boulevard and in a week, she found a job in the office of a downtown Chevrolet dealer. Soon there were strong signs that nei-ther of us wanted to be separated again, ever. Late that summer we decided to get married. After much discussion, we picked Saturday September 8, 1951, for the big event. Bill and Janet Graunke said they wanted to host the reception at their house. My mom and a number of relatives and friends came out from Nebraska. My nephew, Harry Mahoney and his wife, Jean, "stood up" for us. The whole Photo Section came to the wedding, and Master Sergeant Charlie Fetterman, assistant chief instructor at the school, brought his professional Speed Graphic camera and shot lots of pictures, both in the church and at the reception.

Earlier we had found a small apartment on the second floor of a big house on Gaylord Avenue. It was near the base and right on the bus stop for Joan to get to work. During the wedding reception, some clowns removed the front seat from our Buick and of course tied all kinds of things to the rear bumper. On the side they scrolled: "No Sleep Tonight," and "Hot Springs, Here We Come." Of course, "Just Married" was all over the car. The Buick was black and that white lettering really showed up.

After the wedding cake was cut and eaten, and our clothes changed, Joan and I headed for our car and an overnight honeymoon. After opening the car and seeing no front seat, I about fainted. The Graunke car was also a Buick and was parked just behind me on the street, so I ran over to Bill's car, yanked out his front seat and threw it in my car. That was fine except for one thing, it was too wide for the doors to close. By slamming the doors hard, we could get the first latch but that wasn't our only problem. There were two "clowns" from the wedding, half loaded, in our back seat. They said they were going on the honeymoon with us. I replied; "Okay, here we go," and zoomed out into the street. After a block or so, they gave up and asked me to stop where they quickly bailed out.

We both had to be back at work on Monday morning and this was Saturday afternoon. It was going to be a short honeymoon indeed. I had made hotel reservations at the Elks Hotel in Cheyenne and of course, told no one. At the first car wash, leaving Denver, we tried to get the car cleaned up. The white material came off but the lettering could still be seen through the wax. Sunday morning when we came out to get in the car to go to church, the engine wouldn't start. We looked at each other and both said, "Those characters must have followed us here and did something to the car." I looked under the hood and everything seemed normal. I couldn't figure it out but, after a lot of coaxing, the engine finally started.

Our apartment on Gaylord Avenue really looked good when we got there Sunday night. On her last night as a single girl, Joan stayed there with her friend Beverly. They had the foresight to put some provisions in the fridge. When I arrived at work the next morning, my fellow workers teased me that I actually showed up. My boss, Major

Blackburn, mentioned that I looked a little pale. He further stated that I shouldn't fly that day and put me to work in the office. At noon he sent me home for the day.Our first home-cooked dinner as newlyweds was spaghetti and meat balls. The second night we had fried chicken. Today, we still like both very much. The women that Joan worked with taught her how to fix both dishes. Her mother wouldn't let her do much at home in their kitchen. It wasn't long before she became a gourmet cook. The following summer, I was eligible for a 30 day leave. After our original one-day honeymoon in Wyoming, now we would take a long one to the west coast, visiting Yellowstone National Park and other interesting points in the west.

One day at Lowry, when the weather wasn't suitable for student photo missions, another instructor and I took a B-25 up for some proficiency flying. The plan was to fly from Denver to Sterling, to Lamar, to Colorado Springs and back to Denver. We took along a box lunch and it would be a fun day. There was always a thermos of coffee on board too. Somewhere between Sterling and Lamar, I got out of the left seat and was stretching. Soon I noticed a box mounted on the side of the airplane that read "Very Pistol." The other pilot and I decided it was only flares. Nevertheless, it aroused my curiosity and I opened the box and examined its contents. The box contained several flare cartridges of various colors and the pistol to fire them. This was a way of telling someone on the ground the varying degree of distress you were in. Up on the overhead was a port where the pistol could be mounted for firing out the top. Without any reason, except to see if it still worked, I put a red cartridge in the pistol, mounted it in the port and fired it. Each cartridge held five flares. It worked and that was that. After landing from the round robin cross-country, I was driving home and heard over the car radio that an airliner was feared down in eastern Colorado. The reporter said a rancher saw some red flares earlier that afternoon and reported an airliner in trouble. Holy cow! That rancher must have seen my flares! After two days of searching, the authorities found nothing and gave up. The airlines that flew in that area reported no airplanes missing. I said nothing about this and never touched the flare pistol again.

I was preparing to fly a photo mission when the personnel department at headquarters called and informed me that my name had come up for assignment to Korea. I had a lot of B-25 time and they needed B-26 pilots in Korea. The airplanes were quite similar, both being lightweight medium bombers. I was told to get started with my inoculations but two days later, I was informed that there had been a mistake and I didn't have to go to Korea after all. My computer records did not reflect my World War II combat duty. When that error was discovered, my assignment to Korea was rescinded. The policy was to send all pilots who had no combat duty before tapping the pool of those with combat experience, so I got a reprieve. This situation created a lot of dissension among the pilots. Both Major Blackburn and Captain Wasche soon left for Korea and my new boss was Captain Virgil Highstand. He had flown the big B-36 long range six-engine heavy bomber while stationed at Ellsworth AFB in South Dakota. We got along well and I had to quickly check him out in the C-47 and the B-25. He did very well in spite of his size 12 feet. The toe brakes on both airplanes were at the top of the rudder pedals and had to be adjusted to their upper limits to accommodate his large feet.

In the spring of 1954, while on a trip in the B-25, my name came up again for a new assignment. This time it stuck. It wasn't Korea, but Scott AFB, Illinois. As much as I liked my Lowry assignment and the daily flying, I knew it wasn't going to last forever, so the new assignment came as no particular surprise.

My orders to Scott AFB stated that I was to attend an 11-month course in communications. I wondered why a pilot would be sent to a communications course. I discovered that the Air Force had just started cross-training pilots in specialty fields and that was the name of the game. I wasn't complaining. It certainly was better than going to Korea. I had all the combat flying I needed. Being shot at by the enemy was not one of my favorite sports. Shortly after checking into Scott, Joan indicated that she wasn't feeling very well. The doctor at the base hospital said that she was going to have a baby and we were pleased as punch. After three years, we didn't know if we were going to be blessed with children or not.

Base operations at Scott contacted me when they noticed in my records that I had a lot of B-25 instructor time. The base operated B-25s and they wanted me to check out newly assigned pilots. I was happy to do this but could only do it after classes and on Saturdays. One of the many exciting aspects of military life is speculation and anticipation of where you're going next and when. After classes in the communications school, the rest of the guys would go home and study. I was happy to go to base operations and fly for a couple of hours. Most nights, I would still be studying when my wife was in bed fast asleep.

In school, we studied radio theory first; then tackled the workings of a radio receiver. After that, we had to tear down and rebuild and test a large military receiver.. Next, we learned the magic of radio transmission. I found all this fascinating and enjoyed it very much.

My instructor in radio was Master Sergeant Robert Hardy. He was an excellent teacher-very patient and helpful. After Sergeant Hardy retired from the Air Force, he went into radio broadcasting. He spent many years as news director for radio station KMOX in St. Louis. In the early 90s, he suffered an untimely fatal heart attack.

Our training included the study of scrambled communications called "Crypto Graphics." This required secret clearance from the FBI, and I had a special badge to wear to class. I was still flying the B-25 in the afternoons and on Saturday mornings. I lost count of the number of pilots I checked out in that airplane and I enjoyed every minute of it.

Rumors were floating around that the promotion list was out. My good luck was holding up as I was promoted to the rank of Captain. We celebrated that event with a big steak dinner at the officers club. With our first child on the way, I took my wife into Belleville and bought her a new Singer sewing machine. Some lessons came with it and before long, Joan was sewing up a storm, mostly things for the new baby. We had about ten boys names and as many girls names picked out but hadn't come to a decision yet. On the morning of January 19, 1955, we woke up to a miserable day. During the night the rain had turned to freezing rain and left a real mess outside. As I was dressing to go to class, Joan said I had better drop her off at the hospital first. I guess mothers know when it's time. Fortunately our car was in a garage and not out covered with ice. Very carefully, I drove the two miles to the base hospital. After waiting for a while, a nurse came out and handed me a paper bag with my wife's clothes in it-everything.

The maternity ward nurse said I should go on to class as they were going to keep my wife for a while. She went on to tell me not to worry as they knew how to contact me. It felt strange driving over to the school building with my wife's clothes in that paper sack in the back seat of the car. Keeping my mind on "mobile radio concepts" was very difficult that morning. All I could think of was poor Joan up there in the base hospital all alone. At the noon lunch break, I dashed up there to see how things were going. I could have called but never thought of it. The duty nurse told me my wife was doing just fine and I could check again after class at 4 p.m.

About an hour before the end of class, Sergeant Hardy came over and said the hospital just called and I should go over there right away. Icy roads or not, I was there in a flash. The nurse came out smiling and said I was a new father, but to go and see my wife and she would tell me about the baby. As I entered her room, Joan gave me a big smile as she held our new baby. She then said, "Come here and meet your new daughter." She was the prettiest baby I had ever seen. Joan said she felt fine but was very tired. Soon a nurse came and took the baby back to the nursery. Then my wife told me the pediatrician had said that the baby had some kind of heart problem. They were going to watch that very carefully. It took me a long time to get to sleep that night from all the emotion of being a new father and the worry of the baby's condition. The next day I had an important test in radio theory. I should have been thinking of electrons, resistance, impedance, Marconi's laws and all the electrical formulas I needed to know. I just couldn't concentrate on the principals of radio theory that morning.

We named the little girl Sheila Diane. She had 100% of her mother's good looks and features. Before my wife left the hospital, the pediatrician told her not to worry, as the problem with the baby was no doubt minor in nature. We were to bring her back in a week for further examination and monitoring. School was about to end and graduation was planned for April 1. We were not going back to Lowry, but would go on to a new assignment somewhere. Both of us hoped it would be in the Midwest, close to both our families. My mom wrote that she was very happy over the new baby, and couldn't wait to come and see her.

Between final exams and graduation I was informed of my new assignment. Our hopes to stay in the Midwest were shattered. My orders were to proceed by government transportation to Wheelus Air Base in Tripoli, Libya, North Africa. That's not the end of the world but it has been said that you can see it from there. By now the doctors had determined that our little girl had a partial artery blockage plus a hole in one of the upper heart chambers. They said only time would tell and it just might heal itself. Surgery was a possibility, but not now. With today's advanced technology, they would have operated immediately.

I was given three weeks to report to McGuire AFB in New Jersey for transportation to North Africa. The doctors at Scott said, in their opinion, that it was okay for us to take the baby overseas. Joan also wanted to talk to the doctors in Omaha. Air Force policy dictated that I had to go to Wheelus Air Base and secure housing approved by the base commander before my family could join me. My last flight in the B-25 at Scott was a cross-country to Will Rogers field in Oklahoma City and return. I didn't know it then but that was my last flight in the B-25. I had accumulated over 2,000 hours in that fine airplane.

In Omaha, Joan didn't want to stay with her folks so we went out and found a small house to rent. It turned out fine as it was quite close to her folks' house. Back in Denver we had bought our first new car, a

1953 Ford Victoria.   At least Joan and the baby had transportation
when I left for North Africa. The doctors in Omaha also said it was
okay to take the baby overseas since the military had fine doctors and
hospitals over there. The Air Force said that if I were to serve the foreign duty alone, it would be for 18 months. If I later brought my
family over, the assignment would be for three years. We didn't care as
long as we were together.

My nephew, Joe Mahoney, drove Joan and me to the Omaha airport for my departure for over-seas. It was a sad parting and Joe told
me later that Joan cried softly all the way back to her house. Leaving
McGuire AFB, my C-54 transport had to make a fuel stop at Lajes
Field in the Azore Islands out in the Atlantic Ocean. After landing, a
delay was announced; one of the engines on the C-54 had lost an oil
pump just before we landed. I walked over and signed for a room in
the BOQ, and then headed for the Officers Club to relax.. A sign on
the door said they were open 24 hours a day. That was necessary as
flights came in from all directions day and night. The open mess was
located there also. In the club were rows of slot machines that were
kept busy by the waiting passengers. The club had a large bar that was
oval in shape. That night I had my first introduction to Holland's
Heineken beer. It was 25 cents a bottle and I thought it was about the
best tasting stuff I ever had but it nearly got me into trouble.

It was Friday night and the place was packed. On the way from
McGuire, I played cards with two friends and we stuck together at Lajes
Field. At the bar we heard dance music coming from somewhere, so
two of us proceeded to investigate and found a party in progress. Going right in, I soon noticed two girls talking and asked one of them if
she would like to dance. We had been dancing for a few minutes when
someone tapped me on the shoulder. Turning , I was face to face with
a major who was not a happy camper. He informed me that this was a
private affair and asked how I got in. Then he said, "You're also dancing with my wife."

Back at the bar, we had a good laugh over that social blunder.
Also at the bar were three Army nurses who were headed to Germany.
When asked where we were going, I said, "To the Land of Enchantment, Libya, North Africa." The six of us drank beer and talked for a
long time. As the major and his wife were leaving, she gave me a little
wave as they passed the bar. Her husband never saw that. It would be
one more day before our C-54 was fixed and could fly on to the "Land
of Enchantment."

Upon arrival at Wheelus Field, I noticed a lot of MATS (Military
Air Transport Service) airplanes sitting on the ramp. The base was a

big "way stop" for troop movements, and it also had a large gunnery range out on the desert. The 12th Air Force fighter units in Germany would use it on a rotating basis year-round. The fighter units built their own "tent city" on the east side of the base and, after a dispute with the base commander over dress code in the main club; they built their own officers club using a large tent.

I was living in the BOQ and my job was Assistant Base Communications Officer. I worked for a Major Shepherd Schultz and the communications center was located directly across the street from the officers club. I also had two other jobs. One was OIC (Officer in Charge) of the base MARS (Military Airinc Radio Service) radio station. I had a sergeant that operated the station from a trailer on the highest point on the base. Most of their radio traffic was at night when radio wave propagation was better. During the daytime, they were range-limited. A lot of the MARS traffic was to the States at night using radio signals sent to ham operators on the east coast. By using radio-phone patches, verbal messages could be sent to, and received from, almost anywhere.

Base communications was logistically divided into two parts-the inside plant and the outside plant. The inside plant contained the message center, administration and other offices. My office was located in the inside plant. The outside plant contained the storage area which was fenced in and was where all the spare overhead telephone cables, poles and other equipment was stored. In dry weather, everything worked well; but during rare rainy periods, most of the overhead cables were operationally shutdown from the moisture. Using bottles of pressurized nitrogen, we had to pump out all those overhead lines. What a job that was. I had a jeep to drive and was all over the base most days "killing snakes." My third job was on the flight line. Again my records got me a flying job as an instructor in the C-47. The base had four of them. Another instructor was Captain Andy Jackson. We became good friends and went on many good trips in the Gooney Bird as the airplane had been nicknamed. Rated pilots who had a desk job still had to fly a minimum of four hours a month. Base operations liked to have an instructor pilot in command so the co-pilot could come from headquarters, or elsewhere, and didn't have to be rated in the airplane.

Before I could sign up for a trip to Italy or Germany, I had to get Major Schultz's approval. He was a medically grounded pilot and didn't like for me to be gone very much. Until he rotated back to the States, I had a hard time getting the opportunity to fly. Andy Jackson tried to get me transferred to Base Operations for a full time flying job. After several attempts, he gave up trying. One of the trips Major Schultz didn't have any problem with was the courier run down the coast to a radar site located near Benghazi. There the base operated a remote AC&W (Aircraft Control and Warning) site. Using the latest radar, they controlled friendly aircraft and kept track of bogeys. The radar site was due east of Wheelus, about 400 miles away and all over water. Base communications had the responsibility of supporting the radio trailer and its personnel at Benghazi.

Wheelus Field also had an AC&W radar site located on the highest point on the base. A good friend of mine, Captain Ralph Frank, was the OIC of the site. Ralph and his wife, Susie, entertained a lot and Joan and I had many good times with them. About 30 people were stationed at the Benghazi radar site and they were in constant need of supplies, parts, mail from home and a steady and continuing rotation of personnel. They were totally isolated and relied on Wheelus Field for support. The C-47 courier supported them with weekly flights.

On the next Benghazi trip, Major Schultz quickly gave me the okay to fly because he also wanted to make the trip. He said he needed to inspect our communications trailer down there and talk to the people who operated it. The trailer was the radio link to Wheelus Field and Europe. It was a clear day when we departed and the weather forecast was clear with unlimited visibility. The flight took about three hours and, normally, the Site Commander invited us to stay for lunch before heading back home. This day, they served ham and lima beans. Something was wrong because when I sat down to eat, Major Schultz had already eaten and looked pea green. He and a couple of others got sick as dogs, so sick they couldn't fly back with us. The very thought of flying made them even sicker. Thankfully, my copilot and I helped unload the airplane and hadn't eaten with the early group. It turned out the problem was the ham, not the beans. The next few trips to Benghazi, I passed up lunch and ate on the airplane. Our canned K-rations had replaced the old WW II C-rations. They were somewhat better but not by much. At least they didn't make you sick. We always kept a good supply of those rations on board the courier airplane. A week later, Major Schultz rode the courier back and said that was his last trip to that place.

Letters from Joan saying all was well in Omaha were frequent. She said the baby was fine and really looked healthy in spite of her problems. She kept asking if I had found approved quarters yet. I replied that I was searching diligently but had found nothing I liked.

Ralph Frank had a car-well, sort of a car. It was a British Morris Minor and a sad excuse for an automobile. It was tiny and underpowered but it was transportation nonetheless. Anyway, Ralph took me into the city of Tripoli several times to look for housing. Not finding anything, I was becoming somewhat discouraged when one day we came across a new building site in what they called the new "American Sector." The Arabs could only build mud and stick shacks; so the Italians did all the construction in the city. From WW II until 1948, Libya was under Italian control. Then by decree, a very slow takeover from the Italians was started. It didn't work since the Libyans couldn't do anything productive, so the Italians stayed to teach them how to run their country. When I arrived there, no colleges and only a couple of high schools existed. There were, however, some elementary schools. The few affluent Libyans sent their children to schools in England or France, never to Italy.

The city of Tripoli had a beautiful harbor and the new section was quite modern. Entering the old section, you quickly go back 100 years in time. Up until 1948, the country was under Italian control. Now it was an independent nation with no knowledge of how to operate even the simplest business. The Italians had to stay and teach them and it turned into a circus. Every business and municipal office had dual management. Every transaction, no matter how small, took forever because of all the constant jabbering. The Arabs loved to lick the official stamps needed for every piece of paper. Then they would take a big cancellation tool to bang those stamps as hard as they could. They got a big charge out of that. The language barrier was terrible; the Italians didn't speak English, the Americans didn't speak Italian and the Arabs spoke neither. Gestures and pantomime were the order of the day when you had to go downtown. It got so humorous that, at the Officers Club each night we would laugh and laugh over those silly happenings. In the American sector, the Italians were building some four-plex apartments. The construction looked pretty good and one day I located the construction manager. To my surprise, he spoke a little English. At the site, I met Major Ken Frain who had just rented a unit. He took me over to see it and told me one unit was still available. The other two had been rented by Standard Oil and Shell Oil Companies. I found the manager again and, after some discussion, I had an apartment!

It would require a few days to obtain the base commander's approval of the unit. After approval was obtained, the New York Port Authority could be notified, and they would cut orders authorizing my family to travel by military transportation to Tripoli. That night I wrote Joan a long letter describing the new apartment that had tile and marble everywhere. When the Arabs built something, it was hard to determine whether they were building it or tearing it down. It was a sight to behold. The apartment I had rented was not quite finished, and I checked on its progress at every opportunity. It was quite large and would easily accommodate all our possessions, including our big TV set. The base operated a low-power TV station that was on the air a few hours each evening. The news, weather and sports were all we needed. A couple of times a week a movie would be scheduled and that was just great In another letter home, I told my wife to get rid of the Ford and make plans with Offutt AFB to have our furniture picked up from the little house in Omaha, The rest of our furniture was in military storage. Joan had a friend whose husband was a car salesman. He told Joan not to worry as he would take care of the Ford. He took care of it alright; he only gave her wholesale price.

I was excited about having my family with me. Living as a bachelor hadn't been much fun. The officers club had a German band that played six nights a week and they were excellent. Their lead trumpet player could imitate Harry James, Clyde McCoy and other prominent trumpet players of the time. Their female singers rotated every month back to Germany, and each one was better looking than her predecessor. The vocalists could imitate any American female singer of the time. There was a poker game in the club every night. The players were mostly transient air crews; and the pots were huge with script, green, marks and Italian lira-too rich for my blood. I just watched the nightly money exchange. The club had one pool table and I taught the German lead trumpet player how to play "nine ball." That's where the nine and five balls are money balls. The young musician became facinated with the game and was always ready to play.

The weather at Wheelus, located on the Mediterranean coast, was either very good or very bad. When the breeze blew in off the sea we had clear, warm days and crisp, cool nights.. When the wind, known as gibley winds blew off the desert, the weather was hot and miserable day and night. The blowing fine red sand permeated everything. Doors and windows could not deter it. When I woke up in the morning, there was fine dust everywhere, even in my teeth. Life during the sandstorm was pure misery. Because of that, several of us "bachelors" stayed at the club until closing each night just to keep out of those dusty BOQ rooms. I enjoyed listening to the German band and the German singer and drinking German beer. That combination is a welcome respite after a hard day's work.

One day about mid-morning, the sergeant in charge of the message center called to say that I had a telegram. He said he would bring it right over to my office. While waiting for Sergeant Hansen to arrive, my mind was racing. The wire had to be either from Joan saying she was leaving, or from the New York Port Authority giving me arrival details. It was from my wife and I was so excited I could hardly open it. The wire message was dated July 20, 1955, addressed to Captain Thomas F. Gordon, APO 231, Tripoli, Libya and it read, "Your mother passed away suddenly-heart. Red Cross wiring. Joan." Shocked beyond belief, my eyes filled with tears as I couldn't even think for a moment. My poor mother! She wrote to me every week without fail. Each Sunday night, she would sit at her kitchen table and write a three or four-page letter telling me of the past week's happenings, news that my sisters would never tell me. Now there would be no more letters.

With a big lump in my throat and an aching heart, I just sat there at my desk with my face in my hands. In a second wire, the American Red Cross wanted to know if I could come home. I hated being so far away at a time like this, about halfway around the world. Getting my composure back, I went to Major Schultz's office but he was on the phone. I waited in the hall until I heard him hang up, then went in. At first, he acted like he thought I was going to ask him if I could take another flight. I still couldn't talk very well, so I just handed him the wire. After reading it, he changed completely and said he would help me get a flight out to the states. First he said, "Better go up to the MARS station and have your boys arrange for a radio/phone patch to the states tonight."

Back in my office I called Sergeant McPherson, the NCO in charge of the radio station, and told him what I needed. He said I would have to wait until after dark for good propagation of the airwaves. That night, after eating at the club, I went back to my office and did some paper work while I waited for Sergeant McPherson to call. After about an hour, the phone rang. "Better come up here. We have contact with a ham radio operator in Morristown, New Jersey." Sgt McPherson said. My jeep got me up there in record time. If an AP (Air Police) had tried to stop me, I would have just kept on going. When I arrived, the MARS operator said the ham in the States was trying to make a phone patch to my wife in Omaha. Soon the night operator got out of his chair and said, "Captain Gordon, sit down here and start transmitting."

Radio-telephone conversations are always one-way. One party transmits his message and indicates the end of his transmission by saying "over." After hearing "over", the other party takes his turn and transmits his response, again ending his transmission by saying the word "over." This worked well as long as one of the two parties didn't butt in out of turn. I couldn't believe I was actually hearing my wife's voice way back in Omaha. She said she read me 5 by 5 (good readability and signal strength), while I only read her 3 by 3 (fair readability and strength). When I asked her what happened to mom, she replied that she had either a stroke or heart attack, or both. When the doctor arrived at the house, she was already gone. Joan said they could hold off the funeral another three days, and asked if I could get there. I told her I would do everything in my power to do so, but if something should happen to prevent it, I would get word to her some way.

That night lying in my bed, all I could think about was my poor mother. She was so good and did so many nice things for me in my life, and what little did I do for her. I felt bluer than blue. Early the next morning I was down at the MATS passenger terminal with emergency leave orders in hand, thanks to Major Schultz. He had HQ personnel do that during the night so I could get out of there. The sergeant at the terminal desk said all the planes heading for the States were full of active duty people rotating back home. My emergency leave orders did not have priority over them, only over people on ordinary leave. Finally, a Lieutenant came out and said there was another airplane coming through in about two hours, and would check availability of seats on that flight. I was getting very nervous now as time was becoming crucial.

When the westbound MATS plane landed, it had on board a 2nd Lieutenant "courier." That's a person who baby-sits classified material all the way to the States. He cannot leave the airplane until the final destination. His food has to be brought to him and he has to use the "facilities" on the airplane. With some help from my Wheelus friends, I became the new courier leaving Wheelus in just a few minutes as soon as the refueling was finished. I was very lucky to be on that airplane. After a long flight, I landed at dawn at McGuire AFB in New Jersey near Philadelphia. Getting rid of the classified baggage, I took a taxicab over to the Philadelphia International Airport. All the way I kept telling the driver to speed it up. At the airport, United Airlines said they had a flight to Omaha via Chicago leaving in about an hour. With ticket in hand, I paced back and forth at the gate waiting for the airplane to arrive from Newark. When it landed, I almost held my breath that it wasn't broken or something. Near the gate, I spotted a telephone and called my wife. She couldn't believe I got to the States so quickly. I gave her my arrival time and she said my nephew, Harry Mahoney, would pick me up at the Omaha airport and drive me to the funeral. It was to be held later that same morning. I looked at my watch and realized there wasn't much time for me to fly to Omaha, and then be driven up to Cedar Rapids, but it worked! My nephew met me and drove at breakneck speed to the funeral. I arrived an hour before the service after having traveled over 6,000 miles. That whole trip was nothing short of a miracle.

After the funeral and back at the house, my dad asked me to come outside with him. He told me what a shock it was to him, on the night of my mother's attack, when Doctor Reeder told him that she was gone. It was a big shock to me to lose my mother but I'm sure losing a mate must be even a bigger shock. Dad had gone through that same thing years earlier when his first wife died. After a meeting with my dad and my sisters, we went along with his decision to try to stay in the house alone. We didn't like it but that's what he wanted to do; so we decided to let him try it. Three of my sisters lived near and would look after him and bring him cooked food and other necessities like that. His eyesight was failing but he knew his way around the house by memory. Amazingly, he could even walk downtown to get the mail and then to the local cafe for lunch. After that, he daily went to the Blue Moon (local pub) where he played cards all afternoon. In the evening, after a meal my sisters had prepared, he played solitaire until bedtime. That was his daily routine. He refused to use a white cane-he said he knew where he was going. He talked to everyone, and recognized people by the sound of their voice.

When I notified Offutt AFB that I was home on emergency leave, I requested that they contact the New York Port Authority and arrange for my family to return to North Africa with me. It seems that some good comes from every bad situation. Offutt made arrangements to pick up all our household goods and pack them in large conex crates for shipment overseas.. The transportation department issued travel orders for my family and me to catch a commercial airliner for Philadelphia. There, a military bus took us to McGuire AFB and, after one night in family quarters, we boarded a bus to the St. Francis hotel in Brooklyn, New York. We waited there for air transportation to Wheelus Air Base in Tripoli. My wife said she looked at a globe and discovered that Tripoli was on the other side of the world.

It was tough to leave family and friends, especially my dad. As I left him at his house, I gave him a big hug and said, "Take care of yourself God Bless you; and I love you." I cannot remember ever saying that to my dad before. I probably did so as a child but, as an adult, I don't think so. I tried telling Joan all about Tripoli, Wheelus Air Base and North Africa in general. She didn't mind traveling, but not that far from home. When I described our apartment, she thought it would be fine but we didn't have a car now. I promised to buy some kind of a car as soon as we returned there. Italian, British and German cars were available for purchase in Tripoli. During our stay at the St. Francis hotel in Brooklyn, a terrible tropical storm came roaring up the east coat from the Caribbean and it was a bad one. The name of the storm was Diane and when it reached New York City, it was still raging with high winds and heavy rain falling in sheets. Joan, Sheila and I had a room on the 26th floor of the St. Francis hotel. Next door to us was another Air Force wife, Susie Frank. When I told her I knew her husband Ralph over in Tripoli, we formed an immediate bond. One night after Joan fed our baby and Susie fed her four children, we decided that a stiff drink would be nice. To ride out that terrible storm, the three of us felt some fortification was in order.

Looking out the window from the 26th floor, I could barely make out the red neon liquor store sign across the street. Like a fool, I volunteered to go down and get a bottle, rain or no rain, The hotel had a bar but they charged $25 for a $6 bottle of bourbon. It was raining so hard, I could barely make it across the street. Leaving the liquor store, I had a sack of ice, soda and a fifth of Old Fitzgerald sour mash bourbon. Back on the 26th floor, I had to get out of my wet clothes. The two women took the sack and made some needed drinks. For my gallant effort, I received a big hug from each of them. The three of us stayed up and talked and drank until about 2 a.m. Outside, hurricane Diane was venting her fury on New York City as the five children slept soundly.

In the morning all was quiet, as the storm had moved further up the east coast. After lunch we packed up and took the bus to McGuire AFB to catch our airplane. Instead of a regular airliner, it was a chartered airplane - a Flying Tigers Constellation. The four-engine transport had 96 seats and a crew of five. Every seat was filled with either military personnel or military dependents. While taxiing out for takeoff, the plane suddenly stopped. Over the intercom came, "Folks, we have to go back to the ramp as we have a mechanical problem." An hour later, on another airplane, we departed the USA. After a box supper, everyone settled down for the long flight to North Africa with a fuel stop at Lajes Air Base, Azore Islands, in the Atlantic Ocean. An announcement woke me up and over the speaker I heard; "This is the Captain speaking, Lajes Field is below landing minimums due to rain squalls, we are proceeding to Santa Maria Island where the weather is better." I told Joan that Santa Maria was the only alternate available. The required fuel reserve for an island airport is two hours of "holding" fuel. This is to allow any weather to pass on during that time. Over Santa Maria we had to hold for a few minutes to allow airplanes below us to land in a controlled sequence. Finally on the ground, we walked from the airplane to the small terminal in moderate rain. In the terminal cafe, we were served fried eggs, toast and coffee. Nobody was the least bit hungry. The clock on the cafe wall read 3:30 a.m.

Soon an announcement blared over a speaker for us to be ready to board our aircraft in 15 minutes. The rain never let up the whole time we were there. After another long flight, the airplane finally touched down in the early afternoon at Wheelus Field, Tripoli. Everyone on board was dead tired and grumpy. Joan said she didn't think she would ever be this far away from home. A military bus took us into town and we stopped at the Del Wahari hotel. It wasn't the Hilton but it would do. The next day I heard it was owned by Mafia mobster Lucky Luciano. A casino was located off the lobby and on the top floor, female companionship was available for a price.

The next morning I boarded the military shuttle bus to the base to see if I could get some temporary cots and furniture for our apartment until our own possessions arrived. Base Supply provided a truck to take what I could find out to the American Sector. After getting the water and electricity turned on, we moved into our marble mansion. With army cots and makeshift furniture, it was not very comfortable but we managed. It was surely better than hotel living. As quickly as I could, I went to the local car dealer and bought a German Opel convertible There wasn't much to choose from, but I picked the Opel because I knew the Germans made good airplanes and I reasoned that their cars had to be good also.

The doctors at the Wheelus Air Base hospital told us our little baby girl really should be checked by the specialists at the Air Force hospital in Wiesbaden, Germany, as they really didn't have a heart specialist on staff. This would require an air-evacuation flight in a C-54. In a week, Joan and little Sheila would leave for Germany. As the big C-54 rolled down the runway and took to the air, I watched my wife and baby daughter fly away. I said a quick prayer that they would have a safe trip and a good consultation. The Wheelus hospital had a special radio/telephone link with the USAF hospital in Wiesbaden. Soon I heard that they would be back in a couple of days. While they were gone, I got some flying time in on a C-47 trip to Tunis and back the next day.

The doctors in Wiesbaden said they wanted to see our baby again in a month. They weren't sure what should or could be done for her. In the meantime our furniture had arrived with minimal damage and soon we were quite comfortable in our second floor apartment. Everyone in the American Sector had an Italian maid and an Arab boy that watched the place and took care of the courtyard. Each building had a six-foot stone wall surrounding it. When we would drive up, the yard boy took great pleasure in opening and closing the big iron gate. On top of the stone fence, cut glass was embedded in the concrete to discourage thieves, but it didn't always work. The Arab thieves are the world's craftiest and most silent intruders. Our maid's name was Maria and Ali was our yard boy. Each night Ali slept on the floor without any bedding in the marble foyer downstairs.

During my tour of duty at Wheelus, I had the opportunity to go TDY (temporary duty) to the Furstenfeldbruck Air Base in Germany. The Air Force said anyone who flew fighter-type airplanes in WW II could become qualified in jets. The Lockheed T-33A "T-Bird" school was at "Fursty" located near Munich. Four weeks and 40 flight hours later, I was a qualified T-33A jet pilot. It was October, 1955 and Ralph Frank, Dick Gant and myself who went through the school together, attended our first Oktoberfest in Munich. This Bavarian feast is fueled by large quantities of beer, baked chicken and sausages. Five huge tents, sponsored by five local breweries, were set up in the Theresienwiese Fairgrounds. In each tent, a German band played wonderful music for singing and dancing, mostly singing. Legend has it that the festival grew out of the celebrations held when Bavarian Crown Prince Ludwig married Princess Therese of Saxony-Hildburghausen on October 12, 1810.

After several months of taking little Sheila to the hospital in Germany, we were informed by the doctors that we had two choices. We could continue treatment and hoped she outgrew the problem or return to the US for surgery. If surgery was our choice, it should be done in the next six months. In any event, they highly recommended that we take the baby back to Walter Reed Army Hospital in Washington, D.C., as soon as possible. With the doctor's help, the Air Force gave me what is called a compassionate transfer back to the States. Joan and Sheila left for Walter Reed right from Germany on an air-evacuation flight. Back at Wheelus, I arranged for our household goods to be shipped home. Also, I had to turn my Opel in for shipment home since I wanted to keep it.

Before I left Wheelus, I was informed by the base personnel office that my next assignment was to the 305th Bomb Wing at MacDill AFB in Tampa, Florida. The wing flew the Boeing B-47 long-range, six-engine jet bomber. Our household goods would go into storage and catch up with us later. On Labor Day, 1956, I caught up with my family at the big Walter Reed Army Hospital in Washington, D.C. There the doctors said surgery was the only sensible thing to do. If we relied on nature to heal her little heart, she might become an invalid. The next day I bought a used car and we drove to Omaha to spend time with family and friends. We drove up to see my dad and he enjoyed holding his granddaughter on his lap. He was doing okay living by himself. We still had not made up our minds about the surgery and, in a few days, left for our next home in Tampa, Florida.

After a short stay in a motel, I luckily found a furnished house for rent. When I checked in at the base at MacDill, I learned that the 305th Bomb Wing was TDY in England. After telling them I was on a compassionate assignment, I didn't have to go over there. I was allowed to stay and start my training with the 306th Bomb Wing which was on station. MacDill was a busy place since the 6th Air Division was based there as were the two bomb wings and a refueling wing. The airfield was filled to capacity with bombers and tankers all over the place.

When I finished my ground training, I was sent to Wichita, Kansas, to get checked out in the B-47 bomber. Boeing operated a B-47 factory in Wichita so it was convenient for everybody. The training school was at nearby McConnell AFB. Soon, I found a furnished apartment and we were in good shape. Our little girl was doing as well as could be expected. There were days when she was fine and acted like nothing was wrong. Then, some days, she didn't feel well and it tore us up with worry. When I became qualified in the B-47, I felt good about flying a big airplane with six jet engines. Now I was one of the very few Air Force pilots who flew both fighters and bombers. It sure broadened my scope about aviation and its capabilities. As soon as I qualified in the bomber, I was sent to Stead AFB in Reno, Nevada, for the Air Crew Survival Training Course. Joan and Sheila drove back to MacDill and our rented house.

At Stead, the first week was all ground school, learning how to escape and evade after a bail-out over enemy territory. The next ten days were hell. They took us up into the mountains in a six-by-six truck about 20 miles from the base. After dumping us off, we were on our own as in a simulated bailout. We had meager provisions and were expected to live off the land while trying to get back to the base. The only problem was, they had "enemy forces" out there in jeeps, wearing black uniforms, trying to capture us. I lost 12 pounds while escaping, even though we did catch some rabbits and chased a couple of porcupines up a tree. We were that hungry.

Back at MacDill, Joan found a housing area just off the base where new construction was underway. There, we bought our first new home in a subdivision called Gandy Gardens. It was a small house but we were proud of it. I had sold the little Opel to a captain who was going to Guam and needed a small reliable car. Soon I bought a new 1957 Buick sedan. Joan and Sheila made a couple of air-evacuation trips to

Walter Reed but there was no change in Sheila's condition. The very thought of major surgery on that poor little girl almost drove us out of our minds.

Practice bombing missions in the big Boeing B-47 were flown on the average of three times a week. We would take off around 7 p.m. and climb up to high altitude and make a few bomb runs at the Okeechopee bombing range. After that, we practiced refueling. Aerial refueling is very strenuous, especially at night. Formation flying is easy compared to aerial refueling. After taking on the proper amount of fuel, I would fly down to New Orleans and get started on a night celestial navigation leg. The course ran south from New Orleans to a point in the Gulf about a hundred miles out. At that point. I would turn east and head for MacDill AFB on the coast just west of Tampa, all the while navigating by the stars with shots from our sextant. My crew number was R-32, and consisted of Fred Belfay, my copilot, who also operated the sextant, and Jerry McDowell, the bombardier/ navigator. Jerry rode in the nose section where he had an 18-inch radar scope to guide the airplane when not using the sextant. We won crew of the month more than once for excellent bombing scores. When we hit a target dead center, it was called getting a "shack." Few B-47 crews had many shacks to their credit. Every other month my crew went TDY to North Africa to pull ground alert at one of three bases the Air Force built over there. On the flight over, I had to contact a tanker aircraft for refueling, and then fly all night. Things would proceed nicely until the sun cracked the horizon. It was always a beautiful sight but it sure deflated the body and quickly everyone became deadly tired. After coasting into the country, we had to make three bomb runs on a radar bomb scoring site located at Marrakech, North Africa, then go in and land at one of the forward bases. Those kinds of flight were totally exhausting. Of the 17 days I was over there, 10 were spent on ground alert. The airplanes sat on the ramp loaded with two nuclear weapons. Thank God we never had to drop them on our targets deep inside Russia. On the trip back home to MacDill, I didn't have tanker support and had to land at Lajes in the Azores for ground refueling. Our K-System radar was so good, I could make my own radar approach to any airport anywhere. My bomb/nav would get the airport on his radar scope and give me heading corrections and tell me when to start my descent. I was always happy to get back home to my family after those grueling TDY assignments in North Africa.

After many long discussions, Joan and I finally decided to go ahead with surgery for our little girl. We didn't want to, but thought it was the best thing to do. After Joan's last trip to Walter Reed, arrangements were made for us to be at Mayo Brothers Clinic in Rochester, Minnesota, the last week of December, 1957. Our Christmas came early that year because we wanted to stop and see both of our families on the way up to the Mayo Brothers Clinic. Sheila's favorite toy that Christmas was not a big doll, but a red Radio Flyer coaster wagon. The 305th Bomb Wing gave me a 15-day medical leave with option to extend if needed. After a short visit with both of our families, the Gordon family checked into the Mayo Brothers Clinic on December 31, 1957. It was one New Year's Eve we did not celebrate in any form. Sheila was admitted to St. Mary's Hospital and Joan and I found a motel room close by. Open heart surgery was scheduled for 8 a.m. on January 2, 1958. In the following three weeks, a lot was taken out of our lives, mainly our precious daughter. Dr. Kirtland headed the heart team that did the open heart surgery. He claimed the operation itself was a success; but when they restarted her little heart, a heart-block developed. It was an irregular beat and neither medicine, a pacemaker nor anything else helped. The poor little girl fought like a trooper, but 14 days after her surgery, the poor child just played out and was gone. It was the morning of January 16, 1958. She missed her third birthday by just three days. Now we had to take her to Omaha for burial. It would not be easy.

St. Mary's Hospital in Rochester made arrangements to have the body shipped to Omaha by rail. There would be a connection in Sioux City, Iowa, and then on to Omaha. Well, our luck was still running bad, as the connection in Sioux City was missed and her body ended up in Des Moines. It was finally straightened out and we were totally spent, both emotionally and physically.

Back at MacDill, Colonel Frank Johnson, the 305th Bomb Wing Commander, called me into his office about the middle of January and expressed his sorrow. He had been told by the 365th squadron commander what happened. Colonel and Mrs. Johnson had five children of their own, two of which were not even in school yet. A year before, he had transferred in from France after a three-year tour. He told me that there was a very good chance the wing would be moving to Grissom AFB, Kokomo, Indiana. There we would trade our B-47's for the new Mach 2 Convair B-58 Hustler bomber. Then he surprised me, "Tom, I have something that you might like even better. Our three forward bases in Spain need experienced B-47 Aircraft Commanders to be controllers in their command posts. What would you think of that?" When I didn't reply right away, he said, "Go home and talk it over with your wife and if you want it, I'll recommend you to represent the 305th Bomb Wing It would be a concurrent assignment. Your wife will go with you, not join you later." Arriving home that night, I had a cold beer and suggested we have dinner at the newly renovated MacDill Officers Club. While enjoying a dry martini before dinner, I told Joan what Colonel Johnson had offered me. We discussed the pros and cons of both Kokomo and Spain. Before going to sleep that night, we decided that we wanted to go to Spain.

I hated to give up the chance to fly the Convair Hustler, the B-58, at Kokomo, but felt a change of scenery might be good tonic for both of us. The next morning, I sent Colonel Johnson a memo stating that I wanted to go to Spain. Of the three bases there, Zaragoza, Madrid and Seville, I told him I wanted Seville first with Madrid as second choice. Soon, orders were cut assigning me to the Moron Air Base Command Post in Seville. My duty there would be forward B-47 aircraft controller. I would control the aircraft as they came from the States on their TDYs to the forward alert bases. The Air Force allowed us to take all of our furniture and possessions with us overseas. A year later, that was limited to just 2,000 pounds. The rest would go into long-term Government storage in Philadelphia.

One day during the first week in May 1958, Joan and I boarded a MATS airplane at McGuire AFB and flew nonstop to Madrid. I decided to keep our 1957 Buick, and arranged for it to be shipped overseas. After one night in Madrid, we left by train for Seville. The train cars were compartmented and it was rather fun to travel that way. The train left Madrid one afternoon and arrived in Seville the next morning. On the trip, we met up with another fellow controller, Gerry Weimer, from Forbes AFB in Topeka, Kansas. Gerry hailed from Dunkirk, New York and was single. The Air Force in Spain had a sponsorship program for newly arriving people. Our sponsors were Don and Nancy Crowley and they were fine folks. Nancy, a former teacher, spoke fluent Spanish and that really helped a lot. Don worked in the plans and programs section at base headquarters. He was also a rated bombardier/navigator. Don and Gerry both had been in the same B-47 Bomb Wing back in Kansas, but came from different squadrons.

Leaving the Seville train station, Nancy Crowley drove us to the Christina hotel where we stayed until I could arrange for base housing. The air base was 20 miles from Seville but there was an Air Force auxiliary base near the city called San Pablo. The main housing units were located there, as only key personnel lived on the air base. The airfield was joint-use as the runways were shared by the US Air Force and the Spanish Air Force. Strangely enough they flew ME-109 fighters and the Stuka JU-88 dive bomber. Seeing those German airplanes flying around still made me a little nervous.

My primary job as a forward aircraft controller in the command post was to monitor the Atlantic crossing of temporary duty bombers going in either direction. Usually they would come over non-stop, providing they had air refueling support. When the tankers couldn't support them, they ground-staged at Lajes on the way to Spain, and at Loring AFB in Maine when going home. Every two weeks, a new bomb wing would arrive. There were always 10 fully loaded bombers on ground alert.

Controllers in the command post worked in shifts because the control center operated around the clock, seven days a week. Shift work was not a problem, as it gave me some prime time off. Until my car arrived, I had to hitch rides to and from work. I didn't fly the B-47 anymore, but was back with my old friend, the Douglas Racer, the C-47 transport. Every week two C-47s flew the courier runs. One went to Madrid, Zaragoza and back. The other went to Gibraltar, Rabat, Morocco and back. Again, I was given instructor pilot status. Now I could take almost any pilot with me in the right seat on those courier runs. I enjoyed flying those trips very much but the old radios were a problem. I always had a crew chief with me and one of his jobs was to change the radio crystals every time we were given a new frequency. No button pushing like later on. The set was in the tail section of the airplane; so the crew chief would have to run back and change the crystals quickly so I could transmit on the new frequency. It kept us on our toes to say the least. Once in a while, I would get a good trip to Rome or to the Frankfurt/Wiesbaden area. On those occasions, I usually had a day or two to relax and enjoy the culture. The good food and beer in Germany and the good food and wines in Rome were the best in the world in my opinion.

Before long, Joan and I were assigned a new unit in San Pablo base housing. Moving in, we had to be very careful as the sidewalks were not poured yet; we just had some boards lying on top of the mud. Our unit was a duplex and our neighbors were Mary and Jack Terpening, another controller. In Spain, everyone had a maid and soon we found Lola. The only English word she knew was "okay." We didn't even know the Spanish equivalent. Joan and Lola spent hours in the kitchen learning to converse and it was all in Spanish. Soon Joan could speak with vendors at the door and with waiters and clerks in stores. Lola was a good teacher and she was honest. A lot of the families had trouble with their maids stealing food. Joan gave Lola something in the way of food every day when she left for home. To the best of our knowledge, she never stole a thing. To her, we were Senor and Senora Gordon. We had no children, so she had the best job in the world. The tile floors in our duplex were hand scrubbed every day including wet-mopping the cement stoop and walkway out to the carport.

The Spanish had a habit of turning off the electricity or water to our San Pablo units without any prior notice. Usually it was at the worst time, late in the afternoon, when all the mothers were starting to cook supper for their families. Before long everybody bought English-built Aladdin heating stoves. The stoves burned kerosene and did three things: produced light through its glass fire door, gave off heat and had a flat top for cooking. Large families had several. Joan and I had one and used it many times. The Air Force was still letting people take their annual leave in one lump so, in late summer of 1959, Joan and I planned a 30-day vacation to Europe's main continent. I got the Buick tuned up with new spark plugs and borrowed two 5-gallon "jerry cans" for reserve gasoline. They would ride in the trunk and the luggage would occupy the back seat. We needed special coupons to buy gasoline at military-approved petrol stations in France and Germany. The stations were easy to find, as each had a large sign that read "US Military Approved." Traveling through France, Monaco and Germany was a nice experience. We had good friends stationed at Wiesbaden Air Base near Frankfurt, Germany. Burt and Helen Emerson, from Denver, were there and we had a grand time visiting, eating good food and drinking wonderful German beer. Next I headed the Buick towards Brussels and I tried to find the Corso Club from the war. It was gone now but we did stay at the Metropole hotel. It had been restored and was in very nice condition. When I asked the manager about the Corso Club, he said it was torn down shortly after the war. I said to my wife that I just had to visit the old site for nostalgic reasons. She went along with that, and walked over there with me.

Back at Wiesbaden, the Emersons drove us to Rudesheim on the Rhine river. This was in the heart of the Rhineland-the German wine country. Rudesheim is a quaint town and it was a pleasure to stroll through the narrow walking streets. We noticed a lot of taverns; most had a band playing very nice selections. Wine was all they served. Beer was not available, even if you wanted some. Most of the wine stubes (public taverns) had dance floors. The bands played wonderful music all afternoon and into the evening. We had a grand time in that splendid setting.

We left Spain earlier through Barcelona and returned the same way. Driving out of Spain was easy but coming back into the country was a different story. In Spain, all owners of American cars were required to have in the car at all times an up-to-date B-26 book, a folder that contained all the paperwork that established ownership, registration and insurance in Spain. It took an hour to clear Spanish customs because they had to carefully inspect each and every piece of paper in the B-26 book. After that they would examine the car, including underneath, very carefully. I guess they thought Americans were trying to smuggle something into their country.

Spain had a big rat problem-they were everywhere. Driving at night, you could see them running down the street by the curb. In the morning, when I would get up and go to the kitchen to make coffee, I would see them in the yard playing and jumping around in the grass like pets. We also had a problem with them coming up through the sewer system into our units through the bathroom stools. Everybody kept their stool lids closed and covered with a brick or some other heavy object resting on it. American wives became very nervous sitting on those Spanish stools. Once, when I was home during the day, a young mother came running over screaming that a rat was loose in her house. With help from some nearby Spanish workers, we managed to corner and kill it. That was big sport for those Spanish workers.

During one of our vacations to the continent, we checked into the big General Walker R&R hotel in Bavaria. It only cost four dollars a night for a big comfortable room. There was no bar but the dining room served beer and wine and that was just fine. One night while attending a performance of local talent, including a very good ice show, the head waiter brought a young woman to join us at our table. She introduced herself as Helga Brown, and said she was on a personal holiday. The show turned out to be excellent and when leaving, I asked Helga if we could drop her somewhere. She accepted and directed me to her hotel. Upon arriving, Helga asked if Joan and I would like to stop for a night cap. We said that would be nice. The hotel had a small band playing in the lounge. Over drinks, Helga told us of her growing up in Eastern Germany with her parents and one sister. When the Russians started their push into Germany during World War II, all young German girls were scared to death. Helga's parents decided to take the girls out to a friend's place in the country and hid them in the loft of a chicken coop. Food and water were brought to them and they managed to escape the dreadful Russian advance. Soon the dance floor was filled with people. After dancing with my wife, I asked Helga if she would like to dance. I noticed that she danced very close to me. Later, after a couple more drinks, she became emotional and confessed she had run away from her army sergeant husband. She also said that he was no doubt out looking for her. We bade her goodnight and quickly got out of there. While in Garmish, Joan and I rode the cable car up to the top of the Zugspitze Mountain in the Bavarian Alps. The area is very beautiful and the snow was quite deep near the top. After finishing lunch, we rode a cog-train back down and that was exciting too. In the same general area was Hitler's famous hideaway in Berchtesgaden, called the "Eagle's Nest." It wasn't Camp David but was very plush by German standards.

On the way back to Seville, the car's right rear tire blew out. The roads in Spain were very coarse and hard on tires. Now, without a spare, we headed for the city of Zaragoza where I could buy new tires at the USAF base, but we never reached it as another tire blew about 30 minutes later. Now, with only three tires, we were stranded. It was mid-afternoon in the mountains of northern Spain and there wasn't much traffic on the road. A few cars whizzed by and finally a small black car stopped. A doctor and his wife from Madrid asked if they could help. They knew a little English and with our limited Spanish, we were able to converse. After loading the better of the two blown tires in his trunk, the doctor took it into the next village for possible repair. He said that he would ask the repair shop to bring the tire back out to us.

My wife was getting nervous out there on that lonely road as the sun was starting to set and some Spanish road workers were in the area. After a long wait, I saw the headlight of a motorcycle come over the hill. Some way, the repair shop repaired the tire with a bootpatch. With Joan holding the flashlight, the Spanish boy and I got the tire on the car. He didn't know one word of English; so we tried our Spanish to ask how far it was to the next village. No luck. Driving very carefully and slowly, we made it into the village, paid the repair shop and decided to go on to Zaragoza. Sometime after midnight we finally reached the air base. The sleepy billeting clerk let us stay in the VIP quarters. The suite was large and comfortable and had an "honors bar." After a long and strenuous day, the little bar with its contents of drinks and snacks was indeed a lifesaver.

One rainy Sunday night in early October, we heard a knock on our front door. As I opened it, there stood an American Red Cross officer. After verifying that he had the correct house, I asked him to come in. He asked me to tell my wife to wait in a back room as he wanted to talk to me alone. That was strange and I soon found out why. The Red Cross had just received a cablegram from Omaha stating that my wife's father had passed away. The Red Cross man felt that if he told my wife the bad news himself, the shock might have been too great for her. After he left, Joan took the bad news showing good composure. Immediately, I walked over to the chaplain's quarters and asked for Father Lorge. We walked back to our quarters and sat down over some hot coffee and talked about Joan's options.

Father Lorge spoke fluent Spanish and said he would arrange for an early morning flight for Joan on Iberia Airlines to Madrid. Then he would arrange space on a MATS flight to McGuire AFB. I told her how to get to Philadelphia Airport for a United Airlines flight to Omaha. Now the chaplain had to go over to San Pablo and get some emergency travel orders for Joan. As he was leaving, he said not to worry about a thing. All would be ready in the morning. That night we both thanked God for having a friend like Father Lorge. At the Seville airport the next morning, I bid Joan farewell and asked her to wire me when she got to Omaha. Two days later, I received a message that she had arrived safely and would probably be gone a month. She had to relocate her mother from her house to an apartment. While Joan was in Omaha, I flew at every opportunity, taking all the courier flights I could get. Our maid had a key to our duplex as I was rarely there when she came and left. One day I told her, as she was getting ready to leave, to take this and that from the pantry home with her. She was happy with that and said that she was so sorry to hear about my wife's loss.

On the day Joan returned to Madrid, I had arranged to fly the northern courier run. My plan was to pick her up at Madrid on the way back from Zaragoza. Luck was with me as she got there on schedule and so did I. When I checked in at operations in Madrid on my way back from Zaragosa, I received a surprise I wasn't looking for. The 16th AF Inspection Team was in the terminal and they planned to bump people and fly to Seville on my C-47 courier. I had to think fast as I saw my wife in the terminal and waved to her. Quickly I located my crew chief and pointed out my wife and said to him, "See that lady over there in the feathered hat? Take her out to the airplane, through the side door and put her in the radio operator's seat and close the cockpit door. That lady is my wife." Back in the passenger terminal, I told the dispatcher to announce we were ready to board the flight to Seville. Jack Warren was my co-pilot and he guarded the cockpit door during boarding. The crew chief and I checked the outside and the airplane looked ready for flight. I briefed the passengers to keep their seat belts on during the flight because of anticipated rough weather en route. On the flight deck, I instructed the crew chief not to open that door for anyone, no matter who it was.

After landing at Seville the one-star general, and his IG team, quickly left the airplane along with the others. Now I could open the cockpit door and let my prize passenger exit the airplane.

Joan said it sure was good to get back to Spain and I couldn't agree with her more. I thanked the crew chief for his help, and he said, "Don't thank me sir, I was just doing my job."

In the *Stars & Stripes* military newspaper, I read where King Idris of Libya had died. When I was stationed there in 1955, King Idris was the power in force. He was quite old but still had two wives, one in her sixties and the other in her twenties. They each lived in separate castles and the king would go back and forth between the two castles. The Americans at Wheelus Field found this very amusing, and guessed which castle the king spent the most time in.

During the two summers I spent in Libya, the base was asked to fly high ranking arabs over to an RAF base called El Adam near the Libya/Egyptian border. From there, the arabs would go by surface transportation to Mecca in Saudi Arabia for their annual pilgrimage. King Idris was too old to go anymore, but he asked the Americans to fly some of his top people to their shrine. Mecca, the holiest of Muslim cities, is the birthplace of the Prophet Muhammad, the founder of the Islam religion. For a Muslim to live in Mecca, he must follow the Islam doctrine and pray five times a day, facing Mecca, no matter where he is or what he is doing. At the appointed hour, a Muslim must stop what he is doing, drop to his knees and put his hands on his face and bend down to the ground. In that position and facing Mecca, he prays to Allah, the Lord of the Mosque Kabah, the holiest shrine of Islam. Muslims all over the world must visit Mecca at least once in their life-time. Many come more often and some come every year during June when it's nice and hot.

Mecca is a very dense city, 30,000 people per square mile. It's the second largest city in Saudi Arabia and has no airport, no rail station and no water port. Entrance to Mecca is only by car or bus and during the annual summer pilgrimage the city will swell from 60,000 to well over a million. With its location in the dry desert area of Saudi Arabia, nothing is grown or produced there; so everything has to be imported. The only exception is water and the drilled wells are relatively shallow.

Spain is known for its bullfights and Seville has the best bull-fights in the world, bar none. Each year right after Easter, they put on a gigantic event called the Ferria. It lasts for a whole week. Each afternoon at 4 p.m., the bullfights start. The bulls are the big black Muria breed raised just north of Seville. Every afternoon there are six fights and the matador doesn't always win. I've seen bullfights in Portugal and in Mexico and they don't come close to the event in Seville. Matadors even fight bulls from horseback and it's really exciting to watch the bull's horns flying through the horse's tail.

Time passed quickly in Spain as something was going on all the time. I was either at work, flying or we were on vacation somewhere.

Two months before Joan and I were to leave for the States, my orders came in. At the personnel office, I was informed that I was being assigned to the Titan One Guided Missile Program. For a pilot, I wasn't very excited about the job the Air Force was now giving me. I was hoping for a primary flying job somewhere.

My orders further stated that after completing basic missile training at Wichita Falls, Texas, and Vandenberg, California, I was to report to my unit at Larson AFB, Moses Lake, Washington. I knew where the two training bases were, but Larson AFB threw me. Before leaving Spain, Joan and I took one more trip to Lisbon, Portugal. A few miles south of Lisbon, on a sunny shore, was the resort called Estorile. The golf club there was operated by the British and playing that course was pure pleasure. The whole area around Lisbon (Lisboa to the natives) was beautiful. After a week of fun and pleasure, we hated to leave but I had to get back to work. We enjoyed our three years in Spain, but the USA was going to look really good to us.

After spending two weeks with family and friends, we had to leave for my guided missile basic course at Sheppard AFB in Wichita Falls. Eight years earlier when I was there for Army basic training, there was a marching area which had now been turned into a beautiful 18-hole golf course. After a month in Texas, we headed for California and Vandenberg AFB for further missile crew training, including the missile launch simulator. After finding a small apartment in nearby Lompoc, we soon were to experience our first earthquake. On a Sunday night, while watching TV, I suddenly felt my chair move a little. At the same time the TV began flopping. I looked at my wife and she had a strange look on her face. Just then we heard dishes rattle in the kitchen cabinets. That's all we needed and out the door both of us flew. Everyone was outside and all talking at once. Someone yelped and pointed out a crack in the street. When all the shaking ceased, we all went back to our apartments. Sleep for everyone was light and nervous that night. The water at Lompoc came out of the taps light brown in color and it was difficult to take a shower in that stuff. Every other day I would bring home bottled water from the air base.

At Vandenberg, I witnessed my first live guided missile launch. One afternoon in the base exchange, I heard a loud roar and felt the building shake. Thinking it was an earthquake, I dashed out the door. There I watched a huge Atlas Intercontinental Ballistic Missile (ICBM) rising over the buildings from the launch pad near the beach. It left a majestic vapor trail as it rose up and away toward its down-range target in the pacific ocean over 5,000 miles away. It was so loud you couldn't hear yourself think as the ground shook for several seconds.

When finished at Vandenberg, Joan and I drove north to the great state of Washington and Larson AFB near Moses Lake. When I checked in at the main gate, the guard said I couldn't enter as a base alert was in progress. With that we started to look for a motel for the night. Moses Lake is located in the heart of the Columbia Basin about halfway between Spokane and Seattle. Larson had a B-52 Bomb Wing, a KC-135 Tanker Squadron and a Titan One ICBM Missile Squadron plus various base support groups. It was a large and busy place with a lot of flying activity both day and night. In checking into base operations, I was told to wait a minute. Soon the operations officer came out and said he noticed in my records that I had a lot of C-47 time, mostly as an instructor. I mentioned I was an instructor pilot at my last four bases. His only comment was, "Welcome to the club, I can use people like you." No matter what your primary job was, you were always a pilot first and foremost. That's what the Air Force trained me for.

The operations officer explained that the main mission for the C-47's was to fly the weekly courier flights. As an instructor, I could take along a co-pilot who didn't have much or any experience in the airplane. It seems I had done that many times before. The nearest motel Joan and I found was 30 miles north in Ephrata. Back in 1943-44, Ephrata was a P-38 overseas training base. Now I had a nice little commute each day, and all poor Joan could do was cool her heels. Soon I saw an ad in the Moses Lake newspaper listing a house for rent. Right after church the next Sunday, we found it and noticed a line of people waiting to talk to the owner. When our turn came, we put on our best smiles and manners. When we told the owner we had no children and no pets and would care for the place as if it were our own, he said to wait until he talked to the rest of the folks in the line behind us. After a lengthy wait, the owner came over to our car and said we could have the place. We jumped out of the car and almost hugged him before signing the papers. It was a nice little green house with a big fenced back yard. There was no garage but that was okay. In the front yard were two large apricot trees and in the back, a huge cherry tree. The basement even had a finished bedroom and bath for guests. We couldn't have been happier with our good fortune. Soon our furniture arrived from storage and we quickly moved in. Our stuff looked pretty good to us as we hadn't seen it since leaving Spain. There was a little shipment damage but not very much. There is an old military saying: "Three moves are the same as a fire." The missile squadron was just forming and a lot of the people hadn't arrived yet. So I hustled down to base operations and got my "field check" out of the way so I could start flying. Each Tuesday, the courier left Larson AFB and flew to Mountain Home AFB, Idaho, then on to Hill AFB, Utah, for an overnight. The next morning we flew down to March AFB, Riverside, California. The next day I flew to McCord AFB, Washington, for an overnight and then back to Larson. It was a busy four days and I thoroughly enjoyed every minute. Most of the time I had a green co-pilot. Each month, the courier would reverse its route and that made it even more interesting as the course took us over some beautiful mountainous country. One night I landed at Hill in such dense fog that, after touchdown, I had to ask the tower to send a tug. I couldn't see to taxi in to the ramp. The only way we were able to get into Hill that night was through the use of the Air Force GCA (Ground Controlled Approach). GCA is a precision radar approach both for center line guidance and glide path monitoring. It was a popular instrument approach in bad weather.

The missile squadron had three huge silos buried in the ground out in the country around Moses Lake. The nearest silo was 33 miles out and the farthest was 51 miles away. Each silo operated its own power plant, water well and a liquid oxygen generating plant. The Titan One Missile had to be fueled before it could be raised to ground level for launching. When the LOX (liquid oxygen) and the highly refined RP-1 fuel would meet in the missile's engines, it would automatically ignite. Loading the fuel was a very tedious job. Even though I was trained as a missile launch control officer, my records indicated I had three years of command post experience in Spain. That did it. I was yanked from the crew roster and was now a missile controller in the base command post. I was pleased as punch that I didn't have to pull shift work out in those remote silos. My boss was Major Jack Powers, the chief controller. He had three aircraft controllers and now, a missile controller who radioed frequent test messages to the silos. An actual launch would be directed by the JCS (Joint Chiefs of Staff) from their war room in the Pentagon.

Positive communications (positive control) had to be maintained in case of a launch, real or practice. The bombers and tankers could take off on a practice mission but the missiles could only be loaded and elevated to the surface. Obviously you cannot recall an ICBM self-guided missile that is carrying a nuclear warhead, so the missiles could be loaded but not launched unless we received a launch message from higher headquarters. Thank God, it never happened. All our messages from SAC (Strategic Air Command) were color-coded. A message of one color was a test of the communications network, a message of another color was a simulated exercise short of loading, another was a simulated exercise short of launch, and still another meant "light the fuse," here we go.

I worked in the command post from 8 a.m. to 4:30 p.m. five days a week, the exception being an IG-ORI alert (Inspector General's Operational Readiness Inspection) from SAC. When that occurred, everybody reported for duty and stayed there until the exercise was over. During a SAC IG-ORI, everybody pulled 12-hour shifts and all combat crew members were given verbal and written tests. To stay combat ready, we had to pass these tests. The Wing Commander, Colonel Russell Chambers, stopped me in the headquarters hall one day. The command post was located in wing headquarters, for convenience I suppose. Colonel Chambers said to me, "Tom, just what do I have to know about these missiles in case we get hit with an ORI ?" I told him that I would be glad to meet with him, at his convenience, for 30 minutes a week until he had a good grasp of our combat mission and launch procedures. As Wing Commander, he had jurisdiction over the missile squadron. Colonel Chambers was a good student, a graduate of West Point, and I tutored him until he knew our combat mission as well as any of us. It was his job to know that and he was very aware of it. I went one step further with him. I prepared a classified written examination on things I felt the IG would test him on as Wing Commander. When I presented the practice test to him, he grabbed it and looked it over and then said to me, "Tom, you should be a member of that damn IG team." I guess it was a compliment but I wasn't quite sure.

On the next ORI, Colonel Chambers passed his test with flying colors, and that made me feel really good. However, some of my missile crews didn't do so well and I felt badly about that.

As the missile controller, I had two jobs: first, controlling the missile crews when on alert and second, serving as Emergency War Orders (EWO) training officer for the launch crews. The alert crews had a mandatory classified training session with me one hour each week, during which I tried to hammer the procedures into their heads. I gave them lectures, slide presentations, oral tests, written tests and everything I could think of. Still, on the last ORI, three individuals failed the exam.

The apricot trees in the front yard of our rented house in Moses Lake started to bear and they wouldn't quit. Never in my life have I seen such large apricots. They were as big as an average peach and I have pictures to prove it. Joan and I couldn't keep up with the heavy fruit crop. Each evening when I came home from work, there would be apricots that had fallen during the day all over the yard. We canned apricots, made preserves and I even made some apricot brandy. It wasn't quite like the apricot brandy you buy in the liquor store but it was drinkable.

The big cherry tree in our back yard produced a super crop also. The cherries were big and beautiful. People would take them but wouldn't pick them. The same goes for the fruit in the front yard. I even put an ad in the local paper for people to come and pick the fruit at no cost. The only response I got was from a local preacher. He brought his ladder and filled several boxes for his flock.

Two things happened in Moses Lake that added to our family. After five years of having no more children, the Good Lord blessed us with our first son. Michael Thomas Gordon was born on July 10, 1963, at the Larson AFB hospital. It was a sunny summer day in the Columbia Basin and we were very happy over this big event. Michael was a healthy and beautiful baby boy-a bundle straight from heaven. After our loss in 1958, we now were being rewarded and our joy was almost beyond description. The doctors said the baby was in perfect health.

Earlier that year, Joan and I decided we needed to get a dog.   I had seen an ad in the local paper for a German Shepherd from a lady in Spokane. After calling her, we decided to go over the next weekend to see the 4-month old pup. When we arrived in Spokane, the lady took us out back and there was this big puppy running around with his mother. The lady got out his papers and said his registered name was Bellamy Von Lechhausen. His sire was Schaferhaus Bellamy, and his dam was Asta Von Lechhausen. The AKC papers showed Bellamy's heritage going back to the famous movie dog, Rinty Von Rin-Tin-Tin III on his mother's side. We bought a 4-month-old pup that weighed almost 50 pounds. His paws, ears and tail were huge; but he was good natured and warmed up to us quickly. He loved our large back yard in Moses Lake and quickly became a happy camper. When we brought Michael home from the hospital, we didn't know how the dog would take to the new baby. When Bellamy sniffed and licked the baby's bare foot, I could tell by the way he wagged his tail, he liked and accepted the baby without question. They soon became pals and, when the baby was sleeping in his little crib, Bellamy would lie down near it and assumed guard duty, no doubt about it. Any time the front door bell or the telephone rang, there came a deep soft growl from the dog's throat. Bellamy was sending a clear and distinct warning to any stranger.

When Bellamy was six months old, we took him to a dog show in Spokane. On the way he became car sick so we had to stop by the roadside and clean things up. At the show, the poor dog was in misery but was able just to stand for the judges. To our amazement, he won a blue ribbon just for his appearance. As he reached one year in age, the dog weighed more than 100 pounds and resembled a small horse. I taught him to sit up like a squirrel and, when he mastered that, I taught him to catch a well-thrown rubber ball while sitting up. He never missed.

The next time I flew the courier, we made an extra stop at Fairchild AFB in Spokane. I liked that as it broke up the long trip to Mountain Home AFB in Idaho. At Hill AFB in Utah, we always stayed in the base BOQ. When staying overnight at March AFB, Riverside, California, the crew stayed at the famous Mission Inn. Today the Mission Inn occupies an entire city block but that was not always so.

The Mission Inn originated as a two-story, 12-room adobe boarding house built in 1876 by Christopher Columbus Miller on land deeded to him by the city as payment for his services as a civil engineer. The Inn stayed in the Miller family until the last son, Frank, died in 1935. For the next 20 years a multitude of owners operated the hotel. They all had their own ideas about what the Mission Inn should be and how to make it so. Finally, the Mission Inn Foundation was formed to preserve the hotel's historical and architectural integrity. Today, the Foundation and its curatorial staff operate an interesting Mission Inn museum within the hotel.

One day while I was tutoring Colonel Chambers, he casually mentioned that he heard a rumor that the Titan Two Missile Program was progressing faster than expected.. That might mean that the Titan One Program could be shut down, and it was. The Titan Two missile used solid rocket fuel and lay on its side in the silo. When launched, it was simply raised to the vertical position and its fuse was lit like a huge firecracker. Colonel Chambers's information turned out to be correct; the Titan One program was being phased out in favor of the newer and more modern Titan Two ICBM. Everybody in the squadron was buzzing about what was going to happen to them. Morale was low and all of us were speculating about our future in the Air Force. Everyone was glad to get out of the missile program as most promotions were frozen for the past three years. The next time I passed Colonel Chambers in the hallway, he said, "Tom, do you have any place in particular you want to go from here?" This surprised me and I quickly replied that I preferred Offutt AFB in Omaha because my dad lived near there and was not in the best of health. Colonel Chambers then said, "I know Colonel Fullmer there and I will give him a call and recommend you. He runs a large jet aircraft training program there at Offutt."

Three weeks later, my orders came and I was being assigned to the 3902nd Operations Squadron at Offutt AFB. Joan and I couldn't have been happier about this event. Her mother was living there alone also and we needed to be in the area. My work in the missile program earned me a promotion to major. Some of the missile crew members threw darts at that as they said their hard work got me the promotion. I told them in class one day; "What you do in your job, you get credit for. What I do in my job I get credit for. No one gets someone else promoted."

My neighbor in Moses Lake had a car for sale and I decided to buy it. It was a 1956 Oldsmobile 98 coupe and I thought it would make a good "tractor" to pull our station wagon back to our next base in Omaha. On January 28, 1965, Joan, Michael, Bellamy and I left Moses Lake for Nebraska. We drove the Oldsmobile and pulled the station wagon with the big German Shepard riding in it all by himself. The trip east across the country was uneventful except for a highway patrolman stopping us in Oklahoma. It was right at dusk and the officer said my tail lights on the station wagon were not burning. He followed us to the next town where I could get the necessary repairs. The problem turned out to be a broken electrical line. The next morning, after applying some tape, we were again road worthy. We had no more trouble until we reached the edge of Nebraska.

As we approached southeastern Nebraska, we ran into snow. It was coming down heavily so I pulled into a motel in Nebraska City. The next morning I took the dog out for a walk and I needed snow shoes as it was really deep. Both cars were under mounds of snow and it took a long time to clear them. After talking things over with Joan, I decided to unhook the cars and drive them individually to Omaha. Bellamy was so happy to have company in the station wagon that he wouldn't stop licking my ears as I drove along. The first night in Omaha, we stayed in a motel but the next day I found a small furnished apartment near 72nd and Dodge Streets and that was acceptable for the time being.

When I processed in at Offutt AFB, they told me to report to the Commander of the 3902nd Operations Squadron. In my new job, I was a ground and flight instructor in the jet section. The airplanes were the Lockheed T-33A (T-Bird) and the North American T-39 (Sabreliner). I thought this was going to be great duty. I only had four years to go until eligible for retirement. I was very lucky to have an active flying job in my last assignment. Most pilots have to "fly a desk" in the final years of their careers.

Shortly after arriving in Omaha, I received some bad news. My father passed away. He had been living in a nursing home and suffered a stroke. An ambulance took him to the hospital in Albion, Nebraska. Before I could get there, he was gone. Over a foot of snow was on the ground when Joan and I started out for the funeral. First, we had to drop Michael off at his grandmother's, put the dog in a kennel and drive over to Lincoln to pick up my sister, before heading to Cedar Rapids. I really felt badly about not seeing my dad before his fatal stroke. He was 84 and a loving father but his poor eyesight made his last years difficult.

In a few weeks, I found a house in Bellevue near the air base. It had a finished basement and a large fenced back yard. It was perfect for children and a dog, or so I thought. It took Bellamy a week to figure out how to escape from the yard. He wasn't a jumper but an excellent climber.

To keep him in, I had to install 45 degree industrial brackets on the fence posts and after attaching boards, I painted everything silver. My wife said it reminded her of a prison compound.

I really liked my new job and soon I was checked out in both the T-Bird and the Sabreliner. The policy was that after 100 hours, orders would be cut making me an instructor in each aircraft. In addition, I had to teach aircraft systems ground school for newly assigned pilots. Once a month, all the instructor pilots took turns teaching instrument ground school. Once a year, all SAC pilots had to attend the instrument school and pass a closed book written test. The final portion of this annual requirement was an instrument flight check under the "hood" (a curtain to block out the horizon's reference). That was my job and I loved it. SAC headquarters had hundreds of officers assigned to various jobs and most of them were rated pilots. If they weren't already qualified in the T-33A or T-39, they went through my school. The jet section of the 3902nd Operations Squadron consisted of six flight instructors. We would rotate weekly between teaching ground school and giving flying lessons or check rides. SAC had another annual requirement for pilots, it was called a standardization check. A 100-question open-book examination on aircraft systems had to be passed, followed by a flight check of the pilot's airmanship.

No one was "grandfathered" as everyone had to pass satisfactorily. It wasn't easy to fail a full colonel; but it had to be done sometimes in the interest of safety. After a couple years, the good old T-33A was retired to the boneyard (storage) in Tucson, Arizona. That's where all old airplanes spend their last days before being sold or salvaged for their metal. Policy was that we had to instruct in two types of airplanes and I chose the U-3, a Cessna 310 twin-engine propeller driven airplane, as my second plane. Everyone called this bird the "Blue Canoe." It was slow but rather fun to fly.

Shortly after I qualified as an instructor in the U-3, Colonel Edward Crouchley, the Base Commander, called and asked me if I would go with him on a U-3 cross-country flight to Randolph AFB near San Antonio, Texas. Policy was that full colonels and above had to have an instructor pilot accompany them whenever they flew. On the way down, we made a stop at Tulsa for some coffee and rolls. Colonel Crouchley had received his pilot's wings at Randolph many years before. During the flight, he told me all about the famous "West Point of the Air." Flying back the next day, he decided to take a nap and reclined his seat. He knew I would be vigilant while he dozed. Soon I felt the airplane start to vibrate and couldn't figure out what was wrong. In a short time, I found the problem. The colonel was a tall man and, when he reclined his seat, his knee bumped the electrical wing flap switch to the down position. After raising the flaps back up, we were flying smoothly again. I never told him about that one.

On September 18, 1965, Joan and I were blessed with our third child and second son, Steven Joseph Gordon. Joan and I were happy to have two beautiful sons. Young Michael was pleased as punch to have a little brother to play with. They got along extremely well right from the start and still do today. The little fellow was a joy and, after he was baptized, he became "Stevie." Like his brother, he was in perfect health. Not until he was in high school did we start to call him Steve. Like his brother, he was a go-getter and loved all the sports. They played all the sports very well. Like their dad, their first love was baseball. The three of us would regularly play catch in the back yard. They loved playing fungo (bunting and fielding).

Part of the SAC machine was the Joint Target Planning Staff. Its chairman was the Commander of SAC and the Vice Chairman was U.S. Navy Admiral Noel Gayler. One day the admiral's aide called my boss, Colonel Dan Dolan, inviting six officers from the 3902nd Operations Squadron to be the Navy's guests for three days on an aircraft carrier. When Colonel Dolan asked me, I said, "Sure, I'll go." It was official business so I didn't have to take leave of absence. We left on the admiral's airplane, a C-121 Convair transport. It was about as plush as any airplane can be. His seat was called the "catbird" seat and was upholstered in dark red leather. It was electric and did everything. Beside the seat was a private console containing buttons and switches for controlling all built-in functions. Also, he had his own set of flight instruments for speed, direction, altitude and inside and outside temps. On the flight to the North Island Naval Air Station in San Diego, the guests were served a first class lunch by Filipino stewards. The tables were covered with white linen and were set with silver service and crystal glasses. That night in a back room in the North Island Navy Officers Club, a private party was in progress. I decided not to crash that one and stayed at the bar.

The following morning a bus took us to the dock where we toured the battle ship, the USS Missouri. The ship's officers' quarters were small but very plush. After lunch, the six guests climbed aboard a small airplane called a "COD" (carrier on board delivery). Our guide and escort, Commander Art Haley, suggested that we tighten our belts as tight as we could because we were going to make an arrested landing on the aircraft carrier USS Oriskany. The carrier was about 100 miles out in the Pacific on a shakedown cruise following dry dock repairs. I'll never forget that landing. In spite of our tight belts, everyone rose out of their seats when the tail hook grabbed one of the four arresting wires on the flight deck. The airplane stopped dead in about 50 feet.

The personnel complement of an aircraft carrier is about 5,000 men. It's like a small city and what they don't have onboard, they can make and that includes aircraft parts. Commander Haley gave us a grand tour of the ship and it took about two hours to walk, crawl and climb all over it. During the next three days, I watched day and night aircraft operations: catapult takeoffs (cat shots) and arrested landings (traps) going on all the time. We were given quarters in the Flag Officer's space which was also plush. It had its own galley, but we didn't use it. The ship's officers asked us to eat with them in their wardroom. The food was outstanding and included a big bowl of homemade ice cream with several choices of toppings each night. Every morning at breakfast, my napkin was rolled up in a silver holder with my name on it. Beside each plate was a fresh copy of the latest news from around the world.

The flag, or guest, quarters on the ship were just below the catapult. There was no use going to bed until the night operations had ceased. On the afternoon of the third day, we cruised under San Francisco's Golden Gate Bridge. What a sight that was! Across the bay was the Alameda Naval Air Station where we were to dock. Shortly after passing under the bridge, several large tugs came out to meet us as the ship's engines went to idle. The tugs turned her around and gently nudged the big ship backward into the dock. This took a long time but those tugs really did a good job as I could hardly tell when the carrier touched the dock. On the pier, a band was playing and wives and families of the crew were all out waving to us. Buses stood by waiting to take us to the Officers Club. I thought that was strange as it was only early afternoon. On the bus, our escort told us tradition has it that when a ship docks like that, everyone goes directly to their club to party. No matter if it's 3 a.m. or 3 p.m., that's what happens. At the Officers Club bar, it was four deep and the drinks had to be passed back. After an hour of this bedlam, the Offutt guests left to catch the admiral's airplane back to Omaha.

Time was moving right along as I was very busy with my job. I was piling up a lot of flying time as I sometimes flew twice a day. The six instructors had a lot of training and check rides to give. Training was my favorite task as teaching others to fly those jets properly seemed to come natural to me. My philosophy: "If you're going to fly an airplane, whether by yourself or with a plane full of passengers, do it right. Human lives are in your hands." One day in the middle of the week, Colonel Dolan came to my office in the jet section. He recently had promoted me to OIC (Officer in Charge). He briefed me about a special mission the base had agreed to do in the spirit of public relations. The Air Force liked to do that sort of thing and did it rather frequently.

It seemed that a lady from Ewing, Nebraska had written the Offutt Air Force Base Public Relations office asking for an airplane to do a special fly-over the following Saturday morning in honor of the Savidge brothers. On the outskirts of Ewing, a granite historical marker was erected to commemorate the vast contributions the seven Savidge brothers had made to aviation. Just before the fly-over, and as drums rolled, George Savidge, age 89, would unveil the historic marker. Later, the lady who requested the fly-over, Mrs. Jerry Tomjack, wrote a thank you letter to the Base Commander at Offutt. In it, she said, "I wish you could have seen the face of the old man waving his hat and cane as the military jet flew over." When the noise of the fly-over died away, George said to the crowd, "Imagine those pilots coming all this way just for me."

Sixty years earlier in 1909, George Savidge had assisted his six brothers in building and flying one of the first self-powered airplanes. The granite marker signified that Ewing was the scene of Nebraska's earliest experiments with aircraft by the seven sons of Martin P. Savidge. They were Matt, Philip, John, Dave, Joe, Louis and George. The brothers began the study of flight in 1907 with model gliders, then full-size gliders and, finally, a self-powered airplane. They first flew on May 7, 1911. The flight was a big success. and the brothers spent the next five years barnstorming all over the Midwest from Canada to Texas. The Savidge brothers built and flew three different biplanes. In June,

1916, during a test flight in a newly-built airplane, something went wrong and the plane crashed. One of the Savidge brothers, Matt, was killed in the crash. None of the remaining brothers ever flew again. Suddenly, all activity pertaining to their aviation business came to a halt and it was all over. The seven Savidge brothers had done everything the Wright brothers did, only about ten years later.

When Colonel Dolan briefed me on the Savidge mission, I said I would be happy to do it. Then he asked, "Do you have anyone to go with you?" I replied, "Yes, I'm sure Ed Shepherd would be glad to go with me." He then replied, "Tom, I think I'll go with you on this one." Early on Saturday morning we departed Offutt in a T-39 jet trainer for Ewing. As the aerial charts didn't show Ewing, I had to get a Nebraska road map from which to navigate. I told Colonel Dolan I was born and raised about 50 miles south of Ewing, and that this was a very nostalgic mission for me. The road map proved to be a very valuable aid in locating the little town of Ewing.

I briefed Colonel Dolan what I planned to do for this special flyover as I had done these before. First, I would make a normal pass at 250 knots, to let the crowd know the airplane was there; then I would come back around and put gear and flaps out and fly over at an approach speed of 120 knots so that the old gentleman could get a good look at the small jet. For the finale, I would get the ship cleaned up (gear, flaps and spoilers retracted) and come over again at 400 knots, and pull up and do a couple of slow rolls for them. He said, "Tom, are you sure you want to do all that?" I replied that George Savidge was old, the last of seven aviation brothers that had worked many long and hard hours to emulate the Wright Brothers. I figured he deserved it. Colonel Dolan agreed.

I flew another interesting public relations mission when I was asked to fly the Sabreliner to New York City and pick up a VIP (Very Important Person) at Floyd Bennet Field. The VIP turned out to be New York's Francis Cardinal Spellman and a small staff. I had Kevin O'Toole with me as copilot and on the flight back to Omaha, the Cardinal came to the cockpit and marveled at the array of instruments. He said we must be highly trained to fly a complex jet airplane. The objective of the Cardinal's trip to Omaha was the dedication of a new elementary school at Offutt AFB. The school still bears his name today. Upon leaving the airplane, one of the Cardinal's aides gave Kevin and me an autographed picture of Francis Cardinal Spellman.

The Base Commander, Colonel Crouchley came down to the jet section early one morning for his annual instrument check. I made sure that he was scheduled with me for his ride. It went routinely as he was a very good and intelligent pilot. After the check flight, in the debriefing room, he talked about another trip in the "Blue Canoe." I mentioned that we had better do it soon because I was scheduled for my retirement on March 31. The colonel thought for a minute and then said, "Tom, we'll have a big ceremony on the parade field, marching troops, band and all." Well, it was just not meant to be. When the day arrived for the big event, the weather was horrible with rain and strong winds. Colonel Crouchley's secretary notified me that the ceremony would be held in his office. It was a big day in my life after a long career in military aviation. I didn't know it at the time but, after 27 years of military flying, I would continue flying for another 26 years in civilian life

On the morning of my retirement, my sister, Eileen, and her two daughters, Mary and Janice, drove over from Lincoln to witness the big event. Joan had Michael and Stevie all dressed up in their Sunday best. Colonel Crouchley invited all the 3902nd Operations Squadron officers to attend the ceremony. In the military, an invitation from the commander is taken as mandatory attendance. I appreciated that very much as they were all good friends and co-workers. It was unusual, as only two people were scheduled to retire that day. A master sergeant and I stood at attention as Colonel Crouchley read my retirement orders:

"It is my duty and honor as the Commander of Offutt Air Force Base to declare that Lieutenant Colonel Thomas F. Gordon, having served faithfully and honorably for twenty six years, six months and twenty three days, is hereby duly retired from the United States Air Force on this day the 31st of March 1969." Colonel Crouchley then shook my hand and wished me and my family well. After hugging my wife and my two sons, I heard my wife say, "Tom, they're waiting for you." Turning around, the 3902nd Operations Squadron officers were waiting in a long line to shake my hand. It was a very emotional moment for me and my eyes were anything but dry. All of a sudden the thought hit me that tomorrow, I would be a civilian and I wasn't quite sure what I was going to do with myself.

I am an idealist. I don't know where I'm going, but I'm on my way.

—*Carl Sandburg*

My first airplane, a Piper J-5 Super Cub.
Getting ready to go coyote hunting with nephew Harry Mahoney
1946
Author's collection

University of Omaha baseball team, with coach Virgil Yelkin
I am in the middle row - second from the left - 1948
Author's collection

Preparing to fly solo in my first
jet aircraft
Lockheed T-33A Jet Trainer
Furstenfeldbruck Air Base,
Munich, Germany
October 1955
Author's collection

My poor J-5 took a beating from a bad Nebraska hailstorm in the
spring of 1947. It was later restored to like-new condition.
Author's collection

Boeing B-47 bomber I few at MacDill AFB, Tampa, Florida
305th Bomb Wing 365th Bomb Squadron 1957-1958
Author's collection

Lt. Col. Thomas F. Gordon
USAF Retired
1969
Author's collection

North American Rockwell Model 60 Sabreliner 6-passenger jet transport
The best flying Sabreliner of all the five models built 1976
Author's collection

The uniform I wore to the annual
Officer's Dining-In
Offutt Air Force Base,
Omaha, Nebraska 1967
Author's collection

Joan and I are ready to attend the annual formal military ball at
Offutt Air Force Base Officer's Club, Omaha, Nebraska 1968
Author's collection

With my three sons (l-r) Michael, John and Steve
Family gathering, 1995
Author's collection

*This National Business Aircraft
Committee met often to come up with ideas on how to conserve jet
fuel during the 1973 shortage.
Author's collection*

Dromoland Castle, New Market-On-Fergus, County Clare, Ireland
A favorite overnight stop going to and from Europe. 1982
Notice the Stars and Stripes flying from the mast. It was converted
into a hotel and owned by an American from New York.
Author's collection.

Gulfstream III - 12 passenger executive jet transport
Considered to be the Cadillac of the skies, a wonderful airplane to fly
around the world 1982
Author's collection

Someone once wrote that wars create enemies, and the following peacetime creates friends. Here is proof of that saying. Shown is my friend Hans Langer, former Luftwaffe ME-109 fighter pilot and me, a U.S. Army Air Force P-38 pilot..
1992 Reunion, Chino Airport, California
Author's collection

Gulfstream II Paragon Edition, restored to like-new condition by Midcoast Aviation, St. Louis, Missouri. I flew many certification and demonstration flights in this wonderful airplane during the period 1990-1992.
Author's collection

CHAPTER ELEVEN

THE CORPORATE WORLD
OF AVIATION

No bird soars too high, providing he soars with his own wings.

—William Blake

A week after retiring from the Air Force, I landed a job testing jet aircraft for a civilian contractor at the former World War II bomber base near Lincoln, Nebraska. Being only 60 miles away, I could easily commute from my home in Bellevue. The contract called for a fleet of 220 Air Force T-39A and 88 Navy T-39D Sabreliner twin-engine jet trainers to be brought to Lincoln for the IRAN (Inspection and Repair as Necessary) program. I was given the job as Chief Test Pilot because of my many hours in the Sabreliner while stationed at Offutt. When the owning units brought their airplanes in for the IRAN program, I test flew them before they were placed on the inspection line. This was to determine their exact airworthiness. Once on the inspection line, the airplanes were stripped of all paint using a chemical process. The engines were then removed and carefully inspected for wear and tear. Next the plane's complete interior, including all the wiring bundles, was removed and replaced with new components. All the aircraft systems, including avionics, were tested and updated or replaced where necessary. Before the airplane was repainted, each of its engines was run through a complete and thorough test at the remote run-up area of the airport. After repainting, each airplane was then ready for a full functional check flight to ensure that it was ready to be put back in service. After everything was signed off, the airplanes were returned to their owners. These were, for all practical purposes, new airplanes, even down to new tires which set off their fine appearance and they performed as such. The entire fleet of 220 Air Force airplanes were put through this process. The Navy airplanes went through a similar routine except that the Navy didn't allow much upgrading of systems or equipment. Sometimes the Navy couldn't pick up their aircraft, so I would deliver them to the owning units. Flying across the country in a rebuilt Sabreliner was always great fun for me. The program was completed in just over a year and I was again out of a job.

Just before I retired from the Air Force, I attended a lecture on how to prepare a resume and how to get along with civilians. The military has always (chidingly) referred to civilians as "feather merchants." Now all of a sudden, I was one of them. After carefully preparing my resume, I scanned a Fortune magazine for the addresses of the Fortune 500 companies. I picked 92 of those which operate corporate airplanes and sent each a copy of my resume. My first response was from the North American Rockwell Corporation (NARC) in St. Louis, Missouri. NARC was the original manufacturer of the Sabreliner aircraft in Los Angeles. Their distribution and maintenance centers were in St. Louis and Perryville, Missouri. NARC asked me to come to St. Louis for an interview with their chief pilot, Oakley Allen, at Lambert Field.

After a lengthy discussion, Mr. Allen offered me a job flying the civilian version of the T-39 Sabreliner. It was much plusher and with better avionics than the military version. It sounded like a good situation for me, but I asked for a couple of days so that I could talk it over with my wife back in Bellevue. When I got home, and before I could tell her about the job offer, she said, "You're supposed to call Ray Lambertson at General Dynamics Corporation in Fort Worth, Texas." When I called him that same afternoon, Ray asked me to catch an airplane and come down and talk to Dick Johnson, Director of Flight Test. Now I had two responses from my resumes and I was really pleased with my good fortune.

Two days later I was sitting in Dick Johnson's office. We talked and he asked questions covering everything except flying. He said my resume answered all his questions relating to aviation. He then opened a drawer and showed me a huge stack of resumes from pilots looking for work. Dick Johnson only hired people whose background was similar to his own. He came from a farm background in North Dakota. He played baseball from American Legion classification up to, and including, semi-professional. When I said I had done the very same thing, he offered me a job.

The Fort Worth Division of General Dynamics had two Sabreliner jet aircraft which were used for business on an almost daily basis. This job would pay 50 percent more than the one in St. Louis. I accepted the job on the spot, and was given two weeks to report for work. Flying home that afternoon, I was thinking how to tell my wife that we are now moving to Fort Worth and not St. Louis. When she heard me say Texas, she wrinkled her nose. I guess she was thinking of cowboys and Indians, and wide open spaces in a sea of sage brush.

Back in Bellevue, we quickly put the house on the market. At the base legal office, I had them draw up a power of attorney so Joan could handle the sale of our house in my absence. In a week I loaded up my red 1968 Ford Mustang, hugged my wife and two little boys and, with a big wave, drove away for the two-day trip to Texas. The Fort Worth Division of the company dispatched both Sabreliners most mornings at 7 a.m. One would fly west and the other east. I flew managers, engineers and executives to various business meetings all over the country. The schedule had me leave early and get back late five days a week. Carswell AFB was located near Fort Worth and General Dynamics shared the west side of the airfield with the Government. Both used the single, long 12,000-foot runway. When I arrived for work, the 7th Bomb Wing, based at Carswell, was on temporary duty in Guam for three months so I occupied space at the BOQ for $3 a night. That sure beat $20 a night in a motel.

As soon as Joan sold the house, I got a week off to fly up and help her drive the car to Fort Worth. At first, we stayed at the famous Green Oaks Inn as it was near the aircraft plant. All the "visiting firemen" stayed there too. It was a busy place and you didn't need an alarm clock to awaken you. Every morning at 6 a.m., the B-52's and KC-135 tankers would depart to the south and come roaring right over the Inn. In a short time, we found a nice house in the Wedgewood section of south Fort Worth. A doctor had built this very comfortable brick home just five years earlier. We felt fortunate to find such a nice house. It took Joan about a month before she decided she actually liked Texas. I have always liked Texas, especially the wide-open spaces. Those scenes just reminded me of the many western stories I had read in my formative years.

Our neighbors in Fort Worth were very friendly and we got along just fine. Some of them were not natives as they were imported engineers, and the like, for the aircraft plant out at the base. Out in the deep country, you can go back 40-50 years with the sight of cattle grazing on huge ranges. That scene doesn't change much over the years. On business flights when I had a long period of waiting time, I learned to catnap. Those rest periods were a godsend to me on those long days sitting and waiting for my passengers at some lonely airport. No, they didn't have fancy crew-rest lounges like they do today. Like cats, pilots had to find their own soft and quiet spot wherever they could.

The term "general aviation" includes all aircraft not flown by the airlines or the government. "Business aviation," the most important part of general aviation, is made up of companies, corporations and individuals who use aircraft as tools in the conduct of their business.

Corporations and companies can control virtually all aspects of their travel plans using company airplanes. Itineraries can be changed on short notice and business aircraft can be flown to thousands of destinations not served by the airlines. Business aircraft are productivity multipliers that allow executives to conduct business en-route in complete privacy while reducing the stress associated with traveling on commercial airliners. Passengers who travel on business aircraft never have to worry about en-route connections, lost baggage, over-booking, airline security and the usual terminal delays. Business aircraft not only reduce flight time by going point-to-point; they decrease the total travel time because they are able to utilize smaller airports closer to the executive's final meeting site. Travelers do not have to alter their schedule to conform to those of the airlines. Consequently, business travelers have the freedom to change destinations en-route and depart and arrive according to their own schedules.

Business aircraft are designed, engineered and built to the highest manufacturing standards. Companies who operate them have complete control over the readiness of their airplanes. The safety record of business aircraft is equal to or better than the airlines. Business aviation enables a company to maximize its two most important assets- people and time. Some 92 percent of the Fortune 500 companies are business aircraft operators. Business jets can and do fly the nation's airways with the same speed and safety as the nation's air carriers. Pilots in both environments hold the same Airline Transport Pilot (ATP) rating-the Ph. D. of professional pilots.

My wife and I decided there must have been something in the Texas drinking water because, on September 1, 1970, we were blessed with our fourth child and third son in a row. We named him John William Gordon and he came into this world a healthy good-looking boy. After his baptism, he immediately became "Johnny" to his family and friends until he entered high school 15 years later. When Joan and I were married in 1951, our plans were to have four children. God gave us four, but took one back.

Raising three healthy boys is fun as Doctor Spock often wrote. Sometimes my wife and I wondered about that. But they were healthy boys and we had lots of fun together during their growing-up years. When the boys became adults, the association became even stronger. God has rewarded us handsomely.

Because of our military lifestyle, the children were each born in different states, Sheila in Illinois, Michael in Washington State, Steve in Nebraska and John in Texas. It's a shame the children didn't come earlier, so that we could have taken them overseas with us. They would have experienced the different countries' cultures, and that can be an education in itself and had the exposure to and opportunities to learn a foreign language. When in a foreign country, children learn to speak, read and write the language very quickly.

A rumor was spreading that General Dynamics Corporation had hired a new Chairman of the Board of Directors. Soon it was official. Mr. David S. Lewis, President of McDonnell Douglas Aircraft Company, became our new chairman. A few days later, a request came in from the New York Office requesting one of Fort Worth's Sabreliners to fly back there and support the new boss. Dick Johnson called me to his office and said, "You're it." Another pilot, Orrie Heitt, had been offered the job as he had more seniority, but he turned the offer down. Being next in line, I got the job. I took Bill Remley with me as my copilot. We based the airplane at LaGuardia Field in New York and Bill and I found rooms at the old Lincoln Hotel in Manhattan. The building was so old that I'm sure President Lincoln himself might have stayed there on occasion.

David Lewis, a top-of-the-line aircraft design engineer, was a joy to have as a passenger. He was born in Charleston, South Carolina, and had that old southern charm with a slow drawl. I have never flown him without his noticing something wrong in the cabin. After landing, he would give me a slip of paper and say, "Here, Tom. Get these things fixed before we fly again." On a flight one day, Mr. Lewis asked me to get the Sabreliner transferred from the Fort Worth Division to St. Louis as the New York Office was planning to move back there in the spring of 1971. The next time I saw Dick Johnson, I mentioned the airplane transfer. He blew up and said, "If the Chairman wants the (bleep) airplane, he has to ask for it in writing." The Fort Worth Division had a long-standing policy about verbal orders. In fact, they had a special form called the AVO (Avoid Verbal Orders). It was used for everything.

While I was in Fort Worth having some maintenance done on the airplane, Dick Johnson called me into his office and said, "You have been flying the Chairman a lot lately. How would you like to take the airplane on to St. Louis and set up operations there?" He said he would give me a copilot and a mechanic who had a pilot's license. On the spot, I agreed to take the job. It would mean another move but the challenge of starting up a corporate flight operation from scratch was more than I could resist. That night, I talked with my family about the plan and my wife said, "I thought you told me that after we got out of the Air Force, we wouldn't be moving anymore." Two moves in 18 months wasn't what I had expected either. On June 6, 1971, I flew the

Sabreliner to Lambert Field in St. Louis and parked it at the North American Rockwell ramp. A tall man with a quick military gait came out to the airplane to meet us. There I met John Kane, the Corporate Director of Administration, my new boss. Joan had no trouble selling the house in Fort Worth. An attractive house with a nice professionally landscaped yard will always sell quickly. In addition, I had installed a six-foot wooden fence around the back yard for privacy. Texans like to watch each other and the only kind of fence they would put up was chain link. I was in St. Louis 10 weeks before my family finalized things in Fort Worth and were able to join me. During that time, when I had time between flights, a local real estate agent, Margaret Battinger, helped me locate suitable housing in west St. Louis County.

In a short time Margaret and I found a house that I liked, and hoped Joan and the boys would like it too. They did. In August I was given a week off to fly down to Fort Worth to drive my family back to St. Louis. We had just bought a new Chrysler station wagon and it was huge. We needed the room, too, and on the trip up to St. Louis, we all hoped it would be our last move. One of my first duties in the new job was to write a Flight Operations Manual. In Fort Worth, a "pilot's reading file" was used. Each pilot would sign off on any new material every month. That wasn't good enough for me, I wanted the real thing, an operating manual with teeth in it. In a few weeks, while on a flight to Washington, D.C., I mentioned to Mr. Lewis that I had the flight manual ready for his review. He planned to authenticate it with his signature. About a week later, on another flight, he handed me my draft copy of the manual and said, "It's fine, but I want to give you some safety concerns to add to it." In a few days, in the interoffice mail, I received the following memo containing the Chairman's Corporate-Wide Policy on Aircraft Safety:

Tom:
    I want you to incorporate the following safety concerns in your new flight operations manual.
1. Company aircraft offer speed, safety, and security in air transportation for management officials to increase their efficiency and effectiveness.
2. The pilot is in sole command of the airplane and makes the final decision.
3. The history of aviation is filled with accidents where pilots surrendered their better judgment in the face of pressure from otherwise well meaning executives who looked more to the

importance of business commitments or personal convenience, without recognizing the hazards of the operation
intended.

4. All pilots are to be fully qualified and current in the present
   airplane.
5. All pilots must receive periodic FAA proficiency checks.
6. All pilots must operate company airplanes within their certified flight envelopes.
7. Alternate airports must be part of every flight plan regardless
   of the weather.
8. No pilot will attempt to descend and land at an airport when
   the weather is reported to be below landing minimums.
9. Corporate aircraft are available to all company divisions upon
   request by top officials.
10. Key management officials are to avoid traveling on the same
    airplane in such concentrations that an accident would jeo-
    pardize company management.

David S. Lewis
Chairman

Now my operations manual had some real teeth in it and was
backed by the chairman himself. My job in handling the executive
passengers became much easier, even so, I would be tested more than
once in the years to come. In Montreal, Canada, I was tested by a Vice
President of the company. We were there on company business. On
the afternoon of the second day on this particular trip, when we were
supposed to depart for St. Louis, the weather turned sour. It began
raining about noon, the temperature dropped and later sleet was falling.
Sure enough about 4:30 p.m., my passengers arrived chomping at the
bit to go home. One executive asked me, upon getting out of the limo,
if I was ready to go. I told him this weather was not safe to fly in, and
if it didn't stop sleeting, we might have to stay another night. He became very irritated and said that he just had to get home because of a
very important social event. Trying to keep my cool, I said that it was
unsafe to taxi out in the sleet as some of the rain that had not turned to
sleet would stick to the airplane's wings in the form of ice. It was just
unsafe to try to depart in those conditions. The rest of the passengers
didn't argue at all, just this one executive. After some discussion, the
executive said, "Okay, if you won't fly me home, I'll go over to the
terminal and catch an airliner, this stuff doesn't bother them." Good
luck, I thought to myself. The flight home was canceled, as were all

the airline flights. We all headed back to the Chateau Champlain hotel. To my surprise, the next morning dawned with over a foot of snow on the ground. The airport was closed for snow removal and wouldn't be open for another 24 hours. Our executive was fit to be tied. The next afternoon we finally departed for St. Louis. The executive was anything but cordial.

Another time in Montreal, I had to cancel again. This time it was just rain falling but the airport temperature was in the middle thirties. To me, I felt we could depart with relative safety. As I taxied out for takeoff, the control tower said the temperature was dropping. Rain was still falling rather heavily. After takeoff, when I raised the landing gear, the red light in the landing gear handle would not go out. This indicated the gear was not up and locked in place. The procedure was to lower the gear and try to raise it once more. Same thing, the red light still glowed in the gear handle. I told the copilot to ask the control tower for the frequency for the approach controller so we could come back and make an instrument approach and land. Back on the ground, I informed the passengers that it was too dangerous to make any further attempts to depart and we would be staying overnight. From the cabin came sounds of moans and groans. This time no one gave me a bad time, thank goodness, they understood my decision. When pulling the airplane into the hangar that night, I saw why the red light stayed on in the gear handle. The landing gear doors still had a build-up of ice that prevented them from closing. Had I tried to continue the flight home with the gear doors not completely closed, they would have been torn off in the high speed cruise slipstream. One does not continue flight with an unsafe (red) light in the landing gear handle. It was a mandatory abort in my operation.

The Sabreliner that the Corporate Office acquired from its Fort Worth Division was painted white with a green speed stripe extending along the fuselage. It didn't have a service galley or a lavatory installed in the cabin. At the division level they brown-bagged it, used "piddle packs" and rarely carried any women. The new chairman asked me to get some cost figures on a new paint job and to include a new interior that included a galley and a real lavatory. He also wanted the airplane painted white with a red speed stripe that widened at the rear and went up the tail. It turned out to be a very attractive paint scheme.

A year later, the boss decided that he needed a larger airplane so I looked at the new North American Rockwell Sabreliner 75A. It was considerably larger with new and more powerful engines. Out in the North American Rockwell plant in Los Angeles, the new airplane was being finished and painted with the new paint scheme. I went out there for its first flight and, with Evan Myers, the factory test pilot, we planned the acceptance flight. There at the Los Angeles factory I met Jim Vines. His business card said he was Chief, Aircraft Programs Division, Flight Standards Service, Federal Aviation Administration, Washington, D.C. He asked when we planned to fly our acceptance flight. I said we were planning to fly the airplane that afternoon right after lunch. Jim said he would like to go on the flight as an observer. As Chief of the FAA Flight Standards Office, he had the right to ride on any airplane he chose. My feeling was that anytime an FAA examiner was on board, the pilot was going to get an evaluation of some kind. Jim watched everything I did during the preflight right up to departure.

During the flight I followed the acceptance checklist to the letter. To my surprise, everything went quite well. The examiner rode the jump-seat just behind the pilots and said nothing that I could hear. After landing, Jim thanked me and left. Everything worked properly during the flight and my company accepted the airplane. All it needed was a minor tune-up before flying it back to St. Louis. In a couple of weeks the following letter arrived from the FAA:

Dear Tom,
Thank you for the excellent Sabreliner 75A demonstration flight on September 20, 1974.
The exceptional piloting skills that you demonstrated during this flight qualifies you for an FAA Safety Pin, and it is my pleasure to send this symbol of safe-flying to you.

Sincerely,
James A. Vines
Chief, FAA Flight Standards Division

I didn't realize it at the time but the acquisition of this particular airplane was a mistake because it was an early production model. It was serial number 002 and, to our chagrin, a lot of minor flaws began to crop up. I was asked to call John Kane and go look for a replacement, so one day John and I drove to Perryville, Missouri, where North American's new delivery center was located. After looking over their stock, we selected serial number 044-a brand new Sabreliner 75A. We then made arrangements to trade in our SN-002 and hoped that no bugs were in this new one. It turned out there were very few and all were minor in nature.

Some time later, while on a trip in the Sabreliner, the chairman of the Board came up to the cockpit and asked me what I knew about the new Gulfstream II twin-engine long range jet. I replied that I had seen a few of them and read some articles on the airplane. Recently he had ridden in one and liked the airplane very much. I wondered if he had some ideas about getting one. Late in the summer of 1975, the chairman's secretary called and said the boss wanted me to find a charter Gulfstream II for a business trip to London. I called the Gulfstream factory in Savannah to see if one of their demonstrators might be available. Ken Skoglind, from the sales office, said all of their demonstrators were out on trips, however, he would make some calls to see if another airplane could be found.

In a couple of days, Ken called back to ask the exact dates that we needed the airplane. He said that there were a couple of possibilities depending on our requirements. I checked with the chairman and learned that we needed the airplane for about five days starting in about a week. Ken arranged for the Gannett Newspaper Company to support our needs. He gave me the name of the chief pilot, Skip Dubbles, and the copilot was a factory pilot, George Sayers. The engineer/cabin attendant was Calvin Swartz from the Gannett operation. The chairman asked me to go along as an observer, and Ken Skoglind went as a consultant. The trip went very well and I learned a lot about the Gulfstream from those pilots. Seeing London again was very nostalgic to me as I was there during the war. After returning home, the boss said an engineer shouldn't be serving passengers food and beverages-that job belonged to a hostess. Less than six weeks later, another request came to find a Gulfstream charter for a trip to Iran. Again, Ken Skoglind located a Gulfstream II in Mexico City that could meet our needs. Soon the Mexican GII arrived at Lambert Field. Its colors were white with gold and green trim. The interior was not club style, but airline style-rows of seats on either side of the center isle. Sergio Maza, the chief pilot, had a military flying background and his copilot, Jose Marti, was a former Mexicali Airlines pilot. Their crew consisted of two pilots, Sergio and Jose, Jorge, the engineer and Patty, the flight attendant. All spoke excellent English and were very pleasant to work with. I briefed Sergio on the plan; fly to London, spend a couple of days, then fly to Tehran. From there, the itinerary was uncertain as no one knew except the chairman.

The Mexican crew wanted to know the likes and dislikes of our passengers; food, beverages, movies and the like. The crew brought plenty of money to cover any event or itinerary. On their airplane, a steel safe was bolted to the floor inside a small cabinet. The safe contained $10,000 in US green. Sergio asked me if that would be enough. I had heard foreign airports wanted their fees-landing, parking and departure-all in US green. I told him I thought that would be enough money but also to have a lot of trinkets on board to give to ramp-handlers at foreign airports.

The day before our departure for overseas, Ken Skoglind called to say that he was going on the trip just to answer any questions about the airplane. Talk about a friendly salesman, Ken was good at his job. When I mentioned to Sergio that our departure time was 7 a.m. on Wednesday, his eyes got big. The Mexicans don't like to get up early and rarely, if ever, have an early morning departure in their operations. They often fly late at night, but never early in the morning.

On the morning of the trip I arrived at the airport very early with bag and baggage ready to fly overseas. I was very excited because I had never been to Iran and was looking forward to the experience. Soon, the Mexican crew arrived looking very sleepy. They had already filed the international flight plan with the FAA before leaving their hotel. The airplane had been stocked the night before and the fuel truck was just finishing topping off the tanks. Now all we needed was the catering truck and our passengers. The chairman and three of his staff comprised the passenger list.. Ken Skoglind and I were listed as part of the crew.

During the conversation about setting up the trip, the chairman asked me to go along and observe how the Gulfstream was operated. The glint in his eyes indicated to me he wanted one of these airplanes for our operations. I was almost sure of it. When the caterers arrived, it looked like we could feed an army. Promptly at 6:30 the passengers arrived and we were airborne at 7:00 straight up. The first stop was Gander Field, Newfoundland, for a quick fuel uplift. Thirty minutes later, we were airborne again and headed for London's Heathrow airport. The trip across went very well. The air was mostly smooth and the food was outstanding. Patty knew how to flavor food and it was delicious.

When flying internationally, operators normally use a professional aircraft handler. These contracted agents arrange for all the necessary overflight, landing and departure permits. They make sure fuel is ready when we land and arrange for hotel accommodations, ground transportation and aircraft catering for the next departure. These agents are worth every penny they charge. Sergio arranged for Universal Weather and Aviation in Houston, Texas, to provide this service. They were invaluable and gave us real peace of mind. During the night, they check the weather and file the flight plan for the next trip. They perform an invaluable service.

In London, everyone stayed at the Hilton Hotel, which is located directly across the street from London's famous Hyde Park. It was after 10:00 P.M. when we finally checked in. Ken, I and the flight crew went out and found a French cafe. The Mexican pilots told jokes in Spanish, laughed, then told them again in English for Ken and me, and laughed again. No London business will close as long as there are paying customers in the establishment. Finally we got to bed after a very long but enjoyable day. We weren't scheduled to leave for Tehran until Saturday morning; so the flight crew had the next day off. The six of us toured London, ate at nice places, and just relaxed.

The purpose of the trip was to sell the Shah of Iran some of the new F-16 fighters our Fort Worth Division was building for the Air Force. The rumor was that the Shah wanted the fighters, but really didn't have the funds for as large an order as he needed. He offered to pay for the aircraft with heavy crude oil which was abundant in his country. It was foggy that Saturday morning, when we departed London for the Mehrabad airport outside Tehran. I saw nothing but desolate country the entire trip and when we reached the Iranian border, it got worse. The handling agent had booked us into the Hilton Hotel located on a hill at the edge of the city. Our passengers were picked up in a limo and taken away as guests of Riza Shah Pahlavi, the Shah of Iran.

Before leaving the airplane, the chairman told us we would be there for at least three days. Then he shocked us by saying, "We just might continue on and fly around the world." With that he got into the limo and left. Sergio, his crew, Ken and I just looked at each other in disbelief. The first thing Sergio said was, "That $10,000 is not going to be enough money now." Because it was late, the crew, Ken and I decided to eat right there at the hotel. After a relaxing dinner, we went up to bed. We were all exhausted after another long but enjoyable day.

I was impressed with the way Sergio and his crew operated the airplane. They were truly professional in all aspects of aircraft and flight management. The second day in Tehran, the six of us visited the old market that took you back years in time because it was underground and unchanged. Most of the shop stalls were lit by candle power, just like they were centuries ago. That night we found a French cafe located on the top floor of the International hotel. It turned out to be a fine place. The employees were all dressed formally. Our French waiter spoke good English and overheard some of our stories. Later he asked if he could tell some of them to his French cohorts. When he told those jokes in French, it broke us up. It was even funnier than in Spanish or

English. The French waiter asked us to come back the next night for sure.

After two days of concern about going around the world, I received word from the chairman that we were not going to do that, but fly back to London and then on home. During all this flying, the Mexican crew often let me sit in the pilot's seat to get familiar with the airplane. To me, it handled very nicely. Our Sabreliner was a "Buick," but this machine was a "Cadillac" without question. Flying back home across the Atlantic, Ken tried giving Mr. Lewis some pointers about the Gulfststream; instead Mr. Lewis gave Ken a lesson in Aerodynamics 101. Meanwhile, I fell in love with the airplane. I have flown a lot of airplanes that I liked very much but, in my mind, this was the ultimate in a business airplane.

About a month later, the chairman told me that the Board of Directors approved the purchase of a Gulfstream II executive jet airplane He then said, "Ken Skoglind is coming up next Monday and we need to start laying out plans on how we want this airplane to be equipped, both in the cockpit and in the cabin." I couldn't believe my ears. I was in hog heaven.

When Ken and the chairman settled the deal with a letter of intent, things progressed quickly. The company decided to keep the Sabreliner and operate both airplanes. One would operate domestically and the other internationally. What better deal could I have fallen into! Immediately I had to recruit and hire more pilots. I was receiving at least one resume a day from pilots looking for work. Most were not jet qualified, or if they were, it was only a few hours in a small Learjet, or something like that. I guess the word got out because I started receiving resumes from pilots with substantial jet experience. Most were right out of the military and hungry for a flying job. It was a busy time for me as the Sabreliner was flying business trips almost daily all around the country. The "buzz word" was that General Dynamics was going to get a new Gulfstream II executive jet. In the flying industry a GII is known as: "big iron." Now, the phone was ringing daily with people saying they knew me, and were looking for a job. I had never heard of over 90 percent of the people that called.

General Dynamics was a member of NBAA (National Business Aircraft Association), and I decided to call them for some advice on pilot recruiting and equipping the airplane, plus tips on international operations. The NBAA, a trade association headquartered in Washington, DC, was established in 1947 and is totally dedicated to increasing the safety, efficiency and acceptance of business aviation. They represent the interests of over 6,000 member companies that own or operate nearly 10,000 business aircraft. Through its Operations Department, NBAA participates in major aviation industry forums that work on air traffic procedures, aviation weather, long range air navigation, charting, airspace access, hazards to aviation, aeronautical radio frequency use, aircraft equipment specifications and the highest performance standards. These benefits are presented to the general public, and represents Members' interests as the principal advocate and voice for business aviation before Congress, the Administration, state and local governments and the media. As a member of NBAA, I felt that the company should have the latest and the best equipped cockpit if we were to be traveling to the four corners of the world. I also needed some good pilots to help me operate this international airplane. NBAA said they would send me some operational guidelines and advised me to advertise in the Wall Street Journal for personnel. The NBAA operations staff were very helpful with good cockpit layout suggestions. There were a lot of things to do now. First, I had to go to Savannah for two weeks of ground school on the Gulfstream II. Flight Safety International did the training for Gulfstream right there at the factory. I also received 12 hours in the full-motion GII simulator. Each day after class, I would go over to the factory and watch how Gulfstream put their airplanes together. I was very impressed and I also noticed the airplanes were assembled with much pride and care. They were also built as sturdy as a Mack truck. At the far end of the assembly line, our airplane, serial number 188, was just taking shape. To me, it looked like it would be a long time to completion. Before leaving Savannah, I told the production manager that I would be back in a month or so to monitor the progress of our airplane. By now, I knew what I wanted in the cockpit-dual everything.

Back home I was interviewing pilots right and left. NBAA said that in order to operate two airplanes, one being international, I would need eight pilots. Now I had to hire four more, and quickly, too. In just two weeks time, I had eight pilots in my stable. I made sure all the new ones were Sabreliner qualified so I only had to train them in the Gulfstream. They would have to go to the Flight Safety school in Savannah, two at a time, for two weeks. Following that, each had to pass a type-check given by an FAA flight examiner.

On my next visit to the factory to check our airplane. I was surprised to see that it was now number three on the final assembly line The plant production manager said our airplane would really move fast now. The procedure was that when the airplane was finished in a "green" state, it would be test flown by the factory test pilots to make sure it was airworthy. Once the airplane completed a satisfactory test flight, the new owner would ferry it to a completion center of his choice for interior layout, painting and installation of equipment. With my boss, John Kane, we visited five or six different completion centers, located around the country, to find one that both of us thought would outfit the airplane in our best interests. Finally, we decided on the Page-Gulfstream Completion Center in San Antonio, Texas. Back at the factory in Savannah, I arranged for one of the Gulfstream test pilots, George Sayers, to help me ferry the "green" airplane out to San Antonio. As we prepared to depart, George said to me, "Well Tom, it's your airplane, so I suppose you want to fly it out there." Without delay, I jumped in the left seat and strapped in. It would be my first flight as pilot in command of a Gulfstream II. The green airplane had only an austere fly-away package in the cockpit, and I could only fly it in daylight and under VFR (visual flight rules) conditions. George and I picked a good day and it was clear sailing all the way to San Antonio. That doesn't happen very often. The work at the completion center in San Antonio was estimated to take at least three months.

Arriving back home, I got back in the Sabreliner for some long overdue flying. In a short time, I received a call requesting the airplane for a special mission. The airplane was to stop at Dulles Field in Washington, D.C. and pick up the Iranian Ambassador to the US, Ardeshir Zahedi, and three of his staff. They were going to Seattle for a special Iranian exhibition. When the Ambassador and his party boarded the airplane at Dulles, I mentioned that we would have to make a fuel stop en route, since the airplane didn't have the range to fly to Seattle nonstop. The Ambassador said, "That's fine; let's stop in Houston." That wasn't on our route, but I changed the flight plan to Houston. Getting off the airplane in Houston, the Ambassador said a second car was there to take the crew to the hotel where we were staying over night. This was news to me. Now the whole trip was going to be longer than originally briefed. My copilot for this trip was Hal Burt, who was on loan from the Fort Worth Division.

The hotel was located in the middle of Houston's famous medical district. In the middle of the district was a large cancer treatment center. The hotel turned out to be a first class apartment hotel and the silver Rolls Royce out in front was their "shuttle bus" to and from the medical center. The desk clerk said to just sign for our meals and drinks, as the Ambassador was taking care of everything. That night, Hal and I enjoyed a big Texas steak in the dining room.

At 9 o'clock the next morning, I taxied the airplane out to the runway and took off for Seattle. When I asked about provisions for the airplane, one of the Ambassador's staffers told me not to worry as they carried their own provisions in large coolers. They didn't even want American coffee. In Seattle, everyone stayed at the downtown Hilton Hotel. One of the Iranians mentioned that they would not be ready to return for at least two or three days. If there were any change, I would be notified well in advance. Hal and I went out to the International Exposition the next day and it was a spectacular event. The Iranians hosted a huge dinner and it was the first time I had ever seen whole roasted pigs with apples in their mouths. There were two of them and the food was out of this world. The tables held huge platters of everything imaginable. I had never seen such a magnificent spread before.

During the trip to Seattle, I was never told why we stopped in Houston. Later, I learned that the Ambassador's sister was there undergoing cancer treatment. The Ambassador sent word to me that when we left Seattle, we would return to Houston. When I called my office, my secretary, Virginia Mitchem, said my boss, John Kane, wanted to talk to me. He asked how the trip was going and when I told him the Iranians were throwing in side trips, he said to go along with the program as they were paying for it. In Houston, an aide said we would now go to West Palm Beach, Florida, not back to Washington. This was another surprise and there would be more to come. In Florida, I was informed that we were there to pick up over-water gear; life vests and a life raft. Where were we going next, I wondered.

While I was arranging for the over-water survival gear, one of the Iranians found me and said that they wanted to stay in West Palm Beach another day to relax. He then informed me that our next stop would be San Juan, Puerto Rico. The flight to San Juan was a very interesting trip. I noticed tiny little islands all along the route. It was my first time in Puerto Rico and I found the country hot, desolate and poor. Hal and I stayed at the San Juan Hilton and were told just to sign for whatever we wanted. Sitting at the open bar near the pool one day Hal and I noticed the Ambassador out there in a deck chair. Soon he came by and asked how we liked San Juan. He then said, "There are no pretty girls here, let's go home in the morning."

Flying back, we had to stop in West Palm Beach again to drop off the rented over-water gear. Finally, after a long 12 days, I flew the Iranians back to Washington. After landing at Dulles, and as the party was getting ready to depart, an Iranian gave Hal and me each something wrapped up in a box. After they left, we discovered the boxes contained two tins of Iranian caviar and a gold watch.

I was glad to get back home as our new Gulfstream was nearing completion, and John Kane said to get down to San Antonio and see how it was going. When I arrived, I was amazed at the rapid progress. The chairman told me early on: "Tom, you can specify how you want the cockpit to be but I am going to design the cabin." He wanted a club arrangement with nine big soft chairs and a three-place couch. He also wanted a quality stereo system and a TV monitor with a VCR. The chairman and the executive vice president for finance got into an argument over the VCR. One wanted a Beta format and the other wanted VHS. By way of compromise, we installed both. It was, no doubt, the only business airplane in the country with two different types of VCRs. A large galley and lavatory/dressing room was also installed. The chairman insisted that each single chair in the cabin be berthable for long flights. He also mentioned that the couch was his on such trips.

On October 13, 1976, our new Gulfstream II was pulled out of the completion center hangar in San Antonio. Ron Biller, one of the new pilots I had hired, was finished with his GII training and had just passed his FAA flight check. I had him come down to San Antonio to help me fly the acceptance flight of the completion center's work. We had decided to paint the airplane after the acceptance flight, so the airplane still looked "green." Ron and I had to fly the airplane three times before everything was working just right. John Kane was down there with us and rode on each test flight. He was good at checking out airplanes. John, a retired Navy captain, was an Annapolis graduate and had flown a variety of Navy airplanes, including blimps.

The paint scheme on our new Gulfstream II was white with a red speed stripe, very similar to the scheme of (then) Eastern Air Lines. Ron and I flew the airplane to Boston to pick up the chairman after his arrival on an overseas flight. It was his first flight in the new Gulfstream. In a few days, the chairman's secretary called and said that he wanted to be flown to the west coast. The chairman was the sole passenger on the flight to Los Angeles for a meeting with our west coast office manager, Bing Cosby. Taxiing in after landing at Los Angeles, I couldn't get the APU (auxiliary power unit) started. As the chairman left the aircraft, he said, "Tom, let's plan to leave at 8 a.m. tomorrow for San Francisco. I didn't mention anything about the sick APU, thinking it was something minor. Boy, was I ever wrong.

Air Research Company (ARC) operated the fixed base operation at the Los Angeles airport (LAX). Their mechanics determined that the APU problem was a sheared starter shaft. ARC was an FAA approved repair station for the Gulfstream, but didn't have any APU starters, or shafts, in stock. However, they did find one in Long Beach, and it would arrive by air that afternoon. The problem was that the local mechanics got off at 5 p.m. Quickly, I located the Air Research manager and told him my plight. After I agreed to pay double labor time after 5 p.m., two mechanics agreed to stay over and work into the night. I had to let the chairman know right away that it would be late before I knew if the airplane could make the 8 a.m. departure.

Luckily, when I called our Los Angeles office, the chairman was still there. After I explained the problem, he said the local office would make him an airline reservation, just in case. Mr. Lewis had to leave in the morning, one way or another, because of an important business meeting in San Francisco. I suggested that if the APU was fixed in time for our flight, I would have the hotel leave him a note under his door. The chairman said, "No, you can't trust hotel people. Just call me about six and let me know what's going on." After dinner at our hotel, Ron and I went back to the airport to check on the airplane. The new starter had arrived; but the mechanics said it would be around midnight before they would have it installed and checked out. The engines in the Gulfstream were started by compressed air from the APU's air turbine; so it was a vital part of our minimum equipment list. I made the mechanics promise to call me at my hotel when they finished, no matter what time it was. I turned in early and fell right to sleep. It seemed like just minutes passed when the phone rang. It was 3 a.m. and the mechanic said the APU was back in operation. Now, I had to remember to call the boss in three hours. He wouldn't need his airline reservation after all. My alarm clock awakened me at six so I could call the chairman.

At 7:30 a.m., Bing Cosby delivered the chairman right to the airplane, as it was sitting in the number one spot in front of the building. When leaving the airplane in San Francisco, Mr. Lewis said, "Have some food on board tomorrow as I want to fly direct to Groton, Connecticut. Let's leave at ten o'clock." Then he added "It'll be just me again." The flight across the country would take about five hours; so I had the catering people have lunches and dinners for three delivered to the airplane by 9 a.m. That night at the hotel I asked Ron, "How good a cook are you? Tomorrow you'll have to prepare and serve the food. George (the autopilot) and I will fly the airplane." Our GII's well appointed galley was equipped with a high-temp oven, china, silver service and crystal stemware that would serve up to eight passengers.

After departing San Francisco, and while climbing to our cruising altitude of 41,000 feet, I sent Ron back to get the lunch ready to serve. As he was getting out of his seat, here came Mr. Lewis with two trays of lunch all beautifully arranged. He wore a towel around his waist for an apron and had beaten us to the punch. He said he was having a ball back there all by himself. The stereo was playing at a high volume too. I said we had meant to serve him, not the other way around. He replied, "I'm the cabin attendant today, and that includes dinner later on." Ron and I just looked at each other. Not many corporate pilots get to be served by the chairman of the board of a large company.

When the new chairman came on board with the company, I had some reason to believe that, in addition to being a top aircraft design engineer, he was also a pilot. Flying the Sabreliner to New York one day, I asked the chairman if he would like to sit in the right seat in the cockpit for a while. Without hesitation, he climbed into the seat. Soon, I was given a frequency change and was told to contact the New York Air Traffic Control Center. I thought that this would be a good time to let him fly the airplane for a few minutes. As I was changing the radio frequency, I noticed the airplane starting to turn to the right. I said to him, "Maintain present heading," but the airplane just kept on turning. Suddenly I realized that I had been misinformed. He wasn't a pilot after all. Quickly I said, "I have it," and got the airplane back on the proper course. He never mentioned anything about that experience and neither did I.

One day, when I was still assigned to the Fort Worth Division, a call came in requesting the Sabreliner to go on a mercy mission out to Phoenix, Arizona. I was selected to go and my copilot was Bob Myron. At the Phoenix airport a doctor and a nurse would meet the airplane and give us further instructions. This was a surprise as we didn't fly many of these missions. At Phoenix, the doctor said to file a flight plan to the Grand Canyon airport. This was getting interesting now. When leaving the airplane at Grand Canyon, the only thing the doctor said was, "We'll be back in an hour or so to fly back to Phoenix." What was going on anyway, I wondered. We didn't need any more fuel; so the copilot went into the terminal to get a cup of coffee. I stayed with the airplane and tidied up the cabin and then did a visual post-flight inspection of the exterior of the airplane. Soon I noticed a light twin-engine airplane taxing in after landing but didn't give it much attention. Soon, a tall man with a limp in his right leg, along with a shorter older man, walked down the ramp from the light twin. As they came closer, I noticed something very familiar about the taller man. Sure enough, it was James Arness - Marshal Matt Dillon of the "Gunsmoke" TV series.

Regaining my composure, I walked over to them and introduced myself and asked if they would like to look at my jet airplane. Jim and I shook hands and then he introduced me to his father. They based their airplane at the Van Nuys airport and were out for a spin around the Canyon. Jim had a difficult time entering the Sabreliner as his right knee doesn't bend very far. He said it was a WW II injury he received while serving in Italy. I got Jim into the pilot's seat where we talked for a good half hour. He marveled at all the gauges and controls in the cockpit. I told him that I would love to take them both up for a spin but I just couldn't do it. Jim is as friendly and common as an old shoe. I found out later that we share the same birthday - May 26. Soon I heard my copilot shout from the airstairs that an ambulance was headed our way. Oh, oh, that must be our passengers, I thought. I got Jim and his dad out of the airplane just as the ambulance pulled to a stop by the airstairs with lights and sirens going full blast.

The ambulance attendants, very carefully, slid a stretcher out of the vehicle. Laying on the stretcher and cussing up a storm was none other than the famous Senator Barry Goldwater from Arizona. It seemed he was in the big canyon, climbing a wall, when he fell and injured his back. We had a terrible time getting him up the airstairs and into the airplane. Finally we had to carry him up using a fireman's sling, with him cussing all the way. Watching all of this from under the wing of a nearby airplane, were Jim Arness and his dad. It was a short flight back to Phoenix and the Senator's egress from the airplane was much easier than earlier when getting into it. This time he merely shook everyone off and simply walked off by himself. Between cuss words, he said they did more damage to his back getting him into that airplane than the fall in the Canyon did. Nothing ever appeared in the media concerning his mishap.

Before we ordered the GII, and while we were still based at Lambert Field, the chairman had scheduled the Sabreliner to take him and his wife to Washington, D.C. for a big awards dinner. When the line boys at Rockwell rolled our airplane out of the hangar, they got careless and "dinged" the airplane's right horizontal stabilizer. It came in contact with a steel hangar support beam. The beam didn't give but the airplane did. Now I was in big trouble. The chairman and his wife were already in the limo and on the way to the airport. The damage to the airplane rendered it unairworthy. It was grounded and I was afraid I would be grounded with it. I ran into the flight office, called the chairman's secretary and told her to quickly make airline reservations for them. As I went back out on the ramp, the limo came around the corner looking for the airplane. By now, it had been pushed back into the hangar for needed repairs. The first thing the chairman said was, "Tom, why isn't the airplane out here ready to go?" When I told him what happened, he blew his stack and I couldn't blame him. I profusely apologized for his inconvenience and told him that airline reservations had been made. Rockwell offered to take them over to the terminal but the chairman said "No, you have done enough damage for one day." Then he instructed his limo driver to take him to the airline terminal and then take his wife back home. I felt terrible and let Rockwell management know they would have to pay damages; and if I got fired over this, they would be sued. That was Friday. On Monday, John Kane came out to my airport office and said that the boss wanted us to look for a new home for the airplane. Together, we headed out to the only "reliever airport" in town, the Spirit of St. Louis Airport located out in "Gumbo Flats" near the Missouri river west of town. After checking with all the hangar owners out there, we accepted an invitation to become a tenant in the Ralston Purina hangar. They quickly made arrangements to hangar our airplane. On August 14, 1974, I moved the aviation department from Lambert Field to the Spirit of St. Louis Airport.

Everything went fine until we ordered the new Gulfstream II, which caused a problem for Ralston. They didn't have space for the big jet but decided we were a good tenant and promptly enlarged their hangar some 85 feet to the west just for the GII. At the time, we didn't have our own maintenance department and relied on Ralston Purina to maintain our airplanes. With the addition of the GII, another problem surfaced. They didn't have any qualified Gulfstream II mechanics. They would have to send two mechanics to school in Savannah, Georgia, for the four-week maintenance course. A hassle broke out over the cost. General Dynamics finally agreed to pay the tuition expense, if Ralston paid the travel and living expenses. Later on, we set up our own maintenance department and hired the same two Gulfstream-trained mechanics.

All my pilots now had completed their GII training and passed their FAA check rides. When an airplane has a maximum takeoff gross weight of over 12,500 pounds, pilots must have a type-rating in the specific type of airplane. Under 12,500 pounds, a commercial pilot license with instrument rating suffices. All my pilots had to go to Atlanta and meet with the regional FAA examiner, Mr. Lester Cooling, for their type-checks. As manager, I was the first one to get this examination. Mr. Cooling was very cordial when I met him at the Atlanta Hartsfield airport. He said, "Tom, have you had lunch yet?" When I said no, George Sayers, my copilot, Mr. Cooling and I took the Hangar One shuttle bus over to the main terminal for a sandwich. During lunch, not a single word was mentioned about flying. We discussed the weather, sports and almost everything else.

Back at the hangar, Mr. Cooling said my type-rating examination would be in two phases. The first phase would be an oral exam on the airplane systems. The second phase would be the flight check. I had to pass both phases to have the airplane type-rating listed on my Airline Transport Pilot (ATP) license. It's the same license that airline pilots have. During the oral quiz, the examiner asked me question after question about the airplane, even the air pressures of the tires and the oil, hydraulic and pneumatic systems requirements. The final question was the hardest. I was asked to trace a drop of jet fuel that would flow from the tip of the wing fuel tank to the burner cans in the turbine section of the engine. This was a long route as the fuel had to flow through a lot of lines, filters, three different fuel pumps and a lot more. When I hesitated, he asked if I understood the question. I indicated I did and was just going over the fuel system in my mind. Finally, on a piece of paper, I traced the complete travel route that a drop of fuel would have to take to get from the wing tip to the engine burner cans. He then said, "Fine, let's go fly the machine."

The flight check took nearly an hour and he had me do just about everything: stalls, normal and steep turns, unusual position recovery, engine out procedures, emergency descent, engine out landings, engine cut on takeoff and the famous " FAA Waltz." (I will explain that maneuver later in this chapter.) After I completed the waltz, Mr. Cooling asked me to get out of the seat as he wanted to shoot the final landing for his own qualification requirements. FAA examiners have to be qualified in the airplane in which they examine pilots. When we landed, he told me to wait for him in the general aviation terminal. In a few minutes the examiner came back and handed me a piece of paper that said I owned a type-rating in the Gulfstream II aircraft Later, the FAA would send me a new license with the aircraft type (G1159) permanently affixed on it. After all that, I felt very confident in the airplane. I loved it and thought it was terrific to fly. For the next 20 years I would fly that beautiful airplane. It was a Cadillac with Rolls Royce engines.

On the first few flights in the new airplane, the chairman would hand me a list of things to be fixed when we returned home. They were minor problems, usually light bulbs, a sticking drawer, a seat that was hard to maneuver, or a window shade that snaked down on takeoff. His main complaint was a cabin window that would hiss on descent prior to landing. Finally, when he left the airplane and didn't give me a list, I felt wonderful. Now I knew the cabin was in perfect shape. Most CEOs wouldn't do that as they didn't possess the engineering experience.

The Gulfstream was acquired because the company was building aircraft, ships, submarines, tanks and missiles all under government contract. The airplane was needed to make trips overseas to sell and support those products. My first trip was to the Paris Air Show. A major air show is held there every odd year. In even years, the Farnborough Air Show is held in England. Both are major events, as people from all over the world attend these huge aeronautical exhibits. In early June 1977, I flew several company executives over to the big event in Paris. The marketing people from the Fort Worth Division had made hotel reservations for everyone well in advance. General Dynamics was displaying their pride and joy, the F-16 Falcon Fighter. The show lasted for a week and each morning, promptly at ten o'clock, the flight demonstrations started and lasted for two hours. The demonstrations were repeated in the afternoons at 2:00. The F-16 Falcon stole the show each day.

When I joined General Dynamic's Fort Worth Division, in October 1969, they had a sponsorship program going for new hires. My sponsor was Neil Anderson, one of Dick Johnson's pilots. Dick Johnson wanted Midwesterners to stick together. Neil (Andy) Anderson was born and raised in Omaha and we had an immediate and common bond. Andy was the test pilot for the F-16 at the Paris Air Show. Andy did a superb job demonstrating this airplane each day before more than 100,000 people. The F-16 made the competition look rather sad. Each sponsor of airplanes operated a chalet on the airport grounds near the runway. They were first class and each had a full kitchen, dining room with white tablecloths and a beverage bar. Guests from all over the world came in for food and refreshments. Twice a day, these guests would have a "50-yard line" view of the interesting flight demonstrations going on right in front of them.

Earlier, General Dynamics had built the F-111 fighter-bomber and sold some to the Australian Air Force. Soon after the GII was put into operation, a trip was scheduled to Australia to see if the Royal Australian Air Force could use the F-16s. With the chairman, two of his staff, two marketing executives from the Fort Worth Division, we headed for Australia in the Gulfstream II. For international flights I used a crew of four; two pilots, an engineer and a female flight attendant. Gail Myrick, a former Ozark Airlines Flight Attendant, was on the crew for our first overseas trip. Australia is a wonderful country and the people are extremely friendly. The first stop in the country was Sydney, where foreign customs had to be cleared. It was late so everyone immediately checked into the Hilton Hotel. It had been a very long day. After a day of rest, the next stop was Canberra, which is the Australian capital. It is a city that was planned because the country couldn't decide whether to have its capital in Sidney or in Melbourne. After a long period, a truce was called and it was decided to build a new capital city from the ground up. It was located about halfway between Sydney and Melbourne. Laid out like a college campus, it has lots of manicured grounds, lakes and modern buildings, none of which are near each other. Canberra is not on the coast like Sydney and Melbourne; it is located more inland. After three days of meetings, our next stop was Melbourne. After landing, I parked the airplane on Associated Airlines' ramp. During my Gulfstream training in Savannah, I had met two Associated Airlines pilots, Bob Barnes and his chief pilot, Rod Crump. Associated Airlines operated a feeder airline that flew daily flights across the country bringing passengers to Melbourne or Sydney for connections with international flights.

Associated Airlines operated five Gulfstream aircraft. It was a big operation. Their hospitality was wonderful. During the flight over, a couple of things went wrong that needed fixing. A water line in the galley cracked due to freezing, and a cabin window hissed below 10,000 feet. Both items were fixed by the second day. The Associated mechanics wrapped the new water line with an electrical harness so it would never freeze again. It's wonderful to find an operator overseas that operates the very same equipment that you do. Most of the time on overseas trips, you are on your own as far as maintenance goes. My flight engineer, John Rogerson, came up with an innovative idea. He created a "fly-away-kit"-a box containing all kinds of spare parts stored in the tail compartment-known as the hell hole. That kit saved us many times when we were out of the country. Leaving Australia, we were scheduled to stop in New Zealand. What a beautiful mountainous country it is. As we looked down from the air it seemed the country had more sheep than cattle. We spent the night in picturesque Auckland. On the way back to Hawaii, we stopped at one of the Society Islands, Tahiti, in French Polynesia, for some badly needed R&R. Everyone had been on a very strenuous schedule the past week. The capital of Tahiti is called Papeete. Everyone stayed in thatched huts suspended just above the water in the bay.

The huts were not as primitive as they appeared. They were equipped with all the modern conveniences. The waters around the islands are light green. You can see many feet straight down to the ocean floor where many strange looking fish and sea life moved about. The sunset is a big event in the tropical islands because it happens so quickly. When the rim of the sun touches the horizon, you had better be outside if you want to see it, because in seconds, the sun has suddenly disappeard from sight. Darkness then comes very quickly. One morning while I was eating breakfast in the hotel coffee shop, an American couple came in and sat at my table. They had just gotten off a 747 airliner after an all-night flight from Los Angeles. After we talked a bit, I asked if I could look at their copy of the Los Angeles Times. One of the first things I read was that Bing Crosby had died from a heart attack on a golf course in Spain. Due north of Tahiti, some 2,000 miles away lay the islands of Hawaii. That was our next stop. After a day of rest, we headed for home via San Francisco.

The new Gulfstream didn't sit on the ground long after it got back from Australia A week later it left for Europe on another business trip. The first year we had the airplane, it flew overseas 14 times. That's considered very good utilization of a corporate asset. A month later, it was back in Australia. The Australian Air Force were getting ready to select a new fighter-either our F-16 or McDonnell Douglas's F-18. On this trip to Australia, I had a different co-pilot, Frank Beeby; the same engineer, John Rogerson, and a new flight attendant. Her name was Linda Laurestine-an Air Force Reserve Flight Nurse. Australia was so far away that I had to make more than one stop to get there. Hawaii was the first stop and I used the Kona airport on the west side of the big island of Hawaii. That first night, as the crew ate dinner, I asked Linda if she had contacted the catering company for food for the next day. It would be a long one and we needed provisions for breakfast, lunch and dinner.

Linda said she called in a huge food order and that everything was taken care of. It was to be at the airport the next morning at 6:00. The passengers were scheduled to arrive at 6:30 and our departure time was set for 7:00. Bright and early the next morning, the air crew preflighted the airplane, topped off the fuel tanks and, in general, made ready for the big day ahead. It was past 6:00 and no catering truck was to be seen. Soon it was 6:30 and here came our passengers. Linda was in operations trying to call the tardy caterer. As Frank was putting the passenger's baggage aboard, I saw Linda come running out to the airplane in tears. She said the caterer took the food order to the Hilo airport instead of Kona. The airports were on opposite sides of the big Island. Linda swore she told them the Kona airport. Now I had to explain this dilemma to the boss. First, the chairman told Linda to stop crying as tears wouldn't fix the problem. In the small terminal, I called our handler in Houston and asked them to set up some catering at our next stop-Pago Pago.

The chairman got some coins and all but emptied the vending machines. We weren't too bad off as there was juice and coffee on the airplane. We got along just fine. Linda's eyes were red the whole day. It was 2,550 miles from Kona to Pago Pago (called Pango Pango), and it was late afternoon when we landed. Going west we flew into earlier time zones and that helped some. Sure enough, the Pago Pago airport had catering for us and, after refueling, we were off to the Fiji Islands. These islands were only 900 miles away, so it was a short trip. On that leg Linda prepared an excellent steak dinner with all the trimmings.

Eating my meal in the cockpit, I wondered what kind of animal that steak came from, but it was very tasty and Frank thought so too. We stayed the night in Fiji as Sydney, our destination, was 2,100 miles further. The next morning, everyone was still tired so we got a late start. The airport at Sydney had a midnight curfew and we had to make that, as there was nowhere else to go. Halfway there, we crossed the equator where the winds were supposed to be opposite from those north of the equator where winds flow generally from west to east. That night, south of the equator, for some strange reason, I was still flying into head winds. During the evening, I heard air traffic control talking to a Flying Tiger DC-8 that was ahead of us and also going to Sydney. I asked ATC to tell the Tiger to come up on frequency 123.45 mHz. Soon he came on and we talked for some time. The Tiger had a cargo of 12 horses. I mentioned I had a cargo of 6 humans. The Tiger landed in Sydney at 11:30, and we slipped in 15 minutes later-too close for comfort. The approach into Sydney at night is a beautiful sight with all the lights shining brightly. After clearing customs, everyone went to the same Hilton hotel where we had stayed before. The schedule the next morning was to fly to Canberra and we were to leave at 10:00. Being allowed to sleep in a little was a welcome break for the crew.

In Canberra, everyone was booked into the Lincoln Hotel. This time I got the full story of the birth of the city. It was an artificially created city conceived somewhat on the same lines as Brasilia, Brazil. Canberra grew out of the bitter rivalry between Sydney and Melbourne as to which should become the new nation's capital city after the Federation of Australian States was formed in 1901. Canberra is located inland approximately halfway between Sydney and Melbourne. It is the only major Australian city which is not a sea port. Being far from the sea, this new city is hot in the summer and cold in the winter.

The city of Canberra was hatched in the incubator of an international planning competition started in 1911. Unlike any normal city, Canberra was not developed on the banks of a river or under the protection of a mountain range. Even it's graceful Lake Bueley Griffin is man-made. The city is beautifully green and beautifully clean. The 88-year-old scheme has produced results that not only delight planners and architects, but has created a garden city. The locals call it a city in a garden. There is a profusion of trees, little to no industry and no big city smells of pollution. The air is always fresh. There is no white Christmas in Australia. During June and July the ground is often covered with snow. Summertime starts in October and by January, it's blow-torch hot-over 100 degrees Fahrenheit.

One night I asked the hotel manager where we could find a good place to eat dinner. He gave me instructions on how to find Bogart's Steak House. As the crew walked in, the first thing we saw was a huge picture of Humphrey Bogart, the famous Hollywood actor. The picture was so big it almost covered the entire entrance wall. The steaks were just great. On a later trip to Australia, I took the flight crew back there again.

Back home, I was busy in my office doing the never-ending paperwork when the phone rang. John Kane said that he had a request to support our Asbestos Mines Division in Canada. We were to fly some engineers to their northernmost mine near Frobisher Bay, some 1,200 miles north of Montreal. The town of Frobisher Bay is located on Baffin Island. The bay is named for Sir Martin Frobisher, an English sea captain who discovered it in 1576 while searching for a short cut to India. The bay turned out to be a blind alley for Sir Martin. While there, he found some black soil that sparkled and thought he had discovered gold. Back home in England, he reported his find to Queen Elizabeth. Later the same year, she sent him back to Frobisher Bay, however, this time the Queen's miners sailed with Sir Martin. The soil that so excited him lies disregarded today. Geologists call it iron pyrite-fool's gold. During World War II, the American Army Air Force established an air base there and called it by its code name: Crystal II. Another American air base, located across the Hudson Strait, was called Crystal I.

Crystal II consisted of one long runway, a weather reporting station and lots of Quonset huts. There they have nine months of winter, and despite their short summers, mosquitoes are a real problem as it stays light until 11 p.m. The northernmost American base is at Thule, Greenland, 900 miles north of Frobisher Bay. At 700 miles above the Arctic circle, Thule is mainly a US Weather Station and is known as the world's northernmost settlement. During the flight to Frobisher Bay, the weather was clear all the way. Frobisher has an austere airport but I got the GII safely on the ground. The nearby small town of Iqaluit was wild with celebration as we arrived, though I was certain it wasn't for us. I learned later that the Eskimos had beached a big whale in the bay that morning.

The catch would yield enough whale meat and oil to last for a year. They had good reason to be so happy. The mining engineers I had flown up there were later taken to the actual asbestos mine site in a light airplane. There was one hotel in town. It was unusual as that same building housed a grocery store, a bar, a bowling alley, a movie theater, a combined barber and beauty shop and assorted other small shops. During the severe winters, nobody that lived in the hotel needed to go outside. Days of 40 below zero temperature were the norm. That night my crew and I ate a good dinner, and then watched a John Wayne movie. Being that far north, the asbestos mine could only be worked four months out of the year. The ore was taken by the company-owned Three Rivers Railroad to the bay. There it was loaded on ships headed for Germany, where it was processed. From there, the material was dispatched all over the world. Today, OSHA (Occupational Safety and Health Administration) forbids the use of asbestos material for insulation and fireproofing in the U.S.

During the flight back to Montreal, I noticed huge icebergs, in the Hudson Bay, floating out toward the Atlantic Ocean. Each June, they float out of the Labrador Sea and end up in the ocean. I saw one huge iceberg that had a flat top and was so big that right in the middle was a small green lake. The small and medium sized icebergs just show a sharp tip. That trip to Frobisher Bay was unforgettable.

Back home the Sabreliner was flying its wings off. I was told it was gone all the time. For the next two overseas trips I stayed home and got caught up on my paperwork. In a few weeks I was informed that another trip to Iran was in the planning stages. Now I had to line up the crew for this trip. My copilot was going to be John Langer, the engineer John Rogerson and Vicki Werkmeister, another Air Force Reserve Flight Nurse, the flight attendant. The plan was to fly over to Ashland, Kentucky, and pick up two Ashland Oil Company engineers before heading for Iran. Leaving St. Louis, I had four passengers; three executives and a lawyer. Leaving Ashland, I had six passengers. Vicki had fun back there in the galley fixing tasty food for those six men.

Our first stop was London for a quick overnight. The next day we took off for Tehran. The flight went well but it was a long five hour non-stop trip. I did have some helping tail winds.

On the way back I would have to stop in Belgrade, Yugoslavia for fuel. In Tehran, everyone stayed at the Hilton hotel again. The International Hotel was okay, but the Hilton was newer and the staff spoke better English. The flight crew had two free days to look over the old city. When I was in Tehran with the Mexicans the year before, I saw some things but not nearly everything I wanted to. No traffic in the world is thicker than in Tehran. It's a mixture of American cars, fleets of small British taxis, push carts, wagons, buses, war-surplus trucks and plodding burros. Sometimes flocks of sheep, goats and camels, in from the desert, bring traffic to a standstill. Shops are small. There are no department stores and no real grocery stores either. The druggist, not the grocer, sells powdered milk and only the grain man sells rice. Everyone seems to be in business for himself; butcher, baker, vegetable man-all have their own stalls. Someone mentioned that these merchants sleep in the stalls at night-for security reasons I suppose. Most merchants have radios blaring loud and irritating wailing music from the East. Meat vendors (mostly lamb and foul) hang their products on a line in front of their stalls each day. Most are covered with big flies. The sight was repugnant to everyone but the locals, It didn't bother them at all.

Tehran is a city of rags and riches. Big American cars are seen around the walled palaces and villas that dot the city and its northern suburbs. On the outskirts of the city, poor people live in caves much like animals. In the large downtown mart, piles of multi-colored rugs almost reached the ceiling. On display is every type of Persian rug from tribal primitives to silk-backed beauties that look like paintings. From high balconies hang lustrous carpets fit for palaces, their rich colors glowing in the sun. To purchase a rug, one has to haggle over the price for a good while. The merchants love that game and you should never try to buy a rug at sticker price. You just can't do it. At the hotel, the assistant manager told us that Tehran isn't the real Iran. "You must take a long trip to see the unchanged countryside," he said, so we did that in a rented car with a driver who was also a licensed guide. Just a few miles out into the country, one goes quickly back in time. Southeast of the city is 650 miles of formidable desert-trackless waste with huge salt flats, parts of which have never been explored for minerals. It looked like the second day of Creation, before life or vegetation appeared on Earth. Only 10 percent of the land in Iran is under cultivation, and a third of that relies on irrigation. Another 15 percent is grazing land with coarse grass or just gray sagebrush. Mountains, forests and barren land cover the remaining 75 percent of the country. The Iranians use a centuries-old system of getting water for irrigation. Since the water is sub-surface, diggers hand-sink a well in the hills. If they're lucky and make a strike, they tunnel an underground bed for the water to the nearest village. Every few hundred feet, they dig another shaft to bring up dirt to use later for tunnel repairs. With this method, there is very little evaporation, and the water can't be stolen. Our driver/guide spoke reasonably good English, and I asked him where he had learned it. He said that he had gone to school in France, but never studied English. He had brought back a large stack of old English comic books and simply taught himself. An amazing, but true, story. In the old section of Tehran is an underground bazaar and, upon entering it, you think this same setting must have existed for centuries. Soon I saw a rug that I liked, and true to form, it took a half hour of haggling before the merchant and I agreed on the final price. As I started to pull out some local currency, the merchant smiled and said, "I take MasterCard." I almost fell over, and Vicki laughed until tears were running down her cheeks. The merchant finally laughed too, and I doubt that he knew why. He probably laughed because he thought something was very funny to us. The rest of the crew had similar experiences purchasing various things in the old underground bazaar.

Before leaving Tehran, someone at the hotel said we couldn't leave without eating in a local restaurant, so we hailed a taxi and headed for this recommended place. The menu was in Arabic, so we decided to order the evening special. The waiters pushed over a large serving table and began to prepare the Iranian feast. Over a heaping mound of fluffy Persian rice, the chef dropped in several raw eggs and mixed it all up. On top of the mound of (now) yellow rice, he added strips of broiled lamb. With a big grin, the chef told us to help ourselves using our fingers as there were no utensils. After looking at it for a while, everyone declined. We ordered a drink instead. During the fuel stop at Belgrade, on the way back to London, and while checking the weather in England, I noticed the dispatcher had an odd accent when he spoke. He told me he was a retired Russian fighter pilot. When I told him I flew the P-38 during WW II, his eyes lit up, and he said, "Yes, I saw some of those once, when they flew over my airfield very fast."

We had to overfly London because the weather there had turned sour. Our alternate airport was across the Irish Sea where we landed at Shannon, Ireland. Everyone spent the night at a large Irish castle that was converted into a hotel called Drommoland Castle. It was owned by an American from New York City and he flew a large American flag from the roof-top.

Back home, my mail included a letter from Ken Skoglind, our Gulfstream salesman. He informed me that our new Gulfstream III, which had been ordered several months earlier, was near green completion on the assembly line. In two days I was in Savannah and learned that the airplane, serial number 329, was number one on the final assembly line. The factory procedure had been changed since our GII was built. Now, if you wanted the factory's new completion center to finish the airplane, all they had to do was tow it about 100 yards to the new outfitting center. Those airplanes didn't have to be flown until they were 100 percent completed. If they passed the flight check, they could be delivered to the new owner the next day. The owners of green airplanes who wanted their airplanes completed at another completion center had to arrange for the installation of a VFR fly-away-kit before they could ferry it away. The completion center at the factory was brand new and held 12 green GIIIs. We chose to have the airplane outfitted in the factory's new completion facility. It was estimated that final completion on our GIII would take about three months. On the second floor of the completion center were small offices for new owners' chief pilots and maintenance managers. There they could set up shop to monitor the completion of their new airplanes. We were given such an office, and my maintenance manager, John Rogerson, and I rotated there on a weekly basis. Watching the completion of our new airplane was a great experience. It was far different from the military airplanes I had helped build many years ago in Buffalo and Omaha.

The chairman was going to like the new GIII as it had more room in the cabin (six feet longer) and a bigger wing that held more fuel. The result was a bonus of longer range and less frequent fuel stops. The new wing had winglets for added stability, especially on takeoff and during landing approach when the airplane is normally hand-flown. The new cockpit had the very latest in avionics and flight management systems. The dual long range navigation systems used a laser-driven inertial method of stabilization and motion sensing for greater accuracy and reliability. In early spring of 1982 the GIII was delivered and, as manager of the flight department, I flew the first company flight. I flew the first flights on four new company airplanes: Sabreliner 75A, Sabreliner 80A, the Gulfstream II and III. I felt very fortunate to have been in the right place at the right time. Now we had two Gulfstreams but only needed one. We decided to loan the G II to our divisions that operated jet airplanes. Fort Worth and San Diego divisions each used the GII but before they could fly it they were required to send their pilots to the factory qualification school in Savannah. The new GIII was flown almost daily, and it was a dream to fly. Some of the pilots thought it was punishment when they were scheduled to fly the Sabreliner instead of the new large jet. Later that spring, I flew the Gulfstream III on its first international flight. The company had business to conduct in Cairo, Egypt, and Tel Aviv, Israel. Early on a Monday morning, the new airplane departed for a quick fuel stop in Boston. From there I flew directly to Brussels and stayed two days since we had a company business office located there. The next stop was

Athens, Greece, for an overnight. The following day we had an easy flight to Cairo. As usual, Cairo was hot and dusty with sand blowing in from the desert. The purpose of the trip to Cairo was to formally deliver some F-16 fighters to the Egyptian Air Force.

The three ladies on the trip had done their homework as they brought along books on what to see while in Egypt. They decided to take a commuter flight down the Nile River to see some ancient temples. The flight crew were invited to join them, but we declined. Their first stop was at Luxor, 300 miles south of Cairo. Later they continued down the river to Aswan where the famous High Dam is located. Upon their return, the women said their favorite place was the ancient temples of Ramses II, the Great King, located near Luxor. Before leaving Cairo, I read up on Ramses II, and this is what the local historians have to say about him:

"Until the discovery of the tomb of King Tut in 1922, Ramses II was the only Egyptian King whose name, apart from those of the builders of the Great Pyramids of Giza, was familiar to the nonarchaeological public, and, to this day, its bearer remains a prominent figure in the long history of ancient Egypt.

King Ramses II was the third king of the 19th dynasty of Egypt. His 67 year reign from 1304 to 1237 BC was the second longest reign in Egyptian history. His family of non-royal origin, came to power after the reign of the religious reformer, Akhenaton, and set about restoring Egyptian power in Asia, which had declined under Akhenaton and his successor, Tut.

Ramses' father, Seti I, made the crown prince Ramses, the future Ramses II, coregent with him, giving him a kingly household with his own harem, and the young prince accompanied his father on his campaigns, so that when he came to sole rule he already had experience in kingship and war. It would appear, however, that Ramses was not the eldest son, for in a relief at Karnak of his father's Libyan war, the figure of a prince whose name is not preserved was inserted into the scene after it had been completed, but the figure was later erased and that of Ramses substituted. What lay behind these events is not known, but it is noteworthy that Ramses was crowned coregent at an unusually early age as if to ensure that he would in fact succeed to the throne. He ranked as captain in the army while still only ten years old; at that age his rank must surely have been honorific, though he may well have been receiving military training.

Because his family's home was in the Nile river delta and in order to have a convenient base for campaigns in Asia, Ramses built for himself a full-scale residence city called House of Ramses, which was famous for its beautiful layout with gardens, orchards and pleasant waters. Each of its four quarters had its own presiding deity: Amon in the west, Seth in the south, Buto in the north, and Astarte in the east. A vogue for Asian deities had grown up in Egypt, and Ramses had distinct leanings in that direction.

The first public act of Ramses after his accession to sole rule was to visit Thebes when the god of Amon of Karnak made a state visit in his ceremonial barge to the temple of Luxor. It seems that, apart from his extensive building activities and his famous residence city, Ramses's reputation as a great king in the eyes of his subjects rested largely on his fame as a soldier.

In the fourth year of his reign, he led an army north to recover the lost provinces his father had been unable to conquer permanently. The first expedition was to subdue rebellious local dynasts in southern Syria to ensure a secure springboard for further advances. In 1270, Ramses contracted a marriage with the eldest daughter of the Hittite king, and it is possible that, at a later date, he married a second Hittite princess.

One measure of Egypt's prosperity is the amount of temple building the kings could afford and carry out, and on that basis the reign of Ramses II is the most notable in history, even making allowances for its great length. In Egypt he completed the great hypostyle hall at Karnak and the temple started by his father at Abydos, both of which were left incomplete after his father's death. Ramses also completed his father's funerary on the west bank of the Nile at Luxor and built one for himself, which is now known as Remesseum. At Abydos he built a temple of his own not far from that of his father; there were also four major temples in his residence city, not to mention lesser shrines.

The reign of Ramses II marks the last peak of Egypt's imperial power. After his death, Egypt was forced on the defensive but managed to maintain its dominance over Palestine and the adjacent territories until the later part of the 20th dynasty, when, under weak kings who followed Ramses II, internal decay ended its power beyond its borders.

Ramses II must have been a good soldier, despite the fiasco of Kadesh, or else he would not have been able to penetrate so far into the Hittite Empire as he did in the following years. He appeared to have been a competent administrator, since the country was prosperous, and he was certainly a popular king. Some of his fame, however, must surely be put down to his flair for publicity; his name and the record of his feats on the field of battle were found everywhere in Egypt. It is easy to see why, in the eyes of both his subjects and of later generations, he was looked on as a model of what a king should be."

Two days later, the schedule called for us to fly to Tel Aviv for meetings with the Israelis. The distance from Cairo to Tel Aviv is only 250 miles, but politically, we had to fly north towards Cyprus airspace first, then turn east and fly directly to Tel Aviv. That route took us 200 miles out of our direct route, but that was Eastern Mediterranean politics at the time. Today, I'm sure you can fly from Cairo direct to Tel Aviv. It's only about a 30-minute flight. Security at the Tel Aviv airport was the strictest I had ever seen anywhere. Every bag was checked, passengers and crew alike. My flight attendant didn't appreciate the agent opening her baggage and going through her "unmentionables."

At the Tel Aviv Hilton, where everybody was staying, the crew arrived last and checked in at the front desk. The desk clerk, a young American girl from New York, was there on a summer job. She was very nice and handed me a key to my room. As I unlocked the door and entered, I suddenly noticed a young lady lying on the bed in her underwear. As I stopped, she dropped her magazine and said, "How did you get a key to my room?" Apologizing, I quickly backed out into the hall. Going down in the elevator, I could visualize my hands around that front desk clerk's neck. When I confronted her, she just laughed and said that can happen. I was livid and told her I was going to report her to the management. She just laughed again and gave me another key. I found my new room sans a young lady lying on my bed. The people in Israel are very nice and I have great respect for them. Arriving in Tel Aviv on Sunday, a sign in the hotel lobby said that the lounge would not open until after sunset-an ancient custom. In the lobby, near the lounge, people were standing in long lines waiting for the sun to set.

Before leaving Tel Aviv, I arranged for a car and driver to take me to the Holy City - Jerusalem. The trip was only 35 miles. On the way, the driver said I would have to hire a guide to show me around. After arriving, I soon found a guide and we walked all over the area. I was most impressed with the tour of the Church of the Holy Sepulcher, which is where the Good Friday Tomb is located. The sight almost took my breath away. I had always thought the tomb was vastly different from what I saw. It was no more than a hole in the ground that would admit a person. At the time of the Crucifixion, it was known as a tomb. The next day, as we were getting ready to leave Tel Aviv, the same driver, Mr. Guidean, brought out some of our passengers. I gave him a bottle of scotch for taking me to Jerusalem on his own time. Mr. Guidean told me that for an hour every Sunday night, everything stops in Tel Aviv, because everyone watches the weekly "Dallas" TV program. They all had become totally absorbed in the J. R. Ewing saga.

The first stop on the way home was Athens, where we were scheduled to stay a couple of days. The company operated a field office there.

That evening I was relaxing in my room in the Hilton hotel waiting for 6:00 to roll around because the crew members were to meet in the lobby at that time before having dinner. Sitting there reading a book, I felt my chair move a little. Looking up, I saw a picture on the wall move. Immediately surmising that it was an earthquake, I tore out of the room and ran down ten flights of stairs to the ground floor. Going down those stairs, all I could hear were people shouting behind me. It was very frightening, to say the least. Soon, all the people from the hotel were outside standing on the front lawn. The hotel management brought out some coffee, and someone said, "We don't need any coffee. We need a drink." An hour later, they let us back inside as the power had been restored. In minutes, the bar was jammed with very nervous people. In the bar I met an American who said he was from Iowa and worked for the State Agriculture Department. He was in Greece to teach them how to raise clean pigs. The pigs are born and raised on elevated surfaces. They never see dirt or mud in their short lives. The man from Iowa had been in Greece about four months. This was his third earthquake, and he was getting rather used to them, he said.

From Athens we flew to Munich, Germany, and landed in chilly and rainy conditions. The food and beer in Germany are out of this world. Munich, the capital of Bavaria, is the third largest city in Germany, after Berlin and Hamburg. Seven breweries brew over 88 million gallons of beer annually. In 1920, Adolph Hitler had formed the National Socialistic Party (Nazis) in Munich. In three years, he had his own party army, and they always met in their own large beer hall. The building still stands today. Not far from our hotel was another famous beer hall, The Hofbrauhaus. There you were permitted to keep the liter-sized porcelain mug when you drank draft beer. The last stop going home was Shannon, Ireland. The Shannon airport has a large duty-free store that is very popular with all travelers. They sold Waterford crystal at very reasonable prices. I could hardly get my passengers out of there on the morning of our departure for the United States. Flying across the big Atlantic Ocean for the last time, in the Gulfstream III, was very nostalgic for me. My crew on that final overseas trip was Jerry Sonnabend, Co-Captain, John Rogerson, Flight Engineer and Laura Laurestein, Flight Attendant. They were wonderful and Jerry let me fly most of that last trip.

Back home I was working in my office one day when I received a call from a good friend who was the chief pilot for a large company.

Their G III was stopping in St. Louis briefly to offload some passengers and then were going on to Augusta, Georgia, to take in the last day of the Masters Golf Tournament. They had an extra ticket to the big golf event if I wanted to go. Did I ever! This tournament is considered the greatest golf event in the world. Players are there by written invitation only. The only exception being past champions. The Masters, like St. Andrews in Scotland, is all about tradition. The only green jacket that ever leaves the premises is the one worn by the current champion. Past champions only wear theirs at the club. For the past 60 years the Masters week at Augusta is the same. Monday and Tuesday are for player practice rounds, and they may use only one ball during practice. Tuesday night is the past champion's dinner. Wednesday is the par three tournament. Thursday is the ceremonial tee-off to officially start the tournament. On Saturday and Sunday the TV coverage is only allowed four minutes of commercials per hour, half by Cadillac and half by Travelers Insurance. Sunday night is the members dinner with the new champion, and he gets to select the menu. The Augusta National Golf Course is covered with gorgeous azaleas and dogwood in full bloom scattered among the huge pine and oak trees. Golf is at its most poetic high when, on the final nine holes on Sunday, the TV announcers say, "This is where the tournament really begins." The back nine with two reachable par fives and water in play at five of the first seven holes is a perfect setting for the final holes of a huge major championship tournament. Everywhere they go, Masters champions are treated with an extra measure of respect. Tradition means rules, and Augusta has more rules than anywhere. No running on the grounds is allowed, and no autographs can be solicited on the golf course. Augusta National Golf Club has no female members. They finally admitted its first black member in 1990. Inside the large clubhouse hangs a framed sign that simply states:

This is our tournament. If you do not like the way we do business, you are free not to do business with us. If you find our past policies on race or our present policy on gender offensive, you need not attend the tournament, televise the tournament, write about the tournament, or, for that matter, play in the tournament.

The Members Committee

Back home in my small and modest trophy shelf rests my Masters Golf Tournament badge. By now, my scheduled retirement date from the company was just around the corner. I was trying to finalize some travel and aircraft safety business matters when I received notice of a special meeting to be held the coming Friday at 5:30 P.M. after work. It was to be held in the Clayton Inn just two blocks from company headquarters. Walking over there with two of my Travel Section reservationists, Mary Mason and Kris Ross, I mentioned what a strange time for a business meeting. They said they were thinking the same thing-while trying not to give away the secret. When we arrived at the hotel, the desk clerk directed us to the meeting room.

Entering the room my heart raced as it was full of people from headquarters and several divisions, as well as my own family. Everyone was grinning at me. It was a surprise retirement party!! It was a grand affair with great food and an open bar. Mr. Herb Rogers, President of General Dynamics, spoke of my career, both in the Air Force and with the company. I was given many gifts and then was asked to go to the podium and say something. For the life of me, I cannot now remember what I said to them. Mr. Rogers then said he had a letter from Mr. Lewis who had retired some months earlier. He was now living on a 5,000 acre spread near Leary, Georgia, called "Deer Run Plantation." On the large acreage, he raised corn, soybeans and peanuts. The place contained neither stock nor fences. The huge white ranch house was a miniature of the famous Mt. Vernon Plantation House in Virginia. My former boss had a four-wheeler that he drove all around the land. A hired manager operated the place.

Mr. Rogers then read the following letter:

David S. Lewis
DEER RUN PLANTATION
Leary, Georgia, 31762

22 March 1989

Dear Tom,

Congratulations on your 47 years of service to our country and our company. I know first hand how much your 20 years of leadership at General Dynamics has meant. While you have made major contributions to the success of our company in each of your assignments, I think that none was more important than your dedicated and determined development of truly professional flight operations, first in St. Louis and later in the divisions. I know because I saw those operations change from black to white. Dorothy and I are fortunate to have known you so well, having been your companions on many important flights all over the world.

You and Joan have our best wishes for a long, happy and healthy retirement which you have truly earned.

Most sincerely,
(signed)
David S. Lewis

When Mr. Rogers finished reading that letter, the entire Gordon family had very moist eyes. I was very fortunate to be David Lewis's personal pilot for so many years. What a fine man he was. The party went on well into the night.

All the division people had brought gifts and each had something to say in the way of tribute. A lot of the gifts were humorous in nature. Many of the attendees had cameras and many group pictures were taken. The company photographer, Tom Rule, was there and in a couple of weeks, sent me a nice album commemorating the evening's revelry. I never dreamed the company would do this for me. I was truly shocked, humbled and very honored.

For the past 47 years I have seen aviation grow by leaps and bounds, with bigger and better airplanes, more reliable engines with greater power and avionics that makes the pilot work only on takeoff and landing. Business airplanes can now fly from New York to Tokyo and from San Francisco to Cairo. I am very happy to have been a part of that exciting period in our aviation history.

To acquire knowledge, one must study;
but to acquire wisdom, one must observe.

—*Marilyn vos Savant*

CHAPTER TWELVE

AROUND THE WORLD
IN 20 DAYS

Where we come from in America no longer signifies.
It's where we go, and what we do when we get there, that tells us who we are.

—*Joyce Carol Oates*

In May 1982, my aviation career almost came to a screeching halt. During the 1970s, the FAA fostered a regulation that scheduled air carriers (airlines) impose the "60 and Out" rule. That meant that pilots who had reached the age of 60 were suddenly out on the street. Not fired, but mandatorily retired. Everyone in the aviation world watched this event with great interest. Some corporations such as General Motors, Ford, Chrysler and others decided to follow the airline ruling and required their pilots to step down at the magic milestone of 60 years young. Some of the pilots from these major corporations decided they didn't like this one little bit and sued their companies for age discrimination. To my dismay, my company decided to join the other major corporations and impose the same rule. I couldn't believe they would do this. With the airlines, it was a mandatory ruling by an FAA Regulation. Corporations, which operate under a different Federal Aviation Regulation, were not required to do this. Nevertheless, some companies did anyway, and General Dynamics was one of them. My philosophy is that age is relative and some can be old at 40, and others can be young at 60. Many doctors agree with this theory. I was in the prime of my career and healthy as a horse, as the saying goes.

When I was notified that the "60 and Out" rule was now in effect at General Dynamics, I was beside myself with despair and felt strongly that the company did not need to do this. It turns out that the company's insurance department argued that it was a wise business move and the chairman bought it. I was the first pilot in the company to be affected by this new policy. On my 60th birthday, I was scheduled to fly the chairman on a business trip to Dayton, Ohio. On the flight to Dayton, the chairman never mentioned a word about this new rule. Later that afternoon, on the return flight to St. Louis, he came up to the cockpit and asked what I thought of the new policy. I said it shocked me and I didn't think it was right or fair. He didn't comment and went back to the cabin. I was livid, as I had built the headquarters aviation department from scratch. The growth from an empty room at Lambert Field to a three-jet international airplane operation in 20 years should not go unnoticed Upon landing after the Dayton trip, Mr. Lewis said that he had some plans for me down at headquarters. That was fine, but I wanted to stay at the aviation department and continue in my position of leadership, even if I couldn't fly anymore. He said he would rather have everyone in the aviation department, including the manager, on flying status. He went on to say that I would still have a finger in the aviation pie. I would be responsible for the Flight Safety Program for General Dynamics. There were five aviation departments in the thirteen divisions of the company. In addition, the chairman said the company would give me an additional job at headquarters in Clayton.

My second job at Headquarters was to be the commercial travel manager for the company. I was responsible for getting business travelers to their meeting locations around the country. If I couldn't put them on the company jet, then they were sent out on the airlines. When employees travel, there are three things they need; an airline ticket or a seat on the company plane, a hotel room and a rental car. My job required me to secure contracts with these travel service suppliers. Working with the service providers in acquiring airline tickets, hotel rooms and car rentals at the lowest possible rates was interesting work. When I visited the divisions on business, they often would permit me to fly their airplanes. No one was the wiser, and it kept me current as a pilot. That was always a source of great satisfaction.

In the spring of 1979, rumor had it that the chairman wanted the Gulfstream to take him to the Paris Air Show. Sure enough, on the next Sabreliner trip, Mr. Lewis said to get the airplane ready for a big trip. I didn't think a trip to Paris was that big a deal. How wrong I was. It wasn't long before my immediate boss, John Kane, called me to his office at Corporate Headquarters and briefed me on the upcoming trip. He had just returned from a meeting with the chairman, and had all the details. The passenger load would be the chairman, two executives and their wives. He asked me about the crew that I wanted, and before I could respond, he said, "I want you to go as the man in charge." John Langer would go as second in command and my engineer was John Rogerson. I then told my boss that I would recommend Gail Myrick as the flight attendant as she was well liked and very efficient in the cabin. She had worked for Ozark Airlines for several years and knew her job well. Gail was up for the next international trip anyway.

John then said, "Don't we have two young women who are Air Force Reserve Flight Nurses?" The two RNs were Vicki (Werkmeister) Dunn and Linda Laurestein. They flew about three times a month on air-evacuation flights out of Scott AFB in Illinois, about 50 miles away. John told me to see if one of them could go, as having an RN on board seemed like a good idea. I inquired and learned that Linda wasn't available but Vicki was. Now,I had to tell Gail she couldn't go. Gail took the news very hard and never really got over the disappointment and, as a result, quit her job with me. Gail did have two years of nurse's training but had to get out because she became too close to a lot of her (on the job training) patients. When some of them died, she just couldn't take it anymore.

All six passengers and the four crew members had to go to the County Health Department for overseas shots. Each of us received several and nobody felt well for the next few days. About a week before we departed for Paris, the chairman's secretary called and said to take a lot of money and plenty of clothes as the trip just might continue on from Paris, and around the world. That was a shocker. I didn't take $10,000 in cash like the Mexicans did, but I took a good bit of green and a lot of American Express traveler's checks. My engineer loaded plenty of spare parts on the airplane, where he could find room. The airplane's fly away kit was full and then some. The Fort Worth Division shipped us four large boxes of supplies to take along, and it used up a lot of baggage space in the rear compartment. I called Houston and arranged for Universal Weather to be the official handler for the big trip. All the organization and advance planning required for such a trip would have been just too large an undertaking for the air crew. When we landed at an international airport, the contracted Universal agent was the first person to greet the airplane and right behind him would be the foreign customs agent. They were very cordial and would always ask if our ocean crossing was smooth.

I always gave the handler the schedule for the trip; it was imperative that we adhere to it. The permits required for overseas operation are costly, several hundred dollars each. If a corporate operator blows his schedule, the dated permits are useless, and good money goes down the drain. At first, I had a difficult time on this issue with my company. In the states we were spoiled because we were forever changing the schedule, such as departure dates, takeoff times and destinations. It took me a while to convince our executives that, when we are overseas, the schedule must be adhered to at all costs. This was a tough sell, but I finally convinced them. Universal Weather (my agent) was given the schedule as far as Paris, because those were all the concrete plans I had been given. I would need to telex Houston with any additional schedules. Before leaving Paris, I would have to have a telex back from the handler confirming that I had the required permits. If any operator went on an international flight without the necessary permits, his aircraft could be impounded upon landing. A huge fine would result and quite possibly, the impounded aircraft could become the property of the country of illegal entry. Nobody wanted to get into that kind of mess. Several days before the flight, the crew had a meeting on some last minute details. John Langer coordinated the business of planning and scheduling with Universal Weather. John Rogerson oversaw preparation and maintenance and fine tuning of the aircraft. Vicki volunteered to bring along her black bag that she used on her air-evacuation flight with the Air Force. One day, at my request, she brought the bag out to my office and explained its contents. There were a lot of pills which she said were good for any occasion anywhere in the world. Besides the pills, she had a blood pressure kit, a stethoscope, oral and rectal thermometers, a tongue depressor, gauze of all sizes, tapes of all sizes, cotton balls and you name it, she had it all right there, as good as, or maybe better than any country doctor. As an RN, she had access to drugs you couldn't buy over the counter in a pharmacy. Because of her black bag, we called her Dr. Dunn and she loved it.

On the day of departure for Paris, I was up at five o'clock for a 7 A.M. takeoff. All provisions except the catering order had been loaded the day before. I arrived at the airport at 6 A.M. and two of my crew members were already there. The catering was on time and looked good. We had to feed everyone three meals that day. The passengers were told not to eat anything at home, since Vicki would have breakfast on the table 15 minutes after departure. Promptly at 6:30 the passengers arrived with a mountain of luggage. Somehow it was all stuffed on board, and the main door of the airplane was closed promptly at 6:45. After the engines were started, we lumbered out for takeoff. I was right at maximum gross weight (64,800 lbs) for takeoff in the Gulfstream II.

At 7:00 sharp, the heavy airplane lifted off the runway at the Spirit of St. Louis airport headed for Gander Field, Newfoundland, our first stop. Words are not adequate to describe that kind of flight. As the airplane was climbing into the sun, I adjusted the sun visor, and the thought crossed my mind that I was actually getting paid to do this kind of work. I considered myself extremely lucky. As we climbed through 10,000 feet, I turned off the seat belt sign, and I knew Vicki was busy preparing a big breakfast. John, the engineer, decided to go back and help her. After the passengers were fed, Vicki brought the pilots two trays loaded with western omelets, sausages, hash browns, toast, orange juice, coffee and last but not least, an attractive fruit cup - food fit for a king.

In a short three hours, I started my descent into Newfoundland Territory and Gander Field. During World War II, Gander had been an important way-station for flights to and from Europe. The field had three long runways with excellent facilities for quick refueling stops. The Gander stop lasted only 30 minutes and we were off again for two days of business in Copenhagen. Then we departed for Le Bourget Field in Paris, where Charles Lindbergh landed after his famous transatlantic flight on May 21, 1927. The Atlantic crossing went well as there were no specific weather conditions to bother us. When you file a flight plan to cross the Atlantic, Air Traffic Control assigns you a crossing track and an altitude that you have to maintain the entire way. The weather for the landing at Le Bourget Field was just as advertised - rainy and cool. Jet lag took over after we landed. That's when your mind says you're in one place and your body insists you are still back home, but in two days, everyone had adjusted to the Paris clock. This was the 33rd Paris Air Show and was attended by people from all over the world. Our company had a chalet on the field as we were an exhibitor with our F-16 Falcon fighter aircraft. We would remain in Paris for the entire week.

One day at the chalet, the chairman said to me, "Tom, do what you have to do to fly us all the way around the world, this time for sure." Filled with excitement, I sat down with him at a corner table and we roughed out an itinerary to send to Houston for our overflight, landing and other necessary permits. Paris is one of my favorite cities, London, Rome and Munich being the others. There is so much to do in Paris. Each night the flight crew ate at a different type of restaurant, and all were just great. The French wines were wonderful too. One night the flight crew decided to take Vicki to the Crazy Horse Saloon, famous for its skin show. A lot of beautiful, nude women were on the stage but, with clever use of colored lights, little detail was visible. Vicki thought the young women were beautiful and their bodies in very nice shape. That got a good laugh at our table.

One morning I went to the hotel coffee shop and noticed Mrs. Lewis sitting there alone. When she saw me, she motioned me to come over and sit with her. After a cup of coffee and a cherry tart, she said, "Let's go for a walk in the park; it's just across the street." In the park, she knew all the flowers and birds by name. Mrs. Lewis stopped near a group of school children and their teacher to watch them do their art sketches.

The flight crew stayed at a small hotel just off the famous avenue, the Champs Elysees. While I was shaving one morning, the power suddenly went off. The hotel calmly said it was just a strike by the local electricians, and it would be back on in two hours. Strolling up and down the Champs Elysees is quite an experience. You see everything imaginable and then some. The local young ladies wore short skirts with slits, not up the sides, but in front as well as in back. Vicki and I discovered an outstanding German restaurant where we returned before leaving town.

While at the Paris Air Show, Mr. Lewis got his first ride in an F-16. The airplane that was there for demonstrations was an F-16B model, a two-seater trainer. Neil Anderson gave Mr. Lewis his ride, and Neil said later that he pulled at least 6 Gs and the boss never complained once. That last night in Paris, the crew sat at a sidewalk table on the Champs Elysees and just watched the world go by. It's like 42nd and Broadway in New York City, only better. After a long period of watching the night people stroll by, we decided to hit the sack. The next day would be a long one. Our first stop was Bahrain Island, just off the east coast of Saudi Arabia.

Le Bourget Field was choked with traffic on the morning of our departure. After a 15-minute delay, we finally departed and hoped to make up the lost time during the flight. The weather forecast indicated that we would have a tail wind which would give us a boost in ground speed of about 50 knots. It never happened, the strongest winds I saw all day were only 15 knots. The distance from Paris to our destination was 2,807 nautical miles. Because of light tail winds, I needed to set up long-range cruise control to get there safely. Instead of flying at .80 Mach., I had to back off to .72 Mach. Time after time, the chairman came up to the flight deck to ask why I was flying so slow. He could tell by the deck angle he saw out his cabin window. I tried to explain about the lack of tail winds. Flying at normal cruise speed of .80 Mach. would consume too much fuel. He just went back to the cabin and pulled down his window shade so he couldn't see the tilted horizon.

The weather was good all day except for the light winds. After nearly six hours, I started my descent into the Bahrain airport. Near the surface it was windy and dusty, and when I was taxiing in after landing, my fuel gauges indicated a little less than 2,000 lbs. remaining. Emergency fuel state in the Gulfstream II is 1,400 lbs. During refueling, the passengers got out to stretch and walked up and down the ramp. Halfway through the refueling, someone came out from operations and stopped the pumping because my BP (British Petroleum) fuel credit card was invalid, they said. Airport operations wouldn't take any other credit card. The chairman even offered his personal American Express card. I called the BP office in New York and resolved that problem but shortly another problem arose. The airport's ice machine was broken. There would be no more ice that day. The airplane's galley had two ice compartments: a clean one for drinks and the other one for cooling anything. Long before we arrived at our next destination, both ice compartments were empty.

As I descended into the Colombo, Sri Lanka, (formerly Ceylon) airport, everyone was tired from the long flight. To pass the time enroute, the passengers ate, watched a couple of movies, ate some more and then slept. Upon our arrival at Colombo, it was dark and rain was falling. Before the flight crew's taxi even left the airport property for the hotel in town, they were fast asleep. That night, none of us wasted any time getting to bed. At 6:30 the next morning, the desk clerk gave me a wake-up call. Looking out my window, I noticed it was still raining. After a breakfast of greasy eggs and fish, the crew headed for the airport. The next stop was Jakarta, Indonesia, about 2,000 nautical miles away. During each morning's preflight of the airplane, each crew member had a specific job. With the APU running, Vicki would clean and vacuum the cabin, then make a pot of coffee. The US orange juice really tasted good. Soon the passengers were waiting for us in the small terminal as it was still raining. I couldn't taxi over there to pick them up until the inertial navigation system completed its alignment program. Usually, that took 15 minutes, because each way-point had to be inserted into the system for our next leg. The correct time and date (using GMT-Greenwich Mean Time) and the current location of the aircraft (the airport ramp coordinates in latitude and longitude) must be entered. During all of this, the aircraft must not be moved. The passengers were grumpy that morning and I couldn't blame them. All of us got soaked, but an hour after takeoff in the warm airplane, everyone dried out. We climbed out that morning from Columbo in thick clouds, but at about 15,000 feet, we suddenly broke out into the dazzling bright sun and clear blue sky above.

As we broke into the clear, I could hear clapping and shouts of glee back in the cabin. This was corporate aviation at its finest; you have to cope with the good as well as the bad. Halfway to Jakarta, we crossed the equator-zero degrees latitude. We were equidistant from the north and south poles. Everyone had crossed the equator before but the thrill is always there. As the airplane approached the equator, I announced over the PA: "Folks, we are about to cross the equator, five, four, three, two, one, mark!" That always brought a loud cheer from the cabin. It was very hot and humid when we landed at the big airport in Jakarta. The natives were friendly and spoke fair to good English. Approaching the airport, I noticed several smoking volcanos, and wondered about that. Later I was told not to worry, as they smoke all the time. The Jakarta Hilton is supposed to be Conrad Hilton's pride and joy, the best of the best. The rooms were large, and each contained a big basket of strange looking fruit and a bottle of wine. Instead of getting the next day off, I had to plan a flight to Medan in Sumatra. That's 800 miles to the north over some rough looking jungle. Medan is 250 miles north of the equator, so we got to cross the equator going and coming that day. To my dismay, Medan was even hotter than Jakarta. The air was deathly still, and you could almost cut the humidity with a knife.

After landing in Medan, our party was met by a helicopter which took them to where our company's Boston-built LNG tankers were on-loading LNG (liquefied natural gas). Each ship held five huge round thermos tanks which held the gas in a liquid state at a minus 276 degrees Fahrenheit. Each tank was 110 feet in diameter and all were covered with thick thermal blankets. Those ships would take load after load all the way to the market in Japan. The ladies stayed back in Jakarta and were smart to do so. There on the ramp at Medan, I kept the APU running so that the airplane would stay reasonably cool. I was awakened from a nap by our Universal Agent, who wanted me to go into operations with him. The airport wanted their landing and parking fees paid right away. In airport operations I was told they would only accept US Green. I tried my American Express travelers checks which they would not accept, only US green. Soon, two guards took me, in a jeep, to the bank in downtown Medan to convert my US travelers checks into US green. The bank had the nerve to charge me a 10 percent handling fee. Most of the buildings in downtown Medan were constructed of heavy bamboo. There were a few brick and cement buildings, but not very many. Late that afternoon, the helo arrived with our passengers and we departed for the 90-minute flight back to Jakarta. Descending into the airport that evening, we saw that all the fishing boats were at anchor in the bay. Their lights made a beautiful sight with the city lit up behind them. After Medan, the Jakarta Hilton was a sight for sore eyes. The crew got the next day off, and slept late. It's a great luxury for a flight crew to sleep in, as normally they have to get up with the chickens.

The next evening, we saw Hindu temples and native dancers. Everyone agreed that a little of that goes a long way, especially the weird and irritating music. Even after a couple of drinks, it didn't sound any better. The next morning I looked for a barber shop. All I found were beauty shops that would cut anyone's hair. It felt strange to be sitting between two women getting their hair done. The shop had hot water, so I had the young lady give me a double shampoo. One of the clocks in the airplane was left on St. Louis time, and I noticed that Jakarta and St. Louis were exactly 12 hours apart.

On the third afternoon in Indonesia, I flew our group over to Yogyararta, 290 miles to the east. The first night, everyone enjoyed a nice dinner together, and that was nice as the flight crew rarely got to dine with the passengers. After dinner, everyone went to a night spot where there were more native dancers, but the dancing and music were a big improvement over what we had seen the previous evening. At noon the next day, I flew the GII over to the island called Bali. It was 300 miles further east along the coast. Bali is nice, but I liked Tahiti better. The beaches at Bali are coarse and rocky like in Nice and Cannes, France. At Bali, we were all housed in cottages owned by the Petromenia Oil Company. The nights in this part of the world are really like nights on a different planet. It's always clear with big bright stars. Someone pointed out the Southern Cross; it was my first time to see it. Bali enjoys cool nights with softly blowing trade winds. With that kind of night, you just don't want to go to bed. The crew sat out on the cottage lawn late that night just looking at the beautiful starlit heavens.

Early the next day we departed for the Manila International Airport in the Philippines. En route, we crossed the equator for the fourth time. Looking out my cockpit window, I noticed the country of Borneo. It looked even more forbidding than Sumatra. It was 1,650 miles from Bali to Manila. The flight was smooth although I had to dodge some thunderstorms that were in my flight path. We arrived on a Sunday and the Manila airport seemed very quiet. The weather was clear, but very hot and humid. After we waited an hour, the customs agent finally appeared. He offered no excuses for his tardiness and acted like it was business as usual. In Bali, we added two passengers that were to be off-loaded in Manila; they were flying on to Hong Kong on telecommunications business. I had to pay the customs agent $500 in cash, and all he did was stamp some papers and check our passports. The schedule called for us to be on the ground at Manila 30 minutes, but it took an hour and a half to get out of there. For a Sunday in the Philippines that's not bad, the handling agent said.

The next stop was Taipei, Taiwan (formerly Formosa). Departing Manila, I had great views of some WW II naval battle sites. Looking down at Corregidor, I thought of the Bataan Death March. Two good friends of mine survived that terrible ordeal. Chief Warrant Officer Grover Gilbert and Master Sergeant Charles Fetterman helped each other walk some 65 miles to a train station that would take them to a POW camp. I served with both at Lowry Field back in 1951-54. They told me of the Japanese who shot prisoners who walked too slowly or faltered in some way. The Bataan Death March Survivors Association holds a reunion around the United States each year. At each reunion, they use small containers filled with cooked white rice for ash trays. Since Bataan, none of them ever have eaten, or ever will eat, rice again.

The weather was cloudy and cool when we landed in Taipei. Their new airport is an exact miniature of the airport at Dulles Field near Washington, D.C. The whole party stayed at the Grand hotel, one of the ten best in the world, I was told. The first night in Taipei, the crew went to dinner in the old section of town, as recommended by our handling agent. The streets were too narrow for any vehicular traffic, so the taxi left us off and we walked the last two blocks to the restaurant. The place was like the Ginza Strip in Tokyo, only busier. The food was excellent, and the only odd thing was that they served the hot and sour soup last. Rice wine came with the meal, but it was hard to consume. The local beer was some better, mostly because it was chilled.

At the Grand hotel in Taipei, the chairman and his wife stayed in the Presidential Suite. They were told that Madam Chiang Kai-shek had lived in that same suite for a long time. After two days of business meetings, the schedule called for us to fly up to Seoul, South Korea. It would be a short flight of about two hours. When I checked out of the hotel, the clerk handed me several telex messages from our handler in Houston. Now I had all the down-line permits for the rest of the trip. The remaining flight schedule had to be kept intact or the overflight, landing and departure permits would evaporate.

The flight up to Seoul went smoothly, except that I descended into cloud cover and would have to make an instrument approach into the Kimpo airport. On the Kimpo instrument approach plate, I noticed a warning in bold face: "**Any aircraft straying out of the approach corridor to Kimpo airport will be fired upon.**" Wow! That got my attention real quick. The last time I was fired upon was in WW II when I was flying the P-38. I sure didn't want any more of that. I made sure the passengers never knew about that kicker. Kimpo was under heavy guard as it's not far from the 38th parallel. This was my first visit to Korea. I nearly came over in 1951 but, thanks to a computer, I escaped that war. The airport officials wanted their landing and parking fees paid right away. Much to my surprise, they gladly accepted my American Express travelers checks. After the airplane and passengers cleared customs, I was asked to move the airplane to a distant ramp for overnight parking. For unknown reasons, our handling agent had forgotten to meet us but after many calls to the control tower, a crew bus finally came to our rescue. Universal Weather in Houston had contracted with KAL (Korean Air Lines) to be their agent for corporate flights like ours.

It was after nine that evening when the crew arrived at the Shilla Hotel and light rain was falling. Seoul is a jammed packed city of 10,627,790 souls and the density is 1,157/square mile. The tension was high and the Koreans were not exceptionally friendly. One can imagine what the Koreans on the north side of the 38th parallel were like. We were informed at the hotel to not go out into the streets at night as anyone caught out after midnight would be shot on sight. The Shilla Hotel was a brick high-rise and looked quite new. The hotel was managed by the Japanese using Korean help. On the top floor was a French restaurant, and the flight crew couldn't wait to try it. Like most French restaurants, the food was outstanding, as was the wine. A charming young Korean girl played wonderful piano music nonstop all through dinner. She used a younger girl to turn the music sheets for her. Promptly at midnight, she stopped, gathered up her music, bowed and was gone in a wink.

From my hotel window that night, I saw several military vehicles cruising the streets. They meant what they said about catching people out late at night. Underground, the hotel ran several nice shops with quality merchandise. In the three days we were there, none of the crew ever left the hotel. My room had a radio that could pick up the AFN (Armed Forces Network). I was happy to hear some fresh news from home. Every time I entered our airplane, I would look at the St. Louis clock and could pretty much tell what my family and friends were doing way back there-12 hours earlier. Early on the second morning in Seoul, my phone rang. It seemed that one of our executives had left a package on the airplane. He needed the package and would pick me up in 30 minutes. It was still raining as the two of us drove out to the airport where the guards refused to allow us past the terminal gate that led out to the aircraft parking ramp.

No matter how much talking I did, the guards would not let us pass. I even showed them my pilots license, but no dice. KAL operations people soon came to the rescue. The problem turned out to be the fact I was dressed in civilian clothes and not in my flight uniform. Back to the hotel we went where I changed clothes. This time we walked right through with no problem. Don't ever say the uniform doesn't talk. On every international flight, my crews always wore the airline type uniform. The captain had four stripes on his sleeves, the first officer three stripes, the engineer two and the flight attendant wore one stripe. All the crew members wore nice looking wings that I designed using my Air Force wings as a basis. The uniform does wonders at hotel check-ins too. There's never a wait.

There were more problems on the day we were scheduled to depart for Tokyo.. Our KAL agent was nowhere to be found. We had to muscle our way through departure customs just like tourists. Every purchase had to be checked, even those that were gift wrapped. It didn't matter; they still had to be opened. I finally asked KAL operations to arrange a crew bus to take our passengers out to the airplane. They wouldn't let me bring it up front like I normally do at other airports. Our departure was going to be late, and the boss was pacing the cabin aisle complaining. I had to wait for the inertial navigation system to align itself. and there was no way to rush it. In Tokyo, our office manager, George Durr, was probably pacing the airport terminal wondering where we were. Corporate airplanes unfortunately take a back seat to the airlines. The big carriers always get preference. That kind of delay would drive the chairman up the wall. Nothing could be done about it though, as that's the way the system works. The flight to Tokyo's Narita airport would take an hour and a half. Once we were above the clouds, it was clear and smooth sailing. Just before starting my descent into Tokyo, I saw the majestic white cap of Mt. Fiji protruding through the clouds. Everyone ran for their cameras.

Descending into Tokyo Bay , prior to landing, I was reminded of Jimmy Doolittle's famous B-25 raid on the city in April, 1942. That event inspired a movie called "Thirty Seconds over Tokyo." I also noticed the bay was full of commercial shipping awaiting their turn to tie up at the many docks. I have been told that Japan imports everything but rice. Tokyo has two major airports, Narita and Haneda, and both are heavily used. Corporate flights are required to use the newer one, Narita. It's big and modern but a lot further out in the country. The closer in airport, Haneda, is for local carriers only.

Our JAL (Japan Air Lines) agent met us and the customs clearance went smoothly. As soon as we put the airplane to bed, the agent got us a taxi for the trip into town. However, before leaving the airplane, the agent arranged for a guard. He said it was necessary as two US airplanes had been broken into recently. Like the British and Australians, the Japanese drive on the wrong side of the road. After a long taxi ride, we arrived at the large and pompous Imperial Hotel. It's a luxurious place, and in my room beside the customary basket of fruit was a note inviting the flight crew to a cocktail party at six. I immediately called the rest of the crew and told them to meet me in suite 432. When we entered the suite, waiters in formal attire met us and asked what we would like to drink. Vicki ordered a glass of white wine. She said that she served wine on the airplane all the time and it was nice to be served herself occasionally. The room was crowded and noisy and everyone seemed to be talking at once.

George Durr, our Tokyo office manager, welcomed us and introduced his new Japanese wife. She hardly looked Japanese at all because she had the western eye operation . A lot of the young girls in Japan had their eyes surgically changed from "slant" to "round." That made many of them look like beauty pageant contestants. The hors d'oeuvre table was out of this world. Vicki said she surely wished we could have some of that kind of stuff on our airplane sometimes. After about an hour of this socializing, everybody followed George Durr up to the top floor where we all enjoyed dinner in a beautiful setting.

Later that night in my room, I watched Japanese baseball on TV. It was different and having played a lot of baseball myself, I found it very interesting. The Japanese play a good brand of baseball, somewhere between AAA and the majors. Each time a batter comes up to the plate, he bows to the opposition. There is never an argument, the umpires rule the roost-no question.

I was quite impressed with the city of Tokyo. It's a very cosmopolitan city with wide streets and lots of traffic circles with water fountains and statues. The city has many parks with groves of trees and good-sized lakes. The flight crew had three days to relax and enjoy the area, stroll around and take pictures. On the second day, Vicki, John Langer and I were invited to a luncheon hosted by Mrs. Gho. Her husband was a consultant and interpreter for our Tokyo office operations. The luncheon was on the fourth floor of a hotel not far from the Imperial, so the three of us walked since it was a warm and sunny day. John Rogerson, my engineer, is somewhat of a loner and wanted to do his own thing. That was okay with me. John is a good man and I was lucky to have him in my operation. John's nickname is "The Phantom," and he gets kidded a lot because of his unique ability to simply disappear in a wink.

Nobody told us what to wear to Mrs.Gho's luncheon, so we went casual. Vicki decided to wear a dress as she knew all the executive wives would wear nice dresses. On the fourth floor of the hotel, the doorman at the restaurant stopped us. When I told him we were invited guests, he let Vicki go in, but he motioned John and me to follow him down the hall. There he fitted us with a jacket and a tie. We were both very embarrassed about this. My jacket was green and John's was blue, and neither tie matched anything.

The luncheon was very nice and the food out of this world. Every time Vicki looked at us, she had to bite her lip to keep from laughing at the sight of our ridiculous attire. John and I were the only males at the luncheon. Mrs. Lewis introduced us as "her traveling companions." Mrs. Gho talked of her work in the field of art. She said her family had been involved in the arts for years, and their expensive paintings were displayed all over Tokyo, and in other Japanese cities.

After the luncheon, the three of us went over to the famous Ginza which consists of shop after shop for several blocks, both street level and the level below. The street where the strip is located is open only to foot traffic. The place was jammed and I noticed a lot of western people there. Coca Cola and Camel cigarette signs were everywhere. That night George Durr invited the crew to join him at the Gho's town house for cocktails. Mr. Gho is well known in the automobile and truck tire industry as he is the president of Bridgestone Tire and Rubber Company. George told us that when Mr. Gho married his wife, her maiden name, when converted to English, was Stonebridge. Mr. Gho decided to turn it around and came up with the name of Bridgestone to better compete with the likes of Firestone, Goodyear, et al.

The Ghos' townhouse was four stories high, the ground floor was a five car garage. They lived on the other three levels. When we arrived at the house we all had to remove our shoes in the elevator where two rows of white cotton slippers had been arranged for use by guests. Poor Vicki. She had to put on a men's pair as the ladies slippers were too small for her. She was very embarrassed as the elevator took us up to the Ghos' receiving floor. I said to Vicki, "After a drink, you'll forget the slippers." She just looked at me. When we got off the elevator, Mr. Gho met us with apologies, explaining that his wife had to meet with some art buyers from out of town. He told us all the beautiful paintings on the walls were copies. The originals were in a bank vault and I'm sure, worth a fortune.

The town house was resplendent with expensive appointments and decor. He served us each two drinks (indicating that's all we would get) and mentioned that their daughter was getting married soon. Their wedding gift would be a furnished two-story town house, all paid for. The rubber and art business was big time for them in Tokyo. As we left, we all thanked Mr. Gho for a nice time. From there, George took us to an upscale restaurant for a very enjoyable dinner. During the dinner, a string ensemble played delightful music.

After three very enjoyable days in Tokyo, we headed for the USA. The flight plan called for us to fly from Tokyo to Wake Island, Hawaii, San Francisco and then home. Tokyo to Wake was an easy four hour trip. The only problem was that Wake was a pinhead island in the big Pacific Ocean and, even on the map, you could barely see it. During the weather briefing in JAL flight operations, a newly arrived Notam (Notice To Airmen Message) said the ADF (Automatic Direction Finder) radio beacon at Wake Island was out of service. Now, my only way to find the little island was with the inertial navigation system. To say that I was a little nervous was an understatement. The ADF was our main backup to the INS on this leg. During the flight to Wake, the weather was clear and smooth. As we descended to lower altitudes, an undercast appeared. Now I couldn't see the ocean let alone the little island. I was totally reliant on the INS. The rules for reserve fuel when arriving at an island airport were to have two hours of fuel for holding until any weather had passed on. I had the fuel; but first, I had to find the island. If I missed the island, the nearest airport was Guam, 900 miles to the west. I didn't have enough fuel to fly that far. I somehow had to find that little island. The INS indicated Wake Island was dead ahead of us but, being above the clouds, I couldn't be sure. This type of flying is called "pucker time." A pilot hoped and prayed his instruments were telling him the truth. In flying circles, the saying goes, "There are old pilots, and there are bold pilots, but there are no old bold pilots."

On the flight deck it was very quiet as nobody said a word. Both pilots and the engineer knew that when they broke out under that overcast, the little island was going to be there or it wasn't. If the tiny island wasn't there, we were in deep trouble. We had a life raft and life vests on board for everyone. For years I wore a parachute while flying and never once had to use it. Now I carried over-water survival gear and prayed we wouldn't need to use it. During the descent into Wake Island, the airplane entered the cloud layer at 8,000 feet. The weather briefer, back at JAL in Tokyo, said that any clouds we would encounter would not be very thick. Sure enough, at about 4,000 feet, we broke out into beautiful clear weather. Blue sky above and blue water below. As if by divine providence, dead ahead of us at 12 o'clock lay the little snip of an island called Wake.

The Delco Division of General Motors Corporation should be very proud of their superb inertial navigation system that led us directly to that little pinpoint island in the big Pacific Ocean. Wake Island is under military control and only 25 US people live there, with about 100 laborers from the Philippines. Since World War II, Wake has been a way-stop for military operations coming and going. In recent years, corporate aircraft were permitted to stop there but only with prior arrangements. Our handler set this up for us, and all we needed was some fuel. After landing, I saw 18 Air Force F-4 fighter aircraft sitting there on the ramp. It turned out to be the Hawian Air National Guard on maneuvers. During the refueling, Mr. Lewis walked all the passengers down the ramp where the F-4 fighters were parked. There he told them how he was the "father" of the F-4, the chief design engineer for that program at McDonnell Douglas Aircraft Company in St. Louis.

In less than an hour, I was taxiing out to take off for Hawaii 2,000 miles to the east. Flying eastbound normally gives you helping tail winds in the northern hemisphere. Flying to Hawaii that afternoon, my tail wind component was only 25 knots, but it helped a little. It was close to midnight when we landed at Hickam Field and the Customs and Immigration agent was not there to meet us. I found his name and home phone number and when I called him, he said our arrival time had been scheduled for ten. When we didn't show up, he returned home. In half an hour he arrived and performed the required inspections.

The agent wanted to check everything that had been purchased on the entire trip. Everyone was dead tired after flying all the way from Tokyo. After two days of wonderful rest, the around-the-world flight departed for the mainland. The flight actually took off 15 minutes early. It was the first time that had ever happened. The San Francisco forecast called for partly cloudy and windy conditions. The flight to the mainland was in good weather conditions and we cruised along at 41,000 feet. Everyone was in a jovial mood, since we were finally coming home. The San Francisco approach controller cleared me to fly the "Bridge Instrument Approach" and to expect to land on runway 28L. He then gave me a weather report of scattered clouds at 3,000 feet, temperature 61 degrees Fahrenheit, winds from the NW at 22 knots gusting to 28 knots, altimeter setting 29.97. Finally the controller said, "Contact the San Francisco control tower when crossing the bridge."

During refueling in San Francisco, everyone was on the phone calling home. My home phone was busy, so I called my secretary, Virginia Mitchem. She said Universal Weather and Aviation did a wonderful job keeping her informed of our whereabouts at all times. Soon, we departed on the final leg to St. Louis. My third grade teacher was right-on when she told me years ago that the world was round. I had just proven her correct.

The flight to St. Louis went quickly. I had an 80-knot tail-wind component, so the airplane's ground speed was 540 knots. That's 621 mph and moving right along. It was a tremendous thrill to see the big greeting party waiting for us at the Spirit of St. Louis airport as I taxied in to the ramp. The flight crew were cheered and my wife, Joan, standing there waving to me never looked better. She managed to have a "welcome home" cake for us to enjoy and the flight crew appreciated that very much.

When we left St. Louis earlier that month, I had flown an easterly heading. Coming into the Spirit airport that afternoon, I said to John Langer, "John, we're back home and still flying an easterly heading." Boy! Was it ever good to get back home. We arrived home on a Wednesday so I told the crew to take the rest of the week off. They had done an outstanding job. I couldn't have asked for a finer crew. In departing the airplane, each passenger personally thanked each flight crew member for a good job. Mr. Lewis said to me, "Tom, you did a fine job, as always." I have never flown a finer group of passengers. Vicki said they were wonderful to her, and she added, "The pills from my black bag came in handy many times."

When the Gulfstream factory heard about our around-the-world flight, they decided to make up a nice plaque commemorating the event. In a few weeks, a large box came to me via UPS. It contained 11 nicely framed plaques, three for the passengers and two for each of the crew. The plaque showed a Gulfstream jet flying away, and, below it, the route flown traced on a world map.

The inscription on the plaque read:

This memento acknowledges that between June 4 and June 24, 1979, Mr. and Mrs. David S. Lewis, Mr. and Mrs. Lyman C. Josephs, and Mr. and Mrs. Guy W. Fiske circumnavigated the world in a Gulfstream II, flying a distance of 24,687 nautical miles in 51.3 flight hours.

The Gulfstream II followed the route, inscribed below, under the command of Thomas F. Gordon, Captain; John F. Langer, First Officer; John A. Rogerson, Flight Engineer, and Victoria A. Dunn, Flight Attendant.

We are pleased to welcome these persons into an honorary fraternity of distinguished leaders of business, industry and government who have spanned the oceans and continents of the world in a Gulfstream II.

(Signed)
Allen Paulson
President
Gulfstream American Corporation

Thirty Seconds Over Berlin

A mind , like a home, is furnished by its owner,
so if one's life is cold and bare he can blame none but himself.
——-Louis L'Amour

CHAPTER THIRTEEN

TRANSITION TO RETIREMENT

Get the facts first, and then you can distort them as much as you please.

—*Mark Twain*

When I retired from the Air Force in 1969, I had no idea that a second retirement would be offered to me. Not one more time, but two more times. My second retirement came in 1989. This time it was for 20 years of dedicated service to the General Dynamics Corporation as chief pilot and aviation manager. Thinking I was now going to be put out to pasture, I started to look for something to occupy my new free time. In less than a week, fate intervened and I received a call from the Vice President of Marketing for St. Louis-based Midcoast Aviation. They operated a large modification center and paint shop across the Mississippi river in Cahokia, Illinois. I soon met with the VP of Marketing to see what this was all about. Tom Crowell introduced himself and briefed me on his company's decision to buy three used Gulfstream II's from Exxon Oil Company. Exxon had recently upgraded its fleet with new Gulfstream IVs. Instead of trading in their three G II's, they offered them for sale on the open market.

Midcoast decided to purchase all three aircraft with specific intent to tear them down and rebuild each to a "like-new" condition. Then they would be put on the market for a potentially good profit. It sounded like an excellent idea. Tom Crowell said he checked around the St. Louis area and discovered I was the only qualified Gulfstream II jet pilot that was not currently working. He wanted to know if I was interested in flying these airplanes. I quickly told him I was the man for the job and not to look any further.

At the time, Midcoast Aviation was owned by TWA. Carl Icahn was the top executive who approved the purchase of these airplanes. The purchase agreement required Exxon to deliver the airplanes to St. Louis. The sale was contingent upon each airplane passing a prepurchase airworthiness inspection. This is a very detailed inspection taking the better part of a week. The FAA required that an independent third party perform the inspection. Exxon and Midcoast both agreed that the Gulfstream factory in Savannah, Georgia, was the best place for this third-party inspection.

Before the Exxon airplanes arrived in St. Louis, I decided to meet with my lawyer and tax consultant, David Sauerburger. Together, we went over my options in undertaking this new venture. I thought I was through flying, but apparently I wasn't.. I told Tom Crowell that I didn't want to be a salaried employee of Midcoast, but rather an independent contractor. My lawyer suggested I establish my own aviation consulting company. The next day I established Gordon and Sons Consulting, Incorporated.

My newly formed company was duly registered with the Missouri Department of Labor, effective July 1, 1989. It was to be a family-owned and run company. I was to be the president, my wife the secretary/treasurer, and each of my three sons would be board members with full voting rights. The company stock was registered at a par value of $1 per share, and was privately held. My middle son, Steve, became the registered agent for the new company.

When the first Exxon Gulfstream II arrived in St. Louis, the pilots said they had to operate the airplane until after the pre-purchase inspection. Tom Crowell and I rode down to the Savannah factory with them the next day. During the flight, the Exxon pilots invited me to ride on the cockpit jump-seat. That was fine with me as I wanted to observe how Exxon operated their airplanes. They appeared very professional and I was really impressed. The day after we arrived at the factory, the Exxon crew went home. I guess they felt the airplane would pass the inspection and ownership would pass to Midcoast. The airplane passed the inspection and was ready for a test flight. Midcoast, the new owner, arranged for me, accompanied by a factory test pilot to fly the acceptance flight. The airplane flew very well and all systems were in good operating condition. Exxon flew their airplanes almost daily, and that's the key in keeping an airplane in good working order. Leaving an airplane sitting on the ground for very long will cause it to deteriorate quickly. Avionics go first, then the aircraft systems start to go belly-up. Bottom line is to never store an airplane for long periods.

The inspection write-up's (squawks) from the ground and flight checks were minimal. As is customary, the cost of fixing these squawks was negotiated between the seller and the purchaser.

Most of the time the cost was split down the middle, with each paying half. At the end of the flight check, I asked the factory pilot if he would give me three takeoffs and landings to meet my qualifications in the airplane. I made one takeoff and landing at Savannah, and on the way back to St. Louis, the factory pilot supervised two more at

Parks airport. I was now current in the airplane for at least the next 90 days.

Word quickly circulated that Midcoast had some GII's for sale, and the phone lines were hot. Montgomery Ward (MW), based at Midway airport in Chicago, came and looked at the first GII just back from the factory. In two days, they bought it as is. MW had Midcoast update some of the avionics, but that was all. Soon it was in operation and their chief pilot, Dave Barnholtz, was happy as a pig in mud. Dave had previously flown the GII in Saudi Arabia for an oil company and was happy for the opportunity to fly the Gulfstream again. That was MW's first Gulfstream II.

Soon after the first airplane was sold, the second Exxon GII came to St. Louis and, like before, I rode down to the factory to repeat the pre-purchase inspection routine. Both ground and air inspections went well and Don Evitt, the factory pilot who helped me with the first airplane, agreed to help me fly the airplane back to Parks airport in Cahokia, Illinois. Soon after we brought the airplane back to St. Louis, representatives of the Bank of Mexico showed up and bought the airplane on the spot. I offered to fly it down to Mexico City for them, but they already had two pilots on the way to St. Louis to pick it up.

The third Exxon GII arrived in a few days and went through the same inspection and acceptance procedure as the first two. This last airplane had more ground and flight squawks than the previous ones. Again Don Evitt helped me fly the bird back to Cahokia. This time the airplane was not for sale. Midcoast made a little money on the sale of the first two airplanes, but they wanted to put this one through their modification center. Midcoast wanted to show the aviation industry what their modification center could do in turning a used GII into a "like-new" airplane. The Gulfstream was going to be their showcase and was given the name Paragon. Webster defines the word *paragon* as a model of excellence or perfection.

The Gulfstream that was to become the Paragon Limited Edition had been manufactured at the factory in Savannah in the summer of 1969. It was the 89th production airplane to come off the assembly line. Its serial number was 089, and its FAA registration number was N203A. Exxon Oil had been its only owner. When the airplane came to Midcoast, the total time on the airframe was 8,150.4 hours. The left engine had 7,924.5 hours and the right engine log showed 7,919.7 hours. The total number of landings was 5,075. The times on the airframe, engines and number of landings were normal for the airplane's age. No accidents or incidents were noted in the aircraft's logs. SN 089 would be in the modification center until the spring of 1990.

During the tear down, all the wiring harnesses were replaced and wrung out, a very long and tedious job. The factory also found in the wing butt-joints some corrosion which required that a lot of metal and skin needed to be replaced. Instead of the estimated six months to transform it into a Paragon, it took a year. In the meantime, I flew random flights with other companies who had their airplanes in for routine maintenance, or for a new paint job. The Montgomery Ward GII was coming out of the hangar, after some avionics updates, and I flew some training flights with Dave Barnholtz. Dave flew the airplane extensively in Saudi Arabia, but hadn't flown it in more than a year. He hired me to give him the needed training so he could be current in the airplane and qualify him to carry passengers. Before flying the airplane to Chicago, where it would be based, I took Dave to the airport at Columbia, Missouri, where we conducted his training It's a perfect airport for training as there is very little traffic and the runway is long, wide and smooth. The FAA controllers were happy as they needed the business to keep them sharp. If the controllers don't "work airplanes" every day, they are inclined to lose their edge. Dave did ten or more takeoffs and landings and they were fairly good as he had good depth perception and control of the airplane. Now, I told him, we were going to go upstairs and practice the FAA Waltz. If Dave could master the waltz, he could fly the airplane safely in any conditions, anytime, anywhere.

Here is how the FAA Waltz is executed: Operating off the controlled airways at 15,000 feet, the airplane is set up clean on a north cardinal heading flying at 160 knots indicated airspeed. While turning at 15 degrees angle of bank for 30 degrees each side of north, I would start to lower the flaps gradually and put out the gear. All the while, Dave is banking and turning at exactly 160 knots while keeping his altitude exactly at 15,000 feet. Now I would continue my part of the procedure by bringing the flaps and gear back up while Dave continued his turns while maintaining his airspeed and altitude. He did it! Later, on the ground, I told Dave that he had performed that maneuver as well as anyone I had ever seen.

The FAA Waltz is a difficult and demanding maneuver because not only do you have to keep the airspeed and bank angle constant, the altitude must not vary either. I love that maneuver and have asked a lot of pilots to practice it. It is the best maneuver known to keep a pilot sharp. Dave did a fine job after being away from the airplane for over a year. The next day, I flew with him to Midway Airport in Chicago, Montgomery Ward's home base. Their fleet was now a small six-passenger British Hawker Jet and the GII. I checked into a nearby motel and, in a couple of days, we took a trip out to the west coast. I stayed with Dave until he felt comfortable with the airplane again, and then came back home. It was a week of pure enjoyment for me.

Several GIIs at the modification center were having Ground Proximity Warning Systems (GPWS) installed. Before that job could be signed off, the airplane had to perform satisfactory ground and flight checks. I soon got myself involved in FAA's certification process. To test the GPWS, the airplane would be flown over a sharply rising peak which would set off the cockpit enunciator if the system was working properly. In the US, there are eight FAA-approved GPWS flight test areas. The nearest test area to St. Louis was in Arkansas. Squarely in the middle of the test range sat a sharp peak called Magazine Mountain. That was also the name of the test range. I had to obtain permission from the FAA to enter the range. I also had to provide them with a specific date with a range entry time and a departure time. In that area, Memphis Air Traffic Control Center was the agency I contacted for my approval.

The test range was located halfway between Little Rock and Fort Smith on a magnetic bearing of 286 degrees out of Little Rock at 60 miles. In addition to the FAA clearance, the weather had to be no worse than scattered cloud conditions on the range. Normally, below 10,000 feet, airplanes cannot exceed 250 knots indicated airspeed. This test required speeds of up to 380 knots, which had to be approved by the FAA. The test required the airplane to be flown across the sharp peak at various heights starting at 100 feet up to 500 feet. Each pass required different speeds to see if the system would announce warnings in the cockpit: "Terrain, Terrain. Pull up! Pull up!" It was hard work, but also a lot of fun to fly that close to the peak at such speeds. The GPWS also warns you on an instrument approach to the runway if you have descended below the glide path. This warning system was a wonderful invention.

When the Mexican crew came in to pick up their GII, Midcoast asked me to ride to Mexico City with them to make sure that they operated it properly. While down there, I rode one trip with them up to Monterrey. We stayed overnight and the crew took me to a fine restaurant. The food was great, but I had to keep a bottle of cold cerveza (beer) handy, as the food was highly spiced. All during dinner, a mariachi band wandered around the tables and played requests. I had the crew ask them to play "Spanish Eyes." It was beautiful!

Back at Midcoast, I spent a lot of time with the design engineers on the Paragon. I was very interested in how they were going to equip and arrange the cockpit. Honeywell Corporation had been contracted to install their very latest digital instrumentation which included five six-inch cathode-ray scopes, installed on the instrument panel, for various colored digital flight data and radar displays.

The Paragon Limited Edition aircraft was going to be the showcase that Midcoast would use to show the world the excellent work of their modification center and the interior artistry and refinements that only Midcoast can offer. A lot of corporate aircraft operators came to the modification center to observe this transformation. Most said they would like a demonstration flight when it was completed. In the meantime, I was kept busy flying different GIIs. Most operators with airplanes at the mod-center didn't leave their flight crews in St. Louis, it was just too expensive, so they brought them home. When their airplane came out of the mod-center and needed a test hop, Midcoast would agree to do it, and that's where I came in. I flew a lot of test hops and delivered a lot of airplanes to their owners. I also did check-out training for several different Gulfstream crews. When an operator decided to upgrade from a small jet to the GII, the first order of business was to get their pilots to the factory school in Savannah. Learning the GII systems was a two week crash course.. They also flew 12 hours in the full- motion simulator. When the poor souls came out of the simulator, they were handed a piece of paper that said they were GII-qualified with a GII type-rating. Well, not quite. As they hadn't been in the airplane yet, the FAA required that they perform three take-offs and three landings under the supervision of a qualified and experienced pilot. That's where I came in. I performed this pleasant task for a lot of companies that upgraded to the Gulfstream executive jet aircraft.

A significant number of companies were upgrading their equipment to larger jets. As a result, I flew with a lot of them to help their crews gain proficiency and familiarity in the Gulfstream II. Most of these pilots had never flown anything bigger than a Learjet, Falcon or other similar small jets. The GII was considered "big iron" and it required more skill to handle. I always told these "upgrade pilots," that the GII was like a Cadillac, only better, because it had Rolls Royce engines. I have never seen a pilot when he first flew a GII, that didn't shake his head in disbelief. They never knew such a beautiful airplane existed. Flying the Gulfstream would soon make anyone quickly forget what he had flown before. In my flying career, I flew trainers, transports, fighters and bombers, but never have I flown an airplane that I liked as much as the Gulfstream II. I knew the airplane like the back of my hand. I could almost fly it in my sleep. That's why, when I retired from General Dynamics, I was so grateful to have the opportunity to fly this wonderful airplane for six more years. If I had the financial resources, I would have gladly flown the airplane for free.

Later in this chapter, I will list the companies for whom I either worked or trained aircrews from 1989 to 1995. With some companies, I stayed only a couple of days, and left when I felt that their pilots were capable and comfortable in the airplane. Others took longer. One must be comfortable when flying an airplane in order to do it properly and safely. Too many pilots forget there are passengers in the back. I often told pilots, when flying passengers, to fly the airplane as if their 98-year-old grandmother, or the Pope were their passengers. I hope I planted that seed of philosophy in the head of many pilots. Sometimes a Gulfstream would come into Midcoast just for a paint job. They were known for their top-of-the-line paint shop. Operators came from all over, including overseas, just for this expertise. Many times when the painting was completed, the owners didn't have crews available to fly the airplane back to their home base. I was in the right place at the right time as I returned many airplanes with sparkling new paint jobs to their appreciative owners.

I was totally in my element at Midcoast. During my entire military career I had been an instructor and I guess I was just a natural teacher. I loved to fly. And wanted to instill that same love of flying in all my students. I could always land an airplane with ease; it just came naturally I guess. Pride was also a factor. Every time I had an eye exam, the doctor said my depth perception was perfect. I took pride in my ability to land an airplane so that it just kissed the pavement as the main wheels met the runway. In aviation circles, that is called a "grease job." I'm not trying to blow my own horn, but many is the time I landed the Sabreliner and the Gulfstream airplanes when the passengers didn't know we were on the ground until during the roll out. As God is my witness, it happened more than once.

The Paragon was coming along slowly in the modification center. Every few days I would drive over to the hangar on the east side of the Mississippi River and check on it. I was flying some, but couldn't wait to get my hands on the newly refurbished Gulfstream. A lot of the new avionics had never before been installed in a GII, so a lot of testing had to be done. Not only did the manufacturer's specifications have to be met, but the approval of the FAA had to be obtained. It was estimated that between 25 and 40 hours of flight testing would be required to get the airplane "signed off." I gathered up all the operator handbooks for the new equipment in order to familiarize myself with every aspect of the flight test procedure.. Some of the flight checks required an FAA inspector to be on board; some did not. Never before had a GII's autopilot been connected to the new Honeywell-Sperry digital flight directors. I knew an FAA inspector would be on board for that. Finally the Paragon was towed out of the modification center resplendent in its new paint scheme. It was beautiful sitting out on the ramp in the brilliant sunshine. If it had winglets, and if you looked at it from a distance, it would indeed resemble a Gulfstream IV. Before the airplane could fly, the engines had to go through extensive ground checks, as they had not been operated for a year. Even though the landing gear and wing flaps were checked on the ground, they had to be checked in flight with normal air stress loads on them. Smoky Bennett, from Carl Icahn's group in New York, came out to fly with me on the first couple of flights. TWA had a big interest in this airplane, as they expected to sell it quickly and make themselves a nice profit. We all hoped for the same thing, and that many more Paragons would come out the door of the modification center.

On the afternoon of April 14, 1990, I rolled the Paragon down runway 12-R at the St. Louis Downtown/Parks Airport. When Smokey called out "rotate," I eased the nose wheel off the ground and in seconds we were airborne. The flight was a short one since all we wanted to check were the landing gear, flaps, spoilers and controls in general. I hand-flew the airplane because we had to check for proper rigging by noting any aileron and rudder trim requirements. During the modification, the airplane had been pretty well torn down. Both the wings and tail were removed for inspection and repair. The airplane flew pretty well for having sat on the ground for such a long time. There were a few minor squawks. I noted in my flight check report that the rudder needed 1.5 degrees of trim. When an airplane flies straight and true, the ball, in the turn and bank indicator, will sit squarely in the center of its race. When the ball is not centered, trim is required to bring it back to center. Induced drag occurs when an airplane flies out of trim. Drag reduces airspeed and increases fuel burn. Both are monetary penalties.

An average of two test flights a week were flown in the next few weeks to get everything tested. Smokey Bennett went back to New York and I hired various copilots for the rest of the test program. At altitudes in the very cold air (-55 degrees Centigrade), the airplane would shrink slightly. That caused problems with the cabinetry as doors and drawers would stick. At the lower levels and on the ground, everything would be fine. That is a common problem on any airplane until all the cabinets are adjusted for the necessary expansion.

To get the Ground Proximity Warning System to work, I had to fly down to the range at Magazine Mountain in Arkansas four different times. I certainly didn't mind that, as it was a lot of flying experience one rarely gets to enjoy. About the only thing left to be certified was the autopilot-flight director lash-up. When I talked to the FAA in Wichita, they said to be sure and bring along about 20 50-pound bags of sand and two 100-pound lead weights. From that conversation, I learned that the certification had to be flown in three phases. Phase one was flown with the aircraft's center of gravity (CG) exactly in the center of the aircraft wing's mean aerodynamic chord (MAC). Phase two put the CG at the extreme forward end of the chord. The last phase had the CG at the aft end of the chord making the aircraft very tail heavy. I was anxious to be a part of that certification flight test.

On May 15, 1990, I contracted Charlie Bishop, the son of a good friend, to be my copilot on the flight to Wichita. The FAA's Flight Standards Central Region was located there, and you had to bring the "Mountain to Mohammed." The FAA wouldn't come to St. Louis. Upon arrival at Wichita, we had a meeting with the FAA Flight Standards people. They went over all the details of the upcoming flights and then, I got another surprise. Gene Bolin, the FAA pilot who would fly in the right seat with me, said if the airplane was satisfactory in the forward CG configuration, we would then test it in the aft CG configuration. If both those tests were satisfactory, then it's obvious that the airplane would perform satisfactorily with the CG anywhere in between. It made good sense to me. We didn't fly that first day, as the airplane had to be configured with lead bars and sand bags in the nose compartment in order to move the CG to the forward edge of the mean aerodynamic chord- very nose heavy. That night we all stayed at the Hilton Hotel located on the grounds of the Wichita Airport.

Besides Charlie Bishop, I had two avionics engineers along. We all went to the hotel bar and had a couple of beers and talked about this adverse test on the airplane. The engineers thought the FAA should let the airplane fly the ILS (Instrument Landing System) coupled approach with the normal CG first. That would make positive assurance that the new coupling was working correctly. That evening in the hotel bar we watched the Kansas City Royals outscore the New York Yankees on TV.

The next morning, the weather was good and we planned a 10:00 takeoff. Gene Bolin said he would handle the flight clearance and the aircraft radios, and that was fine with me. Charlie Bishop decided to stay on the ground, as he wasn't really needed for this flight. Gene warned me that with the forward CG, I would need a lot of aft elevator trim for takeoff. Normally the GII requires about 10 to 12 degrees of elevator trim for takeoff. I set in 18 degrees of aft elevator trim. The airplane flew better than I expected with such a forward CG. Right after takeoff, we headed north toward Hutchinson, Kansas, where Gene contacted the local approach controller for a clearance to fly successive ILS approaches to the airport. Each approach would result in a full stop landing.

After six coupled instrument approaches, Gene said, "Tom, on this next approach, I want you to cut either engine at the middle marker." This marker is normally one half mile from the end of the runway. On a real ILS in weather, the middle marker is where a pilot sees the runway and lands. If he doesn't see it, he executes a missed approach. He then can make another attempt to land, or fly to his planned alternate airport. Gene also said, "Don't just bring the throttle to idle, I want you to shut the engine down completely." Now this was something I had never done before. I said to Gene, "You just don't do that at the middle marker." He came back and said, "Today we have to do that. It's part of the certification process. I need to see if the GII autopilot can handle the adverse yaw effect from the loss of an engine. If it can, fine, but if it can't, I won't certify the installation." Wow! This was do or die for the Paragon.   As I came around for the seventh instrument approach to the Hutchinson airport, I was worried about the autopilot's capability to cope with the yaw problem. In a twin-engine airplane, a severe yaw problem results when an engine is cut, or lost. If you were manually flying the airplane and this happened, you would immediately apply hard rudder forces to keep the airplane going straight ahead to the runway.   In this situation, when an engine suddenly loses power, the autopilot has to do the job of keeping the airplane on a straight course. This was the acid test for the autopilot

I told Gene that on this important approach, I wanted to intercept the ILS localizer (center line beam) about five or six miles outside the outer marker. That would give me a better chance to get the airplane set up properly for the approach. Intercepting the final approach course, I was hand-flying the airplane. When I got within 30 degrees of the final approach course bearing, I would, then, couple the autopilot to the flight director.   Now the flight director would tell the autopilot to direct the airplane to intercept the final approach course (localizer) and bring the airplane in on that course. Once coupled, all this was done automatically.   At the outer marker, the flight director would tell the autopilot to begin the airplane's descent on the glide path toward the approach end of the runway.   The airplane was now set up to make this important approach. I hoped and prayed the autopilot would have the "muscle" to correct the engine yaw and fly the airplane towards the runway in that last half mile.

The FAA approach controller cleared us for the approach to the Hutchinson airport, and asked us to contact the tower when passing the outer marker. All went well, and between the outer marker and the middle marker (four and a half miles), I decided to cut the left engine and hoped that "George" (the autopilot) would handle the yaw correction. At exactly one half mile from the end of the runway, I reluctantly pulled the left throttle to idle, then closed the start lever valve that shut off fuel to the engine. Immediately the engine quit and the airplane yawed to the left due to loss of power on that side. In less than a second, the autopilot corrected the 10 degree yaw to straight ahead. I heard the FAA pilot shout: "Great." In seconds, I restarted the engine and continued on toward the runway for a landing. I was highly impressed with the way the autopilot handled the correction problem; so was Gene Bolin.

Back on the ground, the airplane's CG now had to be changed to the extreme aft end of the wing's mean aerodynamic chord. We wouldn't fly again until the following morning. To change the CG, a complete new weight and balance form had to be completed and this took a lot of time. Gene Bolin said to plan on a 9:00 takeoff for the next morning. Charlie Bishop and I went back to the hotel to relax.

At breakfast the next morning, Gene briefed me on what we were going to do. He reminded me that with a tail-heavy airplane, if I let my airspeed get too low, a nasty stall would result. Essentially we executed the same procedure as before with the nose-heavy configuration, six ILS approaches at the Hutchinson airport. On the seventh, I would, again, cut an engine at the middle marker, a half mile from the runway. The airplane flew somewhat better with a forward CG than with an aft one. The six coupled ILS approaches were normal, and now the seventh and final one also would be, I hoped. As I cut the right engine at the middle marker, the aircraft rapidly yawed 12 degrees to the right, and I could feel the autopilot struggling to bring the airplane back on course. As I held my breath, slowly but surely the airplane came back on course, and I had to push the left throttle to max power to keep my airspeed at 140 knots.

Back on the ground, Gene Bolin said, "Okay, the airplane passed all the tests, and I'll certify it now." With that, shouts of joy came from all around. After lunch, Gene said it would take an hour or so to complete all the necessary paperwork. That gave us time to put the airplane's CG back to the center of the wing's mean aerodynamic chord where it belonged. Flying back home later that day, I couldn't help but notice how well the airplane flew with a normal center of gravity.

During the certification work at Wichita, the engineers at Midcoast were preparing to install a brand new piece of safety equipment called the Traffic Alert and Collision Avoidance System (TCAS) manufactured by the Bendix Radio Corporation, a division of Allied Signal Aerospace. Locating a copy of the pilot's guide, I studied it thoroughly. This is what TCAS will do for you:

It monitors the airspace surrounding your aircraft by interrogating the radio transponder of any intruding aircraft. The interrogation reply enables TCAS to compute the following information about the intruder:

• Range between your aircraft and the intruder.
• Relative bearing to the intruder.
• Altitude and airspeed of the intruder.
• Closure rate between the intruder and your aircraft.

Using this data, TCAS predicts the time to, and the separation at, the intruder's closest point of approach. Should TCAS predict that certain safe boundaries may be violated, it will issue a Traffic Advisory (TA) to alert the pilot that closing traffic is in the vicinity of your airplane.

If the intruder continues to close, TCAS will issue a Resolution Advisory (RA) to maintain safe vertical separation between your aircraft and the intruder. TCAS bases the alarms on a five second pilot reaction time to achieve adequate separation. Increase or reversal of an RA requires a reaction in two and one half seconds.

TCAS can track as many as 45 aircraft, display up to 30 of them and can coordinate a resolution advisory for up to three intruders at once. The advisories are always based on the least amount of deviation from the flight path while providing safe vertical separation.

Wow! This was something else. The TCAS indicator was to be mounted on the instrument panel right in front of the pilot. It had the usual horns, bells and whistles. Never before had I had the luxury of being told an airplane was under me, and climbing, when I couldn't see it. After the installation and all kinds of ground checks, I would have to take the airplane back to Wichita for another FAA certification flight check. This Paragon airplane was one of a kind with all this latest avionics technology. It was an exciting time for me, there aren't many opportunities for a corporate pilot to fly FAA certification flight checks.

After coordinating with the FAA, Charlie Bishop again helped me fly the airplane to Wichita. This time, another FAA certification check pilot would fly with me in the right seat. His name was Pete

Reynolds.   Gene Bolin was out of town.   While eating lunch at the FAA Flight Standard's cafeteria, Pete discussed the profile of the flight check.   Pete was qualified and current in several smaller jets, but not the Gulfstream II.   In fact, this would be his first flight in a GII.   I asked him to handle the radio and raise and lower the landing gear.   I would do everything else.   Pete said another airplane would be flying with us that day, and would play the role of the intruder aircraft.   He said they could either use a Learjet or a Sabreliner.   I asked to use the Sabreliner as I didn't like the Learjet.   It has always been a mickey mouse airplane in my mind.   Some pilots actually like them.

It was fun flying over the prairies west of Wichita, with the Sabreliner making passes at us from below and from above. The TCAS system seemed to be working well, as it was yakking at me the whole afternoon. Back on the ground, Pete signed off on the FAA certification of our new gadget. While we were flying back to St. Louis, that evening, the TCAS told me there were all kinds of small aircraft around me that I could not see. It was kind of scary, too, thinking of all those years and thousands of hours flying without TCAS.

Finally, the Paragon had passed all its FAA certification checks, or so I thought. Midcoast engineers came up with one final test. It was the Cockpit Voice Recorder (CVR), one of two "black boxes" that all airliners and most corporate jets have mounted in the tail section for it's best survivability, in the event of a crash.

The second "black box," mounted in the tail of the airplane, was called the Flight Data Recorder (FDR). During the latter part of May, I received a call from Jim Thompson-Midcoast's top avionics installation engineer. He wanted me to come over for a briefing on the CVR upcoming flight check. I brought Charlie Bishop with me to this meeting and I was glad I did. Jim explained all the many checks the CVR had to undergo in flight. All the ground tests had already been completed and they were ready to check it out in the air. The CVR records all cockpit conversation during the last 30 minutes anywhere in the flight profile. On start up, it begins recording when power is applied to the airplane. After 30 minutes of recording, it just starts over and records on top of the first 30 minutes. This record-erase-record operation goes on during the entire flight until final shutdown. The final 30 minutes stays on the tape until the next flight, when the process starts all over again. Jim said he would be going along on the test flight to direct the required checks.

All electrically powered instruments in the airplane are protected by resettable circuit breakers which break the electrical circuit in the event of a power surge. In the GII there are over 100 such electrical circuit breakers. When one pops out, you can usually hear the "snap" and its white or red collar shows plainly. Jim explained that he would pull the CVR's breaker before power was applied to the airplane. In this way, he could control the CVR and would reset the breaker when he wanted the unit to start recording. Jim briefed us that the first check would be during the taxi out when both pilots would be talking while using the aircraft's printed checklist. The next test would be at 5,000 feet, and then every 10,000 feet until we reached our target altitude of 41,000 feet. By controlling the recorder carefully, Jim thought he could get all the tests on one 30-minute section of tape. The FAA would accept Jim's written report on a special CVR test form. The form and the sealed black box would be sent to the FAA Test Lab in Oklahoma City for analysis. If all tests were satisfactory, the lab would return the unit with a document indicating that it was duly certified to be put into normal service.

The test flight was set for the next afternoon. I asked Charlie Bishop to file a flight plan that would take us to Columbus, Ohio, and back to St. Louis. Half the tests were done during the climb to 41,000 feet, and half on the descent back to St. Louis. At each test point, Jim was just like a film director. With the breaker pulled, both pilots would rehearse what to say. When Jim would say, "Now," he would reset the breaker and we would do our talking. All modes of talking had to be used: normal cockpit conversation, conversation using the ship's interphone system and the radios. All microphones had to be used, the hand-held mike, the headset boom mike and the oxygen mask mike. Jim was a good director and no retakes were needed.

The National Transportation Safety Board (NTSB) says it's time for FAA to require that all newly-manufactured cockpit voice recorders be capable of recording for at least two hours. In addition, the NTSB says technology now makes it practical to require an independent power source to keep recorders going when an aircraft's power system fails. The NTSB reports that investigations of more than 50 accidents in the last ten years have been hampered because data was lost when aircraft lost electrical power. I hope this prodding by the NTSB motivates the FAA to take early action on this important issue.

Midcoast couldn't wait to get this special edition out on the road to demonstrate its fine craftsmanship. In late May 1990, a three-week marketing trip was planned. A meeting including everyone associated with the airplane was scheduled and all Midcoast executives attended. John Tucker, President of Midcoast Aviation, briefed us that the airplane would fly from Montreal to Mexico and from Seattle to Miami to demonstrate to potential customers this fine example of their craftsmanship. John Tucker asked me to find another qualified and current GII captain to go with me on this junket. His theory was that we would be flying so much that one captain just couldn't do it all. I had no argument with that, so I started searching for a good GII captain. At the time, there were only two local companies that operated the GII-Monsanto and the May Company. My old operation (General Dynamics) had moved to Falls Church, Virginia, earlier that year. Finally I located Bob Quinn, one of the May Company's captains, who had vacation time coming. Bob was willing to give up two weeks of his annual vacation to fly with me on this marketing junket. Final plans were made and we left for Savannah on June 3, 1990 with en route stops at Memphis, Chattanooga and Macon, Georgia. The Gulfstream factory wanted to see what Midcoast was able to do in the refurbishing of this used GII. After a careful inspection, the factory officials agreed that it was very well done. At the same time, they had no interest in undertaking such a project themselves. They were too involved with new aircraft production and completions. Two days later I flew to several places in Florida to exhibit the airplane. Midcoast marketing people had made some very attractive signs, and, at each stop, the signs were set up in front of the airplane for all to see and read.

This was a big public relations effort, and it drew a lot of attention. The first question that everyone asked was the price. When they asked me, I would tell them, "I just fly the airplane; talk to the salesman." Tom Crowell, of Midcoast, was on the trip to take care of things like that. From Florida, we flew out to Dallas and spent two days exhibiting the airplane at Love Field.

The next stop was Houston, where we picked up some more Midcoast people. The following day, we flew down to Mexico City. The weather was clear, not the smoggy conditions that usually prevail there. Everyone stayed at the Americana Hotel located right on the airport grounds. It was my first trip to Mexico City and, to my surprise, everyone at the hotel spoke perfect English and were very cordial. You could tell they learned the language from British teachers as there was never a slang word or any colloquialism. The next day, I had to stay with the airplane as potential customers were coming out to see this marvel from the States. Mexicans don't do much in the afternoon. They like to start about 6:00 P.M., and then are often late. They are night people; they party after the sun goes down, and eat late into the night.

One well-to-do Mexican made a rather good offer for the airplane. Of course Tom Crowell had to pass this offer through the chain of command all the way to Carl Icahn in New York City. The Mexican offer was turned down. I personally thought TWA should have accepted it because another good offer like that might never happen again. And it didn't.

After Mexico City, our next stop was Brown Field near San Diego to clear customs and refuel. We then continued up to the Van Nuys airport, just north of Los Angeles. The next day was Sunday and I ran into two noteworthy people; Robert Redford, the actor, and Mr. Allen Paulson, President of Gulfstream. I didn't bother R.R., but I did ask Mr. Paulson to come out to the ramp and look at the Paragon. He hadn't seen it in Savannah when it was there as he had been away on a trip. Mr. Paulson was in the Los Angeles area visiting his son and was on his way back to Savannah. They had enjoyed some quiet time sailboating. After we talked in the lobby of Clay Lacy Aviation, Mr. Paulson followed me out to the airplane where I gave him a quick tour. He said, after a long and careful inspection, "Midcoast did a very good job. I hope they can sell this one and do some more as there are a lot of used GIIs available. Most of them have corrosion problems." He thanked me and walked over and boarded his private Gulfstream and departed for Savannah.

The next day the Paragon flew up to San Francisco. The Golden Gate Bridge is always a thrill to view, especially from the air. A lot of people came by to see the airplane at Butler Aviation, but, after two days of showing, no one offered to buy it. We left the next morning for Denver, and there were no offers there either, so we came home. After two weeks of "catch up maintenance," I flew the airplane to the Houston-Hobby airport for the annual National Business Aircraft Association (NBAA) convention.

This would be another big showcase for the Paragon as thousands of aviation people attend this convention each year. At the airport, the airplane was put on static display. That meant that all of us had to take shifts staying with the airplane to answer questions from hundreds of curious onlookers. When my shift came around, I answered questions until I was blue in the face, as they say. I had to pull one four-hour shift each day for the three-day event. It was like an open house in the real estate business-a lot of curious lookers and touchers, but no offers to buy. The most often-asked questions were " What's the price, how far will it go?, how fast will it fly and how high can it fly?" These were questions from curious onlookers. Every woman who came through the airplane drooled over the decor and appointments. It was very nice.

Finally I flew the airplane back home where more progressive maintenance was to be done. On each flight, there were always a few discrepancies written up. On the road, these squawks added up rather quickly. The Paragon wasn't going anywhere for a while, since there was a lot of work to catch up on. One day an aircraft salesman friend from Dallas, Barry Smith, called and inquired about the Paragon. He had seen it at the NBAA convention in Houston, and said he might have some interested parties. If the airplane was going to be home for a week or so, he would bring these people to St. Louis to look at it.

When I told Barry Smith that the airplane would be "down" for a couple of weeks, he said to look for him on Monday. While in St. Louis, Barry mentioned that the First Interstate Bank in Denver was foreclosing on a GII. Apparently the party buying the airplane couldn't pay off the note and had to give it up. Suddenly the bank owned an airplane and didn't know what to do with it. They located an aircraft brokerage in Dallas and talked to Barry. He told the bank he would be glad to represent them in marketing it. When the bank learned the airplane had to go through a pre-purchase inspection by a third party, Barry came to their rescue again. He flew to Denver and explained the whole process to the bank's president and his staff. A GII crew was found to ferry the airplane from its location in Ardmore, Oklahoma, to the factory in Savannah for the inspection. After the factory looked it over, the inspection team said that it should be grounded. Almost everything on the airplane was overdue for inspection or replacement. In addition, it had a healthy case of metal corrosion. The factory called Midcoast Aviation in St. Louis, an authorized Gulfstream repair station, and asked if they would do the job. If the factory did it, it would be weeks before they could even get to it. Along with two Midcoast engineers, I flew to Savannah and looked at this sorry mess. The airplane obviously had little or no maintenance for a long time.

To ferry it to St. Louis, I had to obtain a special FAA permit to fly it to the Midcoast mod-center. The permit said the airplane must be flown in daylight and in VFR conditions. It was several days before I had the right kind of weather. The airplane didn't fly; it just limped along the skyways. The people at the factory said it had the worst case of corrosion they had ever seen. The airplane had never been hangared and, as a result, it sat outside in all kinds of weather and caught a bad case of airplane cancer. It took Midcoast five months to get the airplane in flying condition so that it could be sold. During that time, the bank contracted with me (thanks to Barry) to monitor the maintenance progress with weekly written reports. As the bank's consultant, I was paid quite handsomely just to be around the hangar and watch this slow job get finished.

A firm in Fargo, North Dakota, finally bought the airplane for a song. The Denver bank took a bath on the deal. In a few days, I flew the airplane to Denver, picked up some bank officials and proceeded to Fargo. It was December and consequently very cold in North Dakota. Right after landing, I learned of two things that were very wrong. First, the Fargo Drilling Company, which bought the Gulfstream, operated a small twin-engine prop-airplane and were not jet qualified. Secondly, they didn't have a hangar large enough to shelter the Gulfstream. Why did they buy it, was the big question. In talking to their chief pilot and his boss, I explained that, if they left this airplane sit outside in below zero weather, in just one day, all the seals—oil, fuel, hydraulic, pneumatic and everything else would freeze and crack and there would be leaks all over the ramp. I went on to explain that the airplane would be unflyable and the repairs would be very costly. As a result of my discussion with the new owners, I flew the airplane to Minneapolis, where hangar space was available, that same day. I learned later that the airplane sat there for two months before it was sold again. I think the Fargo Drilling Company tried to make themselves a fast buck. I seriously doubt that they did.

The Paragon was away on a three month lease.. Midcoast decided they needed to get some return on their investment. I don't know what they paid for the airplane, or what they spent in transforming it, but the asking price was 7 million.dollars. That price tag probably scared away a lot of potential buyers. In Mexico City, a buyer had made a good offer and Mr Icahn turned it down. I thought, at the time, that Midcoast should have taken the offer and ran. When the Paragon came back from its short-term lease, the plan was for it to be flown to Dulles Field near Washington, D.C. Some potential buyers there wanted to look at it. Tom Crowell was with me and said that after the showing at Dulles, we were to fly up to White Plains, New York. Mr. Icahn wanted a personal look at this expensive machine. After we had waited for over two hours, Mr. Icahn finally showed up with his whole family, his wife and four gangly teenagers. I took the family up for an hour's flight around Long Island Sound while Tom Crowell served them a modest lunch. Getting off the airplane, Mr. Icahn's only question was "Will it fly to London?" When I said it would, with a Gander fuel stop, he just looked at me, and walked away.

One day in early December 1992, representatives from Conoco Oil Company came to St. Louis and looked over the Paragon. When told that Exxon Oil Company had bought the airplane new and had been the only owner, Conoco became interested as they knew that it had been well maintained. Oil companies have a reputation for treating their corporate assets with great care. After some negotiating, Conoco bought the Paragon, and Midcoast breathed a big sigh of relief.

It seemed the U.S. Government had asked Conoco to go over to Russia and teach the Russians how properly to drill for oil. They were using old technology, Conoco said. They planned to make one trip per month flying drilling engineers to Russia. Finally, on December 18, 1992, Conoco was ready to take delivery but they wanted it delivered to them in Texas, not Missouri or Illinois, so I got one more flight in the Paragon after all. The date of delivery was also the 50th anniversary of my first solo flight back in Fort Hays, Kansas. Flying to Houston that day, I was filled with 50 years of aviation nostalgia. On the flight to Houston I thought to myself that maybe I should write an account of all those years of flying. My last landing in the Paragon was a beauty. The Conoco pilot said, "Tom, you really rolled that one on." A fine compliment from a peer is worth its weight in gold.

I did contract flying for three more years before finally calling it quits on November 20, 1995, after I flew a Gulfstream II from Savannah to Cahokia, Illinois, for Midcoast Aviation. It was a night flight in clear weather and the night landing wasn't perfect, but it was a safe one. It's rather ironic that my first landing as pilot in command of an airplane was in broad daylight back in Kansas in 1942. Now my last one in Illinois in 1995 was in the blackness of night.   I had spent the entire six years since retiring from General Dynamics flying GII and GIII aircraft. . During that period, I had flown over 1,000 hours, more than 300 hours in the Paragon alone. I had no incidents or accidents, except for one time in a GIII, when the landing gear failed to retract and lock after takeoff from St. Louis, so I just put the gear back down and flew the short flight back to the departure airport.

During the period from 1989 to 1995, I flew for the following companies, either as a contract pilot, or as an instructor training their pilots:

Apex Oil Company
Avtec, Inc
Bank of Mexico.
Berg Electronics Corporation
Drummond Coal Company
Fargo Drilling Company
Flight Services Group
First Interstate Bank
Kallita Flying Services
KB Aviation, Inc.
Midcoast Aviation
Montgomery Ward
Peninsula Corporation
SDA Enterprises

Slim Fast Foods
Smith Food & Drug Company
Wetterau, Inc.

Before leaving the cadillac of the corporate fleet, I want to show the readers a comparison of the Gulfstream family of superb executive jet aircraft:

GULFSTREAM SPECIFICATIONS

GENERAL	GII	GIII	GIV	GV
Minimum crew	2	2	2	2
Max passengers	19	19	19	19
Engines (2)	RR Spey 511-8	RR Spey 511-8	RR Tay 183-13	BMW/RR BR 710
Takeoff thrust (Total)	22,800 lbs	22,800 lbs	24,900 lbs	29,500 lbs

DIMENSIONS

	GII	GIII	GIV	GV
Length	80 ft	83 ft	85 ft	96 ft
Wingspan	69 ft	78 ft	78 ft	91 ft
Cabin length	39 ft	41 ft	43 ft	51 ft
Cabin volume	1270 c/ft	1502 c/ft	1590 c/ft	1681 c/ft
Baggage capacity	2000 lbs	2000 lbs	2500 lbs	2500 lbs

MAXIMUM RANGE

	GII	GIII	GIV	GV
NBAA IFR	2859 nm	3650 nm	4000 nm	6500 nm
Long range cruise Mach.	.72	.77	.80	.82

PERFORMANCE

	GII	GIII	GIV	GV
FAA takeoff distance	5600 ft	5860 ft	5100 ft	5500 ft

Max cruise speed	.83 mach	.85 mach	.85 mach	.87 mach
FAA landing distance	3500 ft	3400 ft	3200 ft	3200 ft

WEIGHTS

Max ramp weight	65,300 lbs	68,700 lbs	70,200 lbs	89,400 lbs
Max gross t/o wt	64,800 lbs	68,200 lbs	69,700 lbs	89,000 lbs
Empty operating wt	30,363 lbs	32,200 lbs	32,900 lbs	46,800 lbs
Max fuel weight	23,300 lbs	28,300 lbs	28,300 lbs	41,000 lbs
Max landing weight	58,500 lbs	58,500 lbs	58,500 lbs	75,300 lbs

All Gulfstream aircraft are certified to carry 19 passengers; however, for more comfort, especially on long trips, most operators configure the cabin in a club style to accommodate from 12 to 14 passengers. All seats are large and very comfortable. Most single seats will berth for sleeping on long flights. Gulfstream is the hallmark for its large oval picture windows in the cabin. First time passengers often marvel and rave about being able to see the whole world through those wonderful windows.

This book is my second attempt to make a mark in the publishing arena. Back in 1973, during the first fuel shortage, I was the Chairman of the NBAA Energy Committee. The president of NBAA, John Winant, asked me to write a booklet on fuel conservation for business aircraft. I was happy to do that and, after a lot of research and study, came up with a 20-page booklet. It has been listed in the NBAA catalog of publications for many years. In that booklet, I covered the main points of how to conserve fuel when flying an airplane. The preface of the publication states:

"Conservation is not a new concept for pilots. Professional pilots have always concerned themselves with methods of conserving precious gallons for unanticipated problems. The consequences of running out of fuel are too severe for conservation to be treated lightly.

In 1973, however, the Arab oil embargo caused everyone to pause and think about our national situation and future needs. The requirement to conserve vital petroleum resources was brought into sharp focus. In addition to making sure that sufficient fuel was available for in-flight contingencies, pilots must now also be conscious of the need to conserve our aviation fuel supplies for our future flights, tomorrow, next month, and in the years ahead.

The booklet examines many of the techniques for conserving fuel in aircraft operations. It was written by a pilot for pilots and attempts to gather under one cover, all those things pilots can do to increase the efficiency of their aircraft, day by day. We therefore welcome and encourage your comments and recommendations. NBAA lays no claim to knowing all there is to know about conservation and, since the problem of diminishing energy supplies seems to be one which will be with us for a long time, we will not be lacking sound opportunities to revise and update that published herein."

In the booklet I outlined a complete standard flight profile from takeoff to landing, stressing each point in the profile. At the end, I listed the following reminders:

1. Know your flight manual.
2. Keep the airplane light and clean.
3. Take time to properly plan the flight.
4. Compute reserves carefully and correctly.
5. Maximize the use of ground power.
6. Plan taxi routes to cut ground operation time.
7. It costs fuel to carry fuel you don't need.
8. Don't start engines until you are gate released and have flight clearance.
9. Use reduced power takeoffs whenever possible.
10. Climb clean and quickly to optimum altitude.
11. Maximize your specific range.
12. Climb, climb, climb, do not sit on a hard altitude when below optimum altitude.
13. Trim and retrim. Reduce the drag.
14. Fly most efficient speed for best specific range.
15. Hold at maximum endurance airspeed. Use angle of attack.
16. Make sure instruments are properly calibrated.
17. Optimize en route descents. Use profile descents.
18. Use delayed-flap approaches when operationally feasible.
19. Shutdown unneeded engines on the ground.
20. Have your performance audited.
21. Improvement will be the result of good management control.

For the summary of the booklet, I wrote:

"While each of these individual items may not appear to contribute significantly to fuel savings, collectively they can be quite effective. You'll never know if you are actually saving fuel unless you know how much you've been using in the past. As in business, good record keeping in the fuel management area is essential to know what you've done, what you're doing now, and what your goals should be in conservation techniques. Burning some midnight oil can go a long way in helping you find ways to burn less of the other kind." Through the years, I have received many compliments on this fuel-saving booklet.

Once I heard the question asked, "What is a corporate pilot?" Well, a corporate pilot is first and foremost, a true professional, no less professional than a doctor, lawyer, architect or minister. Professional pilots are as dedicated and precise in their work as a surgeon in the operating room. Professional pilots will plan their flights with utmost care. They prepare the tools of their trade and themselves just as a surgeon lays out tools and plans for an operation. Professional pilots are able to settle down an apprehensive passenger as easily as the successful general practitioner.

Professional pilots are as sure of their position as the trial lawyer standing in front of the judge and jury. Just as the trial lawyer must foresee every possible block from the opposition, so the professional pilot must be prepared with an alternate plan at all times Professional pilots are as loyal to their boss and company as ministers are to their Maker. They respect their company and its best interests above personal desires. Professional pilots' respect for safety is as sincere as the architects' regard for proper materials to insure strength of construction. Neither will compromise at any cost. Professional pilots can fly from one airport to another more safely than other pilots. Professional pilots constantly study for improvements and upgrade their ratings. Professional pilots take great pride in their profession without giving the impression of arrogance. Younger pilots should be inspired. Professional pilots recognize the delicate margin between respect and subservience. They are warm but yet not familiar. Professional pilots are honorable people and win the respect of all who come in contact with them. They are a credit to those who call themselves professionals. All of the above components make up a professional pilot

Before adding my final comments about my life in aviation, I would like to share with the reader the following masterpiece from the pen of John Gillespie Magee, Jr.:

HIGH FLIGHT

Oh, I have slipped the surly bonds of the earth
And danced the skies on laughter-silvered wings;
Sunward I've climbed, and joined the tumbling mirth
Of sun-split clouds - and done a hundred things
You have not dreamed of

wheeled and soared and swung
High in the sunlit silence. Hovering there,
I've chased the shouting wind along and flung
My eager craft through footless halls of air.
Up, up the long, delirious, burning blue
I've topped the windswept heights with easy grace
Where never lark, or even eagle flew.
And, while with silent, lifting mind I've trod
The High untrespassed sanctity of space
Put out my hand, and touched the face of God

In December 1941, Pilot Officer John G. Magee, a 19-year-old American flying with the Royal Canadian Air Force in England, was killed when his Spitfire collided with another airplane inside a cloud. Some months before his death, he composed the immortal sonnet, "High Flight," a copy of which he fortunately mailed to his parents in the United States.

Aviation has been my life for the past 55 years, starting with the building of the P-40 fighter for the Curtiss Wright Corporation in Buffalo and ending with my last Gulfstream II flight 55 years later. During that time, I have flown to the four corners of the world and most points in between. I have met and known hundreds of wonderful aviation people. I count my blessings. It's a great privilege to have lived from the Model-T Ford to the deep space age. More has been accomplished in science during my lifetime than in all the years of recorded history preceding those years. My life in aviation has been rewarding and exciting. I survived three major wars but not without fears and close calls. The seeds of aviation were planted in my brain long before I realized it. As this incredible century is closing, I felt that my 55 years of aviation memories just had to be committed to the written word.

This book then is a log of my exciting life in aviation as I both lived and loved it. I envision that the next 55 years in aviation will bring man to accomplish wondrous things in deep space. The Moon, Mars and Venus will all be inhabited with Mars having a giant space laboratory with hundreds of inhabitants. Deep space probes from Mars and Venus will explore the vast unknown galaxies. Beyond that, many light years out there, maybe is where the gates of Heaven begin.

The original Americans (Indians) believe that, when they die, they will go to a place on the other side of the Sun. Maybe so, but I'd like to think God is waiting for us somewhere, way out there far beyond the galaxies, where man has yet to explore.

Transition To Retirement
If you would win a man to your cause,
first convince him that you are his sincere friend.

—*Abraham Lincoln*

FOOTNOTES

1.   The Glenn Miller Story that is described in this book came from various articles in the military newspaper *Stars and Stripes* after Glenn Miller was lost over the English Channel in 1944.

2.   The story of the Glacier Priest, Father Hubbard, also came from the *Stars and Stripes* newspaper after World War II ended in 1945.

3.   The story of the John G. Magee poem "High Flight" came from a story published in the *Stars and Stripes* military newspaper in 1945.

4.   The story of the Egyptian King Ramses II came from a gathering of public facts found mostly in the Egyptian Museum in downtown Cairo. Additional information was found in the National Library and in the American University Library, also in Cairo. 1982.